The Birth of Insight

BUDDHISM AND MODERNITY

A series edited by Donald S. Lopez Jr.

RECENT BOOKS IN THE SERIES

From Stone to Flesh: A Short History of the Buddha
by Donald S. Lopez Jr. (2013)

The Museum on the Roof of the World: Art, Politics, and the Representation of Tibet
by Clare E. Harris (2012)

Bonds of the Dead: Temples, Burial, and the Transformation of Contemporary Japanese Buddhism
by Mark Michael Rowe (2011)

Locations of Buddhism: Colonialism and Modernity in Sri Lanka
by Anne M. Blackburn (2010)

In the Forest of Faded Wisdom: 104 Poems by Gendun Chopel, a Bilingual Edition
edited and translated by Donald S. Lopez Jr. (2009)

The Birth of Insight

Meditation, Modern Buddhism, and the Burmese Monk Ledi Sayadaw

ERIK BRAUN

The University of Chicago Press   Chicago and London

Publication of this book has been aided by a grant from the Bevington Fund.

The University of Chicago Press, Chicago 60637
The University of Chicago Press, Ltd., London

Paperback edition 2016
Printed in the United States of America

25 24 23 22 21 20 19 18 17 16 15 14 13 2 3 4 5 6

ISBN-13: 978-0-226-00080-0 (cloth)
ISBN-13: 978-0-226-41857-5 (paper)
ISBN-13: 978-0-226-00094-7 (e-book)
DOI: 10.7208/chicago/9780226000947.001.0001

Library of Congress Cataloging-in-Publication Data
Braun, Erik, 1972–
The birth of insight: meditation, modern Buddhism, and the Burmese monk Ledi Sayadaw / Erik Braun.
pages cm — (Buddhism and modernity)
ISBN 978-0-226-00080-0 (cloth: alk. paper) —
ISBN 978-0-226-00094-7 (e-book) 1. Ñana, Ledi Cha ra to', 1846 or 1847–1923 or 1924. 2. Meditation—Buddhism. 3. Dharma (Buddhism) I. Title. II. Series: Buddhism and modernity.
BQ974.A3588B73 2013
294.3'91092—dc23
2013014690

♾ This paper meets the requirements of ANSI/NISO Z39.48-1992 (Permanence of Paper).

To the women who have shaped me most:

my mother

my sister

my wife

my daughter

Contents

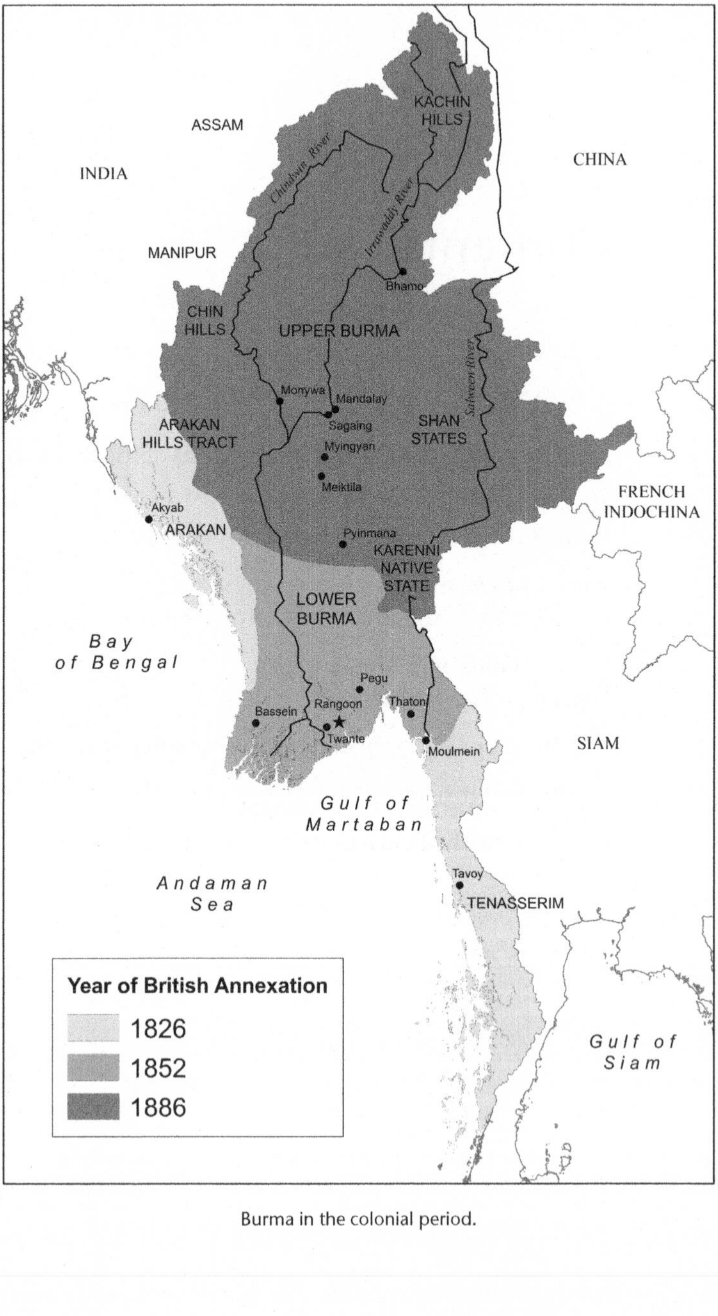

ASSAM
INDIA
CHINA
KACHIN HILLS
Chindwin River
Irrawaddy River
MANIPUR
Bhamo
CHIN HILLS
UPPER BURMA
Salween River
Monywa
Mandalay
Sagaing
ARAKAN HILLS TRACT
SHAN STATES
Myingyan
Meiktila
FRENCH INDOCHINA
Akyab
ARAKAN
Pyinmana
KARENNI NATIVE STATE
LOWER BURMA
Bay of Bengal
Pegu
Bassein
Rangoon
Thaton
Twante
Moulmein
SIAM
Gulf of Martaban
Andaman Sea
Tavoy
TENASSERIM
Year of British Annexation
1826
1852
1886
Gulf of Siam

Burma in the colonial period.

Preface and Acknowledgments

On December 26, 2004, my wife and I joined the morning meditation session in the main hall of the International Meditation Center (IMC) in Yangon, Burma (now known officially as Myanmar). We, along with over fifty other meditators—all laypeople—arranged ourselves in rows on the floor, men on one side, women on the other. The leader of the center, an old and revered layman named U Tint Yee, sat elevated above us in a chair at the far end of the room.

When the session started, we all closed our eyes, and the room sank into a plangent silence. As the minutes crawled past, I struggled to pay attention to the ever-changing sensations within my body. The goal was to use my corporeal experience as the means to gain insight into a universal truth: reality's impermanent, unsatisfactory, and conditioned nature. Hence the term for this practice, insight meditation (*vipassanā*). Acquiring such insight could free one from suffering, from the Buddhist point of view, by enabling one to let go of all attachments to things that are destined to disappear and so disappoint. But I found myself distracted. Thoughts of other places, past events in my life, the intellectual interests that had brought me to the IMC, plans for later travel in Burma—they all crowded into my consciousness. It looked like it was going to be a long hour.

I was just about to peek over at my wife, to see how she was faring, when I felt a strange sensation, as if the floor were shifting underneath me. At first I thought it was just the vibrations caused by some kids fidgeting in front of me, but I opened my eyes to see the whole building starting to shimmy on its foundation. Fellow meditators, silent and composed moments before, cried out and grabbed one another. The waves passing through the earth grew so powerful that I saw the water in a lotus pond outside sloshing back and forth like a seesaw.

All eyes turned to U Tint Yee. Should we flee the building? After all, the doors to the outside were only steps away. Yet, even as the oceanic push and pull intensified, U Tint Yee remained absolutely still, his eyes shut. And, so, though the building swayed back and forth around us, we followed our teacher's lead and we, too, stayed put. Finally, after what seemed an eternity (but was probably only a minute or so), the undulation of the earth stopped. People's cries died down as the floor stopped slipping and sliding. After a few moments, when the tremors did not return, a palpable sense of relief filled the hall. It seemed the earthquake was over, and, remarkably, there was little damage. No one was hurt, though people continued to hold on to each other, some softly crying. Still, U Tint Yee showed no reaction: no opening of his eyes, no movement at all. There were some whispers, but the force of U Tint Yee's example kept the crowd's attention. When another minute passed and it became clear he would not stop meditating, everyone took the cue from him. Each person resumed a meditative position and restarted his or her silent practice. The session ended at its scheduled time, as if nothing had happened.

I start the book with this vignette because it encapsulates for me, in a small but visceral way, the power of meditation that drew me to this project. As the story indicates, meditation is more than a tool for personal transformation. It is also a social force, one that can keep a crowd of laypeople sitting during an earthquake and push them back to practice right after it ends. It is, speaking more broadly, a way to make sense of the world that shapes personal choices, group behavior, and even political acts. Yet the power of meditation has not been an unchanging given in Buddhism. It has a history, and I had come to Burma to understand why an influential insight meditation movement had originated there before anywhere else. And I was at the IMC because U Tint Yee followed in a lineage of teachers who identify the famous and charismatic Buddhist monk named Ledi Sayadaw (1846–1923) as the modern founder of their movement and the key architect of mass insight practice. To focus on Ledi Sayadaw's life, as this book does, is to explore the birth of insight, understood as the start of a modern meditation movement that now shapes people's lives in all sorts of situations—earthquakes included—not just in Burma but all over the world.

Such a project has depended on the assistance of many people. In

Burma, I received invaluable help from U Kyaw Zaw Naing, U Thaw Kaung, Sayama Daw Mar Lay, Saya Kyaw Nyunt, U Thiha Saw, U Aung Mun, Nance Cunningham, U Aung Soe Min, Sayama Yu Yu Khaing, the Thitagu Sayadaw (U Nyanissara), and U Uttamasara. Special thanks go to Dhammācariya U Nandamālābhivaṃsa, who, though busy as an abbot and teacher, met me often to discuss Abhidhamma matters and shared with me his unpublished translation of Ledi Sayadaw's commentary, the *Paramatthadīpanī*. Without U Nandamālābhivaṃsa's assistance, my analysis of the *Paramatthadīpanī*, which forms an integral part of chapter 2, would have been far more difficult.

At Harvard University, Janet Gyatso advised me on the first incarnation of this project; what is concise and convincing in it still shows her influence. She is for me the model of the rigorous and responsive scholar, and I am grateful that our discussions have continued since I left Cambridge for the great southern plains of Oklahoma. Charles Hallisey and Donald Swearer both also went beyond the call of duty to offer comments and assistance that encouraged and enriched my understanding of Burmese Buddhism. At Harvard, other people also helped me a great deal. I thank Eyal Aviv, Beatrice Chrystall, Jason Clower, Karen Derris, Diana Eck, Stephanie Jamison, Holly Gayley, Robert Gimello, Smita Lahiri, Amod Lele, Mark McClish, Arthur McKeown, Robert Orsi, Ryan Overbey, Parimal Patil, Stephanie Paulsell, and Michael Witzel. I extend particular thanks to Anne Monius, who remains an enriching conversation partner. I also thank Harvard University for providing a Sheldon Fellowship that made initial research in Burma and in London possible.

Beyond Harvard and up to the present day, a number of other people, friends and colleagues, have helped me clarify my thinking and do the best work I can. During my undergraduate days, Jonathan Evans guided me through the study of Old English that provided the philological tools for my later reading of Buddhist texts. John Okell and U Saw Tun taught me Burmese at the Southeast Asia Summer Studies Institute in Madison, Wisconsin, and, since then, have answered with unfailing patience my ongoing translation questions. Michael Aung-Thwin, Jason Carbine, Charles Carstens, Jane Ferguson, Rupert Gethin, Gustaaf Houtman, Chie Ikeya, Ingrid Jordt, Alexey Kirichenko, Patrick Pranke, Juliane Schober, Daw Than Than Win, Justin Watkins, and U Zawtika have also given me valuable assistance. Thanissaro Bhikkhu offered perceptive comments on portions of the book manuscript, and U Jāgara carefully read the conclusion; Guillaume Rozenberg, William Pruitt, Ward Keeler, and Anālayo Bhikkhu were each kind enough to read the whole work and offer many helpful comments. Justin McDaniel, who set a daunting precedent as the first fellow student I met at Harvard, read the introduction and pointed the way to a slimmer, better version. Anne Blackburn very generously read the entire manuscript with great care and responded to further questions from me; her input has much improved the work. Special thanks go also to D. Christian Lammerts and Alicia Turner, who read large chunks of this work, brought sources to my attention, and have always been willing to discuss matters raised in the book. Thanks also to Thomas Patton, who discussed many issues of the book with me, did the lion's share of work compiling the index, and who has been, more generally, a welcome friend and colleague in the study of modern Burma. And I give my deep gratitude to Lilian Handlin, with whom I've had many wide-ranging and productive discussions about Burma, and to her late husband, Oscar Handlin.

James McHugh deserves special thanks as a friend and academic conversation partner. Beyond academia, Joseph Usher and Aaron Swatogor must be mentioned as great friends who take a genuine interest in what I do, but do not define me by it.

At the University of Oklahoma, a number of colleagues have been very supportive. I thank Barbara Boyd, Tom Boyd, Rangar Cline, Brent Landau, Kyle Harper, Lee Green, Amy Olberding, Zoe Sherinian, Rienk Vermij, David Vishanoff, and Jane Wickersham. I thank Melissa Scott of the Center for Spatial Analysis at the University of Oklahoma for producing the excellent map of Burma used in this book. I would like also to express my appreciation to the College of Arts and Sciences at the University of Oklahoma and to the Office of the Vice President for Research for fellowships and research funding that insured that this project came to a timely completion. And heartfelt thanks to the chair of the Religious Studies Program here at OU, Charles Kimball, who has given me unflagging support and is a trusted mentor.

At the University of Chicago Press, my thanks to Alan Thomas, who has shepherded this work through the publication process with grace, to Randolph Petilos, who guided me through many publication logistics, and to Richard Allen, who went through the manuscript with great skill and helped me to make it clearer and more accessible. I am also deeply grateful to the Buddhism and Modernity series editor, Donald Lopez, who showed an early and enduring interest in the project and offered thoroughgoing and insightful comments on the manuscript that have improved it enormously. I thank, too, the anonymous readers for the Press, who devoted to the book much care and critical acumen.

It would be remiss not to express gratitude, too, to the man who occupies almost every page of this book, Ledi Sayadaw. If he's looking down from a heavenly realm, I doubt he agrees with all that I say here, but surely he sees that my critical analysis of his life never loses respect for all that he did.

My thanks and deep love to my mother, Catherine Braun, my father, Jerome Braun, his partner, Michael Alewine, and my sister, Katie Hunter. They have given me unfailing support and encouragement. My thanks, too, to my in-laws, John and Constance Wahlin, who have put up with a son-in-law with interests that demand travel to far-flung places (at times, accompanied by their daughter). The power of meditation touched these folks' lives, too, in the wake of that earthquake of December 26. It was only some days later, when my wife and I left the IMC, that we were told the earthquake had caused devastating tsunamis in the region. Our meditation teachers had felt our undisturbed practice took precedence over any immediate need to know such information. This was not a feeling shared by our family and friends, who recalled our vague talk of going to Phuket, Thailand—that week!

My daughter, Annika, is just a year and a half old. Yet from the start of her life, she has shared with me profound conversations that have inspired me and taught me more about living in the now than any meditation. To use John Betjeman's words to speak to her: "You hold the soul that talks to me / Although our conversations be / As wordless as the windy sky."

Finally and above all, my love and gratitude to my wife, Britt Wahlin. She is the lynchpin of my life. While busy with her own work, she has supported me in countless ways—reading endless drafts of this book, sharing in the care of our daughter, even meditating during an earthquake! She has made this book possible (much else besides), and I hope all that is pleasing in it testifies to my incalculable and welcome debt to her.

On Transliteration and Abbreviation

I typically give a Burmese word in a phonetic transcription, either my own or a widely established form, that approximates its pronunciation. This method avoids words bristling with diacritics that often look little like they sound and are therefore hard for many to retain. (For example, *sayadaw,* a term of respect for a monastic teacher, is written *cha rā to* in strict transliteration.) With so many words from disparate sources, there are inevitable inconsistencies. I follow the first appearance of a phonetic rendering of an uncommon but significant term, however, with a technically precise transliterated form that is based upon the conventions of the Library of Congress (LOC) Romanization system (see Barry 1997). In this system, a single open quotation mark at the end of a syllable signifies the symbol in Burmese that indicates the absence of a final vowel. Italicized double and single straight quotation marks signify the Burmese symbols for, respectively, a high tone and a "creaky" tone. I diverge only in two instances from this system: I transliterate the low-pitch vowel "o" as *au,* while the LOC system gives *o',* and I render the low-pitch unstressed initial vowel "a" simply as *a,* while the LOC transliterates it as *'a.* Pali words are transliterated according to the conventions of the Pali Text Society. Except for those mentioned only in passing, Burmese and Pali terms can be found in the glossary at the back of the book.

I refer to some Pali texts with abbreviations. The "long collection" of discourses of the Buddha, the *Dīgha Nikāya,* is referred to by the letters DN; the "middle-length collection," the *Majjhima Nikāya,* as MN; the "grouped collection," the *Saṃyutta Nikāya,* as SN; and the "numbered collection," the *Aṅguttara Nikāya,* as AN. The *Visuddhimagga* (*Path of Purification*) is referred to as Vism.

INTRODUCTION

Ledi Sayadaw and the Gifts of the Buddha

Long ago, two merchants, named Tapussa and Bhallika, journeyed to the middle country (*majjhimadesa*) of India on a trading mission. While traveling between cities with a caravan of five hundred ox-carts, they happened upon the Buddha, sitting under a Rājāyatana tree. The men were, it is said, the first people to meet him after his awakening. Filled with devotion, the merchants offered the Buddha rice cakes and honey. He took the food—his first meal after enlightenment, a most auspicious gift—and accepted the men as his first disciples. At their request, he also offered them a gift. He did not give a doctrinal teaching, though he had spent much of the time since his awakening formulating doctrine. Nor did he teach them to meditate, though meditation had enabled his enlightenment under the nearby Bodhi tree. Instead, the Buddha plucked eight hairs from his head, gave them to the two merchants, and sent them on their way.[1]

The Burmese now claim Tapussa and Bhallika as their own. The story goes that the two merchants returned home to the area of modern-day Yangon and gave the precious hairs, relics of the Buddha (called *rūpakāya*), to their king. The king enshrined them in the Shwedagon Pagoda, which became Burma's most sacred site.[2] To the present day, the Shwedagon draws more pilgrims than any other place in Burma: from the street vendor to the general, from the novice monk to the old abbot rumored to be enlightened. Most go to pray, light incense, chant *suttas* (*sūtras*), offer flowers, and circumambulate the structure in the clockwise direction. For many cen-

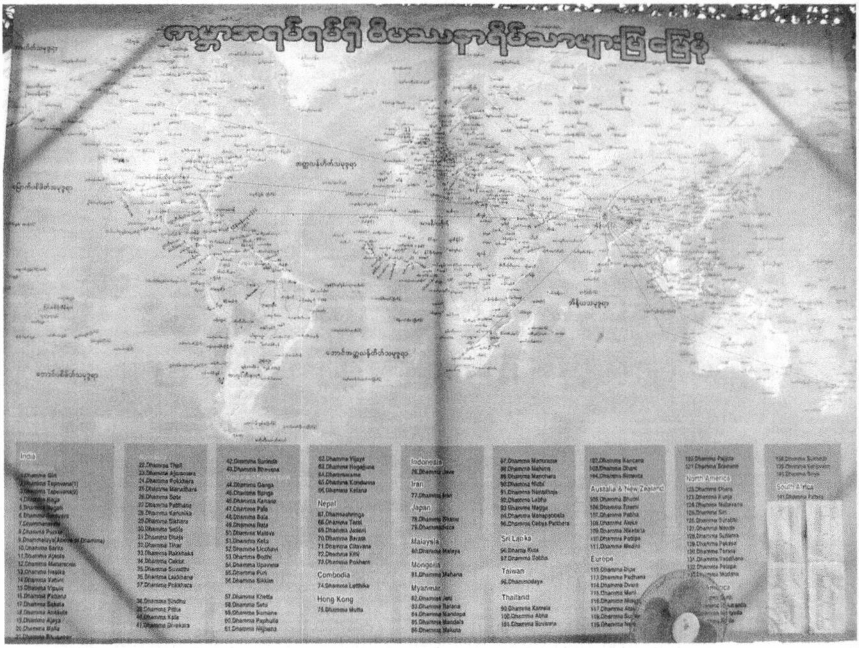

FIG. 1. Map of insight meditation centers around the world located at the Shwedagon Stūpa. Author's photograph.

turies, Buddhist laypeople and monks and nuns across Asia have focused on such devotional forms of practice. While over the course of Buddhist history relatively few people have meditated, many have worshipped the Buddha's relics, as Tapussa and Bhallika did.

Prior to the colonial era, in Burma as in other Theravāda cultures,[3] some monks and even some laypeople studied meditation as a scholarly topic, but this did not lead to its widespread practice.[4] Rather than meditate, monks mostly studied, taught, and acted as "fields of merit" (*puññakhetta*), that is, suitable recipients of the charity of laypeople, traditionally provided in the form of food and robes. In turn, the laity focused on cultivating good karma (*kamma* in Pali) through generosity and virtuous behavior. Both groups oriented their actions around the Buddha as a figure of devotion, still present in his relics.

Yet, in a pavilion on the outer edge of the Shwedagon's broad marble walkway, I recently saw a large Mercator map, entitled "Map of Insight Meditation Centers around the World" (see fig. 1). On it, a wheel, symbolizing the teaching of the Buddha, hovered over India. Red lines radiated out from the wheel to countries around the world with insight meditation

FIG. 2. Ledi Sayadaw, ca. 1907. From Ledi Sayadaw, *Paramatthadīpanī* (1907).

(*vipassanā*) centers.[5] At the bottom of the map in English letters was a list of over one hundred centers, grouped by country.

Today, many Buddhists and non-Buddhists alike assume that most Buddhists meditate. As the map suggests, these days a lot do. (Indeed, in our time meditation is often Buddhism's synecdoche.) Yet, mass meditation, by both monks and laypeople, was born in Burma only in the early years of the twentieth century and at a scale never seen before in Buddhist history. Why did the practice start then and there? The answer to this question is complex, but any attempt to answer it leads one back to a single figure, a Burmese monk named Ledi Sayadaw (see fig. 2). This book is the story of his life and the role he played in the modern rise of Buddhist meditation.

Born in 1846, in a village not too far from the royal capital of Mandalay, Ledi would become one of the most famous and beloved—though also, at times, controversial—monks in Burma. Thousands of people in locations across the country would throng his sermons, drawn to a man who offered the most rarified teachings in a down-to-earth and entertaining way. As one British colonial official observed, Ledi's fame stemmed from the fact that "he had large charity, a thorough knowledge of human nature, a delightful sense of humour and a fine voice. His effortless eloquence held immense audiences rapt."[6] Just as he reached out to people in his talks, he wrote numerous works in a simple style accessible to the common person. Many were bestsellers, and hundreds of thousands of people joined groups dedicated to studying and memorizing them. Indeed, people often welcomed Ledi to their village by chanting one of his poems in homage and saw him off in the same way. By the time he died in 1923, this charismatic and profoundly influential figure's call to lay practice had mobilized a large swath of the population and laid the basis for widespread meditation. The map at the Shwedagon signaled not only meditation's popularity but also Ledi's celebrated part in making it so.

The unique rise of mass meditation in Burma emerged out of the relationship between two spheres of activity: the study of Buddhist doctrine and the effort to protect the Buddhist religion. Ledi played critical roles in both. He empowered regular people in the first decades of the twentieth century to participate in the longstanding, elite practice of cultivating mastery of Buddhist literature. He focused particularly on the philosophical texts called the Abhidhamma.[7] Considered the most complex and demanding of all the Buddha's teachings, these works were held in great esteem among the populace, especially the teaching of the twenty-four conditional relations (*paṭṭhāna*) that explain the origination of all phenomena. Even today, hop in a taxi in Yangon and you are likely to see a CD hanging from the rearview mirror with the conditional relations printed on it in the shape of a wheel, each relation forming a spoke. As the cab drives down the street, you are bound to pass shops and homes with posters and calendars displaying the relations, monks holding fans with them stitched on the front, and monasteries that have them placed over the entrance. Ledi gave people an unprecedented opportunity to gain access to the in-depth study of such highly valued teachings.

Many people during Ledi's life were worried that Buddhism was in decline (as the scriptures predicted) and would soon disappear under colonial influence. The British had seized the most southerly parts of Burma in the war of 1824–26 and the entire lower half of the country in the second Anglo-Burmese war of 1852–53. They then took the whole of the country—including Upper Burma, the portion where Ledi was born and lived—in 1885 (see frontispiece).[8] This protracted conquest gave the Burmese time to observe the disruptive effects of British power.[9] In response to their rule, Ledi promoted the study of abstruse Buddhist doctrine, including the Abhidhamma, as a way to protect Buddhism. He went on to formulate simple forms of meditation as a further line of defense. By dispersing the study and practice of Buddhism among the populace, he made it harder for the British to destroy it. For the first time, serious meditation practice became plausible, appealing, and even patriotic. Like so many religious innovators throughout history, Ledi found a solution to social disruption by carrying the past into the present. His "traditional" view was an integral part of his vision of a modern Buddhism that included meditation.

The English word "meditation" has a broad semantic range. The most general term for meditation in Theravāda Buddhism is *bhāvanā,* a Sanskrit and Pali word that means "cultivation" or "development." It encompasses a continuum of practices that includes study, memorization, chanting, moral effort, and, certainly, relic veneration.[10] Theravāda texts and teachings, however, do not consider all forms of *bhāvanā* as having the same potential. In the canonical and paracanonical texts, two types of meditative practice are understood as indispensable for achieving realization. The first is calming (*samatha*) meditation. This regimen leads to states of great concentration (*samādhi*), even absorption (*jhāna*), because calm and concentration are understood to go together like two sides of the same coin. The second is insight meditation (*vipassanā*). These two sets of practices have a complex relationship with one other, and both Pali-language and vernacular Burmese texts have debated that relationship at length.[11] In later chapters, we will return to the matter of these sets of practices and their relationship, but we can say here that, in general, calming comes first. The meditator cultivates calming prior to insight because it stabilizes the mind and gives it a penetrating focus. According to a classic scheme found in the monk Buddhaghosa's fifth-century magnum opus, the *Visuddhimagga* (*Path of Purification*), there are forty objects suitable for achieving varying degrees of calm and concentration.[12] These include, among others, recollections of the Buddha, the *dhamma*, and the *saṅgha*; disks of colored earth upon which to focus one's attention, called *kasiṇa* devices; and the formless objects of space, consciousness, and nothingness. Once the meditator has finished cultivating a calm and concentrated mind, he or she uses it for insight practice. It is insight meditation that actually gives rise to a liberative understanding of the impermanent (*anicca*), suffering-filled (*dukkha*), and essenceless (*anattā*) nature of all life. Insight meditation, then, is not the effort simply to achieve a temporary state of consciousness, as in the case of calming. It is, instead, the mindful observation (*sati*) of reality that confirms the lessons of Buddhism at a transformative level.

As I noted above, the historical record suggests little practice of such meditation in Southeast Asian Buddhist cultures until recent times. This is not to say that no one meditated prior to the colonial period, but, as I will explore in more detail in the following chapters, such practice was limited, especially among the laity.[13] Ledi sought to change this situation by convincing a wide range of people to take up meditative practice. To do this, he presented meditation as having the potential to benefit anyone, no matter the person's job or station in life. His flexible approach encouraged people to pursue insight, even if they did not have the time or resources to cultivate much calm and concentration first.[14] As Ledi would put it, "Maturity of knowledge is the main, the one thing required."[15] If a person prepared through study, he or she could skip initial calming practices and still make spiritual progress. In fact, mundane life—Ledi used the example of going to the movies, for instance—could become the arena of meditation. This capacious formulation of practice for those living lives as householders played a critical part in forming the Burmese predilection for meditation. And, by developing a model of collective, lay-centered study, he made meditation feasible on a mass scale.

Several practice lineages hail Ledi as a root teacher. This includes the organization of S. N. Goenka, which put up the map at the Shwedagon.[16] Throughout the Buddhist world, lineage is a primary element in establishing religious authority. A teacher is considered legitimate if he can place himself and his teaching in an unbroken line back to the Buddha. This is certainly the case for the insight meditation movement. Yet it is noteworthy that many of the current meditation movements originating in Burma locate the starting points of their recorded histories only in the late nineteenth and early twentieth centuries. For instance, when asked who Ledi Sayadaw's meditation teacher was, Goenka says: "There is no recorded history, but Ledi Sayadaw says he learnt this technique from a monk in Mandalay."[17] The monk U Nārada, known as the Mingun Sayadaw, was another early proponent of lay meditation. Somewhat later than Ledi, and possibly influenced by him (as will be discussed in the conclusion), Nārada also searched for a method of meditation. During his quest, he met a monk in a cave in the hills above the town of Sagaing, who directed him to study the Buddha's teachings in the *Mahāsatipaṭṭhāna Sutta* (the *Greater Discourse on the Establishings of Mindfulness*).[18] Thus began the movement that Nārada's pupil, the Mahasi Sayadaw, would spread so widely in Burma and beyond.[19]

While such movements look to the period that coincides roughly with Ledi's life as the beginnings of their known histories, little scholarship has attended to the events and figures during this time.[20] By focusing on Ledi's life, as well as on his writings and the contexts of their production and reception, this book will show how in the late nineteenth and early twentieth centuries he reformulated the complex of Buddhist teachings and institutions, what Theravāda Buddhists call the *sāsana.* A key part of that reformulation of the sāsana was the popularization of meditation that would in later decades turn meditation into a mass movement that spread around the globe.

The story of Ledi's life and career in the following chapters shows that he did not get his understanding of meditation from a particular teacher, nor did he find it in a book. He developed his presentation of meditation himself, depending on his traditional intellectual and spiritual formation as a young man.[21] He was born thirty-nine years before the end of the last dynasty of Burmese kings (1752–1885), called the Konbaung, and in the middle of the region out of which a network of influential literati at the court had emerged. From the start, his monastic education exposed him to the deep-seated cultural conception of literary acumen as the means to authority and acclaim in Burma. This formation only intensified when he traveled to the capital Mandalay in the late 1860s to continue his training at a royally sponsored monastery. There, powerful monks and lay literati were using textual control and production to gain and wield power, and Ledi's education in such an environment helps to explain his emphasis on learning. Later, when he responded to colonial pressures, he turned to textual study as the basis for meditation. His approach depended on the localized development of an elite Buddhist tradition that stressed the use of texts—those of the Abhidhamma above all others—as the way to answer societal and religious problems.

Ledi's vision of meditation, then, mixes together the old and the new (in other words, his Konbaung-era formation and colonial factors). Such a mixture calls our attention to the problem of identifying what makes a form of Buddhism count as modern.[22] Scholars have suggested many criteria, some related to causes, others to effects, and most place an understandable stress on the impact of colonialism.[23] The wide range of criteria points to the fact that what qualifies as modern and, by extension, as premodern (which is no less if not more variable) changes with approach and subject matter.[24] This variability reminds us to take care before we affix a label. A necessary caution does not mean, however, that we must do away with a distinction between premodern and modern forms of Buddhism. Born during the disruptions of colonialism, large-scale meditation is clearly a product of modern times. We cannot ignore this fact if we want to answer the question of why it arose first in Burma when it did. But Ledi's life points to overlooked continuities between the modern and premodern periods. No previous study of Buddhism has taken such a close look at an influential figure whose life straddles that divide. By examining Ledi's life we have an opportunity to go beyond providing a case study (as worthy as that is), for his life is far more than just an illustration of a larger trend. The analysis in the following chapters will allow us to unpack what really counts in a modern form of Theravāda Buddhism. To do so will show how the past relates to the present—or, to put it in the terms of this project, how the Buddha's first disciples, Tapussa and Bhallika, relate to Ledi and the millions of people who meditate today.

Sources for the Study of Ledi Sayadaw's Life and Work

The works Ledi wrote provide the primary access to his thinking and to his approach to teaching Buddhist ideas and practices. They are the most important sources for this book, and I use a wide range of them. I discuss specific works in detail in the chapters that follow, together with the contexts in which they were written and the genre conventions they display. Other sources include contemporary periodicals, books written in response to Ledi's philosophical works (especially in chapter 2), and analyses of aspects of Ledi's career. Some of these documents are written in English, though most are in Burmese or Pali.

Besides Ledi's writings, the most important sources are his biographies. There are three of particular value to this study. The *Biography of the Great Monk Ledi Sayadaw* (*Lay' tī cha rā to ther' mrat' krī" e* mahātheruppati kathā,* which I will call the *Great Monk Ledi*) was written around 1926, just a few years after Ledi's death. It is the earliest complete account of his life. The other two were written much later. The *History of the Famous People in the Ledi Lineage* (*Lay' tī gantha waṅ' kyau myā" sa muiṅ"*, called the *Ledi Lineage*), by Hla Pain (Hla Puiṅ'), was published in 1967, and the *Life Story of the Great Monk and Benefactor Ledi Sayadaw* (*Kye" zū" hraṅ' lay' tī cha rā to bhu ra krī" bhava phrac' tau cañ'*, called the *Life Story*), by Aung Mon (Oṅ' Mvan'), appeared in 2007.

The *Great Monk Ledi* was written by U Wunnita (Ū" vaṇ ṇi ta). Born in 1892, he became Ledi's student in 1912, when he fully ordained at the age of twenty. Wunnita developed a close relationship with Ledi, following him on his preaching tours and becoming a well-known preacher in his own right.[25] In about 1926, he returned to lay life.[26] His departure from the monkhood did not mark, however, a severing or even a weakening of his involvement with the legacy of Ledi. On the contrary, he returned to lay life so that he could help to manage the publication of a journal founded after Ledi's death called the *Ledi Dhamma Journal* (*Lay' tī ta rā" sa taṅ'" cā*).[27] Its aim was to spread the dhamma by building on Ledi's work. The biography Wunnita wrote likely served the same purpose. Perhaps because of his journalistic experience, he employed a style that could capitalize on the relative freedom of the press in colonial Burma at the time of its publication. Much was being published, especially on Buddhist topics. He produced a book likely to gain attention in a competitive marketplace: The *Great Monk Ledi* is fast-paced, accessible in style, and relatively short at 215 pages. Because the book is well written and by someone who was close to Ledi, and because later biographies do not add anything substantial to the narrative it provides, I have relied on this work more than any other.

While the *Great Monk Ledi* focuses on Ledi from the cradle to the grave, the *Ledi Lineage* is much more concerned with his legacy (as indicated by the work's title).[28] Of the 566 pages of the book, the first 273 concern Ledi; the other 293 pages concern his disciples.[29] But the *Ledi Lineage* does not break with Wunnita's biography—in fact, it can be seen as a natural extension of the earlier work. The *Great Monk Ledi,* as the first lengthy and popular biography of Ledi, served to fix his persona in the Burmese consciousness. The *Ledi Lineage* then consolidates Ledi's contributions by giving further attention to his legacy. The works do not differ in terms of the basic facts they record about their subject's life. As in the *Great Monk Ledi,* close attention is paid to dates, and the book occasionally uses footnotes to provide further information on a particular topic.

In contrast to the *Ledi Lineage,* the *Life Story* by Aung Mon has relatively little discussion of lineage; it ends with Ledi's funeral and memorial activities.[30] It covers the same events in Ledi's life as the previous biographies and does not seek a new interpretation of them. In fact, it often relies on the *Great Monk Ledi* and the *Ledi Lineage.* Its usefulness comes from the detail it provides. Indeed, at 1,001 pages it is encyclopedic. I use it as a resource to check and at times expand the information found in the other biographies.

These books strive for a thorough accounting of Ledi's life, and they show the influence of the modern Western biography in their naturalistic presentations and substantiation of facts. But Western conventions do not entirely determine their concerns or style. Understanding the significance that these works seek to give to events in Ledi's life reveals how he was regarded and portrayed for a Burmese audience. For instance, consider the following passage describing Ledi's birth from the *Great Monk Ledi:*

AN AUSPICIOUS SIGN

When [Ledi Sayadaw's[31] mother] gave birth to him—he who would be like the highest ornament adorning the three jewels—there transpired an extraordinary, auspicious sign, an amazing event. At the front of their house a big rainbow, called by various names, including "Indra's bow," came out of a nearby clump of bamboo poles and went into a tamarind tree in a marvelous way, like fireworks. While all the villagers of Sainpyin [Cuiṅ' Praṅ'] looked on, noisily jostling each other, the aforesaid rainbow then swooped down from the sky and went into [Ledi's] house. From inside the house it flew to the roof, suffusing it with a variety of colors in stripes of blue, green, red, yellow, etc. Then it was said that the rainbow flew up to the sky, hovered there, and disappeared.[32]

The *Great Monk Ledi* tells of the numinous appearance of a rainbow at Ledi's birth not simply to impress the reader or foreshadow his greatness. The biography uses such an event as a means to connect Ledi's life to larger patterns of religious significance constructed in earlier biographies, even to the biography of the Buddha himself, whose life acts as the template used to evaluate the significance of all others.[33] Just as auspicious events signaled the Buddha's birth, so they did for Ledi. This story of the rainbow, then, is a constructive part of the biographical narrative that places him within a sacred arc that begins prior to his birth and stretches beyond his death.[34] In Burmese biographies, operating under the laws of karma and rebirth, there is a robust sense of the past's role in creating the present, and so such works often pass from the genre of personal biography to wider historical study. Biographies tend to include information beyond what bears directly on the human subject; in fact, the commonly used word for biography in Burmese, *atthuppatti,* conveys a range of meanings that include "story," "fable," and "history."[35] Awareness of this more expansive sense of what a biography can be enables us to understand the significance of Ledi's life as part of a collective history that goes beyond the personality of the individual.[36]

The wondrous story of Ledi's birth, especially considering its part in a larger story that includes the Buddha, points to the hagiographical slant of these biographies. While magical or supernatural events are relatively infrequent in them, they do present Ledi consistently in a positive light. They note controversies in which he was involved, but they assume always the propriety of his position. For instance, Wunnita discusses the controversy surrounding Ledi's Abhidhamma commentary, the *Paramatthadīpanī,* in order to demonstrate the vindication of Ledi's opinions by other august scholar-monks.[37] Frank Reynolds has suggested a distinction between biographies of religious figures that "humanize," which is to say those that present their subject with human failings, and those biographies which "spiritualize" their subject, which is done "by expunging references to his human weakness, mental lapses, signs of occasional cruelty, and so on."[38] Wunnita clearly spiritualizes Ledi, as do Hla Pain and Aung Mon. Additionally, it is important to note that official censorship in Burma, which has varied in intensity but certainly exerted an influence on Hla Pain and Aung Mon, promoted spiritualization, because showing signs of discord or controversy in Buddhist matters was officially disfavored.[39] This quality to the works reminds us to pay careful attention to their agendas and contexts, as described above, in order to use their wealth of information effectively.

Ledi as a Child and a Look Ahead

This study is not a biography in the strict sense of the term. Its goals are narrower, to explain Ledi's role in the growth of meditation and to determine what this explanation means for understanding modern forms of Buddhism. Its focus, therefore, is on those of his actions and writings that reveal his seminal part in the development of meditation into a practice widely accessible to laypeople.

The amazing rainbow that accompanied Ledi's birth, described in the passage above, appeared in Sainpyin village on Tuesday, the thirteenth day of the second half of the Burmese month of Nat-taw (Nat' tau) in the Burmese year 1208. This was December 24, 1846. Ledi was named Tet Kaun (Tak' Koṅ'),[40] the first of his parents' children to live and, ultimately, the oldest of five.[41] The name of his father was U Tun Tha and his mother Daw Chum.[42] They were rice farmers, and Tet Kaun grew up in a typical Burmese village with life revolving around agriculture and the local monastery.

When Tet Kaun was ten years of age, his parents sent him to study at the village monastery.[43] Prior to the arrival of the British, this was the usual site of a boy's education.[44] Continuing a common pattern, at age fifteen Tet Kaun ordained as a novice monk (*kui raṅ'* or *sāmaṇera*) in his village monastery under the supervision of the abbot, the sayadaw U Nanda. He took the name Nyanadaza (Ñāṇadhaja), meaning "banner of wisdom."[45] While a pupil of U Nanda, the novice Nyanadaza studied the foundational texts of the Burmese Buddhist tradition, including the *paritta*s (suttas for chanting for the purpose of protection), the *Dhammanīti* and *Lokanīti* (texts of basic ethical training), *nissaya*s (word-by-word Burmese commentaries on Pali texts), grammars, and the *Abhidhammatthasaṅgaha,* the primer used as an introduction to the study of the Abhidhamma.[46] The young monk became well known as an exceptional student.[47]

At eighteen years of age Nyanadaza left the novicehood briefly to help his parents with farming, but he returned to the religious life after eight months in order to continue his studies. He traveled to a nearby village, called Yay-tweq (Rai Thvak'), to study under another monk, U Gandhamā, famous for his knowledge of Hindu texts, literary composition, and astrology.[48] At this time Nyanadaza began to compose various forms of religious poetry. Here we see an early indication of his literary efforts, and it seems likely that from the start of his monastic training his teachers encouraged such a diligent and intelligent young monk to acquire the literary skill so important for monastic success at the elite level.[49] At the age of twenty, in 1866, Nyanadaza took full ordination under U Nanda, and he studied with him and another monk, the sayadaw U Dhamma, until he left his village to continue his education in the royal capital of Mandalay.[50]

Momentous historical events were taking place in Burma at this time. When the boy who would become Ledi Sayadaw ordained as a novice in 1861, the territory ruled by the Burmese king had recently undergone a drastic contraction. In 1853, King Mindon had taken over the kingdom from his half-brother Pagan, partly as a result of Pagan's disastrous war with the British that resulted in the loss of Lower Burma.[51] Ledi certainly must have known about these events. Indeed, a coup led against Mindon in 1866 caused such disruption in the country that Ledi had to delay his journey to Mandalay by about a year. Nonetheless, his monastic education seems to have continued without serious disturbance in the countryside. It was the journey he eventually made to live in the royal capital that marked a radical change in his life, for during his time there he was exposed to the ongoing encounter with the West. Before he left the city, he would find himself an active participant in that encounter.

The next chapter describes Ledi's formative education as a monk in Mandalay and his eventual return to his natal area to found the Ledi monastery. His time in the royal capital impressed upon him a strong sense of the importance of literary mastery for monastic success and for facing the challenges that confronted Burmese Buddhist society. His activities there also made him aware of Western cultures and exposed him to meditation as a scholastic topic that could be used to make sense of the modern world, including scientific knowledge from the West. Ledi left Mandalay in 1883, after the monastery in which he lived and taught burned down, caught up in one of the many large-scale fires that plagued the city in the unstable years that preceded the British annexation in 1885 of the last free portion of Burma. It was around this time that he entered the forest and took up meditation. At that charged moment Ledi said the end of Buddhism was near, and his sense of Buddhism's dire situation pushed him to develop a view of the karmic forces of history that would reappear in his meditation practice.

Subsequent chapters continue the story of Ledi's life as they delve into aspects of his career and writings that contributed to his vision of meditation. Chapter 2 considers a tremendous controversy Ledi caused with the publication of his Abhidhamma commentary, the *Paramatthadīpanī*. The central question of the chapter is why a work that is highly technical, written in Pali, and concerned with a twelfth-century Sri Lankan text would cause fractious public meetings in cities across the country, elicit numerous responses in newspapers and books, and even incite a book burning. The answer reveals the value of the Abhidhamma as a resource for meditative practice, and the story of the controversy shows how Ledi learned the power of print culture and of the spiritual possibilities for lay life.

The third chapter follows Ledi onto the national stage as he puts the lessons he has learned into action as a way to protect Buddhism. During this period, he wrote many popular works in an easy-to-understand style; he preached all over the country, drawing huge crowds with his entertaining sermons; and he tirelessly organized social groups to allow laypeople to act on their own initiative. In all three spheres of activity, Ledi's goal was to enable the laity to take on a new role in Buddhism, one that would empower them to meditate. The cornerstone of his efforts was the Abhidhamma. He taught it comprehensively and continually, "like falling rain," as one Burmese scholar put it. In order to show his creative use of the Abhidhamma in all his spheres of action, the next chapter, the fourth, examines in detail Ledi's most popular work and one of modern Burma's first bestsellers, an Abhidhamma poem called the *Summary of the Ultimates*. This influential poem exemplifies the ways Ledi used learning to revamp lay life, expanding its possibilities and setting the stage for mass practice.

The fifth chapter concerns the culmination of Ledi's efforts. He moved meditation to the forefront of Buddhist practice, using the strategies that were important throughout his career: his emphasis on the laity, his efforts to make meditation simple and accessible, and his reliance on the Abhidhamma. His writings show how he reconfigured meditation and, by doing so, reshaped Burmese Buddhism into a distinctly modern form, one that relied upon precolonial inheritances even as it responded to colonial challenges. Ledi would say that the ideal lay meditator could be called "a monk in the world," suggesting that the birth of insight was the fruition of his vision of modern life rooted in a Buddhist perspective.

The conclusion finishes the story of Ledi's life and, in light of the book's exploration of his transformation of meditation, considers the impact of his vision of modern Buddhism in Burma and beyond. Thousands of years earlier, the Buddha had established devotion as the exemplary practice for Tapussa and Bhallika, not through his words but with a gift given from his own hands. The Shwedagon still draws thousands of people every day due to the power of this practice. In the conclusion, however, we will consider a very different lesson the Buddha teaches in contemporary Yangon. This teaching is given at another *stūpa* called the Botataung. There, insight practice and learning become the Buddha's gift to people, a gift once again given from his own hands. In tandem with a consideration of Ledi's influence on later meditation teachers, stretching into the West and up to the present day, the lesson of the Botataung Buddha will allow us to gain a more precise understanding of the nature of social change that led to a quintessentially modern form of Buddhism. Though the Botataung and Shwedagon stūpas are only a few miles apart, hundreds of years and dramatic historical disruptions separate the lessons given at each. This book traces the distance and time through Ledi's life, as it follows the birth of a simple practice with a complex history.

The story begins in the next chapter during a time of great upheaval, when young Ledi traveled alone to Mandalay to face a crucial test.

ONE

The Best of Times and the Worst: Ledi Sayadaw's Formative Period

In 1869, U Nyanadaza, the young monk who would become Ledi Sayadaw, sat down in a pavilion at the entrance to Thanjaun (Saṃ kyoṅ‘ ”), a royal monastery in the capital of Mandalay.[1] He had traveled many rugged miles from his village and endured many hardships to be there, in the hope of winning a spot in what was perhaps the most prestigious monastic institution in the land.[2] It must have been a daunting scene: before him, Thanjaun's outer walls rose two stories high, enclosing over twenty buildings, many gilded and topped with multi-tiered roofs. As impressive as it must have been, the monastery formed only a small part of Mandalay's dazzling panorama. It sat near the king's ornate palace complex amid numerous large monasteries and mansions. The buildings so sparkled with gilt and semiprecious stones the city was said to resemble Amaravatī, the heavenly capital of the god Indra's realm. Indeed, Mandalay was often called "the city of gems."[3]

Alone at the entrance, Ledi began to chant the *pātimokkha,* the monastic code that guides the life of the ordained. Admission to Thanjaun as a resident monk required a flawless recitation from memory.[4]

In many ways, at the moment he sat there, it was the best possible time for an ambitious and scholarly monk to be in Mandalay: the saṅgha had an unprecedented level of support from the king; intellectual inquiry and literary production flourished in the capital among those scholar-monks who were expert at navigating the complex and immense Buddhist textual corpus, "the ocean of the *piṭakas*," as the Burmese put it.[5] Nearby, lay literati at the court were also commissioning, writing, and studying Buddhist texts on a variety of topics, including meditation, in fruitful collaboration with monastics. Yet it was also the worst time to be a young monk in the capital: the British had split Burma in two, taking control of its lower half and destabilizing the remnant that remained independent; greatly weakened, the king faced the possibility of a total loss of his country to a foreign power; and the saṅgha, unified since 1784, had splintered into contentious factions.[6]

Ledi made it into Thanjaun. Once behind its walls, he gained a position from which he could observe and eventually participate in Burma's conflicted and precarious situation. His formative experiences during this time taught him how monks, the king, and lay courtiers used Buddhist learning, including learning about meditation, as a way to answer Burma's societal challenges. Ledi would depend upon these experiences to shape his own responses to the arrival of British colonial rule. In the process, he would formulate a vision of Buddhism for all Burmese that included the practice of insight meditation.

A Lineage of Learning

Almost a century before Ledi went to Mandalay, a group of monks, who came to be called the Thudhamma (*Sudhammā*), had gained the support of King Bodawpaya (ruled 1782–1819) and instituted a program of monastic reform that would mark Ledi's experiences at Thanjaun.[7] The proximate cause of the reform was a debate over whether novice monks entering a village or formally appearing before the laity should cover both shoulders, as fully ordained monks did, or leave one shoulder bare. This was not a trivial matter, for upon it hinged the issue of whether monastic authority rested upon scripture alone or a blend of scripture and local custom.[8] The Thudhamma monks maintained that scripture alone determined proper behavior, which led them to advocate that novice monks cover both shoulders. King Bodawpaya's decision to side with the Thudhamma monks did not introduce an entirely new valuation of textual authority—monks on both sides of the debate championed textual prowess—but it contributed to a culture in which monastic and court literati won power through the use of texts.[9] This was especially so because the king required all monks to reordain in the Thudhamma lineage and hew to its particular textual focus.[10]

Along with re-ordination came an effort to standardize the educational curriculum of monks throughout the country. This kingdom-wide regularization of the study and use of texts, though never completed, strengthened the ties between village monks and elites at the capital.[11] King Bodawpaya also emulated these Thudhamma textual practices. In conjunction with growing political centralization and literacy among the Burmese populace, a focus on texts led to the rise of lay literati who used the mastery of texts as a means to prestige and power.[12] This further cohered monastic and lay literary practices and would enable Ledi to tap into lay literati knowledge as well as monastic expertise. He also had a particularly strong connection to this literary ethos that went beyond his ordination into the Thudhamma lineage. His early monastic training took place in the heartland of the Thudhamma approach to Buddhism. He was born and raised in the center of the Lower Chindwin River Valley, where this movement began in the mid-eighteenth century. Furthermore, throughout the Konbaung Dynasty (1752–1885) the kings who ruled Burma and the most influential monastic and lay literary figures at the court emerged from this area.[13]

Their origins in the Chindwin region allowed Thudhamma monks to further buttress their claim to authority by presenting their lineage as one that adhered to the strict practices of forest-dwelling (*araññavāsī*) monks. In juxtaposition to town-dwelling (*gāmavāsī*) monks, forest monks were understood to live lives that cleaved more closely to the ideal of the homeless renunciant. It was not that the town-dwelling monk was considered illegitimate or subpar, but, as a rule, forest-monk status conferred added prestige and influence. For it was understood as a monastic lifestyle more rigorously devoted to spiritual pursuits (ideally, including meditation) and freer of the worldly temptations of cities and towns.[14] This gave forest monks greater potency as sources of merit, which drew lay people, including kings, to them. It also gave such monks greater authority to innovate. In Burma and across the Theravāda world, appealing to forest-monk status was a way to justify changes in practice and the assumption of an authoritative role in the saṅgha.[15] At the start of the Thudhamma reformation, the group's peripheral location in the Chindwin Valley, relatively far from the capital, made their claim to be forest monks credible. By the mid-nineteenth century, however, they could hardly claim to be outsiders, as they were the only lineage of significance in Burma. Nonetheless, the trope of the forest monk remained a powerful one in the institutional memory of the group. Ledi would eventually return to the Lower Chindwin Valley to make his own claim to forest-monk status around the time of the arrival of the British.

Life at Thanjaun

Ledi picked Thanjaun because of the fame of the Thanjaun Sayadaw as a learned monk.[16] His choice reflects his ambition, for it went against the usual practice in which a monk from outlying areas joined whatever monastery had a connection to his village.[17] Even if the monastery's intellectual rigor drew Ledi in, however, the way learning and power dovetailed in Burmese Buddhism meant he also had joined an institution at the apex of the monastic hierarchy. The abbots of Thanjaun, appointed by the king, were some of the most powerful monks in the land. The current head, the third Thanjaun Sayadaw, had been a personal teacher of Mindon, was a favorite of the queens, and occupied a dominant position on the king's advisory council of monks, the Thudhamma Council. In addition, his teacher, the The-in Sayadaw (died 1846), had been the *thathanabaing* (*sāsana puiṅ'*), the head of all monks in Burma designated by the king. While Mindon had not tapped another head monk after the death of the preceding thathanabaing (the Maungdaung Sayadaw) in 1865, the Thanjaun Sayadaw's powerful positions and the patronage he received suggests that he had become the *de facto* head of monks in Burma.[18]

Mere recitation of the pātimokkha did not get Ledi access to the Thanjaun Sayadaw. Within the monastery, a monk had to prove himself to win good accommodations and the attention of the senior monks. At the start, Ledi was just a face in the crowd—an especially large crowd, in fact, as he entered the monastery at the start of the yearly rains retreat (*vā* or *vassa*), when many monks had settled down at Thanjaun for the period.[19] Because of this, Ledi's first sleeping place at the monastery was a spot of ground by a water pot, often soaking wet because of spills. All he had to sleep on was a scrap of leather hide and a rough cloth made from gourd, which he rolled up every day so other monks could use the space to collect water.[20]

Such a humble beginning reported in Ledi's biographies accentuates his subsequent success. He knew he had to draw attention to himself as a serious scholar to escape the water pot. He applied himself with vigor to group lectures and personal study, and he made an effort to stand out from the crowd. For instance, when the monks at Thanjaun recited together, Ledi would speak very loudly.[21] The abbot soon noticed the young monk:

> Seeing the monk Nyanadaza, who was very brilliant and industrious, and who also had an intention to gain wisdom, he [the Thanjaun Sayadaw] called him into his presence and said:
>
> Thanjaun Sayadaw: "By what monastic title are you called?"

Ledi: "I am called Nyanadaza, Venerable Sir."

Thanjaun Sayadaw: "Well, that distinguished name is noble!"

When the Thanjaun Sayadaw had spoken in this way, he called for the Salin Sayadaw, U Pandicca, who was a disciple very skilled in literature, and said to him: "Maung Salin, you should pay attention to this young monk and help with his teaching. Young monk, you attend the lessons of Maung Salin, and train with me too."

When the Thanjaun Sayadaw had said this, both the Salin Sayadaw and U Nyanadaza said together, "Yes, venerable sir."[22]

By distinguishing himself, Ledi won further training with a monk "skilled in literature," and one who was powerful in his own right: the Salin Sayadaw also held a seat on the king's council.[23]

What is notably lacking in the description of Ledi's life at Thanjaun is meditation as a practice, the prior claim of Thudhamma monks to forest-monk status notwithstanding. We will see later in the chapter that some monks had turned to meditation around this time, but they had done so as part of a movement that sought refuges for practice some miles from the capital in the hills across the Irrawaddy River above the village of Sagaing. In contrast, monks who remained at the center of prestige and power in Mandalay focused on scholarship.

The King and the Saṅgha

King Mindon had ruled Burma for thirteen years when Ledi arrived in Mandalay.[24] He had ascended to his position in 1853, not long before the Second Anglo-Burmese War ended in the humiliating loss of the entirety of Lower Burma, just like the previous one fought with the British in 1824–26. Mindon sought to strengthen Burma in light of its precarious position, sandwiched between the direct or indirect imperial powers of the British and the French. Because he could not afford to risk open conflict, to prop up his authority he emphasized his role as the *dhammarāja,* the righteous ruler who supports and protects Buddhism.[25] While Ferguson's statement that "Mindon basically tried to solve his nation's problems by becoming a better Buddhist"[26] perhaps simplifies the situation too much, he did rely to an unprecedented extent on Buddhism.[27] By doing so, he emphasized to his subjects, Ledi included, the links between the saṅgha and the state.

Mindon far outstripped his predecessors in his meritorious Buddhist deeds.[28] Among them, the royal record of his reign lists building pagodas, monasteries, and rest houses; gilding pagodas; digging canals and wells; repairing water tanks and ponds; putting his sons into the monkhood;

donating money to monks successful in exams; giving daily food to the saṅgha; freeing animals from death; and sponsoring cremations.[29] One of Mindon's most notable acts was the placing of a new *hti* (a finial) on top of the Shwedagon Pagoda in Rangoon in 1871, deep in British-held Burma.[30] Such an act was a means not just to legitimate his rule but also a way to maintain a sense of the unity of Burmese culture between royal Upper Burma and the British-controlled territory of Lower Burma.[31]

Beyond his role as patron, the dhammarāja had another quintessential duty, to protect the saṅgha, especially from internal decline due to the slackening of monastic discipline. This was of great concern because monks, living in the most auspicious way possible through their adherence to the rules of discipline (the Vinaya) laid down by the Buddha, were the key source of merit (*puñña*), or good kamma, for the lay people who supported them. The purer the monk's fealty to the code of discipline, the greater the merit a lay person gained by giving to that monk.[32] Just as Mindon surpassed prior kings in his patronage, he tried to enforce regulations on monks' behavior that were stricter than in previous kings' reigns, in order to insure good monastic discipline. On February 15, 1856, he sent out a royal order proscribing monks from such practices as farming, asking for money, attending puppet shows and boxing matches, engaging in alchemy, and having sex with women.[33] To insure monastic adherence to his law, Mindon relied upon a system of ecclesiastical administration. The most important figure in this system was the thathanabaing, who was chosen by the king. The king also appointed the committee of eight monks called the Thudhamma Council to assist the thathanabaing.[34] Outside of Mandalay, monks called *gaing-oks* (*guiṇ'" up'*) supervised districts and, under them, *gaing-dauks* (*guiṇ'" thauk'*) administered sub-districts.[35] One of the key duties of these officials was to tally the numbers, location, and disciplinary fitness of the monastic population and report the findings back to Mandalay. Further, in Mandalay Mindon appointed two laymen to assist the thathanabaing, the *mahadanwun* (*mahā dān' wan'*, the officer of religious affairs, sometimes called the ecclesiastical censor) and the *mahadansaye* (*mahā dān' cā re"*, the clerk of religious affairs). These men were instructed to walk the streets of Mandalay in the morning and to apprehend any monks seen to be acting contrary to the Vinaya.[36]

Mindon's efforts show how closely he involved himself in the affairs of the monkhood. But, though monks generally accepted that the king had a role in saṅgha purification, the extent of his control was a contentious matter. Ledi had entered an environment in Mandalay in which the saṅgha and the state were closely related, but hardly in lock-step. Members of the saṅgha could and did resist state control. For instance, many well-known monks, even some members of the Thudhamma Council, balked at Mindon's law of 1856, not because they objected to the prohibitions but because they disagreed with the king's claim to power over the saṅgha implied by the law. They argued that the Vinaya itself had a clear enumeration of all the rules that monks needed to follow.[37] As noted at the start of the chapter, the Thanjaun Sayadaw was serving as a sort of tacit thathanabaing when Ledi arrived in Mandalay, but Mindon may have left the post officially vacant so that he could exercise his authority more directly over what could clearly be a resistant monastic community.

Beyond his efforts to control saṅgha behavior, Mindon took another step in 1859 that profoundly affected Burmese Buddhism. He recognized a monk, the Shwegyin Sayadaw, as the founder of a separate sect (*nikāya*) within the saṅgha distinct from the Thudhamma.[38] Mindon apparently did so because he admired the Shwegyin Sayadaw's reform-minded views, and perhaps because he hoped to use the presence of another *nikāya* as a means to divide the saṅgha and so control it more easily.[39] Yet, rather than making monks more tractable, Mindon's recognition of a new sect further atomized the saṅgha and made it even harder to control. Numerous sects formed during and after his reign, each claiming to adhere more purely to the Vinaya and often invoking the powerful model of the forest monk.[40] This growth of factionalism was exacerbated by the situation in Lower Burma, where the British did not attempt any control over the saṅgha and so allowed dissenting groups a base of operation to draw Upper Burma into further feuding. Although he was the paragon of support for Buddhism, by splintering the saṅgha Mindon contributed to a growing sense among the Burmese that Buddhism was under grave threat.[41]

When Ledi entered Thanjaun, he gained a clear vantage point on this dynamic and interdependent, but fractious, relationship between saṅgha and state. No doubt he had a sense of this relationship when he was back in his home village, but studying under teachers operating at the highest levels of the monastic hierarchy in close collaboration with the king offered him the chance for a more profound exposure to the complex relationship between the two.

King, Court, and Foreign Learning

Mindon and his courtiers recognized the power of Western learning, and key court figures sought to use Western technological and scientific developments as a way to strengthen Burma. The introduction of minted money, the establishment of a regularized system of taxation, the use of a printing press, and the development of a means for transmitting Burmese by telegraph were just some of the measures taken.[42] The literati associated with the court were themselves following earlier developments in the late eighteenth and early nineteenth centuries among Chindwin monks and the king, who sought to use learning as a means to buttress state and saṅgha. They had focused primarily on religious texts at first, but had soon turned to a broader range of materials, even those concerned with ostensibly "worldly" matters.[43]

Particular people at the court became sources of knowledge and expertise.[44] This individualistic aspect of the accrual of Western learning is important to note, because Ledi formed a close relationship with one person deeply engaged with the West, a man named Hpo Hlaing. Born in 1830, he had been a longtime friend of Mindon; they had attended the same monastery in their youth. He advised Mindon in his rebellion against King Pagan and won for his help the right of appanage to the area called "Yaw," hence his title the "Yaw Atwin Wun," or the "Minister of Yaw." Hpo Hlaing was known for combining an expertise in Burmese literature with an avid interest in Western scientific knowledge.[45] His library was said to be stocked with Western books, and in 1870 he commissioned the building of a brick monastery in Mandalay modeled on an Italian building.[46] Hpo Hlaing had a number of European books on technical subjects translated into Burmese, including André-Marie Ampère's French textbook on chemistry and an Italian book on anatomy.[47] He also arranged for ninety students to be sent to study in France, Italy, and England, and Mindon made him responsible for handling all interactions with foreigners at the court.[48] Hlaing thus acted as a key conduit for the king's and the court's knowledge of the Western world.

It had taken real grit to get into Thanjaun, especially considering it was not a monastery with connections to his village. But Ledi, a young monk from a family of farmers, showed an even more brazen determination by gaining the tutelage of this high-placed official. Ledi repeatedly visited Hpo Hlaing's house, even though he was told time after time the minister was too busy to speak with him. Finally, Hpo Hlaing—perhaps in exasperation—came out of his house and asked the young monk why he kept coming by. Ledi replied that he wanted to become skilled in literature like the minister.[49] Impressed by Ledi's intelligence (and perhaps his cheekiness), thereafter Hpo Hlaing met often with him. Ledi subsequently credited Hpo Hlaing with exerting a powerful influence over him, saying: "My ability to write is just thanks to Yaw [Hpo Hlaing]. I write in the manner in which he writes."[50] At the time, most writers added redundancies and the repetition of words for rhyming effect. Hpo Hlaing counseled

Ledi to reject this style and instead write in a way that was "succinct and clear."[51] Ledi took his advice: he later became well known for writing works that broke ground in terms of their accessibility to a broad audience. In addition, Hpo Hlaing was known to say exactly what he thought, whatever the consequences.[52] His attitude may have promoted a tendency in Ledi to be blunt and unsparing. As we will see in the next chapter, Ledi offended many with the brusque writing style he employed some years later in his first well-known work.[53]

Ledi's relationship with the minister gave him the opportunity to acquire knowledge about a wider world of learning, as well as the chance to observe at close hand the ways in which the king and courtiers used learning, both foreign and local, to address the challenges to the state. In one instance, Ledi even participated directly in a court-orchestrated event that attempted to use textual control as a means to spiritual and political strength.

The Fifth Council

From April 15 to September 12 of 1871, a large group of monks, many of them the most senior and revered monastics in the land, gathered together in the royal palace in Mandalay. Ledi, just twenty-five years old, was among them. They convened to hold what is referred to in Pali as a *saṅgīti* or a *saṅgāyanā,* meaning a general council of the saṅgha of monks, in which the Buddhist canon is recited. The holding of such a council was of huge symbolic importance to Mindon, who had ordered the monks to convene from across the realm. There had never been such a council in Burma, and Mindon's was reckoned to be only the fifth since the first was held, just a month after the Buddha's death.[54]

Oddly, the precise reason to hold a council had never been fixed, and the purposes for which they were held had varied. At the first, the monks were concerned to codify the teachings of the Buddha.[55] The second council, which took place some one hundred years later in the city of Vesāli, was meant to settle a dispute over ten points of monastic behavior.[56] The third, held in the Indian king Asoka's (c. 304–232 BCE) capital of Pāṭaliputta, was concerned with disagreements over interpretations of the *dhamma.*[57] Finally, the fourth took place in Sri Lanka in the first century BCE, when monks, concerned the shrinking of the monkhood would lead to the loss of the teachings, committed the canon to writing.[58] As no council had taken place for centuries after the fourth (in the Burmese view) and never in Burma, convening a fifth council was an unparalleled and powerful act on Mindon's part.[59] And because there was no preestablished objective to such a meeting, he could hope to use it to answer the problems of his own time.

To be sure, his problems abounded. As mentioned earlier, the Burmese saṅgha had splintered into disputatious factions. In the political sphere as well, Mindon faced grave challenges. The second Anglo-Burmese war of 1852–53 still hung over the kingdom like a pall. Subsequently, the fighting necessary to quell a coup in 1866 left dead the heir to the throne, the Kanaung Prince, and caused many people to emigrate to Lower Burma to take advantage of its political stability and the free land available there for rice cultivation.[60] This outflow of the population weakened the king's political power and the economy of the kingdom. Around the same time, Mindon was also forced to sign the Anglo-Burmese Commercial Treaty of 1867.[61] The treaty undercut Burmese sovereignty and humiliated the crown by allowing the British to travel freely up the Irrawaddy River and to use royal regalia.[62] In response to these events, the Fifth Council was a way to reassert the stability and superiority of royal Burma by showing the strength of its Buddhism.

Whether the issue was doctrinal disputation, monastic behavior, or something else, the assumption was, however, that a solution required that the saṅgha come together as a single corporate entity in the ritualized act of chanting.[63] As kings had done in earlier councils, Mindon probably hoped to show his strength by reunifying the splintered saṅgha through the process of communal recitation. Yet the council did not bring together monastic factions, for the monks of breakaway sects, such as the Shwegyin, would not take part. Their formation as self-governing groups had put them beyond the Thudhamma hierarchy, and they had no wish to participate in an event that would indicate allegiance to Thudhamma monks under the king.[64]

Because Mindon did not reunify the saṅgha in the council, scholars such as Ferguson have tended to view it as a failure.[65] Yet the record shows that Mindon treated Buddhist issues with sophistication and forethought. He hardly fumbled along in a reactionary way, and he appointed highly capable courtiers to assist him, such as Hpo Hlaing. Given this state of affairs, it seems unlikely that the refusal of some monastic groups to participate would catch him by surprise. In fact, surely he at least suspected that non-Thudhamma monks would decline to take part. The fact that he chose to hold the council anyway suggests well-established objectives for it beyond the hope of totally unifying the monkhood. For one thing, even if unification was not total, the council promoted the participating Thudhamma *nikāya* as the most authoritative group of monks. This perhaps made a virtue out of a vice, accepting the various sects and domesticating them under the authority of the king and his council focused on the prestigious and powerful communal chanting of the canon.[66]

Furthermore, the inability to unite the saṅgha as a whole brought to the fore another purpose of the council. Since its defining activity was the group recitation of the Pali texts, it was natural in the context of a split monkhood to emphasize its function as a means to purify and preserve not the saṅgha but the *tipiṭaka.* This was not a novel purpose for a council either, as the example of the fourth, which put the canon in writing, makes clear. From the Burmese perspective, the Fifth Council's stress on textual preservation was natural enough, and it added to the sense of the sāsana as rooted in its texts that transcended any sectarianism. It seems, too, to have created a sense of the king, as patron of the texts' preservation, as above sectarian squabbles.

There was, in fact, already a long history of royal concern for the texts of the dhamma in Burma. The Fifth Council was made to fit into earlier efforts by Burmese kings aimed at textual purification for political ends. For instance, earlier in the Konbaung Dynasty King Bodawpaya (ruled 1781–1819) had devoted himself to the running of the Royal Library, and he sponsored the editing and production of several copies of the canon because he feared that errors had crept into the texts.[67] It became, in fact, a standard practice for a Konbaung king, upon his accession to the throne, to sponsor the copying of the tipiṭaka.[68] Before the council, Mindon had had copies produced on palm leaf with an iron stylus, on palm leaf in ink, and on gilded palm leaf. Like Bodawpaya, prior to the copying Mindon had also had the texts examined closely for errors in a rigorous process that involved many sayadaws and laymen of the court, including Hpo Hlaing.[69] After the copying on palm leaf manuscripts had been completed, Mindon decided to go one step further. By May 4, 1868, approximately three years before the first meeting of the Fifth Council, he had had the texts checked for errors by senior monks and then incised on 729 marble tablets.[70]

The council took place, then, after all the work to purify the texts and to record them on both palm leaves and stone was finished. This counterintuitive order of events further supports the point that a lack of saṅgha unity caused a somewhat redundant stress on textual purification and control (so far as I know no errors were found). Yet it was hardly mere repetition, for the act of chanting the texts also offered other important benefits. Recitation produced beneficial merit and the ritualized act of chanting assured that the merit bore fruit.[71] Powerful and effective chanting depended, of course, on the proper command and control of the texts, and so the protection of royal Burma through the apotropaic effects of chanting dovetailed with the efforts at purification.

This notion that the purpose of a council was to insure the purity of texts became highly influential, so much so that many sources confuse the order of events of the carving of the tipiṭaka and the holding of the Fifth Council. It is often assumed that the latter led to the former.[72] For instance, in the official souvenir album published by the Burmese government upon the finish of the Sixth Council in 1956, one of the leading sayadaws of the event states:

> The elders of former days, Arahant Kassapa, Arahant Yasa, and Arahant Moggalli-putta Tissa of India, Arahant Rakkhita of Ceylon, and the learned Mahātheras of Mandalay, full of energy, treating the recension of the Texts as a matter of vital importance, had the Texts arranged, classified and recited whenever they saw dangers arising against the Buddha Sāsana; and with the ardent support of the then Rulers had convened the five previous Sangāyanās at the Fourth of which the texts were reduced to writing, and *in the Fifth of which they were inscribed on marble slabs. . . .*[73]

In the mid-twentieth century, at one of the most symbolically charged events of the newly independent country of Burma, an official voice of the Burmese saṅgha in a government publication equates the councils with textual preservation and puts the Fifth Council before the carving on stone. This confusion at the highest level represents the power of the notion that textual preservation is the point of a *saṅgāyanā.* It reflects, too, the dominant sense that the heart of the sāsana is in its texts.

The enduring cultural memory of the Fifth Council indicates that to take part in it was to participate in one of the most important activities of the saṅgha establishment during Mindon's reign, and one that had lasting effects. Even if somewhat compromised by an inability to unify all monastics, the council stood as a powerful example of how the saṅgha and state worked together for the mutual benefit of both: the preservation and support of the sāsana, on the one hand, and the health and endurance of the state, on the other.

Ledi had a prominent role in the council as one of the monks who recited a canonical text. Recitation during the council was not done *en masse.* Instead, a monk would recite a text or part of a text to the assembled monks and, in particular, to a learned senior monk who would listen for errors. One can imagine the pressure a reciting monk felt as he chanted the text in front of thousands of the most respected sayadaws in the land, not to mention famous courtiers and even perhaps the king. Ledi was one of these lone monks. He recited by himself the entirety of the *Kathāvatthu,* one of the seven books of the Abhidhamma Piṭaka, the abstract philosophical works of the Theravāda Buddhist canon. His recitation from memory, done without assistance and without any mistakes, undoubtedly helped to cement his position as a leading young monk. Wunnita describes the following reaction to his recitation: "When one monk [Ledi] in the recitation hall recited by himself the *Kathāvatthu,* it was said that the monks, novices, men, and royal officials were all amazed. They praised him, saying that he had a great deal of courage."[74]

Reciting an Abhidhamma text was particularly significant, given that the Abhidhamma had—and still has—pride of place among the texts of the canon in Burma, as those that contain the complete expression of the Buddha's teaching. We will explore in the next chapter the historical reasons for the development of the Burmese valuation of the Abhidhamma, but here we can note that in such a climate, in which textual mastery was the means to authority, demonstration of mastery of one of the most esteemed texts was a significant accomplishment on Ledi's part. What is more, this demonstration took place in the midst of a gathering of elite monks that lasted for many months. Ledi's deep involvement in this milieu gave him the opportunity to meet and fraternize with some of the most powerful and learned monks in Burma, to familiarize himself with the concerns and activities of the elite echelon of the Thudhamma *nikāya,* and to show off to his elders his knowledge and intellectual promise.

Ledi's biographies do not suggest a specific reason why such a young monk garnered such an important part in the council. They imply, however, that his role depended upon his prior demonstration of exceptional talent in scholarly work, including memorization. He got into Thanjaun on the basis of memorizing the monastic rules of conduct, and we have already seen that the Thanjaun abbot had recognized him as a promising student. Between the time of his arrival at Thanjaun and the holding of the council, Ledi had also been named *sa zo* (*cā chui*) or "head student."[75] This job was given to the young monk considered the best student-scholar in the monastery. The position required him to help teach his fellow students. He had to provide paraphrases of the canonical texts during public meetings, and the paraphrases needed to include a philosophical explanation that required work with commentaries.[76] This role would have often put Ledi in the spotlight. Another possible reason for Ledi's position at the Fifth Council lay outside of the monastery: Hpo Hlaing had an active role in the council's organization. He was thus in a position to help Ledi win an important part in the proceedings. In fact, the text that Ledi recited, the *Kathāvatthu,* was one that Hpo Hlaing had recommended Ledi study with special care.[77]

After the council, Ledi's career continued on an upward trajectory. At the age of twenty-seven in 1873, in recognition of his teaching skill, the Thanjaun Sayadaw awarded him the title of "first teacher" (*pathama cā khya*).[78] Later, in 1880, Ledi wrote answers to twenty questions about the ten perfections (*pāramīs*) of the Buddha that the Thanjaun abbot had set before all the monks of the monastery. Apparently, only Ledi attempted a response, and his answers were collected into his first book, the *Manual on the Perfections* (*Pāramīdīpanī*).[79] Ledi was by this time also known as a voracious reader and an avid student of Abhidhamma literature.[80] In a clear sign of trust and respect on literary grounds, the Thanjaun Sayadaw lent Ledi his own books (no small gesture in a largely pre-print age), and another well-known scholar-monk, the May-aung Sayadaw, asked Ledi to compose a commentary on the notoriously difficult concluding stanzas of an Abhidhamma text entitled the *Maṇisāramañjūsā.*[81]

By his early thirties, Ledi had positioned himself within the highest levels of the ecclesiastical hierarchy in the capital. His part in Mindon's Fifth Council demonstrates his deep involvement in saṅgha activities involving the royal court. His participation in this event, in addition to his relationships with royally appointed monks like the Thanjaun Sayadaw and with the minister Hpo Hlaing, gave him a perspective on the activities involving the king and saṅgha that stressed the importance of learning. Yet a new interest in the practice of meditation was also emerging at this time among monks and at the court. Of particular note, Hpo Hlaing was even bringing his Western knowledge to bear on the conceptualization of meditation. He was thus in a position to impress upon Ledi the possibility of meditation as a means to incorporate Western knowledge into a Burmese Buddhist worldview, as well as to serve as a source of information about Mindon's and his court's activities in regard to meditation.

Meditation

The isolated instances of meditation as an actual practice suggest that it had not generated widespread interest among monks or the laity prior to the nineteenth century.[82] A monk named Waya-zaw-ta, who lived in the Sagaing Hills just across the Irrawaddy River from the royal capital, had started a vipassanā movement in the 1720s and 30s. He even told his disciples that his instructions could lead them all the way to the state of an *anāgāmī,* someone destined only for a heavenly rebirth before the attainment of awakening. But this movement was suppressed when he died, and the government defrocked his monk-disciples (and made them shovel elephant and horse manure in the royal stables).[83] Later, in 1754, a monk named Medhawi (1728–1816), later called the Taung-lei-lon Sayadaw, wrote the earliest example we have of a vernacular meditation manual.[84] He would go on to write over thirty more. There is no indication, however, that this sayadaw taught meditation widely or that his works had an extensive reach.

Nevertheless, the efforts of individuals like Waya-zaw-ta and Medhawi reflected, and perhaps contributed to, an ongoing shift in the conception of meditation's power.[85] The nature of this shift can be seen in the change in the possibility of living *arhats* in Burmese Buddhist chronicles of this period. Patrick Pranke has observed that the *Sāsanasuddhidīpaka* (1784) and the *Vaṃsadīpanī* (c. 1797) take for granted that no arhats exist in the saṅgha. But the 1831 *Thathanalinkara Sadan* states that awakening is possible for meditation practitioners, and the 1861 *Sāsanavaṃsa* goes further to claim that there are monks living in the saṅgha who are arhats.[86] Pranke has suggested that a growing belief in the possibility of awakening, starting in the eighteenth century, stemmed from the political and social disruptions that accompanied the decline of the Nyaungyan Dynasty of kings (1597–1752).[87] As people entered the uncertain time period before the Konbaung Dynasty, old truths broke down along with social institutions, and people began to rethink spiritual (and other) possibilities. Here is an instance, then, in which political destabilization enabled religious change.

The growing orthodoxy of the position that one could achieve awakening marked a crucial conceptual transformation. The belief that attaining *nibbāna* was impossible in these degenerate days was a common one across the Theravāda world at the time. But the growing prominence given to the possibility of awakening in these texts signaled a change that would enable a rethinking later about the potential of meditation practice on a mass scale. While a would-be meditator need not believe arhats exist, or even can exist, in order to believe in the value of meditation for the attainment of a better rebirth, the development of a belief in contemporary arhatship likely supported an increasing interest in meditation as a practical pursuit. With the profound societal disruptions that marked the transition to colonial rule, further changes would take place that depended on what was by that time the well-established belief in the possibility of becoming an arhat.

This change in attitude about arhatship in historical chronicles did not lead these works to promote meditation, however, let alone to argue—as was done abundantly later—that meditation was a necessary part of monks' and even the laity's lives. Such an attitude only began to take shape during Mindon's reign. This was due, at least in part, to the king's attempts to institute tighter controls on monastic behavior. Mindon's proclamation of the 1856 law enforcing stricter discipline pushed monks toward the *araññavāsī* forest practices that privileged meditation as part of a disciplined monastic life. A significant number of monks during the years of Mindon's reign did move to the hills of Sagaing, where they took up lives of contemplation and study in hermitages and caves.[88] For instance, the Htut-kaung Sayadaw (1798–1890), a renowned meditator who lived on Minwun Hill in Sagaing, trained over three hundred pupils in meditation.[89] Another monk, U Thila (1832–1907), adopted strict vegetarianism and emphasized ascetic practices and adherence to the Vinaya. He was rumored to be an arhat.[90] These monks mostly taught meditation to monastics, and neither encouraged meditation on a broad scale, but they attracted the court's patronage and likely spurred the courtly interest in the topic.[91]

At the same time, while Mindon's attempts to exert lay control over the saṅgha may have encouraged some monks, it alienated others. They, too, turned toward forest practices, but as a means to resist what they saw as royal meddling.[92] Some monks even went beyond Mindon's reform efforts to challenge the orthodoxy of the dominant Thudhamma lineage. One of the best-known monks to do this was the Hngettwin Sayadaw (1831–1910), who was at one time a tutor of Mindon's chief queen. By 1867, he, too, was living on Minwun Hill near Sagaing.[93] He is especially noteworthy because he was the first to require monks to meditate every day, and he encouraged lay people to do so as well.[94] The Hngettwin Sayadaw's impact, however, stemmed not from his emphasis on meditation but from his larger revisionist outlook that taught a sort of fundamentalist reform. Such reform included meditation but stressed also the correct understanding of the practice of donation (*dāna*) and proper conduct on the part of monks. The Hngettwin Sayadaw's reforms were a direct challenge to the Thudhamma orthodoxy, and they seem to represent an effort on his part to return the saṅgha to doctrinal purity.[95] This emphasis on purity, rather than on meditation specifically, explains why the Hngettwin Sayadaw established no lineage for teaching meditation that played a serious part in the later efflorescence of meditative practice in the early twentieth century. Neither Ledi nor any other famous meditation teacher invoked the Hngettwin Sayadaw as a model for practice.[96]

Parallel to an evolving monastic emphasis on meditation, court literati cultivated meditation as a literary topic that enabled control of a wider sphere of learning. For instance, Mindon commissioned a work about meditation entitled *Thu-ya-za Meq-ga Dipani Kyam* from the Maungdaung Sayadaw, his thathanabaing, sometime between the mid-1850s and mid-1860s. One of Mindon's queens, Ma-hei-ti, also requested the production of a book on vipassanā, the *Vipassanā kyei-hmon* by Sayadaw Thandima. It was composed in 1883.[97] Deserving of particular attention are two other texts written at the court by none other than Hpo Hlaing, *Taste of Liberation* (*Vimuttirasa*), written in 1871, and *Meditation on the Body* (*Kāyānupassanā*), written in 1875.[98] The texts reveal a concern for a lay readership and an effort to show meditation's relevance to knowledge about the modern world that presage and likely informed Ledi's presentation of meditation.[99]

Hpo Hlaing makes the broad scope of his intended readership explicit in the introductions to both works. He says he wrote *Taste of Liberation* in order to "make happy the people who are [meditation] *yogis,* who desire the path and fruit of nibbāna."[100] A few years later, in *Meditation on the Body,* he identifies his audience even more explicitly, saying he wrote the text "in order to cause all monks, novices, and lay people to easily understand [the subject matter of the book]."[101] Not only does Hpo Hlaing direct *Meditation on the Body* to a wide audience, but the request for the book came from another lay person, Mindon's daughter, the Salin Myosa princess.[102] Such an example of an interest in meditation within the lay sphere, both in terms of patron and author, suggests a nascent step toward a lay-centered focus. Additionally, Hpo Hlaing's intention to make the book, as he put it, "easy to understand"[103] signaled the possibility of Burmese meditation texts as practical aids to the pursuit of insight. Ledi's relationship with Hpo Hlaing may account for the premium Ledi placed on a comprehensible presentation of meditation as relevant to all people.

Easy-to-understand language notwithstanding, Hpo Hlaing's books are highly detailed and complex. In *Taste of Liberation,* he covers dependent origination (*paṭiccasamuppāda*), morality (*sīla*), consciousness (*citta*), the three marks of existence (*tilakkhaṇa*), wrong views (*micchādiṭṭhi*), no-self (anattā), and finishes with a chapter on nibbāna. In *Meditation on the Body,* as the title indicates, Hpo Hlaing breaks down the human body into its component parts as they are detailed in Buddhist Abhidhamma texts. In it he discusses the twenty-eight most basic elements of matter (*rūpa*) and the thirty-two parts of the body, as well as the *kalāpa*s, the subatomic particles that comprise physical matter. Both works seek an encyclopedic coverage. They are not so much handbooks for practice as reference works.

Meditation on the Body is particularly interesting because in it Hpo Hlaing explicitly places European learning within a Burmese Buddhist perspective.[104] I mentioned earlier that Hlaing had had an Italian anatomy textbook (*anātamī ca so roma nuiṅ' ṅaṃ*) translated into Burmese. It is this textbook that he reconciles with the Buddhist understanding of a human's physical makeup in *Meditation on the Body*.[105] Throughout the book Hlaing frequently interrupts his Abhidhammic explication of particular parts of the body to compare the Italian text's description of the same part. So, for instance, he presents the five kinds of *pasādarūpa*s or sensitive matters that form the bases for sense consciousnesses and correlates these rūpas to descriptions in the anatomy textbook.[106] He notes, for example, that the *cakkhupasādarūpa,* the sensitive matter of the eye that enables vision, can also be described in the manner of the Italian text, as functioning on the basis of "a large nerve which runs from the brain to the eyeball, which is an exceedingly delicate mass of nerves, fat, and tissue."[107] In another example, he begins a description of the lungs from the perspective of the Buddhist commentaries, ending with "This is what is said [about the lungs] in the commentaries."[108] The next paragraph begins: "As for the anatomy book . . . ," and proceeds with a description drawn from the Italian work.[109] This same format is repeated again and again throughout the book.

This approach domesticated foreign learning at the same time that it affirmed the superiority of Burmese Buddhist knowledge. In his linking of Burmese and Western knowledge, Hlaing modeled an approach to meditation that subsumed Western scientific knowledge within a Buddhist outlook. Any given comparison between, say, the Abhidhamma description of the faculty of sight and the Italian description of the anatomical structure of the eye, stands in isolation as simple comparison and equivalence. To stop the analysis there, however, would misconstrue the larger purpose of such a work. *Meditation on the Body* not only puts Western learning in a Buddhist framework but recasts its ultimate significance. Hpo Hlaing does not tell us the name of the anatomy textbook, but given his recounting of its information, it seems clear that its central purpose was to impart an accurate understanding of the physiology of the human body in materialist terms. The purpose of *Meditation on the Body* is quite different. Understanding the structure of the body points toward the greater good of awakening, nibbāna or "the taste of freedom" as Hpo Hlaing puts it. His work thus models a way to absorb detailed Western knowledge within a larger Buddhist framework. The Buddhist body puts the Western body in service toward a higher end by showing how the Western anatomical dissection equates to a Buddhist analysis of the body culminating in enlightenment. The book thus suggests that modern learning and modern life can be part of the process of awakening.

Given that Ledi and Hpo Hlaing had an ongoing relationship until

1883, it is not surprising that in Ledi's writings on meditation there is also a focus on the contemplation of the body that connects Buddhist knowledge of the body to Western biological facts. Like his teacher, Ledi presents the body, intimate and particular, as the source of a liberative understanding that is common and universal. But Ledi goes beyond Hpo Hlaing to reflect on British rule and social change. He puts the body of the meditator into history, so to speak, because he explicitly calls for practice that can affect the world. In this crucial respect, Ledi's writings about meditation differ sharply from Hpo Hlaing's texts. Hlaing's books at most foreshadow the call to practice. Neither his, nor the other texts commissioned by the court, stipulate a specific form of practice, and none of the methods of meditation which became popular in Burma, including Ledi's, are based directly on these texts or upon the teachings of the monks in the Sagaing hills supported by Mindon's court.[110] Like the royal support of textual composition, support for such adepts was largely about practices of patronage, rather than an attempt to subsidize the proselytization of practice.[111] Meditation seems to have attracted the court's interest largely as a badge of merit and authenticity, and, in regard to famous meditating monks, the attraction was to the practitioner, not to practice.

Mindon did play a part, however, in promoting meditative practice through his personal example. Houtman's review of meditation practice prior to 1885 notes a few references to meditation by Mindon, most notably in the Burmese Buddhist historical chronicle, the *Sāsanavaṃsa*:[112]

> He [Mindon] himself also always made an effort towards calming and insight [*samathavipassanā*]. But as the kings who are the lords of countries have many legitimate duties, sometimes they do not get a chance to give themselves up to meditation. As such, he would just give himself up to meditation even at the time of letting out the excrement from his body. He would not spend time in vain. He would also bring from the cemetery the bones of human heads, skulls and the like that were called auspicious in the world, and having had them turned into toothpicks or other similar things, he placed them near him and accumulated the merit produced by the meditation on the bones and the like.[113]

Neither the text nor the context in which the passage occurs support a view that Mindon was doing anything that resembles later practices in the insight movement. The description comes within a long section intended to show Mindon's efforts to maintain the health of the sāsana. Meditation is presented as only one aspect of the king's effort to apply Buddhism to every part of his life, and Mindon's actual practices do not resemble the finely grained, schematic systems of mental training developed later. Yet the presentation of meditation as part of the exemplary life of the ruler still gives it a high status that implies the feasibility of lay practice. And the mention of the mundane bodily function of defecating as a worthy means to insight underscored the value of the body for Buddhist truths and the possibilities inherent in everyday life.

Although royal attention did not start widespread practice, Mindon's and his court's activities involving meditation prepared Burmese culture for it through their support of theoretical works and the king's example. Studying at Thanjaun and frequently visiting Hpo Hlaing, Ledi had the chance to absorb the new currents of thought touching upon meditation. He would then carry with him the seeds for innovative ideas about the study and practice of meditation out of the capital and into the forest.

Leaving Mandalay and Caring for Cows

In the final days of Mindon's life in 1878, one of his queens, Sinpyumashin, gained control of the court and promoted her son-in-law, a little-known prince named Thibaw, to be the next king.[114] Following machinations in the court and a bloody succession, Thibaw ruled from 1878 until the end of Upper Burma's independence in 1885.[115] During his weak reign, corruption was rampant—indeed, some court figures were even in league with bandits who took control of large portions of the countryside. The kingdom grew increasingly unstable; villages and towns were burned and even district governors murdered.[116] In his final years as king, Thibaw's sphere of control shrunk to little more than the environs of Mandalay, and it seems that in the seven years of his rule he never once left his walled palace grounds.

Thibaw sponsored the building of several pagodas and made donations to famous Buddha images, but his patronage of Buddhism was nowhere near that of his father. Partially, this was a matter of straightened finances, and an attempt to raise money by instituting a lottery paupered many Burmese and only made Thibaw more unpopular.[117] Fires became frequent in the capital, and one broke out in 1883 that consumed the entire northern quarter of the city, including Thanjaun.[118]

After the destruction of his home, Ledi left the capital for a monastery in the town of Monywa near his village.[119] Up to this point, he had followed the expected pattern of an up-and-coming monk, rising in the monastic hierarchy by distinguishing himself on the basis of his scholastic performance. It seems likely that if Mandalay had not suffered the convulsions of such an unstable period, Ledi would have continued his upward trajectory as a scholar-monk at Thanjaun. Even after the fire, Ledi probably could have stayed in Mandalay. Returning to the area of his childhood, however, meant greater social stability in familiar surroundings. In the first few years after his return to his natal area, Ledi maintained a focus on study and teaching.[120] He moved to the Monywa area, bringing with him several monk-disciples. He stayed first at a prominent monastery in the area, Shwesigoun (Hrve caññ‘" khum), but eventually moved into his own monastery built for him by a lay donor in his home village of Sainpyin.[121] However much his dealings with high-placed monks and literati in Mandalay had exposed him to the growing interest in meditation, the disciples he brought back with him and the patronage he attracted shows that he did not turn to meditative practice at the expense of literary practice or the typical relationships between elite scholar-monks and the laity.

But the social disruptions of the early 1880s—the destruction of Thanjaun, the need to move back to his home area, growing lawlessness—surely impressed upon Ledi the precarious situation of the Burmese people. The arrival of the British in Mandalay on November 28, 1885, capped off the series of calamitous events. The ostensible reason for the invasion was the levy of a large and, as the British saw it, unwarranted fine of 2,300,000 rupees against the Bombay-Burmah Trading Corporation for illegal teak extraction. In reality, the British government was not so much worried about the fine as the growing influence of the French, who had negotiated treaties with the Burmese and were even rumored to have agreed to supply Burma with arms.[122] The British delivered an ultimatum to the court on October 22, 1885, demanding that Burma negotiate over the fine, allow a British resident in Mandalay who would have immediate access to the king, and defer all foreign policy to the government of India.[123] The Burmese suggested modifications to the demands, which were rejected. The third Anglo-Burman War began on November 14, 1885, and lasted only twelve days, ending in humiliating defeat for the Burmese. Royal Burma was not only conquered but became merely one more province of British India. With British troops using the palace as their barracks, the Burmese watched as the king was carried in a bullock cart to a British steamer, the *Thooreah,* to live the rest of his life in exile in India.[124]

The loss of the kingdom to non-Buddhist foreigners was a profoundly disturbing turn of events for the Burmese. It surely was for Ledi, who was in his late thirties by this time with a well-established career that had been deeply connected to the royal court. That same year, in 1885, he wrote a work, entitled the *Nwa Metta Sa* (*Nwā" mettā cā*) or "The Letter on Cows," which offered his first advice on how the Burmese should respond to the situation.[125] In the piece Ledi makes his first call for lay social action. Following a familiar model exemplified in Mindon's efforts, Ledi used Buddhist teachings and a call for Buddhist practice as a means to respond to foreign rule. The "Letter on Cows" reveals Ledi's karmic outlook on the world and the way he understood individual behavior to impact the fate of Burmese society. While the letter concerns a matter of abstention, we can see in it his understanding of the workings of kamma that explains how meditation would fit into a continuum of practices responsive to the contemporary political situation.

The "Letter on Cows" is an example of a literary form in Burma called a *metta sa* (*mettā cā*), which means a "loving-kindness letter." Such letters, often written by monks, are euphonious homilies, usually on matters of morality.[126] It is clear from the first line of Ledi's letter that the arrival of the British forms the backdrop to its composition. It begins: "This letter of advice was written at the request of the leading gentlemen of Monywa at the very start of English rule in 1885."[127] The letter's purpose is to exhort people not to eat beef. This was not an unprecedented call on Ledi's part. Kings in earlier times had afforded protections to cows, because they were understood as important to agriculture.[128] Yet why pick this particular matter to address at such a momentous time? I can find no indication that Ledi knew of the cow protection movement in India, but it could have been a source of inspiration. Dayananda Saraswati and his organization the Arya Samaj had spearheaded this movement, which succeeded in mobilizing a large number of Hindu Indians and could have suggested to Ledi the power of such an appeal on a Burmese Buddhist basis.[129] Closer to home, his mentor Hpo Hlaing had shown that the individual possessed liberative knowledge within himself that fit with modern life. In sympathy with this point, Ledi teaches in the "Letter on Cows" that recent events reflect the same liberative truths, thus bringing Buddhist teachings into the modern world as means to address social problems:

> As for the matters which take place in the present days, thinking "Who do we rely on?" and "Who do we bear a grudge toward?" is not proper, because such thinking is confused. You should think instead about the country of the Sākyans, the 160,000 relatives of the Buddha, who at one particular time were all killed because of the [bad] kamma that they already possessed. They were totally destroyed by King Viṭaṭū, a bad man of wrong views.[130] Despite the fact that the Buddha himself with his bountiful power went to Viṭaṭū three times and tried to stop the king, even he could not do anything. Although the Buddha tried to help, he couldn't. We also cannot accuse the *nats*, *Sakka*, or the *Brahmas* of not caring about us.[131]
>
> Because of his action of cruelly destroying the entire kingdom of the Sākyans, King Viṭaṭū, the master of Sāvatti,[132] and his troops were drowned in their camp in

the waters of the [Aciravatī] river.[133] They became food for fishes and turtles. Considering this teaching that comes from the Buddhist texts, if you accept it, it leads to the conclusion, "The people who were destroyed met their fate, but the people who did the destroying were drowned. . . ."[134]

As for us people in Myanmar, we all continue to face danger at present just because we are not following the basis for the protection of the world, the moral life [*brahmacariya*] of ancient tradition. Harmonious friends among the six types of people[135] have been split up in an extraordinary fashion and we have been listening to false teachings. It should be seen that from the time of our great-great grandfathers the people of Myanmar, as with people throughout the world, have mostly made their living as farmers relying on the power of the cow and the water buffalo.[136]

This passage is a lesson about the communal dimensions of kamma.[137] King Viṭaṭū and his troops obviously stand in for the British, and their wrongdoing leads them to a bad end. This model of karmic retribution was surely appealing to the Burmese, especially just after the takeover of Upper Burma. Buddhist teachings assured them that justice would be done, at least eventually, and the British punished. History was thus on the Burmese side—yet, not entirely. Ledi apportions blame all around; the karmic knife cuts both ways. In the letter the Burmese are equated to the Sākyas. This was a noble association, as the Sākyas were the relatives of the Buddha, but they, too, were guilty of a crime that had brought calamity to them. Viṭaṭū destroyed them because they had tricked his father into marrying a slave woman. Just like the Sākyas, the Burmese had brought about their own national destruction by engaging in immoral behavior. In fact, the Sākyas had colluded to commit a single act (tricking the king) that resulted in collective retribution, but Ledi, in his interpretation of the story, extends the causes of a collective karmic consequence to each individual's behavior. He states that the Burmese face hard times because people have disregarded "the moral life." (He warns the reader later that those who eat beef will be "food for the dogs of hell,"[138] but those who abjure beef "will have happiness in the future.")[139] Each person who does wrong weakens the dhamma as a whole and brings suffering to the country. This belief in karmic consequences for groups of people is what Jonathan Walters has called "sociokarma."[140] Ledi clearly understood Burma to exist within this communal dimension of kamma.

To make the point that cows deserve to be included among those warranting gratitude and respect, Ledi goes so far as to adopt the voice of a cow in another part of the letter, in order to emphasize the work they do for humans and their suffering because of it. Besides being an effective means to get his point across, this device also points to Ledi's talent at writing in an entertaining and effective way. At one point the cow laments:

"After they have laid out all the side dishes and rice in the middle of the table in great abundance, smiling and laughing they enjoy the taste of our meat, liver, and succulent fat. How can a family enjoy munching on us? How can they swallow us up? The rice which we produced and the dishes which are our flesh, these make up the meal which they are enjoying. How hurt we feel!"[141]

Cruel disregard for such suffering led to bad outcomes. Societal events were the collective karmic fruit of the sort of disrespect the cow describes. Proper Buddhist action in this view benefited society, just as bad behavior brought trouble to everyone. This was not limited to beef eating either. Ledi also wrote letters against gambling, lotteries, and drinking.[142] And as his career continued, he would expand the ways that lay people could incorporate Buddhism into their lives as a means of self-improvement leading to social betterment. Included within this view was meditation, which would emerge out of Ledi's growing promotion of lay study and practice. This does not mean, however, that Ledi would come to promote meditation explicitly as a means of collective social uplift. On the contrary, Ledi discusses meditation in his works as the affair of the individual. But the "Letter on Cows" reveals the connection Ledi saw between individual effort and collective outcome, and his belief that Buddhist practice could address modern social issues.

To the Forest

About a year after writing "The Letter on Cows," in February 1887, Ledi entered a patch of dense jungle called the "Ledi Forest." This move into the forest marks the start of meditation as a part of Ledi's life. One of several similar versions of the story of Ledi's entry into the forest is found in the *Great Monk Ledi:*[143]

At that time, in 1887, on the eight day of the month of Ta-po-dwe [Ta pui' tvai], the forest of "Ledi" was a very wild and frightening place. It was said that the big forest was very dense, extremely harsh, and filled with all sorts of ghosts. Thinking, "Today, whether [these statements about the forest are] true or not, I must try," Ledi called together three or four lay observers of the Uposatha day.[144] Looking around with them for a place to live in the forest, he saw a big tazoun tree. This big tree was a very good place to stay; it was suitable for meditation. Having rested at the base of the tree, Ledi said to the lay people: "Now, I did not come here just for a visit, but with the intention that I would enter the forest. When all of you have returned home, I will remain behind here. Please inform the junior monks." Having said this, he gave them leave, and that day and night he stayed under the tazoun tree. . . .[145]

Taking up meditation practice is an important part of the story. From this point on, Ledi's biographers note his regular efforts to meditate as part of his daily life, punctuated by more intense periods of retreat. This was a momentous move on Ledi's part, for he aligned himself with the small but prestigious coterie of meditating monks, such as those on Minwun Hill in Sagaing, and took up the practice he would later promote widely to the Burmese populace. But Ledi's actions do not signal the start of an exclusive interest in pursuing meditation. Four or five young monks soon joined him in the forest, followed by many more. Meditation was a part of life for his junior monks, too, but so was extensive and advanced study.[146] Ledi also wrote many works during this time. Rather than a renunciation of scholarly activities in favor of meditation, his entry into the forest meant an intensification of monastic life in all spheres of activity.[147] He did not break continuity with the stress on learning he had imbibed in Mandalay; he added another activity to it.

Entry into the forest resulted in Ledi gaining his own sphere of control as a sayadaw. It is in this period that the monk Nyanadaza becomes Ledi Sayadaw. Such an opportunity arose because of Ledi's willingness to take the risk to strike out on his own. He surely thought over this bold move into the forest, though it seems likely that he knew that he would receive support from donors with whom he already had relationships in Monywa. After all, he brought laymen with him to stake out the spot where he established himself in the forest, and, what is more, his location was easily reached from town. In fact, not long after he sat under the tazoun tree, the wealthy donor who had built Ledi a monastery in Sainpyin built him another in the forest, and so the Ledi monastery was born that still exists today.[148] Nonetheless, Ledi was taking a chance heading off into the jungle, one that shows the steps he took that would make him a leading figure in the Burmese saṅgha.

Setting himself up in the forest made Ledi more powerful by tapping into the prestige and authority of the long-standing forest-dweller (*araññavāsī*) model, described earlier.[149] While the British takeover of Burma did not directly push Ledi into embracing the life of a forest monk, the event surely promoted his turn to the model in uncertain political times, just as earlier Thudhamma monks in the Chindwin Valley appealed to the same model at a time of political instability before the establishment of the Konbaung

Dynasty in 1752. Viewed from this perspective, Ledi's entry into the jungle to study and meditate depended partially upon the unstable situation which colonial rule created, but also upon patterns of behavior and the valuation of specific objectives (prestige and independence) established long before the arrival of the British.

The period of the late nineteenth and early twentieth centuries was one in which monks across the Theravāda world were taking to the forests to pursue more ascetic and meditative lives. Thai monks, such as Ajaan Mun (1870–1949) and later his students Ajaan Lee (1907–1961) and Ajaan Maha Boowa (1913–2011), wandered from place to place in the jungle, principally in northeastern Thailand but also in Burma.[150] They dyed their own robes with the bark of the jackfruit tree, confronted wild animals (especially tigers), and spent much of their time in meditation.[151] The ready adoption of a peripatetic lifestyle following ascetic practices (*dhutaṅga*), in distinction to the settled and relatively easier life of most village and town-dwelling monks, distinguished these men. For them, the move from the monastery into the forest was a forsaking of the stability of society for the precariousness of the wilds, in order to expedite the attainment of realization. In Sri Lanka, the monk Paññānanda, who was born in 1817, also followed an ascetic forest-dwelling life, starting from the mid-nineteenth century. He had to struggle to reestablish the forest monk tradition on the island, emphasizing meditative practice and devoting himself to teaching and preaching.[152] While monks in the later Sri Lankan forest tradition looked to Paññānanda as a founding figure, not all lived the same sort of life. Some subsequent forest monks, for instance, emphasized scholarly pursuits.[153]

As for Ledi, the almost immediate re-collection of students around him, his continued teaching, and the swift founding of the monastery that would give him his name show that he did not intend to follow an unsettled and highly ascetic quest for awakening, as idealized in the Thai forest tradition. And in contrast to Paññānanda, Ledi tapped into a living model still seen as a viable option for monastic life and one that allowed for scholarly study. Ledi's case, in comparison with these Thai and the Sri Lankan examples, suggests the varied possibilities for the forest monk model. As Carrithers observes in speaking of the Sri Lankan situation, the forest monk tradition, like Buddhism more broadly, is "polysemous, composed of many meanings."[154] The way that Ledi lived the forest monk life fit the particular circumstances in which he found himself and took on the character of his formation. As noted above, the story of his entry into the forest indicates not a sharp turn away from scholarship for the sake of meditation or asceticism, but the addition of meditation to textual practice. Indeed, the forest model offered Ledi a means to improvise, in order to bring these two aspects of the monastic life together. From his independent position in the forest near Monywa he would be able to draw upon both to forge in his later writings a vision of a new sort of lay person, one who, like him, fused learning and practice.

Out into the World

In the years following his entry into the forest, Ledi continued to teach at his monastery. By 1895, now forty-nine years old, he had produced another three books and headed a thriving monastery that he had built from the ground up.[155] Some people might at such a point in middle age be ready to settle into a routine. But not Ledi. As will be examined in the rest of the book, he was about to turn, deliberately and self-consciously, to prolific literary production and frequent traveling that immersed him in wider Burmese society. But the writing of books and his teaching while in the forest suggest that he had never really left the world. The movement outward that takes place in Ledi's life at the end of the nineteenth century, as he attracts greater and greater attention and as he leaves his monastery to preach and organize monks and laypeople, represents not a sudden shift but a culmination. He combined his emphasis on learning and his interest in meditation with a willingness to engage the world on Buddhist terms.

One of the books Ledi wrote during his years at his forest monastery marks the start of his transition to a career that included the teaching of meditation to the laity. In 1894 he preached a number of sermons on the philosophical basis of meditation to a lay woman at her request. Several years later, these sermons were put down in writing as the *Meditation Object of Puṇṇovāda* (*Puṇṇovādakammaṭṭhān'"*).[156] The sermons and its book suggest Ledi's willingness to respond to the interests of lay people and particularly to women, a group who would play an important part in his educational and organizational efforts. In the book Ledi presents an approach to meditation, based upon an analysis of the body's parts, that would remain an important aspect of his technique, perhaps thanks to Hlaing's influence. It would be several more years before Ledi composed a work again specifically on meditation. His activities and his writings in the meantime, however, which will be examined in the following chapters, are vital to understanding his later formulation of meditation and its wide appeal.

In 1895, Ledi traveled to India and visited the sacred sites of Buddhism.[157] During this trip he wrote another work, the *Manual on Dependent Origination* (*Paṭiccasamuppādadīpanī*), explaining the function of the twelve-fold chain of causation understood in Buddhism to give rise to all phenomena.[158] When he returned to Burma in 1896, Ledi decided to stay in a forest monastery near the town of Tuntay (Tvaṃ te", often spelled Twante), just across the Irrawaddy River from Rangoon, and devote himself to meditation.[159] He was now fifty years old. Ledi's biographies say little of his trip to India except that he visited the major sites of Buddhism. But his journey hundreds of miles down the length of Burma from Monywa to Rangoon, his travel across the Bay of Bengal on a British steamship, and his train travel through the heart of the Raj in the only foreign country he was ever to visit must have impressed upon him the extent of British power and Burmese Buddhism's small and fragile place within it. Perhaps the trip inspired him to make further efforts to advance in his meditation. Perhaps, on a more practical level, Ledi also took the opportunity to meditate while in Lower Burma because he was in familiar territory, where he spoke the language and shared the culture, yet was still far away from the responsibilities of his own monastery in the north. Whatever the case, it is at this time that he wrote, so far as I know, his only work that speaks openly about his own meditational accomplishments. Wunnita reports that Ledi gave him the following poem that he had written while practicing near Tuntay:[160]

> Near the end of the sāsana many people are born, but try finding a man like me in Jambūdīpa.[161] Set up the flag of great diligence—proclaim me like no other!
>
> I practice all sorts of meditation. With lion-like intellectual powers, I have completed the path of jhāna.[162] I have mastered and control all five of the masteries [of the jhānas].[163]
>
> In all the realms under and above Brahma,[164] I have set up the flag of power abundantly. I will reside in contentment. In the future I will be brave and unsurpassed during the victory of the next Buddha Metteyya.[165]

Ledi begins the first verse with a shocking challenge: There are many people in the world, but among them "find a man like me in Jambudīpa," which is the human realm in Theravāda Buddhist cosmology. His implication is that he is unique among all Buddhists for his accomplishments—a bold, even brash, opening line. If the first verse is bold, the second is no less so. Ledi flatly states that he has "finished the path of jhāna"—in other words, that he has finished the stages of samatha meditation up to the most rarified consciousnesses possible. The third verse only emphasizes this tone of braggadocio with his claim that in a future life he will be "unsurpassed."

Wunnita did not become Ledi's disciple until 1912, but it is not clear that Ledi waited to share the poem until then. Even if he did, verses such as these are highly unorthodox. Among the four most serious monastic rules of the Vinaya is one forbidding any false claims of spiritual attainment.[166] An intentional misrepresentation would make one a *pārājika* or breaker of this rule, which would entail permanent expulsion from the saṅgha. In Burma both lay people and monastics have taken these rules very seriously. Scott claims that in the nineteenth century monks expelled from monasteries for breaking one of the *pārājika* rules would sometimes be stoned to death by villagers.[167] These doctrinal and even social dangers have contributed to the longstanding and powerful reluctance among meditators to make any specific claims about their accomplishments. Yet Ledi makes the strongest possible statement about his attainments. His willingness to do so is revealing of his confidence in himself, and it also shows his disregard for convention. As the following chapters will show, Ledi was willing to ruffle feathers in his promotion of an innovative vision of Buddhism.

The final verse of the poem also provides a sense of how Ledi saw the Buddhist fitting into the modern world. Ledi positions himself within a Buddhist cosmos with its multitiered planes of existence ("in all the realms under and above Brahma"). The claim that he will live again in the time of Metteyya, the future Buddha of the next dispensation of the dhamma, presents him as moving through a Buddhist conception of space and time in which the future "returns," in the sense that it repeats a cycle, giving Ledi the chance for liberation (nibbāna) once again. As the events recounted in this chapter indicate, Ledi was well aware of the effects of British power. Indeed, his remark that the time is "near the end of the sāsana" indicates that the situation in which the poem is written is one of threat and impending loss. But this loss is not without meaning. On the contrary, Ledi suggests that the threat brought by the arrival of the British only confirms a meaningful vision of reality. Events fulfilled the logic of Buddhism in his view—its own trope of possible decline—and thus set in motion certain responses to social and political events. As "The Letter on Cows" also demonstrates, Ledi engaged the world from a Buddhist perspective, one that could see Buddhist ends to modern history.

Overall, the poem points to his deep involvement in meditative practice and perhaps, during that time, a personal transformation. When he returned to the Ledi Monastery after his meditation in Tuntay, a change seems to have taken place in him. We cannot know for sure, but his experiences recorded in his poem seem to have oriented him more overtly and intensely to meditation. To be sure, this was not at the expense of scholarship, for the next year, in 1897, Ledi finished writing a complex and lengthy work on the philosophical system of the Abhidhamma.[168] This book, the *Paramatthadīpanī* (*Manual on the Ultimates*), would become a source of intense controversy, and its important part in his life is the focus of the next chapter. Nevertheless, meditation had become a newly prominent part of his life. In 1898, near the town of Chait-to in the southern region of Mon state, Ledi went on another extended meditation retreat at the monastery of one of his senior pupils, U Tiloka.[169] Then, in 1900, he took another radical and risky step, relinquishing control of the Ledi Monastery to his disciple U Nyanabatha.[170] Without taking up another equivalent position, he gave away his authoritative position at the monastery he founded, now with five hundred monks in residence—it had grown a great deal from its start under the tazoun tree! That same year he pursued meditation during the rains retreat with another disciple, U Indaka, in a forest monastery in the Sagaing area.[171] He then took up residence for a couple of years in caves near the Chindwin River in his home region, not too far from Monywa.[172] Yet all the while Ledi continued to teach and to write books (five alone during a year spent in one cave). Meditation clearly had become central to his life, but it still did not supersede literary efforts. On the contrary, it is during this time that he began to formulate through his texts a vision of meditation that would be appropriate on a mass scale. As we will see, in his presentation of meditation to lay people, his approach changed radically from his own experience in Tuntay, for he promoted a practice that did not require any jhāna cultivation at all.

Ledi's formative experiences in the Thudhamma heartland of the Chindwin Valley and in Mandalay had stressed the importance of the text, and he carried this sensibility over into the colonial period. He would soon learn how his emphasis on the text could mesh with the power of print capitalism when his book, the *Paramatthadīpanī*, was published in 1901. The reaction to this work, explored in the next chapter, would teach him the potential among the laity to use learning once reserved for the elite. The book was a highly technical philosophical commentary, yet it ignited a fierce controversy that would be likened by one Burmese scholar to a full-scale war.

TWO

The Great War of the Commentaries: Ledi Sayadaw's Abhidhamma Controversy

In 1910, a Burmese veterinarian in government service, writing under the pseudonym Nat Tha (Nat' Sā"), published a book entitled the *Atisundara Kyam.*[1] In it, he likened Ledi to "an enemy with alien concepts"[2]—a grave insult in a country still deeply wounded by the British takeover. To label Ledi in such a way was to lump him with the foreigners seen to be threatening Burmese Buddhism. Nat Tha's book so enraged one of Ledi's students that he bought every copy of it he could find in Rangoon and burnt them all.[3]

Nat Tha's work, however, was just one of many combative, even angry, responses to the publication in 1901 of Ledi's *Paramatthadīpanī,* a commentary on a twelfth-century Abhidhamma handbook.[4] In the years following its publication, over forty books were published to challenge it;[5] a back-and-forth among Ledi's admirers and detractors took place on the editorial pages of popular newspapers in Mandalay and Rangoon;[6] and at numerous public meetings people discussed how to refute the work.[7] Not to be outdone by Ledi's disciple, a monk at one meeting even suggested burning it.[8] It is no wonder, then, that one Burmese scholar said the *Paramatthadīpanī* started "the great war of the commentaries."[9]

Yet, at first blush, the features of Ledi's book make the

response to it surprising. It comments on a medieval Sri Lankan scholastic text, is written in Pali, and delves deeply into abstruse matters of Abhidhamma doctrine. To be sure, the focus of Ledi's commentary, the *Abhidhammatthasaṅgaha* (*Compendium of the Ultimates*), was then and is still today a foundational text of Abhidhamma education in the monastic curricula of Burma. Given this fact, it is not so surprising that some monks and laymen, those schooled in complex Abhidhamma learning, might take issue with a work they saw as misconstruing the authoritative interpretation of the text that had been fixed in earlier commentaries. Nevertheless, the scope and intensity of the reaction—the public meetings, the many response-books printed, the editorials, not to mention a book burning—suggest that the controversy went beyond issues of textual authority within the monastic education system. What made this work, seemingly so divorced from the concerns of most colonial-era Burmese, cause such a stir? Answering this question will help us to understand the development of Burmese Buddhism during the colonial period and the origins of insight meditation as a popular practice.

At the time the *Paramatthadīpanī* appeared, Ledi was in a cave near the banks of the Chindwin River, but he was not a hermit cut off from society. As we will see, his frequent interactions with disciples and others meant he was well aware of the controversy. It seems likely, in fact, that reaction to his work helped to draw him from his cave onto the public stage. The furor over his book showed him the power of print culture and the potential of scholastic textual practice in wider Burmese society. Explaining the controversy, then, will reveal the centrality of the Abhidhamma to Burmese Buddhism and to Ledi in his shaping of an ideal of lay life that included meditation.

The Abhidhamma and the *Paramatthadīpanī*

The term Abhidhamma has two related senses. It denotes, on the one hand, the seven books in the third basket (piṭaka) of canonical literature, the Abhidhamma Piṭaka, and, on the other, the system of thought that develops from the canonical texts and later Abhidhamma literature.[10] Unlike the other two baskets of the canon, the Sutta and the Vinaya, the Buddha is understood to have preached in ultimate (*paramattha*) terms in the Abhidhamma. To speak in ultimate terms means to describe reality only with regard to its genuinely existing constituent parts. Fundamentally, there are just eighty-two genuinely real parts, called dhammas. They fall under four categories in the Abhidhamma system: consciousness (citta), mental factors (*cetasikas*), materiality (rūpa), and awakening (nibbāna).[11]

There is only one dhamma of consciousness (citta). By itself, it is the bare knowing of an object. A consciousness, however, always arises in combination with mental factors (cetasikas) to form a full act of cognition.[12] There are fifty-two of these factors, some good (such as compassion), some bad (such as shamelessness), and some ethically variable (such as feeling).[13] The Abhidhamma system stipulates just eighty-nine possible combinations of bare consciousness with groups of factors.[14] (Here, it would avoid confusion if the Abhidhamma system used different terms for consciousness as the mere knowing of an object versus consciousness as knowing combined with mental factors, but it does not.) Some of these eighty-nine are categorized as either wholesome (*kusala*) or unwholesome (*akusala*). Others are classed as "resultants" (*vipāka*), meaning they are the result of other wholesome and unwholesome consciousnesses. Still others fall into the "functional" (*kriyā*) group, meaning they are neither the result of wholesome or unwholesome consciousnesses.[15] Continually co-arising in eighty-nine possible permutations within these four categories, these cognitive events follow one another so rapidly that they suggest to the unawakened being an unbroken and enduring entity—in other words, the self.

In the same way as the process of consciousness, moments of material existence also arise and pass away continually in a series of linked events. Materiality (rūpa) begins with the four "great essentials" (*mahābhūtāni*)—also called the elements (*dhātū*)—of earth (*paṭhavī*), water (*āpo*), fire (*tejo*), and wind (*vāyo*). These essentials are so called because they represent the fundamental building blocks of matter. They depend on nothing else for their existence, and thus are said to bear their own natures (*sabhāva*). They are not simply physical material, however, but properties of all matter. Earth is the principle of extension and support, or the tangibility of hardness and softness; water is the principle of cohesion that causes matter to stick together; fire is the principle of temperature, both of heat and cold; and wind is the principle of movement in matter.[16] The other twenty-four physical dhammas come into being dependent on these four primary elements, and so are called "derived materiality" (*upādāyarūpa*). Just like the mental states, forms of materiality appear and disappear so fast that the physical world seems solid and enduring.

To investigate and parse experience, both mental and physical, into these dhamma-events that appear and disappear billions of times in the blink of an eye is the means to the one unconditioned and lasting dhamma in the Abhidhamma system, nibbāna. The point of the system, then, is not merely descriptive. Analysis of mental states and materiality forms the basis of ethical prescriptions and practices aimed at liberation.

The canonical Abhidhamma, as an enumeration and examination of the dhammas, led to other works written in the same highly systematized and comprehensive mode of analysis in ultimate terms.[17] This is what Buddhaghosa calls writing with an "Abhidhamma perspective" (*abhidhammapariyāya*),[18] one that is described traditionally as a "literal or unembellished discourse on the dhamma" (*nippariyāyadhammadesanā*).[19] The style of such writing is distinctively dry, detailed, and impersonal. Speaking of this literature, Robert Gimello says: "Among its salient features are a tendency to periphrasis and to the use of a technical rather than a common nomenclature, a preference for intransitive over transitive verbs and for the passive rather than the active voice, and a consistent avoidance of personal pronouns."[20] A large body of works, building off the canonical texts, use this method and write in this style. In fact, as time went on Buddhist authors wrote so many works in this vein that, starting in the fifth century CE, summarizing texts began to appear to help students master the essentials of the system.[21]

As noted above, Ledi's *Paramatthadīpanī* is a commentary on the most famous and influential of these summaries, the *Abhidhammatthasaṅgaha*.[22] Therefore, a brief description of the *Saṅgaha* (as I will refer to it from now on) will also serve as a description of the topics of Ledi's work. The monk Anuruddha most likely wrote the *Saṅgaha* in Sri Lanka between the tenth and twelfth centuries.[23] So well known is this text in Burma that during Ledi's time, and still today, the Burmese refer to the *Abhidhammatthasaṅgaha* as simply the "Thinjo" (*saṅgruih'*). This is the Burmese pronunciation of *saṅgaha,* meaning "compendium." The *Saṅgaha* manages to cover all the basic Abhidhamma teachings with great concision (usually around fifty pages in printed editions), yet also with great precision, and this combination explains its popularity.[24]

The *Saṅgaha* has nine chapters that provide an outline of the philosophical, psychological, ethical, and soteriological categories and concerns of the Abhidhamma system.[25] The first three chapters are oriented around consciousness (citta).[26] Chapter 1, the chapter on the compendium of consciousness (*cittasaṅgahavibhāga*), defines consciousness into its eighty-nine types; the second chapter on the compendium of the mental factors (*cetasikasaṅgahavibhāga*) describes the fifty-two mental factors (cetasikas) that arise in various combinations with a consciousness; and the third, the chapter on the compendium of the miscellaneous (*pakiṇṇakasaṅgahavibhāga*), analyzes in greater detail the co-arising of consciousness in combination with mental factors in key categories.[27]

The fourth and fifth chapters deal with the roles of consciousness in a person's experience. Chapter 4, the chapter on the compendium of the cognitive process (*vīthisaṅgahavibhāga*), describes the active, intentional processes of consciousness, such as perception through the senses and in the absorption of calming meditation. On the other hand, chapter 5, the chapter on the compendium (of consciousness) free of the process (of thought) (*vīthimuttasaṅgahavibhāga*), deals with the passive, automatic functions of the mind.[28] These include the process of karmic fruition, death, and rebirth. At its start, chapter 5 also includes a survey of the cosmological realms of existence. Chapter 6, the chapter on the compendium of matter (*rūpasaṅgahavibhāga*), shifts from mental phenomena to the material world. It covers the twenty-eight dhammas of physical matter (rūpa) and also discusses nibbāna.

The final three chapters of the *Saṅgaha* build upon the information of the preceding ones to explain further the dynamism of the system and its liberative potential. Chapter 7, on the compendium of categories (*samuccayasaṅgahavibhāga*), explains various groupings of the dhammas in Abhidhamma texts as ways to classify ultimate reality and make the entire sweep of one's experience susceptible to insight.[29] Chapter 8, the chapter on the compendium of conditionality (*paccayasaṅgahavibhāga*), lays out how the dhammas arise and interact. It provides an analysis using, first, the twelve-fold chain of dependent origination (*paṭiccasamuppāda*) and, next, the twenty-four conditional relations (*paṭṭhāna*).[30] The last chapter, chapter 9, is on the compendium of meditation subjects (*kammaṭṭhānasaṅgahavibhāga*). It follows in content, though not in organization, the topics of Buddhaghosa's fifth-century manual, the *Visuddhimagga*. It covers the forty meditation objects, aspects of both samatha and vipassanā practices, the nature of the four types of enlightened beings, and the categorization of possible spiritual attainments.[31] The highly scholastic exposition, however, does not provide actual meditation instruction.

Since the *Saṅgaha* is concise to the point of being cryptic, a student almost always studies it with the aid of a commentary, in tandem with instruction from a teacher. Among the many commentaries written over the centuries—at least nineteen well known in Pali and a multitude in vernaculars—the *Abhidhammatthavibhāvinīṭīkā,* written by the monk Sumangala in the twelfth century in Sri Lanka, was during Ledi's time, and remains up to the present day, the preferred key to the *Saṅgaha* throughout the Theravada world.[32] In fact, so well known is it in Burma that the Burmese usually just call it "the Tikajaw" (*ṭīkā kyau*), meaning "the famous commentary."[33] (I will refer to this work as the *Vibhāvinī* in the rest of the chapter.) Such is the popularity of the combination of the *Saṅgaha* and *Vibhāvinī* that in Burma they are often printed together in one volume.

Their close relationship explains why Ledi chose in the *Paramatthadīpanī* to direct most of his criticism at the *Vibhāvinī.*[34] The *Vibhāvinī* represented the dominant interpretive lens through which to view the *Saṅgaha,* and Ledi aimed to replace the *Vibhāvinī* with his work, which he called "a new text on the great commentary, the *Saṅgaha.*"[35] Seeking to do so was another bold move on Ledi's part. As we will explore in detail below, the *Vibhāvinī,* supported by other commentaries, formed a critical part of religious authority in Burma. Ledi's attack on its positions was a challenge to those who had built their claims to authority on the text. He risked inciting refutations that could destroy his reputation. But if he pulled it off, the reward would be the chance to claim a central position in the Burmese saṅgha as an intellectual force of the highest caliber. With his training in Mandalay and years of teaching in his own monastery, no doubt Ledi knew the stakes. At the end of the chapter we will consider further the risks involved in the *Paramatthadīpanī*'s challenge and what Ledi understood he could gain from it.

The *Paramatthadīpanī* and the *Vibhāvinī* follow the traditional commentarial style of etymological analysis (*nirutti*) to explain a passage in the *Saṅgaha.*[36] In defining words and phrases in a particular passage from the *Saṅgaha,* the commentaries naturally follow the order of the root text. This organization highlights these works' dependence on the root text for their structure. Both the *Paramatthadīpanī* and the *Vibhāvinī* have the same chapter titles as the *Saṅgaha,* in the same order, with the same topics taken up within the chapters. Thus, as with the *Paramatthadīpanī,* the summary of the chapters of the *Saṅgaha* above accomplishes a description of the topics explained in *Vibhāvinī,* too.

Yet something made the *Paramatthadīpanī* distinctive. Not in the sense that controversy itself was unprecedented. In fact, the Burmese had a long history of controversial works, including many of fairly recent vintage.[37] But no Abhidhamma commentary, resolutely focused on doctrine rather than practice, had inspired such a reaction. This calls our attention to the style and substance of the work itself. While its organization follows the traditional format of a commentary, within this format Ledi inserted an unusually strong tone of refutation. In the opening verses he describes his commentary as answering the need for a proper explanation of the *Saṅgaha:*

> In this world are found many commentaries on the *Abhidhammatthasaṅgaha,* explained by scholars of old.

But those whose minds wish for the essential meaning do not gain satisfaction from these [commentaries]. Having approached me, they asked for an explanation of ultimate reality.[38]

Ledi never specifies (in the *Paramatthadīpanī* or anywhere else) who exactly asked for "an explanation of ultimate reality" (*paramatthassa dīpanaṃ*). Considering that he compiled his commentary while teaching his disciples in the forest outside of Monywa, his students may have asked for it. Whoever asked, in referring to the request of others he fulfilled a trope of commentaries, in which the motivation for composition, at least ostensibly, comes from an external request. Ledi was doubtless eager to take on such a task. One of his biographies says that he had started preparing a commentary on the *Saṅgaha* while still a student at Thanjaun, but had given up when all of his notes were lost in the fire that razed the monastery in 1883.[39]

Ledi's claim that those "whose minds wish for the essential meaning" (*ye sāratthābhimānino*) of the *Saṅgaha* had not yet gained satisfaction clearly sets his composition apart from the *Vibhāvinī* and other commentaries at the outset. To be sure, other commentaries make claims for the benefits of their use. The *Vibhāvinī,* for instance, states that it "will bring accomplishment in pure and profound wisdom" to those who study it.[40] But Ledi puts a real sting in his words with the claim it will do what earlier commentaries could not.

This tone carries right through the rest of the *Paramatthadīpanī,* particularly when Ledi corrects other works' interpretations of the *Saṅgaha,* above all the *Vibhāvinī*'s. At every one of his many points of disagreement, Ledi first recapitulates the other text's interpretation of the *Saṅgaha,* then tersely states that the other work is incorrect. His most common phrase to make this point is *taṃ na sundaraṃ,* or "that is not good." He uses this phrase so much that Nat Tha titled his book as a direct refutation: his defense of the *Vibhāvinī* is meant to show it is *atisundaraṃ* or "very good." He even dubs the *Paramatthadīpanī* in his work the "*na sundaraṃ ṭīkā,*" implying both that it often used this phrase and that it was a work that was itself "not good."

Ledi also employs a number of other phrases of dismissal. Some of the most common are:

That does not agree (*taṃ na sameti*).

That is not to be accepted (*taṃ na gahetabbaṃ*).

That is not to be relied upon, based on the meaning (*taṃ na sārato paccetabbaṃ*).

That should not be said (*taṃ na vattabbaṃ*).
All that is not fitting (*taṃ sabbaṃ na yuttaṃ*).
That should be thought over (*taṃ vicāretabbaṃ*).
That is rejected (*taṃ paṭikkhittaṃ*).
That is simply groundless (*taṃ niratthakam eva*).
That is baseless (*taṃ akāraṇaṃ*).
That should not be regarded in this way (*taṃ tathā na daṭṭhabbaṃ*).

The Burmese historian Myin Swe characterizes these phrases as "rather harsh" (*khap' kram'" kram'"*),[41] and one reason for the controversy is surely that many found this language insulting. No other commentary has such a resolute focus on correcting its peers. The *Paramatthadīpanī* contains 245 corrections and almost all begin with one of the above brusque statements. There are eighteen corrections in the first two chapters commenting upon the introductory verses of the *Saṅgaha,* fifty-two in the chapter on consciousness, twelve in the chapter on mental factors, thirty-two in the miscellaneous chapter, twenty-six in the chapter on cognitive processes, thirty-four in the chapter on consciousnesses without the cognitive process, twenty-nine in the matter chapter, twenty in the categories chapter, nineteen in the chapter on conditionality, and three in the chapter on meditation.[42] Although the consciousness chapter has the most, it is also the longest, and in the other chapters the number of critiques is generally proportional to their lengths.

The layout of Ledi's text could have also exacerbated the sense of insult to the commentaries. As early as the 1907 edition—the earliest edition I have obtained and well within the full efflorescence of the controversy—every correction is numbered. Adding to the impact, the numbering of the corrections does not start over with each new section or chapter but runs throughout the whole text, thereby impressing upon the reader by the end of the book the hundreds of points at which Ledi has taken issue with some other interpretation of the *Saṅgaha.* There were at this time a genre of texts called *khalita vicāraṇā* that numbered their corrections of mistakes in other texts, but these were technical and brief works.[43] So far as I know, no other full-length commentary before this highlighted its disagreements with other works in this way.

Yet the fact of even such a large number of critiques seems an insufficient explanation, by itself, for a controversy of such intensity and duration. To challenge the interpretations of other commentaries with rather harsh words was not unprecedented. The *Vibhāvinī,* for instance, contains numerous disagreements with earlier, authoritative texts. It dismisses as "worthless" (*asāraṃ*), for instance, the view of those who claim that material dhammas last for sixteen consciousness-moments (*cittakkhaṇā*) instead of seventeen.[44] It disagrees with the *Mūlaṭīkā,* the subcommentary on the commentaries on the canonical Abhidhamma texts, over the nature of time in the process of cognition.[45] And it critiques the *Saccasaṅkhepa* (another compendium like the *Saṅgaha*) in regard to the issue of kamma and what one can perceive about one's future rebirth at the threshold of death.[46] It also refers to the commentator Jotipāla's disagreement with the *Saṅgaha* itself over an issue of rebirth consciousness.[47]

What is more, Ledi was only following the lead of his own teachers in critiquing the *Vibhāvinī.* Ledi says in the introduction to the *Paramatthadīpanī* that he first decided to look at the *Vibhāvinī* because his teachers refused to use it, saying "in the *Vibhāvinī* commentary many bad things appear."[48] As the previous chapter shows, these were royally sponsored monks who occupied some of the most prestigious positions in the Burmese saṅgha. If they taught Ledi to reject the *Vibhāvinī,* it makes it hard to argue that the controversy stemmed from the fact that monastic authorities found it unacceptable to correct the *Vibhāvinī* or, to a far lesser extent, other commentaries. Additionally, Ledi may have had another motivation to write the *Paramatthadīpanī* that would suggest the *Vibhāvinī* was not above critique outside of Burma either. Ledi's biographer Chit San Win says that Ledi, while a student in Mandalay, heard Lankan monks studying at his monastery deriding Burmese monks for still giving "respect to the *Vibhāvinī* commentary which is filled with errors."[49] If it were true that Lankan monks were mocking the Burmese for using the *Vibhāvinī,* it further indicates that the attitude toward the commentary was not monolithically positive.

The very fact of these corrections points to another, more substantive potential source of controversy, however: the specifics of what Ledi had to say. Nat Tha and many other people sought to defend, in detail, the doctrinal positions of the earlier commentaries, especially the *Vibhāvinī.* Confrontational language on Ledi's part may have boosted widespread interest, but the close attention paid to the *Paramatthadīpanī*'s technical arguments suggests that the deeper cause of the controversy was his interpretation of Abhidhamma thought. The account of a large meeting led by the Bingala Sayadaw shows that when people gathered to debate the *Paramatthadīpanī,* they focused on doctrine. The meeting was held in Rangoon in 1905, upon the occasion of Ledi's visit to the city to give a series of dhamma talks. The Bingala Sayadaw first asked the crowd to put forward someone to debate Ledi face-to-face. When no one would volunteer to do so, he recommended that the monks compose a written response: "Present facts on the side of the *Vibhāvinī* which reject the Ledi ṭīkā. Make the effort to collect and compile a ṭīkā."[50] The Bingala Sayadaw's words indicate that he understood that, barring public debate, the way to respond to the *Paramatthadīpanī* was through the well-established tradition of scholastic argumentation. His call to defend the *Vibhāvinī* at the level of technical details suggests that a primary cause of the controversy was a concern that Ledi's critiques distorted fundamental tenets of the canonical Abhidhamma system explained in the commentaries. This would be a very serious matter, for influential misrepresentations could threaten the proper understanding of the Abhidhamma's ultimate teachings, the most perfect and precious of all the Buddha's teachings.

The next step in explaining the controversy, then, is to examine representative arguments to understand what Ledi did that might have threatened the Abhidhamma system. In selecting examples to shed light on the nature of Ledi's positions, however, no particular section or correction stands out. When I reviewed the work in Burma with the scholar-monk and renowned Abhidhamma specialist Dhammācariya U Nandamālābhivaṃsa, he was at a loss to single out any correction as especially controversial. Nor do the texts which respond to Ledi suggest that any single correction attracted particular notice. No section in these reactionary works is outsized, no particular animus is directed toward a particular point or group of points. Later descriptions of the controversy in Ledi's biographies and in other Burmese sources, such as popular monthly magazines covering religion, focus on the social turmoil caused by the controversy and not on any particular matters of Abhidhamma philosophy.

The *Paramatthadīpanī*'s corrections do not hang together to form a larger argument, either. Each stands independently without any attempt on Ledi's part to establish thematic or conceptual connections among them.[51] This narrow approach fits with most commentaries, including the *Vibhāvinī,* which do not attempt larger global arguments about either the root text or other commentaries to which they refer. It is especially noteworthy in the case of the *Paramatthadīpanī,* however, since Ledi makes so many corrections of other texts, and thus has so many more opportunities to speak to the general qualities of the works he critiques. The commentaries in response to the *Paramatthadīpanī* are also written as commentaries on the *Saṅgaha.* So, their defenses of the *Vibhāvinī*—and corresponding refutations of the *Paramatthadīpanī*—come in the course of their explanations of the root text. They, too, do not make larger global arguments.

Because no particular point or section stands out, I selected the following examples to look at in detail in order to give a sense of the range of concerns in these works. The selected matters also focus on the basic functioning of both consciousness and materiality, and thus will be relevant to our study in later chapters of Ledi's use of the Abhidhamma in meditation. Generally, too, they give the stylistic flavor of Abhidhamma argumentation. Beyond the import of the arguments, gaining a sense of this flavor—rather off-putting to many folks' taste[52]—is valuable to understanding the nature of the Abhidhamma as an influence in Burmese Buddhism.

The critiques by Ledi can be at times extremely technical, even captious. This is evident in an example from the chapter on materiality (rūpa). The *Saṅgaha* states: "Matter is twofold, namely: the four great essentials, and material phenomena derived from the four great essentials."[53] The *Saṅgaha* then lists the great essentials (*mahābhūtāni*) of earth (paṭhavī), water (āpo), fire (tejo), and wind (vāyo). As noted above, these four fundamental elements (dhātū) are the basic properties of all matter, and so all other matter is considered derivative of these four elements. Earth (as solidity perceived by touch), fire (as temperature sensed as heat or cold), and wind (as movement experienced as pressure) can be contemplated in order to develop liberative insight. (As the property of cohesion, water is the one physical property the Abhidhamma states cannot be directly sensed, only inferred from the integrity of an object.) Like all dhammas except nibbāna, they continually arise and pass away, and so to observe them closely and directly is to see the impermanent (anicca) nature of the world. As we will explore in later chapters, the possibility of apprehending such qualities in everyday life would make them favored objects of contemplation for Ledi.

If one does not see that these elements are constantly changing (dying and renewing in every micro-instant), the seemingly seamless flow of materiality deceives one into the perception that the objects around us are real and lasting. For this reason, when commentaries give the meaning of the term "great essential," *mahābhūta,* they parse the word as *mahā,* "great," joined to *abhūta,* "deception." Mahābhūtas are then defined as "great deceivers," as they trick one into a mistaken view of the world. Buddhaghosa, in the *Aṭṭhasālinī,* his commentary on the *Dhammasaṅgaṇī* (the first book of the Abhidhamma), refers to the great essentials as like magicians (*māyākārā*). He also likens them to demons, called *yakkha*s, or demonesses, *yakkhinī*s, dangerous creatures who lure people to themselves by taking on pleasant and pleasing appearances.[54]

Following Buddhaghosa, the *Vibhāvinī* defines the great essentials in the same way:

> Alternatively, either because they manifest various extraordinary wonders (*abbhuta*) or various deceptions (*abhūta*), or because in them are great wonders or deceptions,

they are *the great deceivers* (mahābhūta), like magicians, etc. Since they are not by nature themselves blue, etc., and yet they present dependent materialities as blue, etc., they are *great deceivers;* or, as yakkhinīs delude beings with their pleasing appearances and forms, so, as a result of deluding beings by presenting the pleasing forms of men and women, *the great deceivers* are things in which there exist great deceptions.[55]

As in the *Aṭṭhasālinī,* the great essentials are defined here as "deceivers," using the similes of the magician and the demoness (*yakkhinī*). But note that no mention is made of the male *yakkha,* as there was in Buddhaghosa's work. This hardly seems like an important omission, but Ledi critiques the *Vibhāvinī* for it:

But in the *Vibhāvinī,* having made a simile using just the word *yakkhinī,* it is said, "As a result of deluding beings by presenting the pleasing forms of men and women, *the great deceivers* are things in which there exist great deceptions." This does not accord with the commentary.

For in the commentary, in the explanation of the word *mahābhūtasāmaññato* [in conformity with being a "great deceiver"], *mahābhūta* is called three things: magician, *yakkha,* and *yakkhinī.*[56]

Ledi critiques the *Vibhāvinī* for leaving out the male demon when the female is included. He offers no further explanation for his criticism, but it could be supposed he felt that including both genders gave a sense of completeness to the image that was necessary when commenting upon a system that was valued as totalistic. He may have felt, too, that a proper allusion to the *Aṭṭhasālinī* required a full recounting. Still, the matter is of limited scope, and people could have easily seen it as caviling. This example certainly indicates that at least some of Ledi's critiques had no grave intellectual import. Such a critique as this, however, had perhaps another purpose. It allowed Ledi to show his knowledge of Buddhaghosa's commentary at a level of detail that underscored his impressive textual command. As we saw in chapter 1, such command was a preeminent criterion for authority in Burmese Buddhism. To catch the *Vibhāvinī* in such a minute omission only proved his ability.

Not all critiques, however, were limited to perceived textual errors. Others dealt more directly with the substance of the Abhidhamma. To move from matter to mind, let us consider a correction of the *Vibhāvinī* Ledi makes in the chapter on consciousness, and also consider what commentaries defending the *Vibhāvinī* had to say.

Ledi takes the *Vibhāvinī* to task for a statement it makes about the nature of the unwholesome consciousness (*akusalacitta*) rooted in delusion (*moha*). Among the eighty-nine possible types of consciousness, there are just twelve that are unwholesome. These states result from the combination of the bare consciousness (citta) with a negative "root" (*hetu*) of greed (*lobha*), hatred (*dosa*), or delusion (*moha*), along with other mental factors. Of these twelve unwholesome consciousnesses, there are eight rooted in greed (*lobhamūlacittāni*), two in hatred (*dosamūlacittāni*), and two in delusion (*mohamūlacittāni*). Of the two consciousnesses rooted in delusion, one is characterized by doubt (*vicikicchā*) and one by restlessness (*uddhacca*).[57] About these delusional consciousnesses the *Vibhāvinī* says:

> These two types of consciousness [of delusion] have no other root [besides delusion], and, being associated with doubt and restlessness, their nature is instability by virtue of being scattered and diffuse because of delusion; therefore, they always occur free from attachment [*rajjana*] and hostility [*dussana*], and accompanied just by equanimity [*upekkha*].[58]

Ledi understands the *Vibhāvinī* to be implying that the two consciousnesses of delusion do not have the qualities of attachment (*rajjana*) or hostility (*dussana*) *because* they have the quality of equanimity (*upekkha*). In other words, "equanimity" means that the mind of a person in a state of delusion is so "scattered and defuse" as to be unable to fix on anything, making attachment or hostility impossible.[59] Ledi sees this as an argument that equanimity *prevents* the presence of attachment or hatred in the mind. He says this is wrong and supports his argument that a mental state can contain equanimity *and* either attachment or hostility by noting that the *Saṅgaha* says that four of the eight possible states of consciousness with the root of greed (*lobhamūlacittāni*) also contain equanimity. If states of greed can contain attachment and equanimity, equanimity clearly does not negate attachment:

> But it is said in the *Vibhāvinī*: "These two consciousnesses with states of deep delusion and wavering are under all circumstances without attachment and hostility. Therefore, they exist associated just with equanimity." This is not good.
>
> Because of the clear association of equanimity with consciousnesses having the root of greed, connected also with attachment.[60]

Ledi is not arguing that something is present in the consciousness of delusion that the *Vibhāvinī* says is not; that would be a difference profound enough to alter the Abhidhamma system's structure. In fact, he agrees with the *Vibhāvinī* that a person with a consciousness of delusion has no attachment or hostility, only equanimity. Ledi just wants to make the point that attachment or hostility need not be absent because of the presence of equanimity.

In responding to Ledi, Nat Tha, the author of the *Atisundara Kyam,* paraphrases the *Vibhāvinī* in an attempt to make it clear that the text is not claiming that equanimity prevents the presence of hostility or attachment in a deluded consciousness:

> Although there is attachment in the consciousness of greed and although this consciousness has attachment as a result of its weakness, it still has equanimity. Now, the consciousness whose root is in delusion, which is completely free from attachment, should not be spoken of [in the same way]. There is just the existence of equanimity [in it].[61]

According to Nat Tha, just as it is true, as Ledi says, that the consciousness of greed has attachment plus equanimity, it is also true, as the *Vibhāvinī* says, that the consciousness of delusion has equanimity without attachment or hostility. It is simply a statement of the way things are, not why. Ledi is wrong to read a causal implication in the *Vibhāvinī*'s words.

Another response text, the *Inkuraṭīkā,* contains an argument in sympathy with the *Atisundara Kyam* but with a more sophisticated analysis. The author, the Talaingoun Sayadaw, states that the *Vibhāvinī* does not imply that equanimity cancels out attachment and hostility in a deluded consciousness. In support of this, he points out that the *Vibhāvinī* says that equanimity can coexist with all sorts of mental states.[62] To criticize the text by citing the existence of a consciousness of greed with equanimity does not catch the *Vibhāvinī* in a contradiction, but rather only states a fact contained in the *Vibhāvinī* itself:

> But in the Sinhala ṭīkā [the *Vibhāvinī*] it is said that, "Because of great bewilderment and unsteadiness, they [the consciousnesses of delusion] are in every way without attachment and hostility. Therefore, they are associated only with equanimity." Here, "without attachment and hostility" means without pleasant and unpleasant mental feelings.[63] This is said by way of the proximity of causes: because although attachment to a small degree is the cause of equanimity, a lot of it is the cause of pleasant mental feelings; and, just so, hostility [to a small degree is the cause of equanimity, but a lot is the cause] of unpleasant mental feelings. In this case, there is certainly not the fault [on the part of the *Vibhāvinī* of implying] there are no consciousnesses with roots of greed, accompanied by attachment and associated with equanimity. Therefore, the objection of anyone [like Ledi] who says, "This is not good, because of the clear

association of equanimity with consciousnesses having the root of greed, connected also with attachment" makes a bad objection.[64]

The Talaingoun Sayadaw says that the *Vibhāvinī* presents the lack of attachment or hostility as reasons for the arising of equanimity, rather than equanimity forcing them out.

The point of delving into the details of this arcane argument is to understand that Ledi's critique and the defenses of the *Vibhāvinī* raise no matter that would generate significant controversy simply on the basis of philosophical import. Although, in contrast to the previous example of the great essentials, this matter deals with substantive components of the Abhidhamma system, the narrow and technical nature of this dispute over the consciousnesses rooted in delusion exemplifies the philosophically negligible import of all the *Paramatthadīpanī*'s critiques. So, too, the responses to them are of little significance, since they concern issues raised by Ledi, who does not make particularly controversial claims that seriously challenge the Burmese understanding of the Abhidhamma system.

In fact, Ledi is not always hostile to the *Vibhāvinī*. He even disagrees, in part, with an argument made against the *Vibhāvinī* by none other than his lay teacher, the courtier Hpo Hlaing. Hlaing argued that there is contact between the eye or ear and its respective object of perception, while the *Vibhāvinī* claims they never touch one another.[65] Ledi partially sides with the *Vibhāvinī*, saying that while there is actual contact between the eye and a visual object or the ear and a sound, a person naturally does perceive a distance between them. This is because contact with an object depends on light, in the case of vision, or space, in the case of sound. So, Ledi argues, the *Vibhāvinī* is right to call out these two senses as different from the other three senses that are based on materiality—smell, touch, and taste—for which contact with the object is readily apparent.[66] In this correction, then, it seems that Ledi's position mediates between the view held by Hpo Hlaing and that held by the *Vibhāvinī*. Here we have an example of a doctrinal argument by Ledi that, far from being extreme, indicates a tone of conciliation. He even concedes that many other sources agree with the *Vibhāvinī*.[67] While most of the time Ledi bluntly states the *Vibhāvinī* is wrong, this example of mediation goes to show that, in general, his criticisms move within the bounds of acceptable doctrinal disagreement. What is more, he may have had a further motivation not to roundly reject the *Vibhāvinī* in every instance. Balancing differing doctrinal views displayed Ledi's own textual authority, by showing his ability to use skillfully various texts with competing perspectives to establish his own distinctive argument.

The fact that the *Paramatthadīpanī*'s corrections are insignificant, however, is not because inherently they were insignificant, but because Ledi never exploits his corrections as the thin end of a wedge to open up and seriously alter the Abhidhamma system. Examples in other Buddhist traditions show that it was possible to make real doctrinal changes in the system through small amendments. For example, in the Indian *Vaibhāṣika* school of Abhidharma (the Sanskrit equivalent to the Pali Abhidhamma), there was the development of a class of *dharma*s (Sanskrit for dhammas) that straddle the divide between the mental (*nāmaskandha*) and the physical (*rūpaskandha*). These were called *cittaviprayuktasaṃskāra*s. Examples of these are birth, old age, the phrase, and the syllable.[68] These dharmas seem to have come about through a gradual shift in the understanding of what was really real. Aspects of reality originally considered the attributes of other dharmas eventually came to be seen as dharmas themselves, adding to the number of really real things in the world. Because these new dharmas resisted inclusion into a preexisting classificatory system that had split reality exclusively into either the physical or the mental, a whole new category for them came into being. Once considered real, these liminal entities opened up the possibility for a much more complex conception of ontology.[69]

The possibility for real change existed in the Theravāda tradition, too. Commentaries had added refinements to the system up to Ledi's time, and in them we can see examples of significant innovations through small modifications. It is in the commentaries that the lengths of time (*khaṇa*) that mental and physical events exist are first fixed and the process of consciousness (*cittavīthi*) fully described.[70] It is also in the commentaries that the theory of the subatomic particle, called the *kalāpa,* is developed.[71] These seemingly small and recondite changes could contribute to a big shift. Noa Ronkin has argued that the accumulation of such changes eventually transformed the Abhidhamma tradition from a pragmatic system aimed at liberation to a scholastic, metaphysical one concerned with ontology.[72] (Yet, if so, Ledi led it back again to pragmatic uses in meditation, as the conclusion will show.) Ledi never went as far in his corrections as these examples of change. He stays well within the bounds of orthodoxy—indeed, if anything, he polices the bounds of orthodoxy with corrections that substantiate themselves through reference to widely accepted texts and through arguments that confirm preexisting beliefs. In this way, he presents himself as an unparalleled authority on the *Saṅgaha* and does not challenge the fundamentals of the text that were very basis of that authority.

Many works that came out in reaction to the *Paramatthadīpanī* did not favor the *Vibhāvinī* in every single case. One ṭīkā, the *Abhidhammatthasaṅgahavinicchaya,* was written as an attempt to reconcile the *Vibhāvinī* with the *Paramatthadīpanī,* and so it takes a diplomatic approach to both, treating their points equally seriously and adjudicating between them.[73] Even the Talaingoun Sayadaw, who is generally quite critical of Ledi, sides on occasion with him against the *Vibhāvinī,* such as in the matter of the cause of delusion.[74] We see again that Ledi's points of correction were not beyond the pale of acceptability, and even the response ṭīkās that were part of the uproar against the *Paramatthadīpanī* sometimes found its arguments convincing. Of course, even doctrinal points that stayed within the orthodox fold might still have generated interest, but in themselves, that is to say on philosophical grounds, they did not cause a controversy of warlike proportions. In fact, nearly all of the response commentaries, with all of their close and extensive analyses, are forgotten now, for they had very little to offer the tradition in orienting themselves around the refutation of a work that, doctrinally, was not subversive or even extreme.

Overtly complimentary statements about the *Paramatthadīpanī* by well-known sayadaws also add to the conclusion that its critiques were not sufficient to cause such a widespread controversy. It must be borne in mind that the sources for these comments are Ledi's biographies and the introduction to the Burmese edition of the *Paramatthadīpanī,* sources that are inclined to cast his work in a favorable light. Nonetheless, what the sayadaws have to say is interesting and credible, for they do not simply praise the *Paramatthadīpanī* but view it as part of a vibrant tradition of disputation. For example, the Visuddhāyoun Sayadaw is reported to have said that Ledi's commentary was "a good book, which can clear up and purify the errors of the *Vibhāvinī.* They should print and distribute it quickly for the benefit of students."[75] Another sayadaw, the Manlay Sayadaw, a monk famous still today in Burma for his poetry, was asked by a group of monks in Sagaing to refute Ledi's work. He declined by saying: "No lawyer, unless his case is good, will have a name of good reputation. If the nature of the case is not good, although he argues and does well, how will he win the case?"[76] The implication is that Ledi's points in the *Paramatthadīpanī* are sound, and that no matter how well one argues against him, it will be impossible to prevail. Finally, the Myopinji Sayadaw, a famous Abhidhamma teacher who had taught the subject to the Visuddhāyoun Sayadaw and other well-known monks, remarked: "I have seen around sixty points which do not accord with the canonical texts in the *Vibhāvinī.* . . . Since Ledi Sayadaw has found over two hundred points, he has read it more thoroughly than I."[77]

Even if the heart of the controversy over the *Paramatthadīpanī* did not lie in the details of the arguments, however, the details still mattered, for they were the means through which various actors articulated the controversy. Clearly, a value was being expressed in the focus on doctrinal details. As noted at the start of the chapter, the *Vibhāvinī*'s role as the key to the *Saṅgaha* meant that most monks teaching the Abhidhamma relied upon its interpretations of the *Saṅgaha* as the basis for a very important value, their intellectual authority. Ledi's intense point-by-point criticism of the *Vibhāvinī* was, by extension, a criticism of the monks who depended upon it. The sense of having one's authority undermined would be especially strong in the textually centered monastic culture of Burma, and this was surely a factor promoting the controversy.

Yet many laypeople and monks were involved in the controversy who were not in authoritative teaching positions. What drew them into the dispute, particularly if their understanding of the specifics of the texts was only rudimentary? As the examples above indicate, it was not a matter of the niceties of doctrine as such. Yet, again, it would be a mistake to dismiss the technical details out of hand. Complex Abhidhamma argumentation may have been beyond most of those who were interested in the controversy, but that does not mean they ignored or devalued it as a means to answer the challenge the *Paramatthadīpanī* presented. Rather, they looked for surrogate specialists, such as the Manlay and Talaingoun Sayadaws, to take up the challenge of responding for them. In other words, popular interest in such abstruse arguments was not just a trickle-down effect from the elite level, but, in fact, drove disputation that captured in its details an anxiety over the *Paramatthadīpanī*. But if such anxiety preceded disputation, what was its true basis? Could it be that Ledi's acerbic tone and 245 corrections created a sort of "death by a thousand cuts," in which the *Vibhāvinī* was undermined by many small, even caviling, points? But why would this matter when esteemed sayadaws and texts (even the *Vibhāvinī* itself) show that neither harsh language nor corrections were unprecedented or even unusual? To answer these questions, we turn now to the Burmese understanding of the Abhidhamma's place in the sāsana and to social factors in the colonial era that could make the *Paramatthadīpanī* controversial even when its doctrinal content was not.

The Burmese and the Abhidhamma

There is a folk tale told by the Burmese that captures their predilection for the Abhidhamma. It is said that long ago a ship carrying the tipiṭaka foundered at sea. The ship sank, but the baskets of the Buddhist canon floated to the surface to be carried on the ocean's currents. The books of the Vinaya floated to Thailand, and the suttas went to Sri Lanka.[78] As one might suspect, the story tells that the books of the Abhidhamma washed up on the shore of Burma. Regardless of its doubtful veracity, this vignette captures the sense the Burmese have of themselves as distinctive in their appreciation for the Abhidhamma. While inscriptions suggest the Burmese placed great value on the Abhidhamma as early as the Pagan period,[79] most scholars point to the seventeenth century as the time when a pronounced stress on Abhidhamma studies began in Burma.[80] At this time, multiple translations from Pali to Burmese took place, particularly through word-by-word translations called *nissayas*;[81] a system for memorizing the relationships among the dhammas was developed by a monk and subsequently promoted by the king;[82] and a trend to translate religious texts into Burmese extended the reach of Buddhist learning, especially with the development of Burmese-language primers called *ayakauk* (*a ra kok'*).[83]

The curricula of monasteries prior to the twentieth century also reflect the importance of the Abhidhamma in the Buddhist scholarly tradition of Burma, and they offer a link from earlier times to the *Paramatthadīpanī* controversy. Prior to British rule, Burmese monasteries followed no common course of study, but over time a loose standardization had developed in the choice of texts and the levels of the students at which they were introduced. Abhidhamma study usually began for students between the ages of fifteen and seventeen, once they had made the decision to pursue their studies beyond the basic level expected of all boys. Study of the Abhidhamma started with memorization of the *Saṅgaha*. Although not speaking of Burmese culture in particular, the Sinhalese scholar-monk Hammalawa Saddhātissa expressed well the longstanding sentiment in Burma about the *Saṅgaha:* "Trying to study the Abhidhamma without first mastering this book, is like trying to construct a house without a suitable foundation."[84] (Ledi first committed the text to memory while a teenage novice living in his natal village of Sainpyin.) If the student showed aptitude and inclination, he would progress to more complex texts under the tutelage of his preceptor.[85] There was a well-developed textual apparatus to guide the student through Abhidhamma literature. Besides Burmese-language *ayakauk,* monks in Burma codified a group of synoptic compendiums on the Abhidhamma in Pali, which they called "finger manuals" (*lak' san'*") and which we might term "handbooks."[86] This group of texts includes the *Saṅgaha,* the most popular by far, but there are eight others as well.[87] Commentaries on these manuals are typically used to elucidate their teachings and lead the student into further detailed study.

Even for students who did not progress to advanced study, this educational system imparted a basic Abhidhamma literacy that was a fundamental condition for such widespread interest in Ledi's commentary on the *Saṅgaha.* Writing in 1911 at the time the controversy was in full bloom, the English-born monk Ananda Metteyya observed that the Abhidhamma's "profound metaphysics often form the subject of the keenest discussion even by the laity, at the *Uposatha*-day reunions in every monastery rest-house."[88] Of course, an appreciation of the Abhidhamma does not mean that many people would understand the technical details of the *Paramatthadīpanī.* The complex matters argued in it (and in Pali as well) were beyond even the most "keen discussions" of most of the laity—or the ordained for that matter. But the familiarity with basic Abhidhamma teachings among the general populace could have motivated protests against the work. This understanding of the Abhidhamma was not so much about the details of doctrine but about its overall significance. A closer look at this valuation of the Abhidhamma as such—quite beyond the specificities of the doctrinal matters—will provide further understanding of the cultural context which made the impact of the *Paramatthadīpanī* possible.

Ledi states in his *Manual of the Way* (*Niyāmadīpanī*) that ultimate reality concerns what has an actual nature (*sabhāva*).[89] It is knowledge of such ultimate (*paramattha*) matters, what he calls "the light of the Abhidhamma" (*abhidhamma a laṅ'"*), that allows a person to liberate him- or herself.[90] As the repository of ultimate teachings, the Abhidhamma stands apart from works containing conventional (*sammuti*) truth, however useful that conventional truth might be. This contrast between the Abhidhamma and other parts of the canon corresponds to a sense of the Abhidhamma as the complete and perfect teachings of the Buddha.

There are a number of well-known places in the suttas where the Buddha cautions monks to have a certain intellectual humility about what they have learned. For instance, in the *Acinteyya Sutta* (AN 4.77) he lists the four "unthinkables" (*acinteyyāni*) about which one should not speculate, because such speculation is not conducive to the pursuit of awakening.[91] And in the *Siṃsapā Sutta* (SN 56.31), the Buddha uses the analogy of a handful of leaves picked up from the forest floor to indicate how little of the dhamma he has revealed relative to what he knows.[92] Nevertheless, the Theravāda tradition has understood the Abhidhamma as holding absolutely nothing back. In Buddhaghosa's *Aṭṭhasālinī* the story of the origins of the final text of the Abhidhamma, the *Paṭṭhāna,* conveys this sense:

When he [the Buddha] began to contemplate the twenty-four universal conditional relations of root, object, and so on, his omniscience certainly found its opportunity therein. For as the great fish Timiratipingala[93] finds room only in the great ocean 84,000 yojanas in depth, so his omniscience truly finds room only in the great book.[94]

In contemplating the content of the *Paṭṭhāna,* the Buddha finds an infinite reach for his omniscient mind. In the *Paramatthadīpanī,* Ledi echoes this sense of infinite conceptual reach within the Abhidhamma. Also employing an ocean analogy, he says:

Having taken jewels from the great ocean, should one give as many to an islander as he wants, there will still be no lack [of them].

Just so here there are abundant meanings, as jewels in the ocean. Should one explain a hundred times, they would not be exhausted.[95]

In many other works, Ledi reiterates the sense, widely shared in Burma, that the Abhidhamma was complete in its teachings. For example, in the *Manual on Right Views* (*Sammādiṭṭhidīpanī*), he contrasts the totalizing scope of the Abhidhamma with the teachings in the other parts of the canon. Noting the belief in the origin of the Abhidhamma in the Tāvatiṃsa heaven,[96] he even characterizes the full breadth of the Abhidhamma as beyond human understanding:

The noble Buddha did not teach in the world of men this Abhidhamma Piṭaka, in which he explained *in full* such dhammas as wholesome volitional actions and the aggregates of existence. He preached the teachings of the Abhidhamma Piṭaka just in the Tāvatiṃsa heaven.

In this realm of men, he limited himself to just the dhamma of name and form [*nāma* and rūpa], so people can reach with certainty the transcendent wisdom of right views. And he taught the dhamma of name and form just to the extent appropriate for people to attain the transcendent wisdom of right views. He did not teach it in its entirety.[97]

Ledi contrasts the teachings the Buddha gave to men with those given in a heavenly realm, where he gave the teachings "in full." It is only in the higher heavens, in fact, that one can completely grasp these teachings, as only beings there have the capability to listen nonstop for the three months it takes to hear them in their entirety.[98] In the human realm, on the other hand, the Buddha doled out the Abhidhamma in chunks that are understood inevitably to limit understanding.[99] Although the tradition sees the Abhidhamma as complete in its seven books, there is a sense, then, as Ledi indicates, that no unawakened human can fully grasp such a system of infinite reach. Even the title "Abhidhamma" suggests material that goes beyond the normal teachings of the dhamma. When explaining the term, the tradition turns to Buddhaghosa's famous definition of the word Abhidhamma "as meaning 'that which exceeds and is distinguished from the Dhamma' (*dhammātireka-dhammavisesa*), the prefix *abhi* showing the sense of preponderance and distinction, and *dhamma* here signifying the teaching of the Sutta piṭaka."[100] As that which exceeds and is distinguished, the Abhidhamma is thus worthy of special reverence. Indeed, Buddhists must take particular care to safeguard it, especially in times of change.

The takeover by the British was the apotheosis of such change, and it caused intense anxiety over the health of Buddhism, the Abhidhamma included. With the king gone, there was a widespread perception that the monkhood, those most responsible for the sāsana's health through their embodiment of its principles and preservation of its teachings, had no strong check upon their decline into bad behavior. The last king, Thibaw, had muddled the authority of the head of the saṅgha (thathanabaing) by trying to appoint two monks instead of the usual one.[101] With the British takeover had come, initially, the hope the new rulers would promote a single thathanabaing's authority.[102] In March 1886, a group of lay citizens in Rangoon asked the British to appoint a leader, and in December of the same year the leading monks of Burma even offered to pledge official support to the colonial power in exchange for doing so.[103] But the British were reluctant to support Buddhism because of their broader policy of keeping as neutral a posture as possible toward religious institutions and figures among colonial subjects.

In part, this was thanks to a longstanding edict by Queen Victoria to avoid entanglement in religious matters, made in response to the Sepoy Rebellion of 1857 in India: "We do strictly charge and enjoin all those who may be in authority under us that they abstain from all interference with the religious belief or worship of any of our subjects on pain of our highest displeasure."[104] The Burmese did not see this policy position as neutral, however, but as overtly hostile.[105] The lieutenant-governor of Burma in the early years of the twentieth century, H. T. White, remarked: "Now the [monastic] hierarchy complained that, as Government will not enforce discipline, authority is waning, with disastrous results."[106] From the Burmese perspective, the colonial authorities' failure to act was an active injury to Buddhism, because of its need for continual care. Many Burmese sensed hypocrisy on the part of the British, too, for when the Anglican Church came to Lower Burma after the Second Anglo-Burmese war, it received direct support from the colonial government.[107] But the queen's injunction aside, the British were also reluctant to buttress a Burmese institution that might prove troublesome at some point to British rule. Colonial officials did reinstate the scripture examinations for monks in 1895 and funded the publication of the tipiṭaka in 1898—two typically royal forms of patronage—but refused to appoint a thathanabaing directly. Although there were claimants to the office, there was no universally accepted thathanabaing at all between 1895 and 1903.[108] The British did give official recognition to the Taunggwin Sayadaw, who was picked by a group of monks in Mandalay as the thathanabaing in 1903. The changing dynamics in colonial society had irreversibly weakened the position, however, and created the perception that colonialism was undercutting longstanding institutions that safeguarded Burmese Buddhism.[109]

Adding to the Burmese perception of increasing monastic laxity was the common belief that the monkhood was shrinking.[110] A loss in the extent of monks' social functions exacerbated this anxiety over the diminishment of the saṅgha. During the colonial period monks went from a position central to village, town, and national life to being rather extraneous figures in terms of societal functions.[111] In the previous chapter I described the close, if sometimes fraught, interaction between the saṅgha and royal rule. This relationship, in which the monks acted as a balance between the government and the people, ended with the takeover by the British.[112] Furthermore, by resisting the introduction of new subjects into their curricula, the monks, once the preeminent source of learning in Burma, became peripheral to the education of many young Burmese. Because the best jobs were only available to those with training in British-stipulated subjects, which the monks would not teach, parents sent their children in ever-increasing numbers to government-approved non-Buddhist schools.[113] The shift to these schools was especially worrisome to Burmese because so many were under the control of Christian missionaries, who often used their positions of authority to criticize Buddhism and who appeared to have the (at least tacit) backing of the colonial state.[114]

The growing irrelevancy of the monkhood in terms of its political and educational roles developed during a wider societal atomization due to British policies. The reorganization of local governance along alien lines, the sale of intoxicants (such as liquor and opium), disruption of economic practices, the importation of cheap foreign labor from India, the criminalization of traditional activities (like cattle and boat races),[115] and the trend in the civil sphere to marginalize the Burmese language meant it was harder for the Burmese to act collectively to redefine and reintegrate the structures of Buddhism into fragmented lives.[116] All of these factors, but particularly the debilitation of the monkhood, contributed to a sense that the sāsana was in danger.

Coinciding with these developments was the rise of print culture, which heightened worry about Buddhism by reorienting Burmese to a new, expanded, and often pugnacious range of sources of information. The *Paramatthadīpanī* came out in 1901 among a crowd of commentaries on the *Saṅgaha,* just at the start of a massive growth in the print culture of Upper Burma.[117] Printing had existed in limited form in Upper Burma since King Mindon had installed a press in Mandalay around 1870, but royal control and infrastructural capacities had limited the extent of printing.[118] Prior to the British takeover, published books were often on popular religious subjects hitherto copied on palm-leaf, such as the Jātaka stories, histories of famous stūpas, poetry, and stories from the *Dhammapada* commentary.[119] It was only in the relatively free market of print capitalism under colonialism that the print culture of original Burmese works from a wide variety of authors really prospered. This situation started first in British-controlled Lower Burma. As in Sri Lanka, printing first began with Christian missionaries, who brought in presses to produce polemical tracts and materials for the purposes of evangelization.[120] In the 1820s and 1830s, Baptist missionaries in Lower Burma monopolized printing capabilities; their works, mostly copies of the Bible, catechisms, and other Christian tracts, were distributed not only in colonized parts of the country but in royal Burma as well. There was thus already widespread familiarity with books and publications in both British-controlled and independent areas.[121] By the 1870s, Burmese Buddhists, too, could readily access print in Lower Burma.[122] Htin Aung observes, when discussing unorthodox lay preachers and writers: "Some of the lay preachers even expressed themselves in print, and the harm inflicted on the religion became great, because with the introduction of cheap printing presses in Rangoon, their books and pamphlets were widely circulated."[123] Whether laypeople inflicted harm or not, their activities suggest a situation in which people had a relatively unfettered ability to print works.

A more extensive circulation of a wide variety of books and pamphlets developed in Upper Burma after the British annexation in 1885, along with the further growth of printing capacities throughout the land. In 1910, the British colonial official E. J. Colston wrote: "Of late years printing presses have been established in most towns. The output of these presses is enormous, and is mainly of a religious or fabulous character, though books on such subjects as interest young men and song-books are poured out in enormous numbers also. There is nowadays scarcely a home in any village near a large town which does not contain one or more books, and one constable in every five has a broad-sheet of songs in his pocket."[124] The increase in the ability to spread information with the proliferation of presses greatly expanded the audience for doctrinal disputation.[125] This was not just a quantitative change but also a qualitative one. A shift was taking place, from a Buddhism in which expertise centered on a small subset of largely monkish doctrinal experts, to one in which doctrine and learning became the basis for a pan-Burma Buddhist identity.[126]

The *Paramatthadīpanī* controversy signaled this shift. Its mass production meant it could reach a wide audience, one that might react to it in ways different from the coterie of elites who specialized in Abhidhamma study. The nature of the reduplication process in the age of hand-copying meant that what monks and their patrons decided to copy at any given village monastery would tend to be works they already knew or ones they perceived to have local significance. Such a decentralized situation did not support the coordination needed for the mass production of a little-known and potentially abrasive work like the *Paramatthadīpanī.* With the appearance of the printing press, however, monks at peripheral monasteries, amateur lay authors, editorialists in newspapers—all could participate in a countrywide conversation. While the response commentaries, public meetings, and other activities centering on the *Paramatthadīpanī* indicate that the disputes over Ledi's work were largely the concern of the monastic community, the laity clearly took part in the conversations as well. We have looked at the layman Nat Tha's response commentary, and he and other laypeople wrote editorials against the *Paramatthadīpanī* for popular newspapers in Rangoon and Mandalay. While the debate over Ledi's commentary at the granular level of its details was beyond most people, a broader community sustained the controversy through public meetings and appeals to high-ranking sayadaws.[127] The spread of a sense of the *Paramatthadīpanī* as a controversial work reached beyond the elites of the saṅgha, thanks to the power of the growing print culture of books and newspapers.

The participation of new voices, and so many of them, points to a related factor that also augmented the scope and intensity of the reaction to the *Paramatthadīpanī:* the lack of a centralized religious authority to control and contain response. Control of religious information and religious views became radically de-centered through print technology. Due to the British policy of noninterference, monks and laity upset over the attack on the *Vibhāvinī* had no strong system of ecclesiastical and secular power that could adjudicate the matter. This was in contrast to the royal era, in which the king and the monastic hierarchy could more readily check deviation from established views and practices (recall the king who defrocked monks and made them shovel manure because of their claims to spiritual attainments, described in the previous chapter). This is not to say that royal-era ecclesiastical control was pervasive or entirely effective, but there was, nonetheless, a sense of an insuperable authority that could police the bounds of disputation, at the very least, and even try to resolve a matter if the disagreement became too heated. With the king gone and the position of saṅgha leader (thathanabaing) greatly weakened, however, a free market atmosphere ensued, in which every man could add his voice to the clamor. Printed materials reached a level of distribution unheard of in earlier times and spread out at a pace unthinkable in a manuscript-based culture. Moreover, the reaction to the *Paramatthadīpanī* was likely all the more intense because Ledi's work appeared at the start of the efflorescence of print culture in Upper Burma, when the widespread publication of controversial works was still a relatively new phenomenon.

Although it should be no surprise that Ledi viewed the *Paramatthadīpanī* as a positive contribution to Burmese Buddhism, he shared with many Burmese the idea that baleful developments in the colonial period, such as the move of students to non-Buddhist schools and the absence of robust support for the monkhood, signaled the steady decline of the sāsana.[128] The Burmese Theravāda tradition, like Buddhist traditions generally, understands that Buddhism will eventually disappear from the world. The initial basis for this belief comes from canonical passages, such as those in the *Gotami Sutta* (AN 8.51) and the *Saddhammapatirūpaka Sutta* (SN 16.13), in which the Buddha explains that the sāsana will not last forever. Sources differ on the time-span of the sāsana, but Buddhaghosa in the *Manorathapūraṇī,* his commentary on the Aṅguttara section of the Sutta Piṭaka, set the period for orthodox Theravāda at five thousand years.[129] Such a specific number suggests the the decline of the dhamma is inexorable, but there was a strong sense in Ledi's time, as today, that the disappearance of Buddhism could be hastened by the increasing laxity of Buddhists, especially the ordained. This laxity is understood to increase in regard to both behavior and learning, but it is the preservation of the canonical texts, the basis of the tradition of learning called the *pariyatti* sāsana, on which the decline of Buddhism hinged in the Burmese conception.[130]

The first specific reference to the place of the Abhidhamma in the process of decline and disappearance comes also in the *Manorathapūraṇī.* There, Buddhaghosa states that when the canonical texts disappear, the seven books of the Abhidhamma will disappear first, and in the reverse of their order in the canon. Thus, the first to go will be the *Paṭṭhāna*, the text that contains the Buddha's realization of conditionality, the teaching that had given him the full play of his omniscience.[131] Later schemes of decline in Burmese sources describe the same process. Alicia Turner has identified three Burmese texts as key sources for narratives of decline in Burma in the late nineteenth and early twentieth centuries, all of which basically follow the description of Buddhaghosa's *Manorathapūraṇī.*[132] These are: the Burmese historical chronicle, the *Thathanalinkara Sadan* (discussed in chapter 1); a work detailing the process of Buddhism's decline called the *Anāgatavaṃsa;* and an *Anāgatavaṃsa* commentary called the *Anāgatawin Kyam.*[133] These texts were well known, not just in Burmese literati circles but also among the broad Burmese populace. For example, the *Anāgatawin Kyam,* printed in 1907 in an inexpensive edition (for only 6 pyas), sold ten thousand copies.[134]

Ledi made clear in a number of works that he believed the decline of the sāsana was well under way. Recall that in the poem about his meditation given in the last chapter, he remarks that it is almost the end of the sāsana. In 1904 he wrote that Burmese were living in a "waning age" (*chut' kap' kāla*), in which "the bodily and intellectual strength of the saṅgha, which works for the sāsana, is diminishing."[135] And he stresses in this work that Buddhism's survival depends upon study:

> The great tradition of learning [*pariyatti* sāsana], which is the tipiṭaka, is the root of the great tradition of practice [*paṭipatti* sāsana] and the great tradition of realization [*paṭivedha* sāsana]. Only when the sāsana of learning is established can the other two sāsanas also be established. The burden of maintaining the sāsana of learning for five thousand years is really very great.[136]

Certainly, the *Paramatthadīpanī* was published at a time when the Burmese shared Ledi's sense that they lived in an era of degeneration.[137] This sense among the Burmese that their Buddhist tradition was weakening matched a larger anxiety in Southeast Asia, both in Theravāda countries and more widely across the region, that religious values and standards were under threat.[138] The weakening of the moral fiber of the monkhood was precisely so worrisome because monks had traditionally had the responsibility to preserve the texts and teachings.

Most Burmese believed, however, that the sāsana was not yet so degenerate as to be past the point of no return. Buddhists still had the opportunity to reap the benefits of study and practice. This was an obvious fact if for no other reason than the continuing existence of the texts of the dhamma. And while, ultimately, the loss of Buddhism was inevitable, there was a sense that moral and intellectual effort could delay its onset. The Abhidhamma, as the first portion of the canonical texts to disappear, stood (and still stands) in this conception as the bellwether of the decline of all Buddhist learning. Because the omniscient Buddha had decreed that it would disappear first, safeguarding it protected the entire tradition. In this way it served as the "front-line fortress" for Buddhism's survival (to put it in the words of a contemporary Burmese monk).[139]

The Masoyein Sayadaw, who worked with Ledi on a Pali dictionary and became head of the Thudhamma sect of monks in 1956, describes this connection between protection of the Abhidhamma and protection of the tradition as a whole:

> I urge you to teach and learn with great effort the extraordinary Abhidhamma. In the matter of the disappearance of the tradition of learning [*pariyatti*], it is the case that the Abhidhamma will disappear first. . . . The Buddha often warned his disciples: "The sāsana of the Buddha will endure only if the Abhidhamma endures."[140]

The Abhidhamma will go before anything else. This understanding of its place in the tradition led the standard Burmese history of Abhidhamma literature, *History of the Abhidhamma,* to state that "by means of [being] the highest, the teaching of the Abhidhamma is the *main, firm source* of the *Buddhasāsana.*"[141] In Ledi's time, too, the Burmese certainly understood the importance of preserving the Abhidhamma. We have already noted Ledi's participation in the Fifth Council of 1871, which concerned itself with preserving all the canonical texts. A European visitor to Mandalay in 1861, Adolf Bastian, gives us another example of the particular importance of the Abhidhamma to King Mindon. He records that one day he came upon workers in one of the palace courtyards engraving the Abhidhamma on stone posts that the king had ordered set up as milestones along all the roads of the kingdom.[142]

As mentioned in the introduction, the *Paṭṭhāna,* as the very first book to vanish, stood in an exalted place as the bulwark against the loss of the Abhidhamma and, by extension, of Buddhism as a whole. Nine years after inscribing the Abhidhamma on posts, Mindon built a Paṭṭhāna Hall, where a three-month-long discussion of conditional relations, the subject of the *Paṭṭhāna,* was held among respected sayadaws, presumably as a way to insure its longevity and, generally, to avert dangers to the kingdom through its apotropaic properties when recited.[143] In modern times the ascendancy of the Abhidhamma in Burma remains obvious, and especially the great esteem for the *Paṭṭhāna.* I noted at the start of the book that many taxis in Yangon have the twenty-four conditional relations printed on CDs hanging from their rearview mirrors, and that they show up on posters, calendars, monks' fans, and above the entrances to monasteries, among other places.[144] In 2004, when I visited the Shwedagon on the last day of the summer rains retreat, I was reminded that it was an official holiday: Abhidhamma day.[145]

Commentary Meets Context: The Controversy Explained

As the "front-line fortress" preventing the decline and disappearance of Buddhism, the fragility of the precious Abhidhamma in the context of colonialism set the fuse for the explosive controversy over Ledi's *Paramatthadīpanī*. Then, in a Buddhist culture focused on scholastic practices, Ledi's incendiary language in numerous detailed critiques caused the detonation. Disagreements in commentaries had certainly existed, but, thanks to a new print culture, they had never spread with such publicity among so many unused to disputation—and about so sensitive a topic in such a threatening time. In suggesting this explanation of the controversy, I do not mean to reject the possibility of other reasons, including a real interest in doctrinal disputation. The controversy was surely overdetermined. But the explanation given here was at its root: the continuities of intellectual practices of textual mastery and the esteem given to the Abhidhamma met the challenges of colonialism and a new print culture to form a volatile mix.

At the time the controversy was developing in the first years of the twentieth century, Ledi left his cave and began to travel widely across Burma, preaching on the Abhidhamma as well as other topics. He was also continuing to publish many works popularizing the study of the dhamma. We will explore these activities in the next chapter, but it should be noted in the discussion of the controversy that Ledi's travels raised his profile and probably drew further attention to the *Paramatthadīpanī*. The meeting held at the Bingala Sayadaw's monastery, for instance, took place because Ledi was in town for a series of dhamma talks. There was, in other words, a synergy between the controversy and public speeches and other activities that further boosted Ledi's reputation as a leading figure in the saṅgha.

I have not mentioned so far any response by Ledi to the criticisms of others. In fact, he said very little in print. He published his own autocommentary on the *Paramatthadīpanī*, the *Anudīpanī*, in 1916.[146] That book raised no controversy at all, perhaps because it does not set its sights on any other esteemed text, and it follows his first work in organization and in the details of its philosophical arguments. I have found only two statements by Ledi about the controversy. The first captures a sense of coolly dismissive tolerance:

> When the great sayadaw was told, "Venerable sir, there are ṭīkās written such as the *Atisundara Kyam,* the ṭīkā from Mo-nyo, the ṭīkā from Pegu, the ṭīkā from Talaingoun, and the ṭīkā from Chaun-U, which condemn your *Paramatthadīpanī,* criticizing it harshly and using obscene language," he absolutely did not condemn the people [who had written the ṭīkās].
>
> He said, "That's OK. When these ṭīkās and other works are written about my commentary, they put my ṭīkā in an honorable position.
>
> "Later, well, these ṭīkās and other works will all disappear, but my ṭīkā will remain."[147]

Such a statement confirms the idea that one potential product of the controversy was prestige and authority garnered through the display of textual prowess. The controversy tapped into the sense, carried over from Konbaung developments into colonial times, of the importance of textual analysis. The other statement purportedly made by Ledi expresses much the same sense: "They may attack and protest against my ṭīkā now, but in the future in the sāsana which has not yet come, it will remain the only book. At that time they will probably rest their heads on my ṭīkā while they sleep."[148]

At least to a degree, Ledi was right. No work criticizing him, so far as I know, remains in print—most are forgotten—but the *Paramatthadīpanī* was reprinted as recently as 2003 (and is available as part of the Sixth Council Tipiṭaka on the web and in the CD distributed by the meditation organization of S. N. Goenka). As I mentioned earlier, Ledi exposed himself to ridicule and even ruin if his work did not succeed, but it did. The complimentary comments of other famous sayadaws show his success, perhaps above all the telling comment by the revered Myopinji Sayadaw that Ledi had read the *Vibhāvinī* even "more thoroughly" than he had. The *Paramatthadīpanī* made Ledi a force to be reckoned with in Burmese Buddhism on a national level. His remark that ṭīkās against the *Paramatthadīpanī* put it "in an honorable position" raised his own profile as well. His acerbic tone and the large number of corrections in his text drew attention to him and his work, and through the use of so much fine-grained argumentation Ledi displayed his own textual authority according to cultural conventions with roots stretching back to his Thudhamma forbearers and court literati like Hpo Hlaing. Such a display was vitally important in the intellectual culture in which Ledi was trained and in which he participated. He made himself a "member of the club," so to speak. He demonstrated the skills so esteemed in Burmese Buddhism and so put himself in a position to speak with authority.

Even today, advanced students of Abhidhamma in Burma study the *Paramatthadīpanī*.[149] The *Vibhāvinī,* however, has not ceded its position as the key to the *Saṅgaha.* As I noted earlier, Burmese editions of the *Saṅgaha* still often include the *Vibhāvinī* in the same volume. The *Paramatthadīpanī* never really became, as some of Ledi's supporters called it, the *Ṭīkā maw* ("the ṭīkā that surpasses") to the *ṭīkā jaw* ("the famous Ṭīkā," i.e., the *Vibhāvinī*). Ledi had scored an impressive victory, but he had not won the war. Nonetheless, he made his mark on a national scale, and his willingness to start such a controversy also suggests, once again, his confidence in himself and his views. Indeed, so confident was he about his knowledge of the Abhidhamma that he even went so far as to rank his understanding on par with, if not better than, that of the *Saṅgaha* itself. He said: "The *Abhidhammatthasaṅgaha* is an excellent summary . . . but supposing there were a fire or some sort of disaster and there was not even one copy of the book? Give me a paper and a pencil and I will write you a better treatise than that one."[150] This comment puts a fine point on the bold self-confidence Ledi possessed that enabled him to calmly cause controversy and to later promote an innovative vision of meditation.

Beyond the *Paramatthadīpanī*'s power to shape Ledi's reputation, the controversy shows the importance of the Abhidhamma to the broader Burmese populace. That the controversy had negligible doctrinal ramifications should not obscure the fact that doctrinal arguments, drawing impetus from popular wellsprings, not only reflected the notion of the Abhidhamma as the complete expression of the dhamma and its "front-line fortress" against decay, but crystalized that notion in popular consciousness. By drawing attention to the power of the Abhidhamma to determine the fate of Buddhism, the controversy encouraged its prominence, contrary to the common assumption that the Abhidhamma makes little impact on most Buddhists' lives. The widespread interest in the *Paramatthadīpanī* showed Ledi the potential the teaching of the specifics of the Abhidhamma had to engage lay interest—indeed, just a few years after the *Paramatthadīpanī* appeared he would write a poem explicitly for laypeople that translated the *Saṅgaha* into simple Burmese, and this became his most popular work. (This poem is discussed in the next chapter and is the focus of the fourth.) Surely, thanks at least in part to lessons learned through the controversy, Ledi would come to rely upon the power of the Abhidhamma as his most important resource in his efforts to change lay life. In the next chapter we will look at Ledi's public career, no doubt fueled by the renown (and perhaps some infamy) he had garnered through the controversy. It was his efforts in his public role as a preacher, a social organizer, and a popular writer—focused in all spheres of activity on the Abhidhamma above all else—that reconfigured the role of the laity, empowering them to study and, critically, to meditate.

THREE

"In the Hands of All the People": Ledi Empowers the Laity

In 1913, H. T. White, the former head of the colonial government in Burma, remarked upon the devotion and veneration Ledi received as he traveled around the country:

> One of the most striking personalities in Burmese Buddhism is the Ledi Sadaw [*sic*]. This remarkable man dedicated some years of his life to travelling through the country preaching and exhorting. His passionate eloquence drew immense congregations. Wherever he went he was greeted by enraptured throngs. Men and women vied in adoration of the saintly personage, women loosing their hair and spreading it as a carpet for his holy feet.[1]

The *Paramatthadīpanī* controversy had drawn Ledi from relative solitude on the banks of the Chindwin River to prominence on the national stage. Beginning in the first years of the twentieth century (the time when colonialism in Burma was at its high-water mark), he left his fairly sedentary and stable life in Upper Burma for one of nearly ceaseless travel, crisscrossing Burma from north to south and east to west over thousands of miles.[2] (Indeed, in the span of nine years, from 1904 to 1913, he never stayed in the same place two years in a row for the annual rains retreat.) Other monks were touring Burma at the time, too, but no one else moved around so much or achieved such fame. By 1908, a commentator in the magazine *The Burman Buddhist* would say:

> We have no hesitation in saying that no member of the Sangha in Burma stands more prominently before the public eye than the Ledi Sayadaw. This reverend monk has come out of the ordinary groove, and, besides being the most prolific of modern writers, has earned the deep veneration of his co-religionists all over the Province by his eloquent sermons. Everywhere he is received with the greatest enthusiasm, and immense crowds go to hear him preach.[3]

As the reference to his "passionate eloquence" suggests, he did not attract devotion because of elite scholarship. In fact, the attention given to the *Paramatthadīpanī* by the laity caused Ledi to turn to popularizing study and practice. He preached widely; he published numerous books, poems, articles, and other works; and he founded many social groups in various villages, towns, and cities to harness the collective energy of laypeople. Through these actions, he empowered the laity to respond to the sense of the threat to Buddhism revealed in the *Paramatthadīpanī* controversy. In 1917, surveying developments since the British deposition of the king, the lost protector of Buddhism, Ledi said, "Our noble Buddhist religion is in the hands of all the people of the country."[4] His efforts gave people the means to shoulder this unprecedented communal responsibility. As this chapter describes, taking on such a duty would reconfigure Burmese Buddhism and enable Ledi's reconceptualization of meditation as a feasible and even necessary part of lay life.

Ledi's Response to the Threat to Buddhism

Ledi certainly shared with his fellow Burmese a keen worry over Buddhism's survival under colonial rule. After all, he had said it was a time of the degeneration of the dhamma and even wrote—perhaps with a bit of rhetorical high-spiritedness—that the end of the sāsana was nigh. But, as we saw in the prior chapter, he did not believe the decline of Buddhism was a foregone conclusion. He encouraged Burmese to slow the process, even stave it off (at least for a while), through study and self-cultivation. The threat to Buddhism was real but not insurmountable.

Without a doubt, particular policies of the British that encouraged immoral behavior contributed to the sense of threat. Ledi worked against them, acknowledging, for instance, that his preaching against the consumption of intoxicants set him against the British government: "I am not sure the government will approve of my preaching. There will be much loss of revenue; for when I have finished, all liquor and opium shops will be closed for want of custom."[5] In fact, since Ledi's calls for temperance made governing easier, many British officials on the ground were appreciative of his efforts. In June 1908, the Commissioner of the Irrawaddy Division, in thanks for Ledi's efforts to promote morality, presented him with "a book-case containing 24 volumes on Buddhism, a travelling clock, and a printed 'memorial.'"[6] And, in 1912, the government conferred upon Ledi the title of *Aggamahāpaṇḍita*, meaning "foremost great learned one," in recognition of his scholarly accomplishments. The bestowal of the title on him was the first time the colonial rulers had done such a thing.[7] Ledi never became troublesome for the British because their policies were, in themselves, secondary in his view; as in his "Letter on Cows," he kept his focus on the Burmese. Liquor shops would close not due to a change in policy or law but because demand would dry up among the Burmese. Around the same time, the prominent lay organization the Young Men's Buddhist Association (YMBA), discussed below, tried to have intoxicants legally prohibited. As far as I know, Ledi never commented on this effort, though he likely would have approved of such a law. After all, liquor consumption had been illegal in royal times. Ledi's lay teacher Hpo Hlaing had even been placed under house arrest for arguing that alcohol in small doses was acceptable to drink as a medicine.[8] Nevertheless, Ledi focused on personal behavior, not legal remedies. In his view what mattered most for Buddhism's health was the moral renovation of every individual Buddhist.

In this climate, in which colonial policies seemed to stack the deck against Buddhism, Christian missionaries also attracted Ledi's attention. This was especially so because non-Buddhist government-supported schools, often run by missionaries, had become very popular. As noted in the previous chapter, parents often sent their children to these institutions because only they offered the training required for good jobs.[9] Such missionaries did not disturb Ledi so much because they sought to convert Burmese Buddhists (they had little success in that regard),[10] but because they were set up as educational authorities who, at best, neglected Buddhism, but all too often attacked it. Even if a student did not convert, a non-Buddhist educational environment was understood as likely to weaken his or her adherence to Buddhism and hasten the decline of the dhamma. As a 1908 issue of *The Burman Buddhist* put it, such a situation "has in it the germs of an irretrievable national disaster, for it threatens with extinction in but a few generations of men this great and beautiful Buddhist Religion which has formed every nobler feature of the Burmese character."[11]

The English Buddhist monk Ananda Metteyya, writing in 1903 in Rangoon, encapsulates the logic of a focus on Buddhist education in this environment:

> The chief fruit,—and, in our eyes, the best,—of Christian missionary work, is the advance in the general knowledge of Buddhism. Buddhists have heard their old ideals attacked, not always in a spirit of tolerance or courtesy; and they have hastened to learn what their Scriptures could say in reply. They have seen their children taught to deride their parents and their Monks as 'Heathens';—and they have been at pains to learn enough of their own Religion to set matters right; whilst the Monks themselves have been stirred to action in self-defence,—action which has resulted in the people being taught more of the Dhamma than had been necessary for their simple needs before the Missionary invasion.[12]

Ledi joined in this effort to give Burmese Buddhists the educational ammunition to fight Christian attacks. He spoke of arguing with people of "false views" (*micchādiṭṭhi*) and claimed that study could prevent the influence of "foreign religions."[13] That said, he understood that the lure of Christianity was not just a matter of the arguments its proponents made. He observed that missionaries, operating from positions of power, "give money to people who enter the Christian religion from other religions." (And he went on to note dryly that missionaries "have the custom of saying that the eternal lord aids in these matters.")[14] Government-sanctioned schools that ignored Buddhist learning or even allowed criticism of it, missionaries who operated with impunity, the tempting of Buddhists with financial gain—all of these problems added to a sense that Burmese colonial society was biased against Buddhism. In royal times, the king instituted policies to protect the sāsana, but now the situation was seemingly the opposite. As Nicholas Dirks has observed for India, the colonial state tacitly approved missionary actions with its own "missionary" claims to superiority.[15] This was true of Burma, where Ledi saw the sale of liquor and missionary efforts as of one piece. In this situation, Buddhists had to rely on themselves in the fight against non-Buddhist claims to superiority. In response to this environment, Ledi, like others, privileged education as the means to protect Buddhism.

For Ledi, the ultimate—indeed, the "scientific"—resource for Buddhist learning was the Abhidhamma. In a letter to Caroline Rhys-Davids of the Pali Text Society in 1917, Ledi singled it out for its rational appeal to non-Buddhists and the confidence it instilled in Buddhists:

> The philosophy of the Abhidhamma in Buddhism is the recreation-ground for intellectual minds. It gives delight to scientific men of other religions. It can also resist the

interference of foreign religions. Those who are well trained in it cannot be tempted by any other religion.[16]

Given the Abhidhamma's role as the bulwark against decline, Ledi would naturally turn to it as a key means to protect Buddhism. But, as this quotation suggests, it was not a matter of mere rote preservation. The Abhidhamma's ability to armor Buddhists against temptation by other religions suggests the power of its logic, as does the fact that it "gives delight to scientific men of other religions." This power was important, for reason and argumentation were the critical weapons when the fight was taken to non-Buddhists:

When conversing with people of false religions who are logicians and investigators, one cannot budge them with reference to classical texts; one can only prove one's point through logical explanations based upon personal experience.[17]

Ledi says that relying on classical texts—even the Abhidhamma—is not sufficient in itself. It is not that these texts are irrelevant (not at all), but to sway those who do not accept their authority one must confirm the points of the texts in one's own experience, in order to convey them in convincing terms. This was not an argument that only those who personally had gained spiritual attainments could make credible arguments. Rather, Ledi's point is that one must connect the teachings to lived reality.

In many works, Ledi provided examples of such arguments that applied the dhamma to real-world situations. For instance, he states in the *Purification of the Sāsana* (*Sāsanavisodhanī*) that "the Christian religion says that there is nothing of which it is incapable and it has endless power in the Lord."[18] But if that is so, he asks, why do people die ("There are the corpses of Christians all over this earth"), get sick ("But in this world there are hospitals everywhere"), get old ("All over this world are Christian old people"), and refuse to believe in Christianity ("But there are certainly many who do not accept Christianity")?[19] According to Ledi, the answer is quite simple: the Christian religion does not have the power it claims.

Ignorance of karma was a critical weakness of Christianity, in Ledi's view. In a sermon on the evils of intoxication given in April 1908, Ledi argued that the lack of belief in karma rendered Christians unable to engage in the actions necessary to improve materially their karmic prospects. While biblical figures, such as Moses, simply waited for God's help, Buddhists knew they could weaken, if not eliminate, bad karma through moral action on their own initiative.[20] In the *Manual on the Parts of the Path* (*Maggaṅgadīpanī*), Ledi says that those who worship God (and here he may mean Hindus and Muslims, too) must admit that present-day wealth comes from one's own work, which he classifies as "present kamma":

> It is not the way of things in this world that you get goods and property if you pray to and worship an eternal lord. But it is the evident way of things that you get goods and property if you perform your present kamma.
>
> Therefore it is right to believe that in this life getting goods and property does not depend on an eternal lord but just on one's present kamma.[21]

According to Ledi, consequences follow inexorably from actions (kamma). He appeals to reason, then, from what might be called a this-worldly, even seemingly materialistic perspective. (He adds later in the *Manual on the Parts of the Path* that you don't get rid of a disease by praying to a god but by taking medicine.)[22] This was an argument for the vitality of a Buddhist outlook in the modern world on logical grounds and a counter to the missionary claim of Buddhism's "disintegrating tendency."[23]

As much as Ledi stressed reasoned refutations of Christian claims and celebrated Buddhism's logicality, his arguments did not, in his view, represent a modernization of Buddhist teaching that necessitated a break with traditional beliefs and practices. While Ledi used his understanding of karma to criticize Christianity and other religions based on a strictly *causal* vision of the world, he did not have the modernist sensibility that dismissed all supernatural elements from the world or that discounted all apparently "magical" apotropaic practices. On the contrary, he relied on his precolonial heritage that understood a multileveled cosmos in which humans and various spirits coexisted and in which religious rituals, such as chanting, could affect the world. He wrote and recited texts specifically to promote rainfall, for instance, and his recitations were credited with ending droughts.[24] Ledi also performed recitations to banish plagues as he went on his preaching rounds throughout Burma.[25]

The colonial official J. A. Stewart suggested these activities were a sop to the populace: "A visit from him [Ledi] was supposed to exorcise plague. If he took advantage of this belief, it was only to preach Buddhism as a living rule of life."[26] But it is unlikely Ledi was only humoring his fellow Burmese, for he wrote an entire book on how to end plagues through recitation, the *Manual on Plague* (*Rogantaradīpanī*), and gave advice on the recitation of protective suttas, called *paritta*s, as well as the recitation of ritual texts called *kamma vā* (the Burmese term for the Pali word *kammavācā*). His remarks show an unequivocal belief in a universe filled with spirits and ghosts and in the power of the chanted word. For example, he recommended that the reciters of *kamma vā* texts use highly decorated editions, because the sight of such aesthetically impressive dhamma texts would scare away many troubling spirits before one had even begun to read.[27] Such protective practices did not conflict with Ledi's vision of reality because he did not have a "disenchanted" perspective that robbed his universe of unseen forces. In this regard he stands in contrast to someone like the Thai king Mongkut, who in his efforts to reform Thai Buddhism dismissed the Jātakas as folklore and rejected the worldview of the traditional Thai cosmological text, the *Traiphum* (*Three Worlds*).[28]

Ledi's willingness to banish spirits and bring rain, even as he argued for Buddhism's superiority on the grounds of logic, suggests that he felt no sense of conflict between his traditional worldview and Western learning, including science. (Recall that he said: "The philosophy of the Abhidhamma in Buddhism is the recreation-ground for intellectual minds. It gives delight to scientific men of other religions.")[29] As we explored in chapter 1, Ledi had seen his mentor Hpo Hlaing align Western learning and science. Just like his mentor, Ledi understood Buddhism not as coequal to science but as served by it. In describing the relationship between science and religion, Richard Payne has observed that, in the West, much of the conflict between the two stems from an assumption that the methodological materialism necessitated by the scientific outlook requires a metaphysical materialism, too.[30] To put it another way, it is the assumption that sticking to empirically observable facts for scientific research means limiting larger truth claims to the same sphere. For Ledi, however, there was no such assumption:

> At this time, scientists and doctors from Europe and America, with no right view, work only with magnifying glasses and their own observations to posit theories about the origination of existence, which is not a matter within their range of knowledge. But people who have right view, although this matter [of the origination of existence] is one about which they have no knowledge . . . grasp it properly.[31]

Ledi says a scientist, even with his learning and powerful tools of observation, can miss the truth about reality. But a person with right views, even without scientific learning or special devices, gets it right. Science can only reveal phenomena already described in ultimate terms in the Buddhist texts. This was not a hostile attitude toward science and technology, but one that ranked the truths of Buddhism above them—indeed, as insuperable. In this way Ledi protected traditional cosmology and apotropaic practices, such as *kamma vā* recitation. His was not a vision of "nonoverlapping magisteria," science in one realm and religion in another.[32] Rather, Buddhism was *the* magisterium that contains within it all scientific discoveries.[33]

Western modernity carries within itself a sense of conflict between religion and science as competing bodies of knowledge. Charles Taylor has argued that, in actuality, the apparent conflict masks a deeper and more fundamental fight. The most important battle has not been ontological, but moral. On one side there is a modern vision, conflated with science, that allows no room for an outlook that goes beyond what is empirically observable, and, on the other, a religious vision fixed exactly on what goes beyond a materialist view.[34] The true source of conflict, then, has been between two value systems, one expressed in science and one in religion, that Westerners have long struggled to reconcile.[35] At times, it is true, Asian Buddhists have also struggled to reconcile scientific and Buddhist claims about the world, revealing itself, for instance, in the debates over cosmology in Sri Lanka.[36] Ledi's writings, however, reveal no sense of moral conflict and no angst. Indeed, for him scientific endeavors led—poorly in comparison to Buddhist teachings, but nevertheless led—to the spiritual and transcendent. Just as Chakrabarty has noted that South Asian groups could live within the modern world along with the gods, so Ledi could live in the world with spirits and other beings, even as he sought to reshape lay lives to answer the challenges of contemporary times on logical grounds.[37]

As we will see in chapter 5, Ledi refers to technological inventions such as the movie projector and the microscope to explain meditation. He does this to underline the point that scientific knowledge can reveal partially what Buddhist practice reveals fully. As suggested by his confident discussions of chanting to banish disease (along with the use of vaccines, it should be said), Ledi saw science not as a challenge to his worldview but as a support for it. Such a view had wide appeal, because it assured laypeople that science and the modern world it evoked did not undercut their study and their spiritual efforts. Rather, it supported them.

Buddhism as a World Religion

Prompted, no doubt, by his analysis of Christianity, Ledi expanded his view to other religions. In the *Purification of the Sāsana* he also discusses, though less extensively, Hinduism and Islam. It is, in fact, the four religions of Buddhism, Christianity, Hinduism, and Islam that Ledi classifies as "the four great religions" of the world. He maintains that a key reason for the superiority of Buddhism over the others is the fact that only Buddhism has its teachings directly from its founder:

> Among the remaining religions [i.e., the other three besides Buddhism], it is the case that there are vastly varied groups of religious texts. Nevertheless, in Brahmanism [Hinduism], if asked to show the main teachings in words which come from the mouth of Brahma, there is nothing to show, not even one book of a hundred verses. In the same way, in both Christianity and Islam also, if one asks to see the teachings in words which come from the mouths of these great masters, God and Allah, who preached them directly and were seen personally among tens and hundreds of thousands of people, not one book or mantra can be given.[38]

According to Ledi, no other religion has teachings as reliable or authoritative as Buddhism, for it is the only religion with teachings spoken by its founder. Putting Buddhism in this comparative perspective showed its ultimacy on rationalist grounds. Once again, this was a powerful way to defend Buddhism in a time of threat by stressing its logical appeal.

Making such an argument, however, had another, perhaps unintended, consequence. By presenting Buddhism as one system of teaching among others, Ledi played an important part in recasting Buddhism as a religion encapsulated in doctrine. In the *Purification of the Sāsana*, Ledi defines a religion as "various teachings and various sayings," thereby emphasizing Buddhism (along with the others) as quintessentially a system of beliefs.[39] Ledi's choice to use the Burmese word *batha* (*bhā sā*) for religion in this work and many others reflects this idea. Gustaaf Houtman and more recently Alexey Kirichenko have explored the development of the use of *batha* as a term for religion in Burma.[40] Christian missionaries in Burma were the first to use the word, which comes from the Pali *bhāsā*, meaning "language" or "speech." They employed it in order to compare Christianity and Buddhism on equal terms as two species within the same genus.[41] Thus, one would have the "Ka-rit-yan batha" (*kha rac' yan bhā sā*, Christian religion) versus the "Buddha batha" (*buddha bhā sā*, Buddhist religion). In the nineteenth century, Ledi and other Burmese came to use *batha*, or more fully *Buddha batha*, in an attempt to defend Buddhism in the same comparative terms. *Buddha batha* thus came into widespread use as a term reflecting Buddhism as a system of beliefs that was in competition with other systems. Ledi's works, some of the earliest to include this term, supported the adoption of the word and spread its use widely. It is still today the most common term in Burma for Buddhism.[42]

Of course, the doctrinal content of Buddhism has always been of immense importance to Buddhists. After all, the Buddha's dhamma is understood to offer the way out of the round of rebirth (*saṃsāra*), and angst over its potential loss fueled the *Paramatthadīpanī* controversy. But it had not been commonly thought that holding doctrinal teachings defined Buddhism as such, let alone that all Buddhists needed to study the dhamma in depth. The vast majority of young men had typically left the monkhood after just a few years, long before reaching advanced levels of study.[43] Even among those who attained full ordination at twenty years of age, most stayed in their villages, where monastic education did not usually go into great depth.[44] Study by laypeople was generally even more limited. Women, in particular, often received little or no formal education. Burma had a high rate of literacy, at least among the male population, but Buddhist practice was typically a matter of morality and communal life.[45] Although surely idealized, Htin Aung's summation of lay life probably held true: "Buddhism explained that a layman could obtain true happiness and tranquility by fulfilling his domestic and social duties and by the practice of loving-kindness, charity and morality."[46] Whether lay or ordained, for most people in precolonial Burma studying Buddhist teachings extensively or even much at all was not considered crucial. That was only the concern of a coterie of elite monks such as Ledi.[47]

Ledi's efforts at amplifying the education of the laity had a much more profound effect than simply, as Ananda Metteyya put it in the quotation given earlier, "the people being taught more of the Dhamma than had been necessary for their simple needs before the missionary invasion."[48] Metteyya's comment suggests that he believed that the augmented education of the laity in response to missionary critique only added a bit more learning to the prevailing standard but did not qualitatively change lay life or Burmese Buddhism as a whole. But Ledi's stress on beliefs and learning, which had emerged from an elective affinity between the elite monastic culture of his training and a sense of Buddhism as a religion in opposition to Christianity, allowed him not just to add a bit more study to lay life but to reorient Burmese Buddhism around learning.[49]

Ledi presented the true enemy of Buddhists as within their minds: the ignorance or misconceptions that prompt wrongdoing. In the *Manual on Right Views* (*Sammādiṭṭhidīpanī*), he states that all wrong action comes from *attadiṭṭhi*, the view of an enduring sense of self. Until a Buddhist achieves real insight knowledge, he cannot rid himself of this idea of the self, which is, Ledi says, "the seed and root of all bad views, bad dhammas, and bad kamma."[50] In and of itself, of course, this teaching was no innovation on Ledi's part. Moreover, such insight knowledge that extirpated all bad kamma was not simply learning; true insight knowledge went beyond mere intellectual understanding. But what was novel and of supreme importance to Ledi's project was the coupling of the pursuit of such transformative insight knowledge to serious doctrinal study for all Buddhists.[51] Even the improvement of social and political realities, which Ledi had defined as examples of bad kamma in works such as the "Letter on Cows," depended upon the broad Buddhist populace engaging in self-cultivation that necessitated learning.

In 1913, Ledi even founded his own missionary organization to take the fight back to Christian lands, a fight conceived in terms of doctrinal disputation. It was called "The Great Society for the Spread of the Sāsana in Foreign Countries" (*nuiṅ' ṅaṃ khrā" sāsanā pru a saṅ'" krī"*, hereafter called the Foreign Missionary Society). The principal purpose of the organization was to defray the cost of printing the tipiṭaka and Ledi's explanatory works in Europe. In his speech at the founding ceremony, Ledi argued that in countries such as Australia, America, Germany, France, and Italy, "men of wisdom, while investigating and searching for the right scientific system which is in accordance with their views of the nature of the natural world" would convert in large numbers if they had even "a book of Buddhist dhamma worth just two or three annas"—a very small sum and, as a matter of fact, a common price for Ledi's books.[52] This projected popularity of Buddhist doctrine implied that Burmese Buddhism could not only hold its own against external challenges but flourish. Considering Ledi's belief that the Abhidhamma was especially appealing to "scientific men of other religions," it makes sense that he singled out its power to win over Westerners:

> The hearts and minds of Westerners will grasp with pleasure the light of wisdom in the Abhidhamma. Furthermore, a great event will be recorded as momentous in the history of the sāsana, for the great *Buddhasāsanas* of West and East will mix into one entity some time soon, so as to cause in the future in Europe a cry of joy.[53]

The rhetoric of the Abhidhamma's inherent appeal to wise men in the West elevated the standing of Burmese Buddhism. It would not only withstand Christian critiques but conquer the West. And in the hope to appeal to Westerners through doctrine, reactive Buddhist missionary efforts reflected and strengthened the sense of Buddhism as centered on texts and doctrine.

Missionaries' efforts, in conjunction with the policies of the British, turned the focus of Ledi's efforts toward the laity. But the initiative did not reside just with him. As in Sri Lanka (and many other parts of the Buddhist world), the laity in Burma reached out to figures such as Ledi, even while instituting their own lay-run efforts to support the sāsana. For example, laypeople organized themselves into numerous groups in order to assist monks (and to a lesser degree nuns and laypersons) in taking the Pali exams restarted by the British in 1895. And I mentioned in the last chapter that a group of laypeople asked the colonial government to appoint a thathanabaing. When it came to Ledi's own efforts, he also often acted in response to lay requests. Many of his books were commissioned by laypeople, such as his popular summary of the *Abhidhammatthasaṅgaha*, the *Summary of the Ultimates* (*Paramattha saṃ khip'*).[54] Yet, while lay interest drove developments from an early stage, Ledi played a critical role in shaping lay impulses into serious study on a widespread collective basis. In the following sections we explore by what means Ledi popularized learning and, by doing so, made it the genetic basis for mass meditation.

"Winning the Eye of Wisdom among Good People": Print Culture

The *Paramatthadīpanī* had shown Ledi the power of print culture, and he embraced it wholeheartedly. In the years following publication of his commentary, he engaged in what a British official described as a "literary campaign"[55] to educate the masses. In the letter to Caroline Rhys-Davids mentioned earlier, written in 1917, Ledi stated that he had composed many "books called *dīpanīs* in plain Burmese on many subjects which I thought important in Buddhism for the general public, and these spread all over Burma."[56] He wrote on such matters as the different aspects of the Abhidhamma, cosmology, the path to awakening, right views, the four noble truths, the qualities of a good Buddhist, the perfections, and several works on awakening (nibbāna). While the lion's share of Ledi's writings focused on doctrinal matters, he also published poetry, sermons, collections of answers to questions which he had received, works on the Vinaya, and exhortative materials on abstention from meat-eating, liquor, and gambling.

Meditation is also, of course, a central concern of a number of Ledi's works. We will analyze these writings closely in the fifth chapter, but it should be noted here that his meditation texts are not, in the main, practical guides. They share the schematizing and scholastic focus of much of his corpus. Also, these works are interspersed in Ledi's publication record throughout his years before the public eye. He did not hold off arguing for meditation until the last stage of his career. On the contrary, he wrote about meditation early on and often in his public life, though he did turn toward a marked emphasis on the subject in his final years. We will treat meditation in the fifth chapter of this book not because it was the end of a chronological sequence of development in Ledi's career but because meditation was the culmination of a conceptual framework in which he empowered the laity to adopt more virtuous lives and undertake study as powerful preparation for practice.

In terms of the content of his writing, what distinguished Ledi above all else was his emphasis on the Abhidhamma. This should come as no surprise, since he saw it as "the recreation-ground for intellectual minds" and the most effective safeguard against missionary influence. What is more, as the previous chapter showed, the Abhidhamma represented the longstanding site of perfection in Buddhist teachings and thus garnered the most prestige. Ledi had made a name for himself with the *Paramatthadīpanī*, and his much-read *Summary of the Ultimates* was a poem on the *Abhidhammatthasaṅgaha*. In many other publications, too, Ledi took an Abhidhamma approach—what, as I mentioned in the last chapter, Buddhaghosa calls writing with an "Abhidhamma perspective" (*abhidhammapariyāya*).[57] Topics treated in an Abhidhammic fashion include the twenty-four conditional relations, dependent origination, the bases of existence, and, certainly, meditation. Up to recent times, Burmese Buddhists have celebrated Ledi's then-novel emphasis on the Abhidhamma. U Ko Lay, the former rector of Mandalay University and a historian of Burmese Buddhism, said in 1996:

> [Monks had said that] Abhidhamma studies are so difficult that it is not the concern of lay people. Lay people just listen to instructions of the monks about dāna and sīla [generosity and virtue], and that's all they have to do. But Ledi Sayadaw reasoned that Abhidhamma was quintessential among the Buddha's teachings, and that it should be available to lay people.[58]

As we saw with the *Paramatthadīpanī* controversy, most people did not have the opportunity to learn the Abhidhamma system at any depth. Ledi changed that with his writings (and his preaching, too, discussed below). Ko Lay notes that Ledi made the Abhidhamma available as it never had been. This would revolutionize Burmese Buddhism and set in motion the forces leading to mass meditation. In a closer look at Ledi's *Summary of the Ultimates* in the next chapter, we will consider how he made its study a feasible and productive part of lay life.

The method of calculating the number of Ledi's works varies, as sometimes essays would be printed together or would appear in a journal before publication in a volume of shorter pieces. Sources generally agree he wrote between seventy-five and one hundred works of significant length (quite a

FIG. 3. The hall of Ledi's texts inscribed in stone at the Ledi Monastery in Monywa. Author's photograph.

few extending to hundreds of pages).[59] The Ledi Monastery in Monywa has an entire building with his writings inscribed on stone tablets. An inventory of these inscribed works by the Society for the Preservation of Ledi Literature lists eighty titles.[60] Ledi was so prolific that it is said that one of his disciple-monks, named U Revata, had the duty to sharpen between one and two hundred pencils for him each morning so that his writing would not be interrupted.[61]

On the whole, these writings came out in publications that were inexpensive and accessible. In 1928, the colonial government calculated the average monthly income for a Burmese family as 58 rupees, 8 annas, with a balance of 1 rupee, 13 annas left over after typical expenditures on food, clothing, and shelter.[62] Even accepting that the report reflected incomes higher than those of the early years of the twentieth century, the fact that Ledi's books usually cost only a few annas suggests that the average Burmese found his works affordable. And, as Ledi's books usually had print runs above three thousand copies—and some above ten thousand—they were widely available. In fact, Ledi can lay claim to one of print-era Burma's first bestsellers with his Abhidhamma poem the *Summary of the*

Ultimates. In just its first four years of publication, fifty thousand copies were printed, an impressive run even today.

Ledi made his writings accessible to a wide variety of laypeople by using simple language and an unadorned prose style. He did write using literary grammatical forms, which means that, as Burmese is a diglossic language, some particles indicating function in a sentence differ from those used in the spoken language. But these particles, in and of themselves, constitute fairly minor variations. What had really made literary Burmese texts difficult to understand was a propensity, especially in works on Buddhism, for authors to use ornate syntactical constructions, multiple redundant verbs, and abstruse vocabulary, including Pali. Ledi drastically limited these features so dominant in the literature at the time. A missionary claimed Ledi's success was due precisely to his efforts to simplify his message through the use of "simple, homely illustrations,"[63] and J. A. Stewart echoed this explanation when he said Ledi "treated the philosophy of Buddhism in a style intelligible to people of moderate education and also dealt with questions of practical morality."[64]

Ledi refers to his style in the *Manual of the Ultimate Man* (*Uttamapurisa*), justifying it as the best means to a religious end:

> Do not think, "It does not include any Pali!" If one wrote with Pali, then I think it would be really difficult to speak sensibly. Lecturing is not the main thing. Just the winning of the eye of wisdom among good people for themselves—this is the goal.[65]

To focus on enabling readers to get wisdom for themselves was a true innovation. Such a goal meant that Ledi's teachings were not simply old wine in new bottles—in other words, not simply traditional teachings in a more readily available format. Rather, his *dīpanīs* and other writings—particularly those works focusing on the Abhidhamma—were carrying a new message through a new medium. This was not because Ledi presented doctrinal teachings that diverged from what had come before. On the contrary, he never strayed from orthodoxy. But his presentation of classic doctrine in simplified language, in cheap and easy-to-obtain formats, and in large print runs changed the way doctrine would be used. As the theologian P. J. FitzPatrick put it, speaking of the effects of print culture in Europe: "Communication, here as elsewhere, began to fashion what was communicated."[66]

Ledi was a pioneer in the use of print culture, and it enabled him to disconnect doctrinal study from the personal relationship of the teacher and the pupil that was typically available only to monastics. No longer for a tiny elite, the text could stand in for the teacher—indeed, the text could *be* the teacher for the laity.[67] This was profoundly empowering. The Abhidhamma became widely available for the first time in digestible form, and a work like the *Manual of the Ultimate Man* told people to win the "eye of wisdom" for themselves. In the *Summary of the Ultimates,* he even says that he is providing the tools for awakening "in this very life" (*ī bhava hmā paṅ'*).[68]

Putting Down the Fan: Preaching

Ledi focused much attention in his sermons on doctrinal topics, just as in his writings. While, in contrast to print culture, preaching to laypeople was nothing new, Ledi played a prominent part in changing its nature. Traditionally, preaching was a ritualized act in which monks spoke in Pali in an impassive and droning style. The primary value of a sermon came from its potency as a source of merit for the listener, and so its intelligibility was not of paramount importance. Just hearing the Pali was thought to produce merit in the listener by inspiring faith in the dhamma.[69] Those who did understand the sermon would find usually that the topic was limited to a narrow range of basic texts on morality, such as the *Mangala Sutta* or the Jātakas.[70] Monks typically preached with a fan in front of their faces, which further limited any rapport with the audience, and this style came to be called "fan up" (*yap' toṅ'*).[71] This manner of preaching is described in a 1908 article from *The Burman Buddhist,* whose author then goes on to describe a new style that it places in favorable contrast to the old:

> Formerly, we had no sermon proper, no earnest exhortation by priests to laymen, whereby the feelings of *upāsakas* and *upāsikas* [lay men and women] could be roused to activity. Oratory is an art which is eminently necessary for the preacher who has a genuine desire to influence the minds of his flock, but it has not been cultivated in the past by our *bhikkhus*. The old taya-haw-gyin [preaching event] . . . consisted merely of the recitation by the *pongyi* of a well-learnt literary composition, usually containing one or the other of the Jātakas, illustrating the moral which the reciter wished to explain; the preacher's face was obscured by his large fan, his intonation was monotonous and somnolent, and the whole affair was lifeless and colourless. . . .
>
> We have now, however, a number of very able speakers, whose success in chaining the attention of large audiences and bringing home the truths of the law to their minds in plain, earnest language accounts for the revived interest in religion which is daily becoming more apparent. Chief among these we must mention the Ledi Sa-

yadaw and his pupils, notably U Wāyama, who now attracts vast congregations in Rangoon at his numerous discourses on practical Religion.[72]

The new style of preaching was called "fan down" (*yap' hlai*) because the preacher did not block his face with a fan as in the old "fan up" style.[73] *The Burman Buddhist* describes Ledi as integral to this movement, and comments from two British sources contemporaneous with the journal support this description. A missionary named G. Whitehead, in trying to explain Ledi's appeal, claimed that it was due "to his eloquence and simple manner of speaking to the people, as he largely discards Pali and does not merely recite what is written in the books, but preaches matter fresh from his own heart. He does not cover his face with a fan, nor mumble his words."[74] The other source, J. A. Stewart, was mentioned in the introduction. He adds more detail about the particular appeal of Ledi's personality:

> The Ledi Sayadaw was in demand throughout the length and breadth of Burma and in his intellectual prime about 1905 to 1915 there can have been few more powerful preachers. . . . He had large charity, a thorough knowledge of human nature, a delightful sense of humour and a fine voice. His effortless eloquence held immense audiences rapt.[75]

Just as simple language made Ledi's writing accessible, so did his style of preaching. Added to this was another factor to which Stewart alludes that should not be ignored: his personal charisma. Ledi presented transformative content in print and in preaching, but he also made a huge impact through the force of his personality. As much as we attend to the contextual factors that made Ledi's message appealing and sensible, as we should, we must acknowledge the simple fact that Ledi was singularly remarkable—indeed, a genius of his time.

Ledi's fame and skill helped bring the "fan down" style to wide attention, but this trend toward audience engagement and intelligibility had earlier antecedents in Burma. The Thingazar Sayadaw, who traveled on preaching rounds in the mid- to late-nineteenth century, was well known as a speaker who used plain language to teach religious truths. His stories were famous for being entertaining and very funny.[76] Some preachers in the "fan down" style clearly put a premium on being entertaining, in fact, and a few went to surprising lengths. One successful preacher-monk active around the same time as Ledi, U Puñña, adopted the style of a popular actor named Thazan. U Puñña even took the stage name of "The Monk

Thazan."[77] In another example, the author Thein Pei Myint has a scene in his 1937 satirical novel *Modern Monk* (*Tak' Bhun'" krī"*) in which an older monk teaches a younger one what to do to please an audience. In a summary of the book Mendelson describes the scene: "The book opens with a *sayadaw* (Mr. Parrot) teaching a *katika* (preacher) novice how to preach. Parrot refers the young man to books providing scriptural explanations; stresses the need for elegance, refinement, sweetness of voice; urges the use of double entendre in pleasing women listeners; suggests dwelling on old maids' problems in sermons to flatter them; and recommends imitating the great actors such as Po Sein."[78] Ledi never went so far as U Puñña or the "modern monks" of Thein Pei Myint's novel, but his talent for preaching, in conjunction with his writing, were factors that put him "out of the ordinary groove" (as we saw him described at the start of the chapter) and led to huge crowds at his appearances.

As in Burma, in Sri Lanka reformist monks often preached in simple and engaging language. At the debate in 1873 in the town of Pānadurē, near Colombo, the Buddhist speaker Mohoṭṭivattē captured the attention of large audiences, at least partially on account of his willingness to stand up and gesture as he spoke, movements that broke with traditional norms of preaching.[79] This style may have developed through the influence of Christian missionaries.[80] Working roughly a generation later (indeed, he listened to Mohoṭṭivattē at the Pānadurē debates as a young man), Dharmapala (1864–1933) clearly modeled his preaching on the Christian sermon. He usually spoke for less than an hour and at a regularly scheduled place and time, often on Sunday.[81] This Christian influence contrasts with Ledi, who, like other Burmese preacher-monks working around the same time, spoke for long stretches and at times and in places that would vary with his travels. There is, so far as I can tell, no indication that Ledi modeled his preaching on Christian exemplars, though it seems likely that a sense of competition and threat from missionaries promoted the "fan down" style.

Like the large print runs of his books, Ledi's ubiquity as he preached around the country extended the transformative effects of his presence and his message. An entertaining style and a simply worded message were not just more efficient means to convey an old message. Like his writing, preaching on heretofore neglected topics and in a new way conveyed a new sense of lay life engaged with Buddhism at an unprecedented level of sophistication. He could, furthermore, inspire people who might not have the time or inclination to study his books. Besides this, preaching further knitted together the populace in a visceral way his books could not. At the time, as is true today, the laity were not homogenous. The interests among different groups, such as the urban, rural, poor, middle class, and rich, overlapped but were not entirely the same. No doubt print materials supported the development of an imagined community among the laity, but preaching added a personal connection to the charisma of Ledi—with his "large charity, a thorough knowledge of human nature, a delightful sense of humour and a fine voice"[82]—that united disparate constituencies. Preaching set up Ledi as a bridge between different groups.

The anthropologist Guy Lubeigt reports that an informant in recent times still retained a sense of the effect Ledi's visit had on her family:

> In 1885, Ledi Sayadaw wrote in poetic form an advisory letter concerning the consumption of meat and went all over Myanmar to preach about it. At that time my mother was only five. She said that when Ledi came to Zigon her parents took her with them to listen to the preaching. After hearing the Sayadaw they obeyed his advice and also engaged her to do the same. The whole family definitely abstained from eating meat. Until her death in 1954, at the age of 74, she kept the promise given to her parents.[83]

This quotation reminds us that Ledi did not neglect issues of moral behavior.[84] He shared with the Thingazar Sayadaw a concern for morality and, like him, used homespun tales to illustrate the value of the virtuous life.[85] In Sri Lanka, too, influential figures such as Dharmapala and Palane Vajiragnana placed an emphasis on moral teachings that applied Buddhism to daily life, and many of Ledi's sermons fit with their approach.[86] But, in addition, his preaching expanded beyond such topics to matters of complex doctrine.[87] Indeed, as Hla Pain put it, during his preaching tours Ledi "gave Abhidhamma like falling rain."[88] By traveling widely and communicating in an easy-to-understand manner, he drew large crowds to hear sermons that, in tandem with his published works, opened up to the laity sophisticated presentations of Buddhist learning that reshaped their role in Buddhism.

"A Marvelous Influence": Social Organizing

Ledi's preaching and his writings, interrelated in content and purpose, presented to the laity doctrinal matters which had been the preserve of the elite. But Ledi's preaching rounds gave him another opportunity: the chance to organize laypeople into social organizations for self-directed study, along with moral self-cultivation, that collectivized lay action. He founded groups in an *ad hoc* fashion as he traveled across the country.[89]

Members would undertake study of whatever subject Ledi had addressed in his sermon, often using a text he had written on that topic as an organizational anchor. In 1905, for instance, Ledi established groups in the town of Myingyan (Mraṅ‘ khraṅ‘), in central Burma, to study dependent origination (*paṭiccasamuppāda*), the Abhidhamma, and vipassanā.[90] (The mention of the founding of a vipassanā group is particularly intriguing, though it seems the purpose of such a group was the study of a text about meditation, not actual practice. As I will explore in the fifth chapter, Ledi presents meditative practice as an individual pursuit that rides the crest of study done individually and collectively.)[91] The most common group activity seems to have been collective recitation, for memorization through recitation was (and is) a key means of learning throughout a person's schooling in Burma.[92] It was also a longstanding and popular practice for acquiring merit, and beyond the possibility of learning doctrine to a depth heretofore not possible, the chance to gain merit was likely a powerful appeal of the groups. The cultivation of merit also connected such study groups to those Ledi founded to promote moral behavior.

In addition to numerous social groups, Ledi also accepted the donations of a number of monasteries as he traveled. Monasteries were donated in Rangoon, Pyi, Pyinmana, Thaton, Sagaing, and Mandalay, among other places.[93] These were places Ledi stayed during the rains retreat or when he was in a place to preach or take part in some other activity. Thus, their existence as institutions connected to him came into being through his travels, deepening the impact he made. As monastic institutions, however, they did not take lay activities as their focus (let alone the lay pursuit of meditation). Rather, and naturally enough, they focused on the lives of the monastics who lived in them. They do not figure, therefore, as central to the story of the transformation of lay Buddhist life in Ledi's biographies. Yet these monasteries' wide geographic distribution and ties to Ledi undoubtedly made them an aid in the spread of his message and his programs of social action. Although it seems they never acted as the primary engines for the localized development of collective lay action, such institutions offered infrastructural support and, what is more, another meritorious connection to Ledi. Just as his preaching tours offered the chance to connect directly with his prestige and power, monasteries associated with him did too, further tying the country together and strengthening his lay social organizations.

In 1910, a British colonial official noted Ledi's "marvelous influence" (particularly over young men, according to this observer), and linked his preaching to his social organizing:

No review of religio-social work would be complete without a mention of the *Ledi Sadaw* [*sic*]. His sermons and visitations have a most powerful effect in the country. He has a marvelous influence over young men, and has done much good by preaching on their faults. And he is an able and broad-minded reformer, and has taken up questions of clubs and general combination when laid before him and preached on them himself.[94]

This passage suggests that the impetus for social organizing on Ledi's part came, at times, from the people to whom he was preaching, when they "laid before him" an issue. As I noted earlier, while Ledi channeled lay interest in the direction of study and moral efforts, his efforts were stoked by lay requests and interactions that reflected a preexisting drive among the laity to act collectively. Indeed, most social organizations of the time were lay-founded, lay-organized, and lay-run.[95] This initiative among the laity reminds us that they were not simply a passive and inchoate mass waiting for direction, but active agents in expressing the need for innovative responses to the challenges to Burmese Buddhism.

Ledi's groups appeared around the same time as many other lay associations. The Buddhasāsana Samāgama (known as the International Buddhist Society) in Rangoon, the Society for Promoting Buddhism, based in Mandalay,[96] the Sāsanādhāra Society, based in Moulmein, the Dānapaccaya Society in Rangoon, the Yaundawbwin Society of Rangoon, the Asoka Sākyaputta Society, based in Bassein, the Sediyingana Society of Minbu, the Rangoon College Buddhist Association, based in Rangoon, and the Buddha Kalayama Meikta Athin of Myingyan were just a few among many.[97] The best known and most influential of all lay organizations was the YMBA, founded in 1902 in Arakan but based in Rangoon from 1906. (It is this group that published *The Burman Buddhist*).[98] These groups sought to respond to the shared sense of the existential threat to Buddhism. They organized to support the monkhood by providing material necessities and to promote moral behavior. But most had Buddhist education as their central concern, based on the worry reflected in the statements of Ananda Metteyya above, that colonial and missionary influences were leading to Buddhism's decline.

Setting up printing presses, publishing journals, and running schools that included Buddhist education in the curriculum were common efforts to check this possible extinction.[99] Perhaps because many of the YMBA's high-level members were well connected to the center of power in Rangoon, the organization was an especially strong advocate at the level of government policy.[100] The organization argued for the teaching of Buddhism in government schools and for funding private Buddhist schools at the same level as those of Christian missionaries. The organization also worked to have basic education made compulsory in rural areas.[101]

At the time, people in Sri Lanka were also coming together in groups—"voluntary organizations" in Malalgoda's phrase[102]—to address a host of issues concerning the response to missionaries and education.[103] It may be, in fact, that Sri Lankan activities inspired social organization in Burma. The two colonies shared information through steamship traffic, mail services, and travelers.[104] In the pages of the 1903–1904 issues of the Rangoon-based magazine *Buddhism*, Ananda Metteyya provides an overview of organizations active at the time in Sri Lanka as well as in Japan. His reporting could have inspired and promoted lay activity in Burma. And the YMBA notes in the 1908 inaugural issue of *The Burman Buddhist* that the journal was inspired by the Sri Lankan magazine *The Buddhist*.[105]

Ledi was undoubtedly in sympathy with the objectives of organizations such as these. But his groups differed from the others in that they commonly had a wider distribution among the populace, yet were much more specific in their particular scopes of activities. Rather than coming together to accomplish a number of goals or to work for policy change, Ledi organized his groups around a single Buddhist issue or activity. Individual groups were largely autonomous, with no headquarters and thus no central organization to unite them. The narrow range of any one group meant numerous groups could co-exist in a village or town, each oriented to its own doctrinal topic or moral end. Perhaps because of their focus on particular objectives, his groups never played a visible part in the development of a nationalist political movement. This is in deep contrast to the YMBA, which served as the seedbed for such movements.[106] Ledi did not ignore social and political realities, but, as we saw above in his comments about liquor consumption, his response to challenges was based upon a karmic outlook that understood the intellectual and moral development of the Burmese Buddhist as the most effective means to fix religious and social problems.

The Laity's Place in Burmese Buddhism

Preaching was a means to instruct and inspire; just as important, it also provided a venue in which to institutionalize study in a disciplined and standardized way through social organizations centered around a text (also by Ledi). Ledi's spheres of activity were thus interconnected and mutually supportive.[107] Together, they reoriented Burmese Buddhism to put laypeople center stage. In the final part of the chapter we can now consider more broadly the nature of the transformation that the laity underwent. Scholars who have examined the role of the laity in Buddhism during this period, both in Burma and in Sri Lanka, have tended to characterize it as undergoing either a process of laicization or, seemingly in contradiction, a process of monasticization. Laicization means the process through which Buddhism becomes more focused on lay concerns and activities, such that the laity come to predominate.[108] When describing monasticization, scholars are still concerned with the laity, but mean to describe a process in which the laity come to resemble more closely monastics.[109] The terms appear to conflict—does Buddhism became more lay-like or more monk-like?

Laicization and monasticization, however, do not refer to exactly the same thing undergoing change, and this divergence dissolves a direct opposition between the two terms. Laicization typically refers to a transformation in Buddhism as a whole toward more of a lay centrality, while monasticization describes a process of change in the nature of the laity as part of a larger tradition. This disparity suggests that neither term is solely adequate to describe the transformation of Buddhism in Ledi's time. In fact, both are valid, depending on the perspective one takes. Looking at Buddhist social change from one vantage point, laicization rightly stresses the growth of lay responsibility and the profound expansion of lay activities well beyond the typical activities of merit-making and the veneration of relics and monks. These new activities, such as study and also the possibility of meditation, took shape through a communal sensibility, born from Ledi's activities and the efforts of the YMBA and other groups. But monasticization is a useful term from another angle, for it calls our attention to how these new aspects of lay life caused laypeople to do things that previously were almost entirely limited to monks.[110] In this sense laypeople became more like monastics. As Collins and McDaniel observe in the case of nuns in modern Thailand, it is perhaps best to speak of a pluralization of practices and statuses that could potentially blur the lay/monk boundary.[111]

Yet the distinction between the layperson and the monk remained critically important to Ledi. In a speech given in 1913, he suggests a way to understand lay Buddhists' contemporary role in the sāsana that reconciles the processes of laicization and monasticization. His approach indicates that he neither undercuts the sharp differentiation between lay and monastic in Burmese society nor seeks to weaken the respect laypeople give to the ordained. He was speaking at the founding of the Foreign Missionary Society, the organization mentioned earlier in the chapter that he created to spread the dhamma in Western countries.[112] In his promotion of support for missionary activity by all Buddhists, he lays out his understanding of the logic of lay action based on the absence of the king. We saw in chapter 2 that the lack of a king worried many Burmese terribly (as it did many Buddhists across Southeast Asia).[113] Ledi uses this worrisome lack as a way to justify a shift in responsibility primarily to the laity:

> As for the people who must honor and spread [the sāsana]:
>
> 1) If there were a king to spread the Buddhist religion [*buddha bhā thā*], it would be his duty to spread it.
>
> 2) If there were no king, then it would be the duty of all the people of a country, both Buddhist monks and lay Buddhists.
>
> Among the two choices, in our country at present the king who spreads the sāsana has become silent. As our noble Buddhist religion [*buddha bhā sā sāsanā*] is in the hands of all the people of the country, it is the duty of every person in the country, we people of Myanmar, to strive to make it famous long into the future and to spread it to other regions and countries.[114]

Ledi speaks particularly of spreading the dhamma, but he connects propagation to the protection of Buddhism's overall health, a job once the responsibility of the king. He includes monks in this program, but in his view laypeople, as much as monks, have in their hands "our noble Buddhist religion." This was a profound elevation of their role. Indeed, the onus of action fell especially on the shoulders of laypeople, since the king, to use Steven Collin's phrase, was "the epitome of the householder."[115] Ledi's invocation of the model of the king stressed the agency of the laity and justified their revised role in Burmese Buddhism.[116]

Such a model indicates that the empowerment of the laity caused an *intensification* of lay life and, for Burmese Buddhism as a whole, a *leveling*. The intensification of lay life did not mean that laypeople were necessarily any more religious than before and certainly not that they were more authentically Buddhist. But it meant that the demands put upon the laity grew to include many more roles and activities than in the past. In Ledi's program, merit making, moral action, and generosity were only a start. As he said, Buddhism was "in the hands of all the people," and this meant that the laity, in addition to traditional activities, needed to engage in in-depth study. As we will see in the following chapters, meditation would emerge out of such study.

This new, more intense lay Buddhism did not spell a weakening of the divide between the layperson and the monk. On the contrary, the inspiration for the new sort of layperson was the very figure understood to preserve conformity with tradition, the king. This was a decidedly lay figure—in fact, the layman *par excellence.* As the model for the dutiful supporter of the saṅgha, he was certainly not an inspiration for a more laicized saṅgha as a whole. But since the king was involved in Buddhist practices and in saṅgha affairs to a degree most laypeople had never been, appealing to the model of the king supported a leveling through a heightened lay involvement.[117]

The symbolic power of the king would resonate in the field of meditation, too. In his 1904 *Manual on Breath Meditation* (*Ānāpānadīpanī*), discussed in detail in chapter 5, Ledi begins by describing a long line of kings who practiced meditation successfully. He concludes by saying that laypeople in the present day should act as these kings.[118] Overall, this approach meant that the divide between layperson and monk was much narrower than before, but still very deep. Rather than breaking down the clear distinction between monastic and lay, what interested Ledi was applying the principle of strong lay support for the sāsana, once expressed through the singular figure of the king, to the new situation in which Buddhism was under threat and old modes of response were unavailable. His writings, his preaching, and his social organizations show how he used a longstanding Burmese emphasis on learning, particularly of the Abhidhamma, as a powerful resource to answer the threats to Buddhism in colonial Burma.

Yet, for all the symbolic value of the Abhidhamma, Ledi had described it in his *Paramatthadīpanī* as being as full of meanings as a great ocean, inexhaustible, well beyond the full ken of all but the enlightened. The next chapter takes a closer look at Ledi's most popular work, the *Summary of the Ultimates,* to explain how he made in-depth, text-based study of the Abhidhamma, something seemingly so forbidding, appealing and practical in a group setting. And it considers the transformative effects such study would have, for the *Summary* prepared the way for widespread insight meditation by offering laypeople the tools for awakening "in this very life."

FOUR

"In This Very Life": Lay Study of the Abhidhamma

Around the time that Ledi stepped onto the national stage in Burma, a student of his named Maung Gyi—the very same person who burnt the copies of Nat Tha's book critical of the *Paramatthadīpanī*—composed a poem to celebrate his teacher's efforts to transform Burmese Buddhism:

THE RADIANCE OF ABHIDHAMMA WISDOM

Great qualities, so rarely experienced and so pleasing, blaze forth gloriously in the town of Monywa in Upper Burma.
The force of noble Ledi's power and glory shakes the world with a thunderous roar.
Because he beats the big drum of dhamma for all beings who can awaken to hear, they cross to the other side.
So people can reach [awakening] quickly and easily, this noble monk supports them.
Because [Ledi] has set up the radiance of Abhidhamma wisdom in the realm of Myanmar, it shines bright throughout this world.
These great qualities [of Ledi] that blaze forth, they are incomparable.[1]

This poem captures the key feature of Ledi's effort to transform Buddhism in colonial-era Burma. No longer is enlightenment just a remote possibility, as the earlier historical chronicles presented it (discussed in chapter 1). Now, all those "beings who can awaken" can "cross to the other side"—in other words, to nibbāna, thanks to Ledi's "support." This is because he has made Myanmar the bastion of Abhidhamma learning—clearly, the most powerful learning—that "shines bright throughout this world."

We saw in the previous chapter that Ledi fought on multiple fronts—preaching, social organizing, and writing—to transform Burmese Buddhism. As this poem suggests, the Abhidhamma was the lynchpin of this country-wide program. While many of his works address Abhidhamma topics or work in an Abhidhamma vein, one book, called the *Summary of the Ultimates* (*Paramattha saṃ khip'*), had a dominant role to play in "beating the big drum" and making such a daunting topic accessible and appealing. (I will refer to it hereafter as the *Summary.*) It focused on giving laypeople an overall Abhidhamma literacy by translating the *Abhidhammatthasaṅgaha* into easy-to-understand Burmese. People already esteemed the Abhidhamma as the site of Buddhism's perfection and its front-line defense against degeneration, and the reaction to the *Paramatthadīpanī* had shown Ledi the widespread interest in the Abhidhamma as a topic of study. But, as we have seen, relatively few people knew Pali or had the training needed to follow the *Paramatthadīpanī*'s extensive and complex arguments. The *Summary* shows how Ledi changed his approach to the *Saṅgaha* as he shifted his focus from elite Pali scholars to the broad Burmese populace. In fact, Hla Pain says in his biography that the *Summary* inspired Maung Gyi to write the poem above, as he understood Ledi's work to provide everyone the "dhamma tools" (*dhamma a chok' a ū*) to achieve awakening.[2] In fact, Ledi went so far as to say that study of the poem could even poise the learner for awakening "in this very life" (*ī bhava hmā paṅ'*).[3]

The *Summary* and its Appeal

The *Summary* is a poem in a genre called in Burmese *saṃ khip',* a term cognate to the Pali *sankhepa,* meaning "gist," "condensed version," or "summary." Ledi says in the *Summary* that its purpose is to give the reader "a basic knowledge of the *Saṅgaha* . . . quickly."[4] It seeks in 690 short verses to provide a translation of the entirety of the *Saṅgaha.* Like the text it translates, it is divided into nine chapters and covers the same topic as the *Saṅgaha* does in each chapter. The first three chapters deal with the makeup of consciousness (citta), the mental factors (cetasikas), and how the two combine. The fourth and fifth chapters deal with the processes (*vīthi*) of consciousness, and the fifth chapter also covers cosmology. The sixth chapter explores material reality (rūpa). The final three chapters cover modes of classifying reality (*samuccaya*), the conditions (*paccaya*) giving rise to physical and mental phenomena, and meditation (*kammaṭṭhāna*). (For more details on content, see the description of the *Saṅgaha* in chapter 2.) Ledi also wrote an autocommentary for the *Summary,* restating the verses' meanings in discursive prose.[5]

As I noted in the prior chapter, Ledi wrote the poem in 1903. According to the British colonial government's list of books published in Burma, it was first printed in 1904 and became a bestseller. Fifty thousand copies of the text were printed in its first four years of publication.[6] This would be a remarkable number even today, but in its time such numbers were extraordinary. So popular was the *Summary* that Hla Pain says that it was on the tip of every Burmese person's tongue in those years.[7]

As with many of his works, Ledi explains in the *Summary*'s autocommentary that he wrote the poem at the request of laypeople:

> People, who understand the difficulty of obtaining a human birth, of obtaining birth in the time of the arising of a Buddha, and the very great difficulty of getting the chance to hear the dhamma, want to master the *Compendium of the Ultimates* [*Abhidhammatthasaṅgaha*]. But they cannot do so because of the difficulty in three areas: its Pali language, the meanings [of words], and the [overall] sense. Having been asked to provide a means for people to master easily all nine chapters [of the *Saṅgaha*], I will speak a memorization-aid [*saṃ pok'*] poem which can be quickly mastered by women, men, students, and children, if they strive for three to four months.[8]

This quotation captures the elements of the *Summary* that made it resonate with a broad audience. Ledi claims that people are eager to learn the *Summary* because of an awareness of the difficulties enumerated above. This sense of the precious rarity of the sāsana was particularly poignant in the colonial context, when many worried it might soon disappear. (Ledi would stress the rarity of encountering Buddhism in his other works, too, including those concerned with meditation.)[9] To take advantage of the chance to learn the Abhidhamma was the most powerful way to participate in the safeguarding of Buddhism, not to mention the opportunity it offered to improve one's own spiritual well-being.

As we saw in the last chapter, Ledi was spurred by lay requests to formulate such responsibilities for the laity through the model of the king. But to enable people to take part in this kingly project, he needed to provide a way for them to overcome the stumbling blocks of Pali and the complexity of the Abhidhamma system. Indeed, the *Paramatthadīpanī* represented perfectly these challenges, as it is in Pali, makes long and complex arguments, and assumes a deep knowledge of the Abhidhamma. The *Summary* in many ways is its antithesis: the verses are short, gloss Pali terms in simple Burmese, and are explained in clear prose in the autocommentary. Furthermore, by assuring the reader of a time period of just three to four months to learn the *Summary,* Ledi reemphasized its accessibility and promised relatively quick mastery of a comprehensive view of the entire Abhidhamma system. In his letter to Caroline Rhys-Davids, he put an even finer point on this goal: "I have written a book called *Paramattha-saṅkhepa* (a rhythmical Burmese translation of the *Abhidhamattha-saṅgaha*), which even girls can learn easily in four or five months."[10] Ledi's reference to "even girls" being able to learn the *Summary* was probably not a low estimation of women's abilities on his part, as he had many interactions with female devotees on in-depth matters of dhamma. Rather, the statement indicates the poem was meant to reach even those who were likely to have little prior training in Buddhist philosophy.[11] In fact, in his list at the end of the passage of the sorts of people who can master the *Summary,* he begins with women, typically the most marginalized and least educated segment of society. To address them explicitly was highly unusual and likely contributed to the poem's great popularity among women. *The Burman Buddhist* recognized his text, as well as the social organizations connected to it, as groundbreaking in their focus on women:

> Recognizing the great value of female education, which has been so sadly neglected in the past, he [Ledi] and his disciples have instituted Than-Keik [*saṃ khip'*] societies in all the large towns, whereby girls of all ages up to 20 are taught the Paramattha Sankhepa and the fundamental moral doctrines of Buddhism.[12]

This passage suggests that the *Summary* was understood as a foundational tool of education, including for those who traditionally did not have access to the Buddhist education system. We saw in the previous chapter that missionary critiques prompted more in-depth study as a defensive measure. This reaction promoted a stress on the learning of doctrine by laypeople, who had hitherto studied relatively little. But even within the community of laypeople it should be noted that there was also an unprecedented empowerment of a particular group, women. For laymen, increased study was not just a matter of degree, as amplified study, often framed within collectives, caused a profound intensification of Buddhist life and a leveling vis-à-vis the saṅgha. The transformation for laywomen, however, was even more momentous, as they had not had even the possibility of the same level of access as laymen under the old paradigm. This change in the possibilities of women's religious life is a critical factor in the *Summary*'s appeal and its far-reaching effects.

Allied to these socio-religious transformations was, as *The Burman Bud-*

dhist notes, the focus on young people. This, too, would account for the appeal of the *Summary* (and the groups organized to study it, which will be discussed at the end of the chapter). The *Summary,* as a tool to teach the young in a climate of anxiety over the health of Buddhism, offered a means to pass on Buddhist learning to succeeding generations. As with adults, such learning was not just the addition of a bit more information, but a reorientation of the education of youth to include the full breadth of the Abhidhamma system, at least in translation and summary form. This sort of reorientation—a sort of doctrinization of Buddhist lay life—was also an intensification that shifted the laity toward what had once been elite practices.

This connection to elite practice accounts for another factor in the *Summary*'s popularity. Despite its accessibility as a translation, the text maintained links to elite textual practices represented by the *Paramatthadīpanī.* It brought the world of Pali learning into the domain of a Burmese-language text. This was done principally through the feature of the abbreviation of Pali words. Such abbreviation was not just a way to pack in more information but a prestigious pedagogical tool.[13] Abbreviation systems were part of the processes of scholastic training in monasteries. In order to speed memorization, monks would often use memorization-aid texts called *saṃ pok',* the very term Ledi applies to the *Summary* in its third verse.[14] These texts reduce complex terms and concepts to single syllables (sometimes two) that act as mnemonic devices.[15] For instance, there are twenty-four conditional relations (*paccaya*) that give rise to all mental and physical phenomena. Within these twenty-four relations, the seven which co-arise simultaneously with certain conditioned states are classified as the "conascent" (*sahajāta*) group. They are *hetu* (root), *adhipati* (predominance), kamma (karma), *āhāra* (nutriment), *indriya* (faculty), jhāna (absorptive state), and *magga* (path).[16] These terms would be memorized by the respective syllables *ho, dhi, kaṃ, hā, iṃ, jhā,* and *mag'.*[17]

The *Summary* has the same sort of mnemonic abbreviations. For example, in verse 389 Ledi says "*pa, ā, te, vā*" for paṭhavī (earth), āpo (water), tejo (fire), and vāyo (wind).[18] We first encountered these four fundamental forms of materiality, the so-called "great essentials" (*mahābhūtāni*), in chapter 2. In the *Paramatthadīpanī,* Ledi discusses them in detail and critiques the *Vibhāvinī*'s handling of their definitions. Here, they are given in abbreviated forms without any hint of dispute. The focus is practical, intended to enable memorization. As I mentioned in preceding chapters and as we will see in detail in the next, the elements of earth, water, fire, and wind are particularly important in Ledi's system of meditation for laypeople, but such examples of abbreviation can be found in all parts of the poem.[19]

In all cases, Ledi provides the full term of any abbreviation in the autocommentary. The autocommentary thus serves not just as a key to the *Summary* but plays an integral part in educating the reader without the need, necessarily, for a teacher to decode the poem's obscure bits of words. *Saṃ pok'* had not been readily available to laypeople up to this point. Only with the advent of print culture was such a study system put in their hands on a widespread basis—and the *Summary* was one of the first works to do this. Getting to study a text emblematic of the prestigious text-centric world of monastics was a strong draw to the *Summary,* besides the fact that such pedagogical tools surely aided memorization of the poem. No longer were laypeople on the outside looking in, as was largely the case with the dispute over the *Paramatthadīpanī.* Now they had a text that empowered them to take part in the rarified world of Abhidhamma learning.[20]

But even a cursory skim of the *Summary* shows that Ledi included Pali abbreviations even when a Burmese word could convey the meaning and when there was no intention to provide a mnemonic list. For example, verse 636 reads *"nussati hrac' | saññā ek' | tac' hlac' vavatthā,"*[21] meaning "Eight recollections, one perception, one analysis."[22] Note Ledi's use of numbers. He gives the Burmese word for eight, *hrac',* but the Pali word for one, *ek'* (slightly shortened for Burmese pronunciation from *eka*), and then the Burmese word for one, *tac'.* There is no apparent reason why Pali numbers would need to be used in the text, for they convey no sense different from Burmese numbers. Of course, another number system simply adds richness and variety to the modes of expression in the poem, but why add the difficulty? The poem is, after all, meant to be a translation into Burmese.

One likely reason was that many Pali terms have specific meanings within a network of Abhidhamma vocabulary. This is not to say that Burmese could not convey the meaning of a Pali term. A long list of Abhidhamma publications in Burmese demonstrates that authors did translate Abhidhamma texts fully into Burmese. But Ledi could rely upon Pali to convey precisely complex entities.

Beyond technical accuracy, the use of Pali also connected the poem viscerally to the *Saṅgaha.* The frequency of Pali abbreviations is so great, in fact, that it almost makes the reader feel as if he or she were reading the *Saṅgaha* itself. For instance, Ledi says in verse 620, *"Me, ka, mu, u | pvā" myā" hmu | le" khu pamaññā."*[23] *Me* stands for *mettā* (loving kindness), *ka* for *karuṇā* (compassion), *mu* for *muditā* (sympathetic joy), and *u* for *upekkhā* (equanimity). These are the four "immeasurables" or *apamaññā*s (Ledi cuts off the first syllable of this word in the verse for metrical reasons).[24] All the terms are Pali, linked by the Burmese phrase *pvā" myā"* *hmu le" khu,* meaning "nurturing, the four." Put in sensible English, the phrase would read, "Nurturing loving kindness, compassion, sympathetic joy, and equanimity is the practice of the four immeasurables." But the combination of Pali abbreviations and Burmese words is not meant to produce an immediately sensible phrase; it is a device to memorize Pali and make its meaning retrievable in Burmese.

The heavy use of Pali terms and phrases brought laypeople into the world of Pali learning, so important to authority in the Burmese saṅgha. As Steven Collins has observed, Pali has had a unique place in the Theravāda Buddhist conception of language.[25] Commentators came to see Pali as the "root language" (*mūlabhāsā*) which all human beings would naturally speak if not instructed in some other tongue. This idea was based on the belief that Pali actually inhered in an object as its true designation.[26] From this perspective, the word *citta* is not simply a convenient label but the real word for what we arbitrarily call in English "consciousness," and the word *tejo* for the element of fire is the true designation of the property of heat. This belief in a direct connection between the Pali word and its denoted object led to the idea that Pali was the most efficient language for soteriological purposes. The Abhidhamma, which provides the naturally given terms that correspond to ultimate reality, was considered the most efficacious of all for meditation.[27] The *Summary* offered the reader a way to access this power of Pali by means of everyday Burmese language.

This idea of Pali as the really real language aligns with its place as a cosmopolitan language juxtaposed with the Burmese vernacular. Readers of the *Summary* could feel that the use of Pali gave them access to a world beyond their village, beyond even colonial confines.[28] For Ledi and his readers of the *Summary* in the early years of the twentieth century, the vernacular had overwhelming dominance in terms of the contemporary production of religious literature. In fact, Ledi's *Paramatthadīpanī* was one of the last significant Pali works published in Burma.[29] In practical terms, Pali was not a resource for a cosmopolitan cultural order for laypeople. This is abundantly evident, of course, in the fact that the *Summary* is, by and large, a Burmese text, albeit one that contains a great deal of Pali terminology. Creating a text in which the author provides the *sense* of reading Pali, but not the actuality of reading Pali, underscores Pali's secondary place as a vehicle for meaning in the *Summary.* Yet even if relegated to playing second fiddle grammatically in the *Summary,* its presence still evoked the sense of a spiritual realm that was unbounded, one that moved beyond all borders. Collins describes this power of the Pali text:

A text in Pali had *ipso facto* trans-local and trans-temporal reference, linking the here-and-now spatially to the broader world of Buddhism as a contemporary whole, and temporally to the past Gotama Buddha (which modern scholarship accepts as historical), and to the deeper and further temporal horizon of past and future Buddhas (which is, for scholarship, mythological).[30]

This universal sense would have a specific cultural appeal. To learn at least key Pali terms and to have a sense of "reading" Pali allowed a student of the *Summary,* at the high moment of British colonialism in Burma, to assert his or her identity as a Buddhist. This was especially so when anxiety about the perceived decline of Buddhism made the Burmese particularly aware of "the difficulty of obtaining a human birth, of obtaining birth in the time of the arising of a Buddha, and the very great difficulty of getting the chance to hear the dhamma." The use of Pali in the *Summary* provided a feeling of access to an expanded world. In the specific context of a recently arrived print culture and a revivalist laity, laypeople using the poem could feel part of a trans-local community among nation-states and cultures which still looked to Pali literature as the veritable words of the Buddha (*buddhavacana*).

This appeal, however, was as much about exclusion as inclusion. It was a sort of Theravāda parochial cosmopolitanism. Ledi's construction of a Burmese vernacular text, liberally sprinkled with Pali words and phrases, gave the reader a sense of boundaries being crossed, but for the purpose of asserting an exclusive identity as a Burmese Buddhist. Pali becomes a marker of difference rather than a way to a world without borders. Indeed, in one final way it seems that Ledi's use of Pali emphasized the Burmese reader's identity as Burmese. At this time the Burmese language itself faced the prospect of falling into disuse, as the policy and practice of the British to promote the use of English in civil spaces had relegated Burmese to rural areas and the domestic sphere.[31] In this context, the *Summary* was also a means to rejuvenate Burmese, made all the more powerful by its use as a vehicle for the Abhidhamma. Ledi's deployment of Pali accentuated the use of Burmese and legitimized it by virtue of its association with a prestigious canonical language.

Focusing on the Laity

The factors enumerated above—the *saṃ pok'* abbreviation system, simple Burmese combined with prestigious Pali learning, and the focus on a lay readership in a colonial context—were important reasons for the *Summary*'s immense popularity. But the power of the poem's appeal went beyond these factors to revisions of the *Saṅgaha* itself. There is an irony in the fact that the combative *Paramatthadīpanī* never diverges from the organization or subject matter of the *Saṅgaha*, but the *Summary*, which engages in no disputes and caused no controversy, departs at key moments from its mother text precisely because of its explicit focus on its audience. As mentioned earlier, the *Summary* follows the broad topical organization of the *Saṅgaha*, but within that structure it shifts the focus at crucial points. These shifts reorient the Abhidhamma system to lay concerns. Examination of a couple of key divergences will show how Ledi did this and what the ramifications would be.

Considering these passages from the *Summary* will also more fully impart the poem's aesthetic flavor. Poetry may be what gets lost in translation, as Robert Frost said, but my translations below capture the literary effect of the *Summary*. It is, quite clearly, a didactic work. Its scholastic character, however, was by no means considered a weakness. On the contrary, it was held to be one of the poem's great strengths, for it was meant, as Ledi said at its start, to enable one to "master quickly" the precious dhamma, not to appeal on literary grounds.

We begin with the *Saṅgaha*'s and *Summary*'s fifth chapters. The difference in the titles of the chapters exemplifies how the *Summary* emphasizes human life within the Buddhist cosmological system in a way the *Saṅgaha* does not. The chapter title in the *Saṅgaha*, *vīthimuttasaṅgahavibhāga*, means "the chapter on the compendium (of consciousness) free of the process (of thought)." As I noted in chapter 2, this chapter explains all consciousnesses that occur automatically in an individual, as what we might call autonomic functions. There are four sets of these, with each set having four components: (1) the four planes of existence (*bhūmicatukka*) are the different levels of possible rebirth;[32] (2) the four modes of rebirth-linking (*paṭisandhicatukka*) are the types of consciousness (citta) that lead to the four planes of existence;[33] (3) the four kinds of kamma are the classes of volitional actions that shape the possibilities of future events and lives;[34] and, lastly, (4) the fourfold advent of death concerns the karmic reasons for death.[35]

The *Saṅgaha* proceeds in order through these four sets of four, beginning with the planes of existence. It treats each plane as equally important. In contrast, while the *Summary* does discuss all matters treated in its root text, the title for its chapter is "The Chapter on the Planes of Existence" (*bhuṃ puiṅʻ"*). This change in title clearly privileges the topic of cosmology. The significance of the difference becomes clear if we compare Ledi's and the

Saṅgaha's treatments of the "woeful plane" (*apāyabhūmi*) and the "blissful plane" (*kāmasugatibhūmi*), two of the four levels of possible rebirth. The discussions of these planes are combined in the texts' analyses because together they comprise the "sense-sphere" realm (*kāmadhātu*). Within these two planes of the sense-sphere realm are various sub-planes which contain different sorts of beings. First, the *Saṅgaha*'s description of this multitiered realm:

Among these, the woeful plane is fourfold, namely:
(i) hell;
(ii) the animal kingdom;
(iii) the sphere of the petas;[36] and
(iv) the host of asuras.[37]

The blissful plane is sevenfold, namely:
(i) the Human Realm;
(ii) the Realm of the Four Great Kings;[38]
(iii) the Realm of the Thirty-Three Gods;[39]
(iv) the Realm of the Yāma gods;[40]
(v) the Delightful Realm;[41]
(vi) the Realm of the Gods Who Rejoice in [Their Own] Creations;[42]
(vii) the Realm of the Gods Who Lord over the Creations of Others.[43]
These eleven realms constitute the sense-sphere plane.[44]

This is a morally graded continuum, in which the higher levels are superior to those below, and hell, the lowest realm, is the worst place one can be. Life improves in each level as one moves up, and one's place in this cosmos is determined by one's past deeds (kamma). Thus, this cosmological map is an ethical map, too.[45] As suggestive as this sketch of the sense-sphere of existence is, however, it leaves out a great amount of detail.[46] Contrast this with the same topic in the *Summary*:

THE ELEVEN PLANES OF THE SENSE-SPHERE

264|| 960,000 [*yojanas*], | the total depth | of the base of air.[47]
265|| 480,000 [*yojanas*], | the total depth | of water which lies on the air.
266|| 240,000 [*yojanas*], | the total depth | of earth which lies on the water.
267|| Stone, soil— | these two earths | are divided in equal parts.
268|| Sañjīva, Kāla, | Saṃghāta, | the two Roruva,[48]
269|| the two Tāpana, | Avīci—| these are the hell realms,[49]
270|| separated into eight parts | of equal amounts, | each 15,000 (*yojanas*).
271|| *Baṅ', prā, lak', than'*— | surrounding in order | are the four projecting hells.[50]

272|| *Baṅ‘, prā, lak‘, than‘* | (and) a surrounding river—| this is the system, [comprised of] five parts.

273|| Hells, animals, | *petas, asuras*— | these four lower abodes are the woeful planes of existence.

274|| *Lū, ca, tā, yā* | *tus‘, nimmā,* | *vasā, vatti*—the realms of power.[51]

275|| 42,000 [*yojanas*]— | the distance | in succession from the realm of men.

276|| The seven blissful [*sugati*], | four woeful [*apāya*] abodes— | the eleven sense-sphere planes.

This is the end of the eleven planes of the sense-sphere.[52]

These are the first verses of chapter 5 in the *Summary*, emphasizing the importance of the sense-sphere realm of existence that includes human beings. In the *Saṅgaha*, the description of the cosmos follows the list of the four sets of process-free consciousness.

Human beings take center stage in the cosmos in the fifth chapter of the *Summary*. Ledi starts lower down in the cosmos than the *Saṅgaha*—in fact, as low as one can go, listing the material bases of air, water, and earth upon which all realms rest. He starts out, then, with a more detailed and comprehensive description. He moves up to the hells next. Unlike the text he is supposed to be translating, he provides specific names, sizes, and spatial relationships among the various hell planes. Such information was not simply of intellectual interest to his readers; the hells were a reality. Up to the present day, numerous gruesome paintings of the various tortures that await miscreants in these hells adorn the walls of temple buildings throughout Burma.[53] In his other works, Ledi also often dwelt on the sorts of hells that awaited people who had committed bad deeds. In the "Letter on Cows" discussed in chapter 1, he remarks that people who eat beef will be "food for the dogs of hell."[54] And in a sermon on the evils of liquor consumption, he spends much time describing the ways people will experience agony for indulging in intoxicants.[55] The schematic map of the hells, then, was of keen interest to many as a description of real and threatening possibilities and made the *Summary* of immediate relevance to one's spiritual condition.

In the Theravāda scheme of the cosmos, the human realm lies between the woeful abodes below and the heavens above (i.e., the realms of power). So, if Ledi were going to continue his cosmological accounting in a consistent and accurate fashion (as in the *Saṅgaha*), he should have mentioned the place of human beings after verse 273. But he does not. Instead, he describes next, in verse 274, the "realms of power," which are heavens. He then jumps back to end the list of the realms of rebirth with the place of human beings. By ending with the human realm in this out-of-sequence order, he gives pride of place to people within the grand sweep of the cosmos.

It is also telling that Ledi gives much more information about the hells than the heavens. The literary pull—and perhaps he wants to imply the karmic pull, too—is down, not up. This emphasis on woeful abodes colors the cosmological description with an existential threat that could more actively shape behavior than the far more expository and brief accounting in the *Saṅgaha.* This is made all the more evident by ending the list with the human realm and thus drawing attention to the reader's precarious position on the knife-edge between heaven and hell. Ledi's amplifications and rearrangements thus demonstrate that the *Summary* is more than simply the translation it purports to be. His presentation makes the Abhidhamma relevant to the reader as a resource for understanding one's role in the cosmos, and, by implication, appropriate action in it.

It is Ledi's rearrangement of chapter 9, the chapter on meditation, that offers, albeit in theoretical and abstract terms, discussion of how to behave in light of one's place in the cosmos. The *Saṅgaha* divides the chapter on meditation into two sections, the first on calming (samatha) meditation and the second on insight (vipassanā). In contrast, the *Summary* follows an entirely different organization, that of the seven purifications (*sattavisuddhi*) found in Buddhaghosa's *Visuddhimagga.* These seven purifications map the journey from basic practice to awakening through seven progressive levels of self-cultivation and realization. The first is the purification of virtue (*sīlavisuddhi*), which concerns moral practices. The second, purification of mind (*cittavisuddhi*), describes calming (samatha) and concentration (samādhi) practices that lead to deep states of absorption (jhāna). The subsequent five purifications concern the stages in the development of wisdom (*paññā*).[56] By beginning its chapter with the purification of virtue, rather than the *Saṅgaha*'s discussion of types of objects for meditation, the *Summary* moves the reader right away into a discussion of self-cultivation. In addition, to start with moral self-cultivation was to start with the most common arena of lay effort. As noted in the previous chapter, attempting to live a moral life was the preeminent form of practice for laypeople. Virtuous behavior was a powerful means to develop good karma and insure an advantageous rebirth among the many possible outcomes in the complex Buddhist cosmos.

The *Saṅgaha* only analyzes the purifications more than halfway through its chapter on meditation, at the start of its second half covering the practice of insight (vipassanā). It describes four kinds of purification of virtue:

CHAPTER FOUR

(1) virtue regarding restraint according to the Pātimokkha;
(2) virtue regarding restraint of the sense faculties;
(3) virtue consisting in purity of livelihood; and
(4) virtue connected with the use of the requisites.[57]

This is the entire section on virtue in the *Saṅgaha*. The first and the fourth means of purification apply only to monks: The pātimokkha—recall that Ledi had had to recite it from memory to win a place in Thanjaun—is the list of 227 rules followed by fully ordained monks, and the requisites are the four items (robes, food, lodging, and medicine) a monk is allowed to use.[58] Framing the other two aspects, these monks-only restraints indicate that the *Saṅgaha* is focused on the behavior of the ordained. In the commentaries to the *Saṅgaha*, including the *Abhidhammatthavibhāvinīṭīkā* and Ledi's own *Paramatthadīpanī*, there is also no mention of these restraints in regard to the laity.

The *Summary*, on the other hand, has a much more inclusive and detailed approach to virtue. As in the example from the cosmological section of its fifth chapter, the poem expands the text it purportedly translates. By providing a broader scheme in which virtue leads to awakening, Ledi creates a richer and more inclusive discussion of virtue, one for monk and laity alike:

PURIFICATION OF VIRTUE

611|| Higher virtue | consciousness, wisdom— | the three trainings of the sāsana to be noted.

612|| "The fundamentals of good conduct" and | "praiseworthy conduct"— | these two, | the tradition of virtue [sīla sāsana].

613|| The eighth way of life, | given in synopsis, | "the fundamentals of good conduct":

614|| The three of the body | the four of the mouth, | the eighth, right living.

615|| Duties of the rules of conduct and optional ascetic practices [*dhutaṅga*]— | praiseworthy, | pure "praiseworthy conduct."

616|| Restraint: the pātimokkha, | purity of living | the requisites, | and the six senses— | these four purifications are the cause of security.[59]

While the *Saṅgaha* starts its discussion with the pātimokkha, the *Summary* does the opposite, not mentioning the monks' rules until the last verse of the section (and Ledi's autocommentary discusses the pātimokkha only at the end of its long exegesis of the *Summary* verses). This reversal in the *Summary* signals a different focus from its mother text.

Ledi begins with the three trainings (*sikkhā*) of higher virtue (*adhisīla*), higher consciousness (*adhicitta*), and higher wisdom (*adhipaññā*) that map the way to awakening.[60] (This threefold scheme is another way, then, of tracing the journey to enlightenment mapped also through the seven purifications.) Within a discussion of virtue as part of that map, he analyzes behavior first into a category called "the fundamentals of good conduct" (*ādibrahmacariya*). This sort of behavior, defined in verse 614 as eight actions of body (not killing, stealing, or engaging in sexual misconduct), speech (refraining from lying, malicious speech, harsh speech, and gossip), and livelihood, clearly apply to both laypeople and monastics.[61] Next, he gives the complementary category of the actions which are "that of praiseworthy conduct" (*abhisamācārika*). These actions are of two sorts: "rules of conduct" (*kyaṅ' vat'*) and ascetic practices (*dhutaṅga*). At first blush, one might presume that such "praiseworthy conduct," unlike "the fundamentals of good conduct," can pertain only to the ordained, and, in fact, Buddhaghosa in the *Visuddhimagga* correlates "praiseworthy conduct" to the rules given in the Vinaya.[62] In the autocommentary to the *Summary,* however, Ledi explicitly applies this term to laypeople as well as monastics: "Among monks . . . the collection of thirteen *dhutaṅga* rules and the collection of rules of conduct which start with the duties of an *upajjhāya* and *ācariya,* these are called praiseworthy conduct. Among the laity, the eight *uposatha* sīlas, the ten sīlas, and some of the *dhutaṅga* comprise praiseworthy conduct."[63] Going beyond the *Saṅgaha,* the *Summary* redefines terms of moral behavior to give a much finer gradation, just as it gave a much finer explication of the cosmos. Thereby, it speaks to a much wider audience. This sort of added detail, along with reorganization of the material, empowered lay readers as members of the sāsana addressed in the text.

Such empowerment was not a matter of specific instructions on how to behave in Burmese society; the exposition remains at a theoretical, impersonal level. In the same way, meditation, in terms of calming/concentration (samatha/samādhi) and insight (vipassanā), is treated analytically without a practical discussion of actual practice. Ledi would not explain in extensive fashion how laypeople could incorporate meditation into their lives until later works, which will be discussed in the next chapter. And, because meditation as a scholastic topic in the *Summary* does not bear specifically on lay lives, it does not open up to a discussion of lay behavior in the same way as the section on morality does. Thus, the *Summary* shows the most significant divergence from the *Saṅgaha* in the chapter on meditation in its discussion of the cultivation of morality. Indeed, the verses in the section on virtue have some of the most extensive commentary in the chapter. By placing attention on the laity in the area of morality, Ledi empowered their lives as an explicit and integral part of the meditative path of purification traced in the whole chapter through seven stages. (Again, remember that this is a different organizational structure than that of the *Saṅgaha*.) Study thus became appealing not just because it was intellectually plausible and prestigious, but because the inclusion of lay experience within Abhidhamma teaching provided a sense of its relevance to lay lives as part of a process leading to awakening.

These examples show that the *Summary* was not a straightforward translation of the *Saṅgaha* but a "retranslation" that refocused Burmese Buddhism on lay life. It is not that examples such as those given here were in themselves radical transformations, although they were significant. More to the point, they formed part of the construction of a particular modern ethos. To see the cosmos oriented around your life, to understand moral action in your life as a robust part of the process of spiritual development outlined in the most rarified texts—such examples show how the *Summary* made all the details of the Abhidhamma relevant to laypeople's experience, and so made laypeople's experience relevant to the Abhidhamma as a powerful path to awakening.

The approach of the *Summary* in all its features and examples is not something that readers would pass over quickly, either. As we will discuss below in more detail, this work was typically memorized and chanted, both individually and collectively. The information was internalized and practiced not only as an intellectual endeavor but as a bodily and social experience. Moreover, the *Summary* was not consumed in a utilitarian fashion or used as a mere vehicle of information; rather, it was treated with care as a source of immense prestige and power. As Paul Griffiths has observed, religious "reading" (understood here as an oral as well as a textual practice) was a deliberate and reverential use of a work that insured its deep inculcation and transformative effects.[64]

The reorientation of Abhidhamma study by the *Summary,* toward a certain readership and with the amplification of certain areas of concern, was not an arbitrary choice on Ledi's part. The subject matter of the *Saṅgaha* as a comprehensive Abhidhamma text framed his efforts and, naturally, caused him to present study and lay concerns through an Abhidhamma outlook. This was just what he and his readers wanted, of course, and the inclination to the beloved Abhidhamma reminds us that Ledi's innovations worked with his precolonial influences, supporting traditional learning proactively even as he bent it to contemporary concerns. This sort of reinvention of tradition would shape, too, his subsequent presentation of insight practice.[65]

Ramifications for Study

While study of the *Summary* had real value for oneself, Ledi suggests in a short poem in the epilogue that its value goes beyond the individual to the community:

1|| Six hundred and ninety [verses] of adorned poetry, the poem ends here.
2|| In 1208 [1846], | the Sakka era, | the writer of the book was born,
3|| the Mahāthera Nyanadaza from the Ledi forest monastery of Monywa.
4|| This work was finished in the month of Ka-soun in 1265 [1903].
5|| It is entitled the *Summary of the Ultimates.*
6|| Among those who learn by rote this summary of the two piṭakas,
7|| they get the big prize of basic wisdom, [and are] a means of support for others.
8|| Because of the merit of having written this book, I pray that the end of the suffering of all people and animals comes to pass,
9|| that all be free from injuries, that rains be plentiful, that all countries look after the dhamma and be at peace.
10|| May the 84,000 rays of the dhamma shine out, dispelling the darkness; may the sāsana be caused to shine out very brightly.[66]

Ledi says that those who study the *Summary* serve as "a means of support for others," because the one who makes spiritual progress through the attainment of wisdom becomes a resource for other people. This is what Maung Gyi meant in his poem given at the start of the chapter, when he says Ledi "supports" those who can become awakened. Indeed, just as Ledi makes the whole of Myanmar shine bright with Abhidhamma wisdom, the *Summary*'s epilogue suggests that the merit gained when people engage in the study of the *Summary* could be a means of support for the karmic health of Burmese society as a whole. Ledi's wish for "all countries to look after the dhamma" in verse nine invokes the prevalent sense of the threat of colonialism. It seems possible, given the context of the work, that he is implying that, just as the merit he has generated by writing the *Summary* may lead to social, even political, ramifications, so could the merit generated by those who study the *Summary.* Ledi uses the Burmese word *nuiṅ' ṅaṃ* for "country." This word had long use in the language. It can refer simply to "lands" or "territories," but early on it came to mean also a country with a clear sense of bounded territorial control.[67] I am not sure if Ledi's choice of the word indicates a hope that modern nation-states would protect the dhamma, but, if such is the case, the epilogue would suggest that merit serves political ends. This fits with Ledi's approach in the "Letter on Cows"—a work he continued to promote at this time—which stresses the point that one's behavior as a Buddhist affects social outcomes. Such a sense of potential implications to study could have added impetus to the endeavor and to the social organizing that would take place around it.

Ledi also states in the epilogue that his poem (again, purportedly a translation of the *Saṅgaha*) is a "summary of the two piṭakas." He elaborates in the autocommentary:

> The consciousness (citta), mental factors (cetasikas), miscellaneous (*pakiṇṇa*), process (*vīthi*), materiality (rūpa), and conditions (*paccaya*) chapters—these six chapters are those which abridge the seven books of the Abhidhamma.
>
> As for the planes (*bhūmi*), categories (*samuccaya*), and meditation (*kammaṭṭhāna*) chapters, these chapters abridge the Sutta Piṭaka.
>
> Those people who manage to learn all nine chapters, they have managed to memorize the two piṭakas in abridged form.[68]

The *Summary* is thus a means to acquire at least a shorthand mastery of two baskets of the canon. Accepting that the Abhidhamma garners the most prestige among Buddhist texts in the Burmese Theravāda tradition, it hardly casts a pall on the *Summary*'s appeal to add that the gist of the suttas is included here, too. That the *Summary* could capture the essence of both would appeal greatly to the pressing need felt among laity to protect the endangered sāsana. As chapters 2 and 3 showed, a strong sense of a threat to Buddhism had mobilized the laity to action. To master such a text ensured that at least the basic information of the suttas and the Abhidhamma were preserved, the first two baskets prophesied to disappear. In this regard, the *Summary,* more than any other work Ledi wrote, served as a single means to a comprehensive preservation of Buddhism by the laity.[69]

But as powerful as preservation would be as a motivation to learn the *Summary,* its power went beyond its function as a vehicle for sāsana protection. The epilogue also promises salvific benefits for the individual. Here is where Ledi makes explicit that readers who have managed to learn all nine chapters of the *Summary* are equipped for real spiritual attainments:

> They [who have learned the whole *Summary*] are endowed with the dhamma tools to liberate themselves in this very life. If they do not liberate themselves in this life, they will free themselves in the realm of the spirits.[70] As for others remaining from this sāsana, in the next age when there is no sāsana they will be solitary Buddhas (*paccekabuddhas*) and will liberate themselves. As for others, in the sāsana of the next

Buddha they will be very famous disciples known for being such things as preeminent in wisdom or preeminent in supernatural abilities, and they will liberate themselves.[71]

Study of the *Summary* provides the necessary "dhamma tools" for liberation. Study is not the same as the pursuit of liberation, to be sure. Burmese Buddhism had long held the triumvirate of *pariyatti* (study), *paṭipatti* (meditation), and *paṭivedha* (realization), and Ledi did not subvert it. What is distinctive about the *Summary,* however, is that it provided to people a practicable means to prepare for a journey across the border from study to practice. Enabled by study of the *Summary,* the lay person could make real headway to awakening—indeed, Ledi says even "in this very life." The expression "in this very life" would become a hallmark of Buddhist modernist claims about the possibility of awakening in the here and now.[72] So far as I know, Ledi uses the term for the first time in regard to lay practice. And he uses it to describe the potential inherent in the study of a text. This sense of study's organic segue into practice set the stage for meditation, and it provided the means through the Abhidhamma's fine-grained and deconstructive analysis of experience.

Awakening in one's current life was only one possibility, however. Others could trust in gaining awakening as "solitary Buddhas" in the next age that would have no sāsana.[73] Failing that, the *Summary* would enable them to distinguish themselves during the time of the next Buddha, Metteyya. (Although presumably one could not hope to be the Buddha's preeminent disciple, at least by Ledi's lights, since he had claimed in his poem given at the end of chapter 2 that during the time of Metteyya *he* would be "brave and unsurpassed.") These references to future lives show once again Ledi's assumption of a complex cosmos that aligned an innovative popularization of Abhidhamma study with a longstanding worldview of karmic outcomes over innumerable lives. Study of the *Summary* could shape such outcomes, and not just as an individual effort. In public talks Ledi stressed the fact that if laypeople came together in groups they could insure both worldly and spiritual benefits, and, just as he would do for many other texts, he vigorously promoted *Summary* groups to actualize the benefits that could be derived from study.[74]

The *Summary* Groups

Ledi was the first person to organize laypeople systematically to study the Abhidhamma, and the lay groups to study the *Summary* that he created as he traveled around Burma were among his earliest and became his most widespread.[75] The historian U Ko Lay remarked that Ledi created groups in almost every town he visited.[76] U Wunnita claims that there were over 300,000 *Summary* students for the years 1903 to 1926; Hla Pain says there were 400,000.[77] Whether either number is accurate is hard to assess, but it does suggest that *Summary* groups were very popular, and it accords with the multiple printings of the text and the statement in *The Burman Buddhist* that Ledi and his disciples had established *Summary* groups "in all the large towns."[78] This distribution made the collective lay study of the Abhidhamma a reality throughout Burma.[79]

Often, the village headman would become the leader of a *Summary* group, symbolically fusing local authority with study, and every group would have a committee, comprised of local laypeople, to oversee its operations.[80] Lay leaders meant that one had the chance to become not only an Abhidhamma student, but a teacher. The observation of an Inspector of Schools in the *Quinquennial Report for the Years 1902–1907* gives an example of a woman acting as a *Summary* teacher: "The Inspector instances also the case of a Thugyi's [headman's] wife who holds a class in her house in which she reads and explains to the village children the moral lessons contained in the Paramatta Thankheit, an epitome compiled by the [Ledi] *Sadaw.*"[81] The role of the teacher in Burmese society was (and still is) a highly respected one. That a lay person, and particularly a woman, had the ability to become a teacher of the Abhidhamma suggests the empowerment the *Summary* and its groups provided.

As it was with many of Ledi's groups, recitation was the key activity. In the epilogue, Ledi refers to "those who learn by rote this summary."[82] The verb "to learn by rote" (*hnut' ṅuṃ*) literally translates "to keep in the mouth" and this sense underscores recitation of the text as part of the process of memorization, for the verb implies that those who have learned the text by heart have the ability to recite it. This accords with recitation's important part in learning and its function as a source of merit. But recitation as part of the *Summary* societies went beyond the norm. As with his groups using his other texts, Ledi provided an institutional context in which laypeople through recitation of the *Summary* took on *ganthadhura,* the duty to study the holy texts.

The prestige and authority conferred by the *Summary* groups was buttressed by examinations to judge how well members had learned the poem. Members could choose to recite particular portions or the entire work. If one mastered all nine chapters, the reward was a certificate with Ledi Sayadaw's portrait and a small amount of gold.[83] This chance for social recognition and through it connection to the powerful persona of

Ledi (at least through his picture) probably motivated *Summary* study and *Summary* group membership. Ledi often presided personally over recitations as he traveled on preaching tours. It is important to remember that as appealing as study might be because of prestige and the protection of Buddhism during colonialism, social pressure was also a force for participation. It is likely that there was often a complex mixture of motivations at play. Not to mention that many children taking part likely did so because their parents made them.

Whatever the reason, public events in which *Summary* students displayed their learning were immensely popular. A periodical from 1907 describes a *Summary* recitation in Moulmein (now Mawlamyain) that required seventy-five horse carts to accommodate all the women taking part.[84] As noted in the introduction, laypeople often heralded Ledi's arrival in a town by reciting the *Summary* as he approached. In the town of Sittwe, forty male and more than thirty female students recited the poem's verses as Ledi arrived for a preaching festival.[85] And when he left a place, young women would often follow him along the road, chanting the verses of the *Summary* in farewell.[86]

Such powerful study in a group setting moved the Abhidhamma more fully into the lay practice of Buddhism. This is thus a preeminent example of the intensification of lay life. No longer was the Abhidhamma an object looked on from afar as something admired but largely unknown by most monks, let alone laypeople. Abhidhamma study through the *Summary* became one of the most powerful ways to reconstrue what it meant to be a lay Buddhist. The *Summary* stands in this sense as a case study for Ledi's broader program of the doctrinization of Buddhism that we saw in chapter 3. But the *Summary* shows also that Ledi promoted study for more than just protective preservation. The lay study of the Abhidhamma served as a tool for spiritual development as well. The emphasis in the *Summary* on the learning of the *Saṅgaha* as a tool for the laity's progress on the Buddhist path—even awakening "in this very life"—would predispose the laity to take up meditation, which depended upon this Abhidhamma-informed context. To use the image at the start of this chapter, the "big drum" Ledi beat to make all people hear the Abhidhamma was struck to the rhythm and content of this poem, which spread far and wide in Burma. The transformation of Abhidhamma study it enabled, from an elite monastic practice of commentarial exegesis in precolonial times to one of lay study for self-cultivation in the colonial period, would form the basis for the birth of insight meditation as an influential practice, described in the next chapter.

FIVE

The Birth of Insight

In 1904, the same year the *Summary of the Ultimates* (*Paramattha saṃ khip'*) was published, Ledi was already urging laypeople to take up meditation:

> As for some people, they say they will be freed easily when the proper time comes with the fulfillment of their perfections, but that they cannot take up the burden [of meditation] now, when they do not know whether or not they can become freed. They are scared of the burden. They do not seem to compare the suffering of making an effort in meditation now for thirty years with the suffering that will occur if they descend to hell for one hundred thousand years before getting the chance to free themselves easily.[1]

The previous chapters have shown that, in Ledi's view, cultivating virtue and studying the dhamma were critical components of a Buddhist's life. But they did not suffice. As the quotation above indicates, one also needed to meditate, and the time to meditate was *now,* not in some future life when one's perfections were complete. No longer was meditation just for a select group of monastic virtuosi. Through his writings, Ledi recast the burden of practice as plausible for every Buddhist. This was the culmination of his ideal of an intensified lay life explored in the previous chapters.

Ledi enabled those living fully in the world to pursue the awakening he had promised in the *Summary of the Ultimates* "in this very life." Indeed, as we will see, he argued that the lay meditator could "be called a monk, even though a normal lay person."[2] This assurance signaled Ledi's turn toward mundane experience as the arena of meditative practice and the site of liberation. This turn would have profound ramifications for all Buddhists, even the majority who would never meditate. It marked the birth of insight meditation as a popular movement that would reshape notions of Buddhism in modern Burma and eventually grow into a global phenomenon.

Meditation up to Ledi's Time

Nowhere else in the Theravāda world did a trend toward widespread lay practice develop as early as in Burma, and in most other Theravāda societies Burmese influence has been strong.[3] The Sri Lankan reformer Dharmapala had urged laypeople to meditate in his writings, but he did not engender much enthusiasm and started no significant meditation movement.[4] Forest monasteries, where meditation practice often is assiduously pursued, mostly appeared in Sri Lanka after 1950.[5] And a significant lay meditation movement did not begin there until the 1950s, when some laity, having formed a meditation society called the Lanka Vipassanā Bhāvanā Samitiya, formally requested that the Burmese government, and the monk Mahasi Sayadaw in particular, send meditation teachers to them.[6]

Until recently, meditation practice in Thailand remained largely the pursuit of ascetic forest-dwelling monks, such as Ajaans Mun, Sao, Tate, Lee, and their monastic pupils. These monks were part of a tradition that was highly influential in terms of its symbolic importance in Thai culture, and they did teach meditation to laypeople. Yet, relatively few monks took up their actual practices, and there never developed a widespread practice movement among the laity.[7] The reformist king Mongkut (ruled 1851–68) had pursued ascetic *dhutaṅga* practices and calming and insight meditation as a monk, but he promoted textual study during his rule as part of an educational program meant to promote national cohesion.[8] Ajaan Chah (1918–92), one of Ajaan Mun's students, and Bhikkhu Buddhadasa (1906–93) were influential monks who taught meditation to Thai laypeople and many foreigners. The extent of their influence, however, was limited until the latter half of the twentieth century.[9] Even today, some of the most popular methods of meditation in Thailand remain those imported from Burma, though home-grown movements have gained prominence, such as that of the Dhammakāya organization.[10] Thus, while there was certainly an interest in meditation among monks and laity in Thailand as in Sri Lanka, it seems that the impetus for collective lay practice on a widespread basis in the modern period began first in Burma.

As I mentioned in chapter 1, the Burmese Buddhist chronicles from the eighteenth and early nineteenth centuries reflected a growing belief in Burma in the possibility of living arhats, and this suggests a shift in the conception of meditation's potential during this time. We also noted a few isolated instances of interest in meditation practice prior to the nineteenth century among some monks and possibly among a small segment of the laity. The commission and production of books about meditation at King Mindon's court indicate that it had become a topic of scholarly interest at the elite level by the mid-nineteenth century, which fit the literary ethos of the milieu. The courtier and Ledi's lay mentor Hpo Hlaing wrote three books on meditation, and court figures commissioned a number of other texts on the subject. But actual meditative practice did not generate nearly the same interest, though Mindon and some monks in the Sagaing Hills were said to be meditating. The only example of a monk at this time who taught that meditation as a practice was required (to some degree) of all Buddhists was the Hngettwin Sayadaw, but his sect, focused on monastic reform, did not engender widespread practice among either monks or laity.[11]

The list of publications maintained by the British colonial government in Burma, the *General Catalogue of Books,* also shows the development of an interest in meditation. From 1868 to 1900, the catalogue contains twenty-four works focusing on meditation. Although monks comprise the majority of the authors, laypeople are also present from the earliest period. In fact, the first record, in 1877, of a book on meditation, the *Bawah-naw-wadah Deepanee* in the colonial transcription, has a lay author, Po Maik Tha, and two more lay authors follow in 1881.[12] The early start to the publication of works dealing with meditation and the participation of lay writers point to significant and broad-based interest in the topic. Yet, as with the court and its patronage, this interest in meditation did not translate into widespread calls for practice.

Ledi's writings thus represent the first pervasive and influential call to practice. His efforts to inspire meditation, particularly among the laity, were motivated by the same impulses that fueled his calls to study and virtue examined in the previous chapters: namely, the precarious position of the sāsana under colonial rule and the fact that its fate rested in the hands of all Buddhists as the collective stand-in for the king. Meditative practice in this context served as another way to strengthen Buddhism by spiritually strengthening individual Buddhists. Preservation of doctrine had canonical and commentarial sanction as a means to safeguard the sāsana. But the health of Buddhism also increased with each person's spiritual progress, for Buddhism waxed and waned with society's morality, and morality stemmed, ultimately, from the right views developed through study and, critically, practice. What is more, in a climate in which Buddhism was seen as dying, Ledi felt an impetus to encourage all people to profit from the precious teachings while they could—to make hay while the sun shines, or, to put it in the Burmese fashion as Ledi did, "Spin cotton while the moon is bright."[13] For these reasons, he reformulated meditation as a practicable endeavor and made large-scale practice possible.

Most of Ledi's writings at least touch upon meditation. In the analysis that follows I have focused on those that treat meditation extensively and enable me to describe his transformation of its place in Burmese Buddhism: the *Meditation Object of Puṇṇovāda* (*Puṇṇovādakammaṭṭhān'"*), the *Manual on the Path to Knowledge* (*Vijjāmaggadīpanī*), the *Manual on No-Self* (*Anattadīpanī*), the *Manual on Breath Meditation* (*Ānāpānadīpanī*), the *Manual on Meditation Objects* (*Kammaṭṭhānadīpanī*), the *Manual on the Factors of Awakening* (*Bodhipakkhiyadīpanī*), the *Manual on Meditation* (*Bhāvanādīpanī*), the *Big Book on Meditation Objects* (*Kammaṭṭhān'" kyam'" krī"*), the *New Book on the Meditation Object of the Elements* (*Dāt' kammaṭṭhān'" kyam'" sac'*), and the *Manual on Insight Meditation* (*Vipassanādīpanī*). Highlighting and cross-referencing themes and concerns in these works will allow me to identify the features that emerge as critical to Ledi's re-envisioning of meditation.

From Hunters and Fishermen to the Scientific Men of Other Religions

Ledi wrote all but one of the works on meditation examined here for a lay person or a group of laypeople.[14] The earliest was composed in 1894, pointing to the fact that meditation was long a concern of his. As in other arenas, laypeople likely encouraged Ledi to promote meditation in print. Their solicitation of texts may well have stemmed, in part, from the long-standing practice of commissioning works as a means to display one's power and prestige. Additionally, such patronage was another way to preserve the teachings. Yet, with so many texts and topics to choose from, the amount of attention paid to meditation suggests a novel and growing lay interest in the subject in the early years of the twentieth century. As with the controversy over the *Paramatthadīpanī* and the composition of the *Summary*, the requests and feedback Ledi was receiving likely underscored to him that there was a genuine motivation among all sorts of people to learn about meditation and its practice.

Patrons from an urban, male elite predominate, but not exclusively. Indeed, Ledi wrote the earliest work, the *Meditation Object of Puṇṇovāda*, at the request of a sixty-year-old female donor named May Poun, and he followed it in 1898 with the *Manual on the Path to Knowledge,* a work written for a group of hermits living at the Kuthinayoun (Ku si nā ruṃ) Stūpa in the town of Bilin (Bhī" laṅ‘").[15] After that, more elite patrons come to the fore in the texts, perhaps because of Ledi's growing national reputation. He produced two works for a traditional Burmese medical doctor named Saya Myo, the *Manual on Meditation Objects* in 1903 and the *Manual on Meditation* in 1904.[16] That same year he wrote the *Manual on Breath Meditation* at the behest of two people, the son of the courtier Kin Wun Mingyi as well as a government official.[17] The year 1904 was, in fact, a very busy one for Ledi: he also wrote the *Manual on the Factors of Awakening* for a businessman and a government official in Pyinmana, and the *Big Book on Meditation Objects* for a lay Abhidhamma teacher.[18] A work on the material elements, the *New Book on the Meditation Object of the Elements,* followed in 1906; it is Ledi's only work focusing on meditation that does not contain publication information. Aung Mon reports, on the basis of a 1955 edition of the text, that Ledi wrote it in 1906.[19] It is probable that it, too, was intended for a lay audience, as it includes verses to be recited to protect one's children. Finally, Ledi wrote the *Manual on Insight Meditation* for European Buddhists in 1915 in Mandalay during the annual meeting of the Foreign Missionary Society (described in chapter 3).[20]

This range of patrons suggests that meditation was understood to benefit all types of people, and Ledi makes this point explicitly in his writings. He does so most powerfully in the *Manual on the Factors of Awakening*; it is here that he calls on all people to take up the "burden of practice." In the work Ledi uses the suttas and the Abhidhamma text the *Puggalapaññati* to analyze different sorts of people, graded according to spiritual potential, in order to argue that all can take advantage of the rare chance of being born as a human and in an age in which the dhamma is accessible—the precious factors he mentions, too, in the *Summary* as needed to make some spiritual progress. At the very least, one could stave off bad possibilities for future existences.[21] To make this point as strongly as possible, Ledi criticizes those who say that some types of people, such as hunters and fishermen, should not bother to attempt meditation because of the bad kamma created through such professions. Indeed, it was commonly believed that hunters and fishermen were destined for the lowest Avīci hell when they died, and this led to the argument that any meditative effort on their part was pointless.[22] Ledi disputed this in the strongest terms: "One should not even say that hunters and fisherman should not practice calming, insight, and reflection if they cannot give up their work. If one says such a thing, one is implicated in creating danger toward the dhamma."[23] Ledi was making a heavy charge against those who discouraged such people from meditating, for the previous chapters have shown that danger to the dhamma was the great religious concern of the time. The message is clear: no matter what a person does, he or she can still benefit from meditation.

Ledi intended his call to practice to be accommodating to different levels of training and stations in society, and so to broadly counteract the dominant, often exclusive, focus among Burmese Buddhists on practices of giving (dāna) and morality (sīla):

> Therefore, people who, at present, have met with the sāsana, if they hope to obtain the seeds of path and fruit knowledge [*maggañāṇa* and *phalañāṇa*] necessary to free themselves in a future life in the sāsana of a future Buddha, should strive with all-out effort for wisdom of the ultimates [*paramattha*], which are very difficult to meet with, more than they make an effort in morality [sīla] or concentration [samādhi].[24]

It is unlikely that anyone would be taken aback by the general claim of the superiority of wisdom over morality or concentration. Wisdom is, after all, awakening. To tell laypeople, however, that striving for wisdom in their current lives is *more important* than morality was surely surprising, even shocking. As we have noted in previous chapters, to focus on generosity and to seek to build up merit for a better rebirth through moral practices were the typical activities for laypeople to undertake. To argue for meditation was to expand lay activities beyond the longstanding norm, just as Ledi's argument for textual study did. He is by no means dismissing morality, of course. I noted in chapters 2 and 3 that he spent much time promoting abstention and other moral practices. But they were only a start and, in fact, of no special importance if one sought awakening in one's current life. Ledi goes on to say in the *Manual on the Factors of Awakening* that a person intent on achieving the first level of awakening, that of the "stream-enterer" (*sotāpanna*) who has gained the first irreversible level of spiritual attainment, does not have to put any special effort toward almsgiving (dāna).[25] But even the less ambitious Buddhist, he argues, must make some effort to meditate, no matter how much they give or how many meritorious works they do. In other words, here Ledi is adding meditation as another factor in a reformulation of Burmese Buddhism that intensified, in the ideal, lay life for all.

In the passage above Ledi also downplays the cultivation of concentration (samādhi). This was because his approach emphasized meditation as a practice that depended on learning rather than on the cultivation of states of absorption. We will return to the issue of his deemphasis of concentration below, but here we should note that, as with morality, this downplaying did not mean he dismisses or discounts concentration practice. In fact, he often stresses its value and states a bit later in the *Factors* that an individual should ideally do all three: practice morality, cultivate calm, and accumulate the seeds of wisdom.[26] The question for Ledi is not whether one needs calm and concentration, but how much. He accepts a range of approaches, from those dedicated to deep samatha practice to those who cultivate almost none. What is noteworthy, however, is that in his works he presents ways to minimize the amount needed. Just as he empowered laypeople to study, so too he wants to enable everybody to meditate on the basis of that study, even if they are not capable of much calming and concentration. This was why in the *Manual on the Path to Knowledge,* for instance, Ledi urges people to study further any matter they do not comprehend until they understand it.[27] Even mastery of just the basic dhamma teachings could empower practice. He wrote *The Manual on the Factors of Awakening* around the time he was traveling and promoting the study of Abhidhamma through his *Summary of the Ultimates.* The *Factor*'s combined emphasis on meditation and a basic knowledge of the Abhidhamma may have emerged out of his exposure to a wide variety of Burmese eager to understand how to relate textual study to practice.[28]

The *Manual on Insight Meditation,* Ledi's last work on meditation, reveals most clearly the ideal of the lay person who combines study with practice.[29] As I noted above, the book was written for Europeans. It was printed in English translation in Burma in 1915, the same year it was written. It is not clear to me how extensively, if at all, it was distributed in Europe, but it gained notice in Burma and came to be published in Burmese numerous times.[30] Certainly, the intended Western audience did not cause Ledi to change his presentation of meditation in any fundamental way. On the contrary, based on his conception of Westerners, he only sharpens his preexisting approach to it as a plausible part of Buddhist lay life, rooted in study. In the decade prior to writing this work, Ledi had corresponded regularly with Westerners, mostly about matters of Buddhist doctrine and philosophy. The Westerner with whom Ledi corresponded most frequently and at the most sophisticated level was Caroline Rhys-Davids—he called her "the London Pali Devī." He discussed with her a wide range of complex Abhidhamma topics, involving such matters as epistemology and the mind's role in causality.[31] His answers to her questions about the *Yamaka,* the second book of the Abhidhamma, were printed in the 1913–14 volume of the *Journal of the Pali Text Society.*[32] In addition to his communications with Rhys-Davids, he also corresponded at some length with Edmund J. Mills, a chemistry professor in London who was chairman of

FIG. 4. Photograph of Ledi included in Ledi Sayadaw, *The Vipassanā Dīpanī or The Manual of Insight* (1915).

the Buddhist Society of Great Britain and Ireland, the organization which distributed Ledi's texts in Europe.[33] The questions Ledi received from these interlocutors and others likely impressed upon him the idea of a Western inclination toward analytical analysis that prompted him to say, as noted in chapter 3, that the Abhidhamma "gives delight to the scientific men of other religions."[34]

But, however much delight was shared, these interactions certainly did not lead Ledi and his Western correspondents to think of Buddhism in the same way. For a scholar such as Rhys-Davids, a focus on philosophy fit an Orientalist vision of a Buddhism shorn of cosmology, focused on the early texts, and aligned with Western philosophy. While Ledi emphasized doctrinal learning, too, previous chapters have shown us that he saw the study of Abhidhamma as embracing a wide textual lineage and fitting comfortably within a traditional cosmology. In the *Manual on Insight Knowledge* he frames practice, in fact, in terms of the dire threat of the endless round of rebirth (saṃsāra):

> The four realms of misery down to the great Avici Hell, stand wide open to a *Puthujjana* [an ordinary person] who departs from the abode of men, like space without any obstruction. As soon as the term of life expires, he may fall into any of the *Niraya*s or realms of misery. Whether far or near, there is no intervening period of time. He may be reborn as an animal; as a Peta, a wretched shade; or as an *Asura* or Titan, an enemy of Sakka the King of the gods, in the wink of an eyelid.[35]

In a moment of mutual and overlapping influence, a Westerner such as Rhys-Davids could take from her interaction with Ledi the philosophical knowledge she sought, even as he shaped her approach to Abhidhamma study along Burmese lines.[36] For Ledi, the correspondence reinforced the way he popularized meditation as a close observation of reality informed by Abhidhamma learning. But his cosmological vision coexisted with it, one in which, as he put it in the *Manuals on the Factors of Awakening,* "How very fearful, scary, abhorrent, detestable, and sickening is the state of an ordinary person."[37]

The Dhamma Tools for Awakening: The Abhidhamma

The prior chapters have shown that Ledi promoted textual study as the foundation of lay life, and as the previous chapter demonstrated, the *Summary of the Ultimates* was the keystone. In a complement to this effort, he explained and justified meditation from a perspective that privileged the study and memorization of doctrine, particularly the Abhidhamma. This is not to say that earlier Buddhist thinkers failed to establish clear links between study (*pariyatti*) and practice (*paṭipatti*) or to see the value of the Abhidhamma to insight practice. Buddhaghosa, after all, presents meditation as a practice which depends on its rooting in the "soil of wisdom" (*paññāya bhūmi*), which he gives in a highly schematic, Abhidhammic presentation.[38] But Ledi's vernacular works were the first to popularize the message that learning could be, as he put in his *Summary of the Ultimates,* the veritable "dhamma tools" (*dhamma a chok' a ū*) that enable a meditator to relate ultimate truth (*paramattha*) directly to perceptual experience as the means to awakening. As noted in chapter 2, the goal is to see the continually changing combinations of the eighty-one building blocks of conditioned reality, the dhammas, which constantly arise and pass away in every instant. To do so is to realize the impermanent, insubstantial, and suffering-filled characteristics of all conditioned things and so achieve the final, eighty-second dhamma in the Abhidhamma reckoning, the one unconditioned entity, nibbāna.

This approach explains why Ledi's meditation texts focus on the exposition of Abhidhamma categories and concepts—so much so that they verge into the genre of scholastic primers like the *Summary*. As in it, lists upon lists fill these works. Partly, this fondness for minute categorization is the heritage of a literature first formed in an oral culture in which the list (*mātikā*) was a device to aid memorization and instruction. But lists were much more than that. They provided a way to itemize all reality and so gain control over it.[39] Thus the *Summary* was powerful learning, and Ledi's later meditation texts became the way to enact such learning in one's life. Indeed, the *Big Book on Meditation Objects*, discussed below, is an expansion of the *Summary*'s chapter on meditation, and many of these books, such as the *Manual on Meditation*, have abbreviated phrases like those used in memorization-texts (*saṃ pok'*) to aid learning the material by heart. We should remember that the *Summary* was an immensely popular and formative text. In fact, that work and Ledi's books on meditation were mutually supportive. The *Summary*'s influence, however—in terms of the general ethos it presents of laypeople as Abhidhamma scholars and in terms of the specific information it conveys—can be seen as undergirding the Abhidhamma quality of his works on meditation. This is particularly so because most of these works were composed after the *Summary*.

Over the course of the ten books on meditation surveyed here, we can see Ledi's efforts to inculcate a comprehensive Abhidhamma perspective (*abhidhammapariyāya*) in the reader, so that the very content he or she seeks to realize in meditation informs the meditative pursuit. This approach, however, does not mean that the terms and categories he employs only appear in Abhidhamma literature, though certainly many are distinctly Abhidhammic, such as the list of the eighty-two dhammas. Nor does it mean Ledi avoids speaking in conventional language or giving instructions that draw from the suttas; his use of the factors of enlightenment (*bodhipakkhiyadhammas*) and the *Ānāpānasati Sutta* (MN 118) shows his willingness to do both. Indeed, Ledi stresses that the suttas as practical aids are indispensable to the practice of meditation.[40] Nevertheless, his emphasis on the Abhidhamma—he often refers to the teachings he provides as part of it—and his use of its scholastic, list-driven style makes his works Abhidhamma-centric. Given the esteem in which we have seen the Burmese held the third basket (piṭaka) of the canon, this approach to meditation surely added to its appeal and the sense of its potential efficacy.

The *Meditation Object of Puṇṇovāda* analyzes sensory stimuli as a means to detachment, basing its analysis on a close examination of physical phenomena that divides them into their basic elements (*dhātus*)—in other words, the "great essentials" (mahābhūtas) discussed in earlier chapters—of earth (paṭhavī), water (āpo), fire (tejo), and wind (vāyo).[41] It is telling that Ledi focuses extensively in this, his first work devoted to meditation, on the four great elements, for these become the fundamental taxonomy meditators are to use in their practice in all of his works. As we will discuss in more detail below, Ledi singled out the elements because a novice meditator could perceive them relatively easily in his or her mundane experience.

The *Manual on the Path to Knowledge* also begins with the four great elements, but adds further lists (*mātikā*) to be used in analysis: the six material bases of the senses (*pasādarūp'*);[42] the ten kinds of the element of fire (*tejodhāt' mī"*);[43] the ten essences of nutrition (*āhāra dhāt' a chī*);[44] birth (*jātidhamma*); old age (*jarādhamma*); death (*maraṇadhamma*); the mark of impermanence (*aniccalakkhaṇa*); the mark of suffering (*dukkhalakkhaṇa*); and the mark of no-self (*anattalakkhaṇa*).[45] Even the *Manual on No-Self,* which takes the feelings (*vedanā*) as its subject matter, still begins with an explanation of meditative mindfulness of the body (*kāyagatāsati*) and its physical elements as a preparatory exercise.[46] In this work he also introduces the category of the three "profound knowledges" or *pariññās.*[47] These three knowledges, which mark stages on the path to full awakening, allow Ledi to chart how understanding, formed first in study, transforms into full realization. He will use these terms again in his final work on meditation in 1915 to frame a comprehensive view of practice.

Ledi's next work, the *Manual on Meditation Objects,* serves as a sort of supplement to his earlier works, for he states that he wrote it to cover topics he had not yet addressed.[48] By filling in the doctrinal gaps, as it were, covering the issues of the rare chance to be born as a human in the time of a Buddha, the five aggregates (*khandha*), the physical senses (*a tvaṅ'" āyatana*) and their respective objects (*a pa āyatana*), and the eighteen elements (*dhātus*) that constitute the bases for perception, he completes an initial Abhidhammic presentation of meditation.[49] Having treated meditation in some detail in this span of works, the *Manual on Breath Meditation,* an explanation of the *Sutta on Mindfulness of Breathing* (*Ānāpānasati Sutta*), provides Ledi's only extended discussion of technique.[50] I will explore the details of the method he describes in the next section, but we can note here that even this, his most practice-oriented work, delves into Abhidhamma categories. Ledi stresses again awareness of the elements, saying "it is the wisdom of ultimate reality which perceives fully each of these four key elements,"[51] and he finishes by explaining that the wisdom of ultimate reality understands how both mind and matter come into existence depending on temperature (*utu*), nutriment (*āhāra*), karma (kamma), and consciousness (citta).[52]

The *Meditation Object of Puṇṇovāda* had focused on materiality, the *Manual on the Path to Knowledge* on categories of analysis, and the *Manual on No-Self* especially on feelings; the *Manual on Meditation Objects* then filled in the remaining gaps, and the *Manual on Breath Meditation* explained a means to actualize learning in practice. Having covered so many aspects of meditation, in his next work, the *Manual on the Factors of Awakening,* Ledi synthesizes his teachings into a coherent whole. He explains that he uses the summarizing list of the thirty-seven factors of awakening (*bodhipakkhiyadhammas*) to do this because they distill the Buddha's forty-five years of teaching into one set of terms, divided into a number of subsets, that allows one to develop all aspects of the path to awakening—not just morality (sīla), but calm (samatha) and insight (vipassanā).[53] In a complement to *Breath Meditation,* which presented a technique in detail—in fact, they were printed together in one volume in 1905—the *Factors* makes the general case for "the burden of practice" as part of a lay life already grounded in study.

In accord with his earlier works, Ledi stresses as primary the realization of the four elements (mahābhūtas):

> At least, one should strive just to realize the division into four parts within his own body of the four great elements of earth, water, fire, and wind. Although one does not become skilled *in any other part of the Abhidhamma*, if one masters the four elements, one will gain the seeds of wisdom which are very difficult to acquire.[54]

He explains that people who get no benefit from meditation fail to do so because they "have only small ability in the knowledge of learning [*pariyatti*]."[55] The suttas are an important resource for such learning, of course, and Ledi makes ample reference to them in his works. He encourages people to use Suttanta discourses, in fact, to support their practice.[56] The elements, in particular, receive extensive discussion in suttas.[57] Yet, here Ledi classifies materiality within the Abhidhamma. This classification is not meant to supersede the use of the suttas but points to the fact that salvific knowledge is, quintessentially, found in the third basket of the piṭaka. As the quotation above indicates, however, the knowledge he expects is not high, for just command of the four elements is enough to gain "seeds of wisdom" (*paññā myui" ce'*). It is at this point in the text that Ledi argues even hunters and fishermen can meditate, and he points out that they can do so, too, on the basis of study. To prove his point, he says he knows a fisherman who can recite the whole *Abhidhammatthasaṅgaha* and the twenty-four conditional relations of the *Paṭṭhāna.*[58]

A few months later, Ledi wrote the *Manual on Meditation.* Perhaps because it builds on the detail of his prior works and the synoptic view of the *Manual on the Factors,* it is one of his most encyclopedic and complex works, emphasizing the importance of *pariyatti* from an Abhidhamma perspective. It focuses on insight (vipassanā) meditation through an analysis of the five aggregates (*khandha*), impermanence (anicca), suffering (dukkha), and no-self (anattā).[59] The rest of the book is comprised of a detailed analysis of each of the entries in the list, one after the other, geared toward realization of the three marks of existence.[60] In just another month, the *Big Book on Meditation Objects* followed. It repeats the leitmotif now evident: the importance of the study of terms and categories, found above all in the Abhidhamma texts and presented from an Abhidhamma perspective, as the means to enable practice. The importance of the Abhidhamma is particularly evident here, as this work is an autocommentary on the chapter on meditation in the *Summary of the Ultimates.*[61] The *Big Book on Meditation Objects,* like earlier works, emphasizes a focus on the material elements as the basis for practice, devoting its last two chapters to their use by people of middling or keen abilities.

His subsequent work, the *New Book on the Meditation Object of the Elements,* drives home the importance of the use of the elements by taking them as its explicit focus. In that work, Ledi explains the origination of the "great essentials" (mahābhūtas) of earth, water, fire, and wind, and he defines the twenty-eight kinds of physical matter (rūpas).[62] In the *Manual on the Factors of Awakening* Ledi had said that gaining insight into the elements in one's own body was the meditator's most vital skill. In this book, he stresses that a meditator who does not understand the four elements cannot gain insight, only merit.[63] This is not because knowledge about the material world is all that is needed for insight. In fact, one must fully realize the impermanent, suffering-filled, and essenceless nature of both matter *and* mind. But establishing an awareness of the elements is essential. Here, Ledi also offers a way for readers to understand intellectually how the elements relate to bodily experience by correlating the elements to the thirty-two body parts.

The *Manual on Insight Meditation,* Ledi's final work on meditation, distills his vision into perhaps its purest form. More than any other, this work makes a synoptic grasp of the Abhidhamma the basis for insight practice, and he discusses in it all eighty-two ultimate realities (dhammas): consciousness (citta), the fifty-two kinds of mental phenomena (cetasikas), the twenty-eight forms of physical matter (rūpa), and nibbāna. He explains that a comprehensive grasp of the Abhidhamma is so valuable because the ultimate truth it contains "is the diametrical opposite of the hallucination (*vipallāsa*) [of perception, consciousness, or views], and so can confute it. One who is thus able to confute or reject the hallucination can escape from the evils of *Samsāra,* the evolution of life."[64] To claim that such information is a prerequisite for awakening is not an unorthodox view. But, as with his use of print culture more generally, the medium changes the message; the emphasis on learning telescopes the path by connecting Abhidhamma teachings more immediately to liberative insight. Considering our study of the *Summary of the Ultimates* in chapter 4, we might say that that work reached out from the realm of study to that of practice through its claim to provide the dhamma tools for awakening. In turn, these meditation works—especially *Insight Meditation*—reached out to the realm of study from the realm of practice to effectively complete the linkage.

To explain the relationship between knowledge and awakening, Ledi returns to an analysis of the levels of comprehension of ultimate reality that he first gave in the *Manual on No-Self* under the rubric of the "profound knowledges" (pariññās). Such levels of knowledge allow for a spectrum: from learning facts to achieving awakening that depends throughout on Abhidhamma study. These profound knowledges are well established categories in Buddhist literature, but the stress he places on them in *Insight Meditation* as the categories through which to understand meditation reveals most clearly the novel, intellectualized slant he gives to practice.[65]

Each of the three profound knowledges builds upon the other to move one further toward liberative realization. The first, *ñāta-pariññā* or "realized profound knowledge," means the awareness of the nature of the world in line with Buddhist teachings on ultimate reality, worked out on the basis of overt intellectual reasoning.[66] The second, *tīraṇa-pariññā* or "the profound knowledge of analysis," understands not just the nature of reality but grasps it in terms of the three marks of existence as inherently unstable (anicca), full of suffering (dukkha), and not-self (anattā).[67] The first knowledge understands the dhammas that constitute ultimate reality as veritable objects, but with no dynamism. In contrast, one who achieves *tīraṇa-pariññā* sees the arising and passing away of the dhammas in every moment.[68] With this apprehension of ephemerality, an understanding of the nonexistence of self is acquired. But such understanding is not complete until one achieves the third profound knowledge, *pahāna-pariññā* or "the profound knowledge of dispelling." Here we have reached the bedrock of realization. *Ñāta-pariññā* enables *tīraṇa-pariññā,* which now poises the meditator on the cusp of full realization: "*Ñāta-pariññā* is relevant to *tīraṇa-pariññā,* which in turn is relevant to *pahāna-pariññā,* the one sole necessary thing."[69] With the acquisition of *pahāna-pariññā,* one rejects all hallucinations and achieves awakening.[70]

From Ledi's earliest work to his last, the strong link between textual study and meditative practice remains evident. Steven Collins has observed that scholars have often overlooked the highly discursive nature of meditation in much Buddhist literature.[71] In an article on the oral aspects of Pali literature, he relates how ancient Pali texts, operating in an oral environment, advise the would-be meditator to learn a text by heart through verbal recitation as a strict precondition to successful "mental recitation" that leads to full realization (*paṭivedha*).[72] Textual memorization had a close link to meditation—they could be nearly equivalent. Even in Ledi's colonial context, in which he exploited the power of print, memorization remained highly valued and practiced (as it does even today). We noted in the prior chapters that laypeople gathered to study and recite Ledi's texts from memory, above all the *Summary of the Ultimates.* While Ledi never gives an indication that he saw such study and recitation as leading to an internal recitation of the text, he stresses in the works just surveyed that a detailed knowledge of the ultimate parts of reality, especially the four great essentials (mahābhūtas), enables liberation. As he says in the *Manual on the Factors of Awakening,* "Men and women, who cannot study assiduously and at length the dhammas of mental and physical reality, should thoroughly study the four great elements for their whole lives, *reciting them from memory,* discussing their meanings, and observing their presence in their own bodies."[73] It was in this sense that such information served as the "dhamma tools" for awakening, for study could lead to the achievement of insight through, to use Paul Griffiths's phrase, "a radical interiorization of Buddhist metaphysical categories."[74] To be sure, learning was not in itself equivalent to wisdom (*paññā*), but it was the essential catalyst.

This sense of the integral part Abhidhamma learning plays in meditation has endured up to the present day. In a talk given recently, contained on a website about Burmese Buddhism, the well-known Burmese monk U Nyanissara, known as the Thitagu Sayadaw—who, not incidentally, wrote a biography of Ledi—said the following: "Since *Vipassanā* meditation takes the *Abhidhamma* as its sole object of contemplation, *Vipassanā* and *Abhidhamma* cannot be separated. And while it may not be said that one can practice *Vipassanā* only after one has mastered the *Abhidhamma,*

Vipassanā meditation and the study of *Abhidhamma* remain one and the same thing."[75] The popularity of this approach to meditation, one that nearly conflates it with the Abhidhamma, stems in large measure from Ledi's efforts.

"While Living a Householder's Ordinary Life": Simplifying Practice

Ledi would have wholeheartedly agreed with the Thitagu Sayadaw that no one should think that mastery of the Abhidhamma was necessary before starting to meditate. As much as Ledi pushed study, he sought to make its application in meditation a feasible proposition by simplifying its use. As I have noted, he spent relatively little time discussing techniques of meditation in print. He was interested in the larger issue of framing such practice as the natural outgrowth of formative learning. His references to method are intended to make the point that an educated perspective—an Abhidhamma perspective—is the most powerful tool for awakening, and that even a relatively small amount of learning can go a long way. Learning thus stands as the most fundamental aspect of technique. This is not just because a proper understanding of ultimate reality is the most conducive to realization, but, as we will see, because an Abhidhammic outlook allows a streamlined approach to practice in which any experience can be ripe with the potential for spiritual attainment.

One of Ledi's most extensive discussions of method is in the *Manual on Breath Meditation*, where he discusses the *Ānāpānasati Sutta*, the *Sutta on Mindfulness of Breathing*. Following the organization of the sutta, he presents a four-stage process of meditation. As would be expected for a text explaining the Buddha's discourse on the mindfulness of breathing, paying attention to the breath as the object of one's meditation has a role in each of the four stages of the method. Stage one involves paying attention to the sensation of the breath as it enters and leaves the body at the tip of the nose or on the upper lip. This stage of practice contains four progressive steps within it that lead to greater and greater concentration up to "access concentration" (*upacārasamādhi*), the state of a calm and collected mind just on the threshold of absorption (jhāna).[76] The first step is "counting" (*gaṇanā*), in which one focuses on the feel of the breath at the tip of the nose and counts each breath. In the next step, "connection" (*anubandhanā*), the meditator assesses the breaths, noting whether they are long or short; this step culminates in the appearance of the "counterpart sign" (*patibhāganimitta*), which is an image in the mind's eye of one's object of meditation (here the breath), purified of all flaws and defects.[77] The third step is called "fixing" (*ṭhapanā*). Here, one focuses attention on the counterpart sign until it can be generated easily and clearly. The fourth step is actually concurrent with the first three steps and reflects deepening concentration. It is marked by the breath becoming subtler and subtler until, once access concentration is achieved, the breath seems to disappear altogether.[78] Although this stage culminates in a highly concentrated mind, Ledi does not consider it to be actual calming meditation (samatha). Proper samatha comprises jhānic states, which the meditator pursues in the next two stages. In contrast, this first stage involves mindfulness of the body (*kāyagatāsati*) established through a focus on the breath. It is noteworthy that mindfulness, contrary to presentations by many later meditation teachers, is not a quality emphasized as more properly in the domain of insight practice. In fact, it also lays the basis for calming meditation.

Yet the meditator need not go on to true calming meditation, for Ledi presents an option here in the first stage of practice that would be extremely important to the development of mass meditation: if the meditator wishes, he or she can skip stages two and three (that is, the cultivation and mastery of the deep states of absorption called the jhānas) and proceed immediately to stage four, the practice of insight meditation. In fact, one does not even have to go beyond the counting step of stage one (the very first step of the four in this stage). If a meditator can count the breaths for the entire meditation period by using the relatively low level of concentration needed to keep a moment-by-moment focus on the object—called "momentary concentration" (*khaṇikasamādhi*)—he or she can jump straight into insight practice:[79]

> The suttas and the commentaries say that one can move to the fourth stage [of practice, which is vipassanā] only after attaining the four jhānas through mindfulness of breathing. If one can proceed in this way, it is best. But if one cannot, one can also move to vipassanā from the third jhāna, from the second, or from the first. If one has not reached the jhānas, one can move to insight practice from access concentration or from the stage of noting the long and short breaths. One can also move to vipassanā from the stage of counting the breaths, when you have pacified the thoughts of the mind that run hither and thither.[80]

To be sure, the mental control needed for momentary concentration is not a negligible accomplishment. But such control is far less than that needed for access concentration, let alone the absorptions. Thus, in one of the earliest how-to manuals of modern meditation that had wide distribution, written in 1904, Ledi promoted an unusually inclusive vision of participation in the pursuit of insight.[81] In Burma, as elsewhere in Southeast Asia, meditation practice had been typically considered too difficult for ordinary people. It was too much of a "burden" because the process was complicated and required a high level of concentration, even the jhānic states.[82] By telling his readers that only a simple form of practice and a relative modicum of calm were necessary, Ledi opened up vipassanā to a much wider audience.

This approach was only one option, for, again, Ledi does not discount the value of more advanced calming for those inclined to it. He says, after all, that if one can achieve the jhānas, it is best to do so (and we saw in chapter 1 that he himself claimed to have mastered them). Nevertheless, the organization of the work privileges the perspective of the meditator practicing insight meditation without deep calm and concentration. By favoring this more accessible approach, Ledi was not departing from the possibilities for practice in canonical and post-canonical texts.[83] The divide between methods of meditation that begin with insight and those that start with calm and concentration is well established in the earliest literature.[84] The *Visuddhimagga* expresses the authoritative view: there is the meditator who begins practice with the cultivation of the jhānas, called one who follows the "way of calm" (*samathayāna*). Then, there is the meditator, called *sukkhavipassaka* or "dry-visioned," who starts work toward realization on the basis of "pure insight" (*suddhavipassanā*) without deep concentrative states; this practitioner follows the "way of insight" (*vipassanāyāna*).[85] While the *Visuddhimagga* acknowledges this possibility of choosing between first cultivating calm or first pursuing insight, its structure suggests it prefers the former. It presents the purification of consciousness (*cittavisuddhi*) through the cultivation of deep calm just after the purification of virtue (*sīlavisuddhi*), and Buddhaghosa says that these two purifications are the roots which are to be perfected before turning to the purification of view engendered through insight practice.[86] Mention of those who work without the jhānas are few. What makes Ledi's approach distinctive, then, is that it gives preeminence to the "dry" technique that was seemingly a secondary option in Buddhaghosa's view.[87] Ledi was one of the first teachers in the modern era to offer this approach of pure insight practice as a viable—even preferred—option. What is more, he was the first to do so on a widespread basis in popular writings.

In *Breath Meditation,* insight practice is the fourth and final stage of meditation. One shifts from observing the breath to analyzing its nature. In accord with his focus on the four elements of earth, wind, fire, and water as proper objects of basic study, Ledi instructs the *sukkhavipassaka* or "dry-visioned" meditator to analyze the breath in terms of the qualities of these elements. He explains that the elements take center stage because their contemplation does not require any prior development of a deeply calm and concentrated mind (as is necessary to meditate upon mental factors).[88] The touch of the breath indicates the tangibility of the earth element; the perception of a breath as a discrete entity gives rise to a realization of its cohesive integrity through the water element; the temperature of the breath is the element of fire; and, finally, the movement of the breath in and out of the body is due to the wind element. (The wind element is breath's most noticeable feature, Ledi says.)[89] To perceive these fundamental material dhammas is to see that objects we assume are real—the breath and, depending on the breath, the body—are really contingencies arising from things that are themselves constantly changing, just as the Abhidhamma teaches.[90]

As with dry meditation, this explanation of the use of the elements within the breath as the means to an understanding of ultimate reality is not an innovation. The *Visuddhimagga* explains that a meditator can start with meditation on the physical elements, which then leads to knowledge of objects in the mental sphere.[91] Yet Ledi's stress on their use in *Breath Meditation* does not just clarify but simplifies practice. The point is to enable all people to capitalize on relatively simple Buddhist teachings that go beyond morality, for this ensures that the Buddhist does not waste the opportunity of access to the sāsana. The emphasis on the elements is evident in many of the works surveyed above. To recall just a couple of examples, in the *Big Book on Meditation Objects* Ledi argues that material objects are suitable even for middling or run-of-the-mill people (*majjhima pugguil'*), in the *Meditation Object of the Elements* he makes the elements the overall focus, and in the *Manual on the Factors of Awakening* he positions insight into the elements in one's own body as the key skill of the meditator.

In his *Manual on Right Views,* Ledi even warns beginners against rushing to put into practice more complex Abhidhamma teachings, such as those found in the *Visuddhimagga:*

In the chapter on *diṭṭhivisuddhi* [purification of view] in the *Visuddhimagga* of the Abhidhamma Piṭaka, there is a presentation of the taking up of the characteristics of physical and mental phenomena. It is very deep and lays out the dhamma of mind and matter fully. This presentation of the taking up of the characteristics of physical and mental phenomena given in the *Visuddhimagga* is just a matter for people who are specialists in Abhidhamma, and who have mastered its wisdom. It is not a matter for beginners who have just begun the work of vipassanā.[92]

Ledi's point is not to warn people away from study. As we have seen abundantly, he understood learning as critical to a person's success in meditation, and he goes on after the passage above to say that, when it comes to study, one should learn all the teachings in the Abhidhamma.[93] But he is also clearly sensitive to the danger that too high an expectation for the application of study to practice at the outset of meditation can become an impediment—a sentiment the Thitagu Sayadaw echoed in his comment above that one should not think mastery of the entirety of the Abhidhamma was necessary for practice. This is why Ledi also encourages study of the suttas, which not only provide techniques but can leaven complex philosophy with simpler (though not necessarily simple) teachings.[94] And, though Ledi supplies detailed Abhidhamma teaching in many works—the *Summary* and its autocommentary stand out in this regard—he repeatedly offers the reader a way to simplify its initial use, particularly through a focus on the four basic elements.[95]

Ledi's simplification of practice reaches its apogee in the *Manual on Insight Meditation.* It not only suggests a preferential option for the dry approach but justifies this approach as the logical choice on the basis of Abhidhamma knowledge. In this work he says that "those whose perfection of knowledge is ripened" (*pāramī ñāṇ' nu sū myā"*) need not cultivate concentration.[96] Except for a reference to samatha made in order to contrast its field of inquiry with the much wider arena of contemplation in vipassanā, Ledi mentions samatha only one other time in this, his final work on meditation, when he briefly explains the cultivation of supernormal powers (*samathābhiññā*). When one considers that the originally intended audience of *Insight Meditation* was Europeans, this absence of discussion of concentration is especially noteworthy. Given Ledi's missionary work, it is highly probable that he expected such people to be relatively uninformed about doctrine and practice. To present them with a text on meditation that barely mentions samatha indicates even more clearly than earlier works, such as the *Manual on Breath Meditation,* his emphasis on dry insight practice that intellectually prepared people can start right away.[97]

Such a simplified focus carries meditation into the everyday world, making regular life the arena of practice:

> The Insight exercises [*vipassanā a lup'*] can be practiced not only in solitude as is necessary in the case of the exercise of Calm or Samatha, but they can be practiced everywhere. Maturity of knowledge is the main, the one thing required. For, if knowledge is ripe, the Insight of Impermanence may easily be accomplished while listening to a discourse, or while living a householder's ordinary life. To those whose knowledge is

developed, everything within and without oneself, within and without one's house, within and without one's village or town, is an object at the sight of which the Insight of Impermanence may spring up and develop.[98]

This passage underlines the possibility of practice for people "while living a householder's ordinary life."[99] Since Ledi wrote this work for readers in Europe, where there was not yet a saṅgha of monks to speak of, this emphasis on lay practice was especially germane. Specifically, the stress on the ability to practice everywhere, using everything, streamlined meditation and made it accessible to those in the world. Daily life provides the fodder for insight: typical feelings and forms, perceptions and smells. Ledi says that such observation was to take place during the course of a normal day, so that one can "discern the arisings and ceasings of the Four Elements innumerable times" as one moves about in the world—walking, standing, sitting, or lying down.[100] Ledi likens such observation to watching a film:[101]

If we carefully watch the cinematograph show, we will see how quick are the changes of the numerous series of photographs representing the wonderful scene, all in a moment of time. We will also see that a hundred or more photographs are required to represent the scene of a moving body. These are, in fact, the functions of *Vipariṇāma* and *Aññathābhāva* [large- and small-scale change], or the representation of Impermanence or Death, or cessation of movements. If we carefully examine the movements in a scene, such as the walking, standing, sitting, sleeping, bending, stretching, and so forth, of the parts of the body during a moment of time, we will see that these are full of changes, or full of Impermanence. Even in a moment of walking, in a single step taken with the foot, there are numerous changes of pictures which may be called Impermanence or Death. It is also the same with the rest of the movements. Now we must apply this to ourselves.[102]

Insight meditation, then, can be as mundane as going to the movies. Ledi stresses that all experience, viewed in an Abhidhamma perspective, gives rise to liberative insight. The everyday world of lay life, seen with an educated eye, becomes the ground of awakening.

Insight Meditation stresses meditation as an observational attitude during regular life. Notably, it makes no reference to the *Satipaṭṭhāna Sutta*—a text which would become of paramount importance in later meditation movements—or any other sutta on meditation. Nor does it mention the use of the breath (*ānāpāna*) or the four establishings of mindfulness (*satipaṭṭhāna*s). This was certainly not because Ledi rejected these approaches to meditation. As we saw, the *Manual on Breath Meditation*'s focus is, naturally, breath meditation, and the *Manual on the Factors of Awaken-*

ing deals with the four establishings of mindfulness as part of the thirty-seven factors (indeed, the first four). But in *Insight Meditation* Ledi opts for an approach to meditation that uses a strict Abhidhamma taxonomy of reality's ultimate constituent parts (dhammas) as a means to make all life the potential ground of insight. In the *Manual on Breath Meditation,* as well as in the *Manual on the Factors of Awakening,* Ledi had argued for the necessity of gaining control over the mind through mindfulness of the body (*kāyagatāsati*). It seems that in *Insight Meditation* there is a tacit understanding that such control develops naturally through an informed awareness of experience in regular life.

Other works show, however, that Ledi did not see the potential in normal life as necessarily a replacement for explicit meditative exercises. In fact, in the *Manual on Right Views* he warns against mere intellectual contemplation and encourages the reader to find a meditation teacher.[103] And in many of his works he recommends an intense regimen of practice. In the *Manual on Breath Meditation* he suggests three to four hours of meditation a day.[104] He says in the *Manual on the Factors* to fix one's attention for an hour or even two on the object of the breath for mindfulness of the body and, if possible, to set aside three hours every day to meditate on the three marks of existence present in the five aggregates.[105] Practice, then, could be time-consuming and require serious effort and discipline. And such practice could include samatha, if one were so inclined, or focus on mental factors such as feelings, perceptions, and volitions, if one were ready. Nonetheless, presenting, even privileging, "dry" meditation using the four elements represented a profound change, as it made practice plausible to those living in the world. Without the need for deep trances—or, indeed, much concentration at all beyond normal consciousness—practice informed by learning could fit more easily within everyday life, especially if life outside of dedicated practice offered great potential, too.

This practice certainly depended on mindfulness (sati). As we have seen, mindfulness of the body gave one the power over the mind to direct it successfully to practices of calm or insight. But the quality of mindfulness does not dominate Ledi's presentation of meditation in the way it does in many modern forms, especially in Western cultures today. (We will trace the genealogy of this domination in the West in the conclusion.) Mindfulness for Ledi fits with its characterization in the canonical texts as the ability to bring knowledge of the dhamma to bear on the present moment, rooted in one of the establishings (*upaṭṭhānas*). In other words, it is a sort of double-faceted mental state: recollection of Buddhist truths combined with awareness of immediate sensate experience.[106] It is not simply "bare awareness," as one finds it often defined in later literature.[107] That characterization of mindfulness emerges from the teaching tradition of Mahasi, discussed in detail in the conclusion. Ledi does not conceptualize mindfulness as the touchstone of practice in the same way. It is only one factor—crucial, no doubt, but only one—among others that is understood to develop in the course of cultivating knowledge and insight.

Ledi concludes *Insight Meditation* with the assurance that practicing vipassanā will lead all toward awakening, even in their current lives:

> If meditators practice these exercises for the whole term of life, their knowledge will be developed till they have passed beyond the *Puthujjana-bhūmi* [the realm of ordinary people] and arrive at the *Ariya-bhūmi* [the realm of the noble ones] either before death or at the time of death, either in this life or in the life following, in which latter they will be reborn as Devas.[108]

Ledi bases this promise on a proper understanding of reality, on "knowledge developed." One begins with the cultivation of the intellect through learning that leads to more profound levels of understanding through practice. This approach stresses intellectual understanding as the foundation for insight. Close observation of experience, particularly bodily experience, stems from an educated perspective; it depends on knowing what to look for, and this knowledge comes, above all, from the schooling Ledi provides in Abhidhamma teachings. His earlier works had tended toward this learning-centric depiction of meditative practice, but the *Manual on Insight Meditation* provides the most integrated and comprehensive vision of this practice as an indispensable and eminently feasible part of life in the modern world.

The fact that meditation emerged out of Abhidhamma learning explains why Ledi spent so much time promoting study groups but did much less to organize explicit meditation practice in a group setting.[109] As noted in chapter 3, he formed social organizations to study insight meditation, and he accepted the donation of monasteries as he traveled, which became places where he and others taught meditation and where subsequently practice was pursued. But neither his organizations nor his monasteries were sites specifically for lay meditation, let alone on a group level. Furthermore, the monasteries were not dedicated solely to meditation practice. Ledi's ideal of meditation was one in which it was an individual pursuit. It was his students and other monks a generation later, discussed in the next chapter, who would found numerous "meditation centers" (*rip' sā*) strictly for practice and make meditation a social reality on a collective level.

"A Monk in the World": The Birth of Insight

The creation of the potential for mass meditation depended on Ledi's efforts. He used a distinctive Burmese focus on the Abhidhamma as the quintessence of learning to present meditation as a sensible endeavor for a large group of people engaged with the world. The simplifying stress on the observation of materiality articulated through Abhidhamma categories, alongside an obviation of extended calming practices through powerful learning, made meditation understandable, accessible, and portable to any setting or situation. In short, mass meditation began in Burma as nowhere else because of the Abhidhamma. Ledi used it as the lever to shift meditation from a rare pursuit to a practice poised to become a mass phenomenon.

This was the birth of insight, and it developed out of the meeting of Ledi's heritage of an elite, text-centered educational formation in Mandalay and the challenges of colonialism. Even though his life—and Burmese culture generally—suffered a massive disruption through the arrival of British rule, old ways endured, though changed by circumstances to produce a new cultural product.[110] The new thing in the case of Burma, created through Ledi's responses to the challenges he faced, would be the transformation of Abhidhamma perspectives into daily practices of meditation for both the ordained and the laity. It marked the fruition of an influential form of modern Burmese Buddhism. The lay meditator could become, as Ledi put it in the *Manual on the Factors of Awakening,* "a monk in the world, even though a normal lay person."[111]

By saying this, Ledi had no intention to denigrate the distinctive place of the ordained or to create a literal equivalence between monk and layperson. As chapter 3 showed, he used the symbol of the king to intensify lay life by encouraging activities once monopolized by monks, but he did not use it to dissolve the division between ordained and unordained. Rather than the blurring of a boundary, the rhetorical impact of this phrase "a monk in the world" lies in its suggestion of the profound possibilities for a lay life *as a lay life.* The possibilities stretched to awakening, and this fact reoriented the laity to an expanded range of practices and the power and authority that went with them. Laypeople had not been excluded categorically from the pursuit of awakening before this time, but there had not been systematic and authoritative encouragement. As we saw at the start of the book, Tapassu and Bhallika modeled a life of devotion, not meditative practice. Now Ledi was arguing that all laypeople "should strive with all-out effort for the wisdom of the ultimates . . . more than they make an effort in morality or concentration."[112] The possibility of being a "monk in the world" meant intensified forms of lay religiosity that reshaped Buddhist lives and social structures.

This approach appealed to so many—even that majority who did no actual practice—because it assumed that being modern was in consonance with being Buddhist. In fact, the two were inseparable. Meditation in Ledi's presentation was not just the site at which one responded to the demands of the modern world, as if such a world stood apart from Buddhist practice. Meditation was not, in other words, a means to reconcile or accommodate Buddhist values to modern values. Rather, Ledi's Abhidhammic vision of meditation formed, along with moral action and study in groups, an enframing vision of modernity in Buddhist terms. This was a vision that was fundamentally different from Western modernity in a way that reveals the distinct character of a Burmese Buddhist modernity among multiple versions. Prototypically, the Western modern outlook, whatever its variations in local circumstances, is marked by a sense of a spiritual disenchantment, a feeling of the loss of a larger meaning to existence. This sense is well expressed in Matthew Arnold's nineteenth-century poem "Dover Beach":

> The Sea of Faith
> Was once, too, at the full, and round earth's shore
> Lay like the folds of a bright girdle furled.
> But now I only hear
> Its melancholy, long, withdrawing roar,
> Retreating, to the breath
> Of the night-wind, down the vast edges drear
> And naked shingles of the world.[113]

Charles Taylor has used this poem to call attention to a common view that understands the loss of meaning in modern life as a loss of explicit beliefs, in this case the loss of those of the Christian faith pushed away by the perceived conflict between science and religion. But, as Taylor goes on to argue, this sense comes not from an alteration so much in consciously held beliefs as from a reformulation of the unexpressed "background understanding" that makes such a sense of change and loss powerfully resonant as never before (for the possibility had always been there logically).[114] Thus, in the West, the transition to modernity was not simply hearing the "melancholy, long, withdrawing roar" of a faith based in explicit beliefs; it was the fundamental transformation in a shared background understanding that made such a loss of meaning not just possible but seemingly as inevitable as the tide.

Ledi certainly did not share this understanding. We saw in chapter 3 that Buddhism, for him, underlay scientific pursuits. In practice, the two were allies; in essence, the two were one. In the brash poem of his own (given in full in chapter 1), written at the time of the colonial takeover, he felt confident speaking of his future life in which he would "be brave and unsurpassed during the victory of the next Buddha Metteyya."[115] Life was meaningful for Ledi in Buddhist terms and, what is more, filled with the possibility of awakening—profound knowledge (pariññā) could arise in the most mundane circumstances. Dipesh Chakrabarty has observed that political actors in India could see politics as legitimately having religious ends.[116] Gandhi provides a clear example of this perspective in his statement: "Those who say religion has nothing to do with politics do not know what religion means."[117] This is a radical inversion of expectations from the typical Western perspective. In much the same way as Gandhi, Ledi—and, in his view, all meditators—could see colonialism and the particularities of life within British rule as having Buddhist ends. A layperson could move through mundane life as a sort of monk, seeking and finding wisdom in quotidian experiences, such as watching a movie or walking through one's village or town. Recall that Ledi said in the *Manual on Insight Meditation:* "To those whose knowledge is developed, everything within and without oneself, within and without one's house, within and without one's village or town, is an object at the sight of which the Insight of Impermanence may spring up and develop."[118]

One could find significance, too, in larger, traumatic events. As uncomfortable as the arrival of the British was, it still fit comfortably into a perspective, emerging from a Burmese "background understanding," that saw their presence as a logical part of a historical progression in which, as Ledi said, the Burmese were living "near the end of the sāsana."[119] Living in the end-times of the dhamma might be regrettable, but it was sensible and even, perhaps, given the causal forces of karma, reversible (or, at least, retardable). In a world that made Buddhist sense, actions to protect the sāsana—cultivating virtue, studying, and meditating—would be seen as all the more logical. To be sure, one did not need to meditate to see the modern world as meaningful in Buddhist terms—indeed, as I have said, most Burmese did not meditate (and most do not up to the present day). Moreover, though insight meditation became a defining feature of Burmese Buddhism in the colonial period, analysis of this development should not obscure the fact that Burmese Buddhists have understood there to be various possibilities for practice besides the pursuit of awakening through vipassanā. For example, there are the esoteric practices of wizards or *weiksa* (*vijjā*), men who cultivate supernatural powers, often using samatha meditation, to protect the sāsana as well as accomplish worldly ends. The scope of this study cannot include such matters, which, while far less extensive than the growth of insight practice, were also developing and remain vital aspects of Burmese Buddhism up to the present day. But discussion of Ledi's cosmological vision here and in prior chapters is meant to suggest that the emergence of vipassanā as a predominant feature of so many Buddhists' lives occurs within a complex cosmos that contained varied options for practice. Within this rich understanding of the world, insight meditation became a preeminently valuable symbol even for those who did not practice, for it exemplified a practical way to live out Buddhist truths in modern life that depended on a valuation of learning and an emphasis on textual mastery that had deep roots in precolonial Burmese culture.

In light of this situation, the fact that U Nu, independent Burma's first prime minister, promoted meditation a few decades after Ledi's death as a political tool should not be seen merely as the result of personal piety, simply as the vestiges of a defunct traditional society, just as the product of the nationalist fervor of the post-independence years, or, finally, only a mercenary attempt to control the saṅgha. Whether it was a wise policy on his part, given Burma's tense ethnic and religious divisions, is questionable.[120] Regardless, the turn to meditation made good sense in a milieu that shared the outlook in which Ledi had justified and celebrated practice in the world, not just for its personal benefits but for its social effects as well. Such was the power of this Burmese understanding of Buddhism's relevance to politics and society that even the avowedly secular and socialist military government that removed U Nu from power in 1962 had to operate within a Buddhist cosmological perspective and, eventually, justify its rule by supporting outright Buddhist projects, including mass lay meditation.[121] These pressures on the government emerged out of a view, expressed and promoted by Ledi, not so much that Buddhism fit modern life, as modern life fit Buddhism.

Later teachers and societal developments reflect the fact that Ledi's most pervasive impact in terms of meditation was as the architect for the reconfiguration of the role of the lay Buddhist, such that meditating made sense in the modern world (and the modern world made sense in meditation). Subsequent teachers depended upon a vision of Buddhism, shaped materially by Ledi in his popular publications, his preaching (especially on Abhidhamma), and social organizing that made his text-centric and doctrine-heavy vision of Buddhism a social reality. As we have touched upon, teachers after Ledi would carry developments fairly far from his presentation of meditative practice, but they stand as the heirs to his efforts that gave birth to insight and reshaped the lives of lay Buddhists. Having explored the birth of insight, we can, in the conclusion, finish by briefly considering what its subsequent life tells us about modern Buddhism at the time of Ledi's death and up to the present day. At the start of the book, we saw that the Buddha chartered devotional practices in his first interaction with laypeople soon after his awakening. At the end of the book, we find that he is teaching a very different lesson in modern-day Yangon.

CONCLUSION

The Death of Ledi and the Life of Insight

Tapussa and Bhallika began this book. The continuation of their story sets the stage for the end: When the merchants returned to Burma from India with the eight precious hairs of the Buddha, King Okkalapa met their ship on the banks of the Irrawaddy River. In a tale that has gained currency in Burma since the 1950s, it is said that the king reserved one of the hairs and placed it in a stūpa at the spot where he met the merchants.[1] That stūpa, the Botataung (Buil‘ ta thauṅ‘), is about four miles from the Shwedagon in Yangon. By virtue of its Buddha relic, it is a highly auspicious site to visit. While it is not nearly as popular as the Shwedagon, a great many people go there every day to engage in the sorts of devotional practices first chartered by the Buddha, so long ago, for Tapussa and Bhallika.

On the grounds of the stūpa there sits a large bronze statue of the Buddha, built just a few years ago. In most ways, the statue seems similar to the many others there and, for that matter, across the Theravāda Buddhist world. The Buddha is seated cross-legged, wearing robes, with his eyes open and fixed in the middle distance. However, he is holding both of his hands at chest level with his palms out and fingers up. This is odd. There is a set of typical hand gestures (*muddā*) for Buddha statues, each of which conveys a specific meaning. This gesture is not exactly like any of them. It seems the Buddha has a new message.

What the Buddha means to convey becomes clear upon a closer look at his hands. On the palm of the right hand the

FIG. 5. The Athi-Thati Buddha at the Botataung Stūpa in Yangon. Author's photograph.

Burmese word *athi* (*a si*) appears in raised letters. This word means knowledge or knowing, implying, in the context of its presence on the Buddha's hand, an understanding of the dhamma. On the left is the word *thati* (*sati*), meaning mindfulness, and, by extension, insight meditation. Although a singular design, the statue receives the obeisance of many people, and its presence on the grounds of the Botataung suggests that its message is not considered unorthodox. The *Athi-Thati* Buddha represents materially the degree to which learning and insight practice have become defining features of Burmese Buddhism, such that the Buddha can have the very words emblazoned on his upraised palms.[2] As the preceding chapters show, Ledi played an important part in the development of this state of affairs. He drew on learning (*athi*) from the precolonial past, popularizing an elite culture of textual mastery, to justify lay practice (*thati*) as part of a larger program of response to the challenges of his times. His efforts profoundly shaped Burmese Buddhist sensibilities in the years after his death, making possible the development of meditation as a mass movement.

Ledi died in the town of Pyinmana in 1923 at seventy-seven years of age, after fifty-seven years as a monk.[3] He succumbed to unintentional poisoning, when he was given a laxative herb by a visiting Thai monk in an effort to help him regain his strength.[4] At the time of his death, he lived in a monastery that a wealthy couple had donated to him, named the "Ledi Thanjaun," a title which includes the same name as the monastery where he had studied as a promising youth in Mandalay. Ledi had gone blind at the age of seventy-three, reportedly due to the strain of reading and writing so much in poor lighting conditions. He devoted his remaining years to teaching meditation at the monastery.[5]

Ledi left behind a remarkable legacy of books and other writings, not to mention the influence of his preaching and the social organizations that he established. He had played a critical part in making the study of Abhidhamma and meditation real possibilities for the laity, and he had empowered the laity to take on a broader role in Burmese Buddhism. Such empowerment depended upon configuring a new form of Buddhism in the modern era that appealed to values about learning and practice from the precolonial period. As Charles Taylor notes in discussing the transition of non-Western premodern cultures to cultures of modernity: "Outside of those cases where the original culture is quite destroyed, and people either die or are forcibly assimilated—and European colonialism has a number of such cases to its discredit—a successful transition involves people finding resources in their traditional culture which, modified and transposed, will enable them to take on new practices."[6] Ledi is a prime example of someone who modified and transposed Burmese Buddhist resources to enable new practices. Now, at the end of the book, we have the opportunity to assess more precisely the relationship between his particular genius and the forces that constrained and even determined, at least in part, his actions. Remaining aware of both freedom and constraint will help us to understand the nature of his influence and his formation of modern Buddhism in Burma. It will also make his life relevant to considerations of other forms of modern Buddhism with very different local circumstances.

Our examination in the prior chapters has shown that events before Ledi's life shaped its possibilities and outcomes in a process of *path-dependency*.[7] It was the social and institutional environment in which he was educated, particularly in Mandalay, that set him on a certain path by forming his worldview and giving him the intellectual resources he employed in the colonial period. Looking at Ledi's life from this perspective is more than just an awareness that "history matters" or that "the past influences the present," for it highlights how earlier events narrowed the range of possible subsequent events in his life, creating for Ledi a kind of "situated freedom."[8] The makeup of such a freedom included institutional structures, material capacities, and the accepted range of rational choices. But such a process went beyond the intellectual and institutional to include also the formation of emotional tendencies that predisposed Ledi in certain directions. We see this, above all, in his love of the Abhidhamma and his dread of the loss of the sāsana—neither merely an intellectual concern—that drove his push for widespread study and practice.[9]

Remaining aware of the past's enduring power in Ledi's life undercuts the common assumption that colonialism marks a "ground zero" for the start of colonized people's modernities.[10] Marx played a critical part in making this view so influential, and he expressed it in clear terms, speaking of India under the British: "England has broken down the entire framework of Indian society, without any symptoms of reconstitution yet appearing. This loss of his old world, with no gain of a new one, imparts a particular kind of melancholy to the present misery of the Hindoo, and separates Hindostan, ruled by Britain, from all its ancient traditions, and from the whole of its past history."[11] This idea that a person can be separated from the whole of his or her history has shaped the critical perspectives of many scholars. It has led many to see colonialism as totally reconfiguring colonized people's worldviews. To quote Marx again: "All that is solid melts into air, all that is sacred is profaned."[12]

Those subscribing to this view of radical rupture have not ignored the fact that colonized people used practices and texts from the precolonial period to respond creatively to colonial pressures. They tend to assume, however, that subjected people's interpretations of the relevance of their cultural, including religious, resources depend on colonial discourses, whether through contestation, negotiation, appropriation, reorientation, hybridization, or a mixture of these sorts of coping strategies.[13] To be sure, a keen awareness of the disruptions of colonialism has produced much valuable scholarship, for there is no denying that colonialism caused huge societal disruptions.[14] And the preceding chapters show that Ledi found himself in a competitive environment in which he had to fight, regroup, and reorient Buddhism to colonial-era challenges. The path-dependent course of his actions revealed in prior chapters, however, challenges the assumption that colonialism had such power that it caused Ledi to reconfigure his Buddhist worldview on terms set in the colonial moment. It calls us to balance our assessment of the effects of colonialism with precolonial factors still at play in the colonial moment. Ledi's formative years in Mandalay and the controversy over the *Paramatthadīpanī* demonstrate that a colonized subject could hold on to resources and views that depended upon the precolonial past.[15]

Yet, even if the colonial disruption was not quite as far-reaching as often assumed, change did take place in reaction to colonialism. It is the case, then, that large-scale events, both precolonial and colonial, constructed Ledi's situated agency. He was shaped before he acted by explicit ideas, material realities, and, most fundamentally, by a background understanding that saw the world in Buddhist terms.[16] In this situation, he did not produce new ideas or social forms out of whole cloth. Rather, he improvised to apply Burmese Buddhist ideals—the survival of Buddhism, the celebration of learning, and the pursuit of awakening—to his context.[17] Understanding his career as form of *improvisation* allows us to balance enduring social and religious forces with the freedom of the individual to react to immediate concerns and pressures.[18] This book has argued that the improvisations on Ledi's part which departed most significantly from past practices were his endeavors in the social sphere to bring new practices to the laity. As we have seen, he opened up doctrinal study to a wide lay audience through his social organizations, his composition of works in simple Burmese, his use of print technology to distribute his works widely, and his preaching on all manner of doctrinal topics, above all on the Abhidhamma. And it should be no surprise that he also improvised his approach to meditation relying upon the pivotal resource of the Abhidhamma. The inheritance of Abhidhamma learning allowed him to streamline meditative practices outlined in the Pali texts, for the purpose of making them relevant to a new vision of being Buddhist in the modern world.

None of this analysis that puts Ledi's actions into context is meant to negate his individuality. The chapters show that his mixture of boldness, intelligence, diligence, and leadership amounts to genius. His distinctive actions are thus not simply the result of the past and the challenges of his colonial present. There is, quite simply, the mysterious "x factor" of the man's originality. As Wendy Doniger put it: "People are not merely the product of a zeitgeist; Shakespeare is not just an Elizabethan writer."[19] Yet, however brilliant Ledi was, he did not work in a vacuum; he fashioned his ideas and took action within a preestablished worldview and social circumstances, even as he shaped them.

This argument for path-dependent continuities revealed in Ledi's improvisational actions enriches our understanding of what makes up the modern. The Burmese emphasis on textual mastery was the result of a particular cultural outlook continuing to change but set along a certain line of development by earlier events. One may be tempted to see this as an argument for tradition, but to call Ledi's actions traditional would be misleading, unless we qualify that term carefully. It is important to remember that the word "traditional" is not typically neutral, but a way to separate beliefs or practices seen as somehow poised for the future (and so "modern") from those judged to be aligned with (and ultimately consigned to) the past.[20] Ledi was clearly not traditional in this dismissive sense, for his reliance on the past opened up possibilities for the future, as we will see below in the survey of his influence. In fact, his life subverts a simplistic opposition between the traditional and the modern, for his works maintain the view that a Buddhist can be modern in a way that accepts a precolonial Buddhist perspective.[21] Parallel to what Ranajit Guha observes about "traditional" political consciousness among subaltern groups in colonial India, Ledi presented a view that was "traditional only insofar as [its] roots could be traced back to pre-colonial times, but by no means archaic in the sense of being outmoded."[22]

Showing the roots in Ledi's life undercuts a sense of colonialism as a totalizing power, while analyzing its disruptive effects in a more nuanced way. British rule certainly made a difference in Ledi's life and, for that matter, in all Burmese lives. But it did not negate the power of precolonial Burmese history. Ledi's traditional view was an integral part of his vision of modernity. Tradition in this perspective contains reason and freedom within it. It is this conscious agency to choose to preserve thought and practice that signals the use of the past as a rational choice in response to present circumstances.[23] Ledi's life shows how the forces of continuity enabled improvisational changes that made a powerful impact on later conceptions of Buddhism.

Ledi's Influence

A genealogy of Ledi's influence up to the present day and stretching into the West will allow us to see his far-reaching impact. At the same time, such a survey reveals the ongoing improvisations by others who have continued to reshape Buddhism and insight meditation. Indeed, the Buddha at the Botataung with his upheld hands announcing "mindfulness" (sati) and "learning" (athi) represents the distillation of a vision of Buddhism dependent upon but ultimately beyond Ledi's vision. Contextual pressures continued to change after he died, particularly as the economic situation in Burma worsened in the 1930s and nationalism grew.[24] Meditation as a collective practice rode the crest of such forces, but it was positioned to do so thanks to its emergence as a resource with a particular character during Ledi's life.

Although Ledi taught many people, monastic and lay, here I will discuss only those influential followers who allow me to chart prominent trends in the development of mass insight meditation. Among them, one finds the same simple Abhidhammic approach, particularly the practice of observing the physical elements in the body. The Mohnyin Sayadaw (1872–1964) was an extremely popular monk in the 1930s, reportedly attracting crowds of ten thousand, sometimes twenty thousand people.[25] Before Mohnyin allowed his students to practice meditation, he required that they learn the Abhidhamma as an intellectual system, in order to ensure that an Abhidhammic understanding of reality would guide insight practice.[26] In a talk included in Jack Kornfield's *Living Dhamma,* Mohnyin divides his instructions into two parts: first, a section of Abhidhamma theory, and then a section on how to apply this theory in practice. In the section on theory, he begins with the four elements in order to explain the nature of physical matter (rūpa). Following this, to describe what should be observed in terms of mental phenomena, he outlines the six classes of consciousness (citta). These two groups are the same ones that Ledi singles out in the *Manual on Insight Meditation* as the fundamental objects with which to begin vipassanā, starting with materiality. When the Mohnyin Sayadaw turns to the topic of practice, he stresses the need to begin with contemplation of the body: "It is through the examination of the body and bodily sensations, especially those involved in various postures, that the yogi can best understand the ultimate Dharma."[27] This emphasis on the observation of physical phenomena accords with Ledi's approach that urges the meditator to see the constant changes in one's movements like the frames of a movie.

Another direct disciple of Ledi, U Po Thet, known as Saya Thetgyi (1873–1945), is noteworthy because he is one of the earliest examples of a layman empowered by a monk to teach meditation.[28] Designating a layman for such work fit Ledi's approach to meditation that stressed its feasibility and suitability for the laity. It also fits in his broader efforts to empower laypeople to take on new responsibilities in Buddhism. In fact, it is said that Ledi even approved Thetgyi's teaching of monks, a total upending of the usual roles for monk and layperson. Ledi is reported to have told a group of monks at his monastery: "This layman is my great pupil U Po Thet, from Lower Burma. He is capable of teaching meditation like me. Those of you who wish to practice meditation, follow him. Learn the technique from him and practice. You, Dayaka [lay donor] Thet . . . hoist the victory banner of Dhamma in place of me, starting at my monastery."[29] For Ledi to equate Thetgyi to himself and to put him in a position of authority over monks were radical moves, a real leveling of the lay/monk divide. Up to today, the lineage of teachers that follow Thetgyi is the only one in Burma that is headed by laypeople.

Saya Thetgyi never wrote his own works on meditation, but one biography says:

> When he [Thetgyi] died in 1945, he could be confident he had followed Ven. Ledi Sayadaw's instructions to him. Even though he was not learned in the Pali texts, through his own experience, and with the aid of manuals written by Ven. Ledi Sayadaw, he had been able to teach the Dhamma to many. *He had thoroughly mastered the texts written by Ven. Ledi Sayadaw and almost knew them by heart.* By comparing his own experiences with what was written in them, he had been able to see how he was progressing and teach himself.[30]

This quotation highlights the importance of textual study as part of meditation. Indeed, we see the text acting as teacher, and it reminds us that Ledi himself may have derived his approach from texts, perhaps especially Hpo Hlaing's. Here, Ledi's writings actively guide and shape realization. Thetgyi's training-by-text shows that the dissemination of printed matter and popularization of lay study were not just convenient and efficient means of transmitting the dhamma widely, but transformed the possibilities of practice.

U Ba Khin (1899–1971) became Saya Thetgyi's most famous disciple.[31] He, too, was a layman, but far more engaged in mundane life than his teacher. While Thetgyi did not ordain as a monk, he took up residence away from his wife and children and ceded all worldly responsibilities to them, in order to live a celibate life devoted to meditation.[32] U Ba Khin, on the other hand, was a family man with six children and fully immersed himself in a career as a government official. He rose to a position of prominence in independent Burma as its Accountant General, and he combined meditation with this active life of government service, even creating a meditation room for workers in his office.[33] Setting up such a room was, no doubt, a pious act on his part, but it also supported a nationalistic movement, for this happened during the U Nu years of the 1950s when Buddhism and the state were explicitly linked.[34] (In his later years, he focused more exclusively on teaching meditation at the independent center in Yangon he founded in 1952, called the International Meditation Center; this is the place mentioned in the preface where I was meditating in 2004 when an earthquake struck.)[35] His fusing of an active lay life and insight practice represented a step beyond his teacher toward a fully laicized focus on meditation as a practical, even this-worldly, endeavor.[36]

U Ba Khin's approach to meditation also depended upon Abhidhamma concepts and stressed observation of impermanence in the body. His teachings, however, simplify the technique further than Ledi had. In U Ba Khin's presentation of meditation, there is a focus on the kalāpas, the basic subatomic structures out of which all physical matter is composed, rather than the four elements, which together comprise the kalāpas.[37] The use of kalāpas indicates the strong link to Abhidhamma learning, for the Abhidhamma commentaries are the first sources to posit the existence of such entities. U Ba Khin taught students to focus on the kalāpas because they are evanescent, disappearing almost as soon as they appear, but are also understood to be perceivable through meditation. The direct observation of such fleeting entities teaches that all things are in a constant state of flux.[38] This method is not a dramatic divergence from Ledi, but such a fine-tuning points to the fact that meditation teachers who considered his teachings to be authoritative did not necessarily preserve exactly the same approach to meditation.

The most salient difference between Ledi and U Ba Khin, in fact, is not in the theory of meditation but in the practicalities of its teaching. In sharp contrast to Ledi's flexible approach to meditation instructions, U Ba Khin established a rigid timetable for practice throughout the day at his center. When first learning to meditate, students were (and still are) required to take a closely regimented ten-day course that introduces more advanced teachings on method progressively. One practices samatha for the first few days (there is some variability in the number of days, based on the individual's progress) through a focus on breathing at the nostrils. Then, one turns to vipassanā by passing one's attention through the body bit by bit from head to toes in order to, eventually, observe the rise and fall of the kalāpas within it.[39] This standardized and simplified approach represents a sharp turn toward a stipulated technique and away from Ledi's combination of study with flexible possibilities for practice. Indeed, U Ba Khin would say that anyone can realize the salvific truth of impermanence (anicca) through practice, even if they "have no book-knowledge whatsoever of Buddhism."[40]

It is not the case that U Ba Khin rejected the study of the dhamma by laypeople, but his approach downplayed its value for practice. The emphasis on method rather than on theoretical knowledge makes meditation less broad in terms of the range of its initial application and the specifics of technique. It is also no longer an activity that has the same transformative potential to bring up realization in the midst of daily life based on the perfection of knowledge, as in the *Manual on Insight Meditation*. But, on the other hand, it became more accessible for those who had little inclination or time to study or memorize teachings. A stress on a method with sparing reference to doctrine also meant meditation could be more congenial to non-Buddhists. U Ba Khin felt he had a special mission to teach Westerners and others from non-Buddhist parts of the world.[41] This is why he called his meditation headquarters the International Meditation Center, and he did teach many non-Burmese at his center.[42] This welcoming of all practitioners regardless of background or beliefs signaled a strict emphasis on practice that downplayed or ignored other aspects of the Theravāda tradition.[43] This was a modernizing move toward what U Ba Khin called a "practical Buddhism" that could be more readily applied to any religious or cultural context.[44]

The appeal to non-Buddhists through a focus on practice becomes even more evident in U Ba Khin's student, S. N. Goenka (born 1924).[45] It is his organization that put up the world map of meditation centers at the Shwedagon described in the introduction. Goenka's teachings represent a further development in the conception of meditation that positions it explicitly as *the* fundamental teaching of the Buddha. Indeed, the Buddha never taught Buddhism or any religion, according to Goenka; the Buddha only taught a way to live, rooted in meditation.[46] He calls meditation, in fact, "an art of living," and this phrase captures a sense of meditation not only as part of worldly life but as justified in terms of what it offers here and now for psychological (and even physical) wellbeing.[47]

Goenka has matched his emphasis on vipassanā as the heart of the Buddha's teaching with an emphasis on a particular technique that he characterizes as handed down without any change whatsoever from the time of the Buddha: "Five centuries after the Buddha, the noble heritage of Vipassana had disappeared from India. The purity of the teaching was lost elsewhere as well. In the country of Myanmar, however, it was preserved by a chain of devoted teachers. From generation to generation, over two thousand years, this dedicated lineage transmitted the technique in its pristine purity."[48] So far as I know, Ledi never made such a claim, nor did Thetgyi or U Ba Khin put so much stress on a perfectly preserved technique. With Goenka's stress on a method came a growing emphasis on lineal authority through its preservation, in lieu of the saṅgha's traditional authoritative role of preserving the more expansive dhamma found in the canon as a whole.

Regardless of these developments, the Goenka tradition certainly does draw from Ledi's teachings (not to mention that it identifies Ledi as the first known teacher in its lineage, as noted in the introduction). The method is essentially the same as that of U Ba Khin, following a ten-day schedule with progressive instructions and focusing on the kalāpas.[49] But meditation is now no longer taught as part of Buddhism and reference to doctrinal teachings is further minimized. Interestingly, however, the Goenka organization by no means rejects the Pali canon, and the reader will note the organization is responsible for the extremely useful and well-done digitization of the Pali canon. Moreover, the dhamma talks given by Goenka through taped lectures during the standard ten-day retreat in this tradition are filled with traditional doctrinal teachings. Space prevents here a consideration of the group's complex relations to Theravāda Buddhism (a book-length study is needed), but the sketch here makes evident the departures from Ledi's vision. Insight meditation has become a nonsectarian and universal practice explicitly available to all religious adherents.

The unswerving focus on a single technique and the appeal to its universality has proved a powerful means to spread the teaching, particularly outside Buddhist cultures. Goenka was born in Burma but came from a family of Indian extraction. In 1969, he emigrated to Mumbai, India, and began to teach meditation there, first to his family but soon to others as word of mouth grew. His courses, offered free of charge, were popular with Westerners, particularly young people on the "backpacker trail."[50] The spread of his ten-day retreats first in India and then throughout the world influenced many who would later become teachers in the West.[51] In 1982, Goenka appointed his first Western-born assistant teachers, and in later years he traveled to Europe and the United States to promote his method of insight meditation. At present, there are over 120 permanent meditation centers within the Goenka organization on every continent, with other courses held in temporary locations.[52]

In Burma, about a generation after Ledi, other meditation teachers came to prominence who did not have a lineal connection to him. Their backgrounds and approaches vary considerably. For example, the Sunlun Sayadaw (1878–1952), who many Burmese believe achieved arhatship, developed his practice largely on his own, without much educational training. He did acknowledge Ledi's teachings, however, as beneficial to his spiritual progress.[53] In contrast, the Mogok Sayadaw (1899–1962) was renowned for his learning, and he fashioned a meditation method rooted in a highly scholastic analysis of dependent origination. Like the Mohnyin Sayadaw, he required extensive study prior to practice. It is interesting to note that Mogok studied the Abhidhamma in depth and even preached on the subject with one of Ledi's disciples, suggesting, at the least, his exposure to Ledi's teachings.[54] His method has remained quite popular up to the present day in Burma.[55]

But, among teachers without direct links to Ledi, the most influential meditation lineage has been that of the Mingun Sayadaw (1870–1955), mentioned in the introduction.[56] Most modern-day teachers of vipassanā in Burma look either to Ledi or to Mingun as the root teacher of their lineage.[57] Mingun did not travel as widely or with such fanfare as Ledi attracted, nor write so prolifically, but he was the first person to set up a center to teach meditation to laypeople in a group setting, in 1911.[58] I have not found any information about interactions between Ledi and Mingun. Nor does Ledi mention the Mingun Sayadaw in his writings or vice versa. Given the fact that Mingun was junior to Ledi by twenty-four years, however, it is likely that he knew Ledi's pervasive and popular writings.

The Mingun Sayadaw's most famous student was the Mahasi Sayadaw (1904–82), who would become Burma's best known meditation teacher, in large part due to the promotion of his technique by the prime minister U Nu. Ingrid Jordt reports that her Burmese informants claimed that the Mahasi Sayadaw studied with the Mohnyin Sayadaw.[59] If such is the case, then it establishes a direct link to Ledi. But even setting this possibility aside, the popularity of Ledi's writings and Mahasi's wide knowledge of Buddhism means he probably had read Ledi's works.

Mahasi shares with Ledi a penchant for an Abhidhammic approach to meditation. While he puts a strict emphasis on one specific technique and includes in his introductory teachings only spare reference to doctrine and study, the method partakes of general features of the lay meditation scene that Ledi shaped through his actions. The Mahasi method is to focus first on observation of breathing at the abdomen, and then to expand observation to all the processes of perception through the six senses of sight, smell, hearing, taste, touch, and mind (as a sense that perceives thoughts). Each impingement upon a sense is inventoried by noting the cognitive event with a simple label before letting it go. So, for instance, if one were sitting meditating in the Mahasi style and heard the sound of a car go by, one would simply repeat "hearing, hearing" and then let the perception drop and return to the breath (or move to labeling another perception if one arose immediately). This process is understood to develop a deconstructive moment-by-moment awareness that leads the meditator to see reality in its ultimate terms.[60]

Broadly speaking, this approach follows the process of the seven stages of purification (*sattavisuddhi*) outlined in the *Visuddhimagga* and shares its Abhidhammic perspective.[61] There is, however, one important difference with Buddhaghosa's work. As mentioned in the last chapter, Buddhaghosa gives pride of place to a process that includes cultivation of the jhānas. In contrast, the Mahasi method privileges a "dry" (*sukkha*) practice that uses only the lower level of momentary concentration (*khaṇikasamādhi*). Thus, all the bedrock conceptions of lay meditation revealed in Ledi's work remain: an Abhidhammic approach, a downplaying of concentration practice, and an emphasis on the observation of everyday reality. I do not want to suggest that Mingun or Mahasi (or any other teacher outside his lineage) covertly or unconsciously lifted their technique from Ledi. In fact, the Mahasi method stresses the "pure insight" (*suddhavipassanā*) approach without deep concentration to an even greater degree than Ledi did or his direct lineages do.[62] Nonetheless, the commonalities in approach between Mahasi and Ledi suggest that Ledi had a profound influence, insofar as he shaped materially the context and parameters in which the Mahasi movement and others developed.

Just as Ledi and Mingun were the two principal bases for meditation groups in Burma, so these two lineages formed the bases for the internationalization of insight practice and its spread to the West. In continuing to trace the influence of Ledi, I now want to turn specifically to the transmission of practice to the United States, in order to show both continuities and transformations in a cultural context quite different from Burma. In fact, the careers of Western proponents of insight meditation show that they have participated in a global exchange network in which multiple teachings and teachers have flowed between Asian and Western countries and between Buddhist sources and other perspectives in American culture.[63] Out of such a complex network of influences and associations would develop transformed practices. Set on a path that depended on Ledi's actions, people within this network moved beyond his conceptions and even beyond Buddhism.

Three American-born teachers, Jack Kornfield (born 1945), Joseph Goldstein (born 1944), and Sharon Salzberg (born 1952), can be identified as the key "reverse messengers" (to use the sociologist Wendy Cadge's expression), who established a particularly influential strain of insight practice in America. They have certainly not been the only teachers; it should be noted that Goenka's organization, for instance, now has deep roots in the U.S. (The first center in the Goenka lineage outside of Asia, in fact, was the Dhamma Dhara Vipassana Meditation Center, founded in 1982 in Shelburne Falls, Mass.) But the Goenka organization in America, because of its conservative focus on maintaining a particular technique and its claim to teach, not Buddhism, but a way of life taught by the Buddha, has not had the influence on the wider American culture of teachers like Goldstein, Salzberg, and Kornfield.

Would-be American teachers of insight meditation found themselves in a situated freedom, just as Ledi had. Jack Kornfield and Joseph Goldstein both journeyed to Asia as Peace Corps workers in Thailand in the 1960s. They stayed in Asia after their service to study Buddhism and meditate, and in Kornfield's case to ordain with the Thai monk Ajaan Chah. Although they never met in Asia, both men practiced extensively in the Mahasi lineage. Kornfield traveled to Burma and trained at the Yangon Mahasi center under Asabha Sayadaw;[64] Goldstein practiced in India, training under Anagarika Munindra, a Bengali teacher who had spent years in Burma meditating under the guidance of Mahasi Sayadaw. Both men trained with other teachers, too. Goldstein practiced under Goenka, and Kornfield received training from the monk who ordained him, Ajaan Chah. Sharon Salzberg went to India in 1971, where she met Goldstein during her first retreat.[65] She, too, practiced with Goenka and Munindra, though also with other teachers, including some in Mahāyāna traditions.

All three met in 1974 in Boulder, Colorado, where Goldstein and Kornfield joined forces to teach a meditation course at the Naropa Institute, newly founded by the Tibetan lama Chogyam Trungpa.[66] Goldstein and Kornfield went on to teach together around the country. On May 19, 1975, they founded, along with Salzberg and another insight teacher, Jacqueline Schwartz, the Insight Meditation Society (IMS). The aim of IMS was to "provide a secluded retreat environment for the practice of meditation in the Theravada Buddhist tradition."[67] In January 1976, they purchased a site in Barre, Mass., where IMS is still located.[68]

These lay teachers, teaching in America to an almost entirely lay audience, emphasized bare practice to an even greater degree than their Asian masters. Outside of a Theravāda culture and without direct links to traditional Theravāda practices, they dispensed with almost all rituals and activities other than meditation. Although Goenka claims not to teach Buddhism but only pure dhamma, he assumes a traditional cosmological worldview that includes rebirth. Such assumptions—indeed, practically any serious engagement with Theravāda doctrine—are eschewed in the IMS approach. The intention was to leave behind "cultural baggage" in favor of forms of practice understood as the authentic teaching of the Buddha.[69] Goldstein explained: "I'm not so concerned with any labels or the cultural forms of the tradition, although I do appreciate the many ways the dhamma has evolved in Asian cultures. Instead, what inspires me is the connection with the original teachings of the Buddha—with what, as far we know, he actually taught during his lifetime."[70] Above all, meditation was presented (and still is) as the heart of those original teachings.[71] Like Goenka, for these teachers authority comes from practice, and the saṅgha comes to be construed as the community of (mostly lay) meditators.

Around this time, fully fledged Theravāda Buddhism arrived in America. Its first permanent institutional presence came in 1966 with the founding of the Washington Buddhist Vihara in Washington, D.C. The founding of this monastic residence and temple by Sri Lankans was made possible by changes in immigration laws that allowed a large number of Asian immigrants into the country.[72] The ongoing influx of immigrants from Theravāda countries brought in train the establishment of many more temples and monasteries. Typically, immigrant communities and their organizations, however, focused on traditional activities, such as festivals and merit-making, and did not interact with the mostly white practitioners in the insight meditation scene.[73] Up to the present day, though the two groups have cross-fertilized one another as mutual sources of support for itinerant monastics, they have remained largely separate.[74]

The basis of instruction at IMS was the Mahasi method, but with the addition of other teachings, including that of U Ba Khin.[75] In a retrospective look at the experience of setting up IMS, Kornfield wrote:

> When we started IMS, it was primarily a Mahasi-oriented center. I brought in the flavor of Ajahn Chah as well. But because Joseph [Goldstein] and Sharon [Salzberg] had done most of their practice through the Burmese lineages of Mahasi Sayadaw and of U Ba Khin, and we shared this training, this is mainly what we taught. From the very beginning we offered the practices of both Mahasi Sayadaw and U Ba Khin, with Ruth Denison and John Coleman leading retreats. We also asked U Ba Khin's great disciple Goenka if he would come and teach, because Joseph, Sharon, and others were very devoted to him. He responded in a letter saying, "If you open a center and have more than one lineage teaching there, it will be the work of Mara, and it will be the undoing of the dharma." Goenka's teacher U Ba Khin believed this. However, his letter came the day *after* we signed the mortgage—fortunately, it was too late.[76]

The quotation indicates the importance of both the Mahasi and the U Ba Khin lineages to Goldstein, Salzberg, and Kornfield, and through them to subsequent teachers at IMS. This double-pronged influence suggests that the teachings depended upon the Burmese context shaped by Ledi's reformulation of Buddhism. Yet Goenka's disapproval of blending techniques, even if just by having more than one taught in the same place, highlights IMS's innovative qualities. While Kornfield's statement that it was fortunate that Goenka's letter came only after they were committed to running IMS suggests a sense of allegiance to one of their teacher's wishes, ultimately there is clearly a willingness to deviate from them. Kornfield goes on to say: "While we are dedicated to preserving and sustaining the core teachings of our lineage, we are also willing to be innovators, as indicated by our willingness to learn from many lineages."[77] This willingness to draw from many sources has gone beyond the combining of different Theravāda techniques. It has included the use of teachings from

Mahāyāna Buddhism, such as the great perfection (*dzogchen*) teachings of Tibetan Buddhism, and from non-Buddhist traditions, such as Sufism and the non-dualism of Hindu Advaita Vedānta. It should be noted, however, that these teachings are used as instrumental resources for the refinement of practice, not as the basis for extensive philosophical reflection. This eclectic borrowing has been true, too—in fact, is perhaps even more pronounced—at IMS's sister center on the West Coast, the Spirit Rock Meditation Center, which Kornfield helped to found in the mid-1980s.[78]

Within this blending of teachings there remains a focus on practice, framed as a therapeutic tool for one's current life.[79] In the introduction to her recent book *Real Happiness,* Salzberg, after describing a number of Americans trying meditation in order to solve specific psychological problems, says: "As I've learned through my own experience, meditation helps us to find greater tranquility, connect to our feelings, find a sense of wholeness, strengthen our relationships, and face our fears."[80] The stress here—and this quote exemplifies a tendency in all three teachers—is on the psychological health meditation brings to one in the here and now. The appeal of this practical approach fits well with a deeply seated American sensibility that values religious practice as a means to both bodily and mental wellbeing.[81] In affinity with the affective pull toward meditation as a kind of this-worldly self-help, the justification of meditation in terms of psychological benefits makes sense, too, in a context with little traditional doctrinal teaching. In traditional settings, karma justified practice as an escape from the round of rebirth. (Think of Ledi's ruminations on the burden of practice as a way to escape hundreds of thousands of years in hell, noted at the start of the previous chapter.) Without this sense of karmic threat hanging over one's head, the reasons to practice change radically, and pragmatic goals come to the fore.[82]

To be sure, it is not the case that meditation is presented as having this-worldly benefits only in America. Gombrich and Obeyesekere observed in the 1980s that in Sri Lanka many laypeople had come to understand meditation as a tool for success in daily life.[83] And, what is more, teachers in Asia, including U Ba Khin and Goenka, have noted the practical benefits of meditation. Goenka relates how meditation rid him of debilitating migraines, for instance. But Goenka always notes when recounting this fact that U Ba Khin was adamant that he would not teach meditation only for the purpose of healing, and Goenka himself discourages meditation for such an end.[84] Unlike many American teachers, meditation traditions in Asia have not justified practice so emphatically or exclusively in therapeutic terms.

The therapeutic approach to meditation has drawn support from the field of psychology. Kornfield, who has a Ph.D. in psychology and is a practicing therapist, has been an especially strong proponent of the blending of the two: "Of the Western 'inner practices,' the one that is having the most significant impact on Buddhism and on all contemporary spiritual life is the understanding and practice of Western psychology. Many serious students and teachers of the spiritual path in the West have found it necessary or useful to turn to psychotherapy for help in their spiritual life. Many others who have not done so would probably benefit by it."[85]

Kornfield is a prominent voice, but only one among many now seeking to link, if not conflate, the two fields.[86] Indeed, the psychologization of Buddhism has formed an elective affinity, in turn, with the Buddhicization of psychology. At present, a large and growing number of psychologists and therapists, including many without Buddhist allegiances, study and use Buddhist concepts and techniques of mental cultivation. There is a particular emphasis on the practice of mindfulness (sati), understood as a nonjudgmental state of choiceless, present-moment awareness,[87] that has its roots in the Mahasi-inflected lineage of IMS teaching. As noted in the prior chapter, mindfulness in the orthodox Theravāda conception is not conceptualized as merely neutral observation; it includes a governing awareness of Buddhist truths about the nature of the world. Nonetheless, the understanding of mindfulness as just bare awareness has led in recent years to a wealth of psychological studies and secular movements extolling its benefits.[88] Mindfulness has become a separate, healing practice in its own right, rather than one mental factor among others in successful insight practice. This presentation of mindfulness alone as a practical form of therapeutic self-improvement has moved insight practice beyond Buddhism for many. As Kornfield recently said: "More and more, we're teaching meditation not as a religious activity but as a support for living a wise and healthy and compassionate inner life. A number of the people I teach don't consider themselves Buddhists, which is absolutely fine with me."[89]

One of the most influential of the teachers who present mindfulness practice from this secular, psychologized perspective is Jon Kabat-Zinn (born 1944). He forms another step in the lineage we have been tracing, as he has been a student of Kornfield and Goldstein and received instruction from a Western disciple of U Ba Khin, Robert Hover. (He was, as well, a student of the Korean Son master Seung Sahn.) Kabat-Zinn founded the Stress Reduction Clinic at the University of Massachusetts Medical School and has developed a program, called Mindfulness-Based Stress Reduction (MBSR), that aims to teach people to cultivate mindfulness in everyday experience as a means to lower stress. As Kabat-Zinn puts it, the training in the MBSR program is "mostly vipassana practice (in the Theravada sense as taught by people like Joseph [Goldstein] and Jack [Kornfield] etc.) with a Zen attitude."[90] The program involves three formal aspects that combine influences from the U Ba Khin method with Mahasi-style teachings. Participants lie down to "scan" the body from the head to the toes to develop an awareness of the sensations in the body; they meditate on the breath in a seated posture to bring themselves into the present moment through respiration; and they engage in slow movements in yoga-like postures and stretches to strengthen their mindfulness while active.[91] The overall goal is to develop in the participant a mindfulness—what Kabat-Zinn calls "a way of being"—that allows the person to stop the unconscious, prereflective reactions to stimuli that cause stress. This secular form of mental cultivation, rooted in mindfulness for psychological health, demonstrates the complex ways Buddhist influences, including those of Ledi, have promoted developments but certainly not determined them.

Space here precludes a fuller consideration of the nuanced ways the secular and therapeutic uses of meditation reorient practice. It is sufficient for our purposes to see that the psychologization of meditation as a secular technique has led to its use as a tool for self-cultivation and personal flourishing outside Theravāda goals for practice. And it has become very popular. Goldstein's, Kornfield's, and Salzberg's books are spiritual bestsellers. Kabat-Zinn's have been translated into over thirty languages, and he appears frequently in the popular media, such as on the Oprah Winfrey Show, and has received numerous awards. MBSR programs are taught all over the world. More broadly, and thanks in no small part to Kabat-Zinn's influence, mindfulness has come to be applied to a wide variety of circumstances and to address a host of issues. Books and workshops are now available for mindful eating, mindful child-rearing—even mindful sex.[92]

This progression in America has carried insight practice's ethos and worldview very far from a vision of life like Ledi's, in which he would promote meditation by saying, "How very fearful, scary, abhorrent, detestable, and sickening is the state of an ordinary person."[93] Now meditation is meant not as an escape-hatch from rebirth but as a way to make life more enjoyable, richer, more stress-free, even sexier. It is not the case, of course, that meditation practice in the U.S. has developed along only one trajectory. As noted above, Goenka courses are held at centers throughout the country, and many other organizations promote practices in virtually every variety of Buddhism, some highly traditional. But the trend of a secularized and therapeutic form of practice has been particularly influential, and it is valuable to highlight it because of its genealogy that includes, in no small measure, the Burmese Buddhism shaped by Ledi's career. The connections are extremely complex and we certainly would never arrive at a book on mindful sex through Ledi alone. It is a long, long way, in many senses, from Thanjaun to IMS and Spirit Rock. Much of the development in the United States must be credited to American culture's emphasis on well-being, a Romantic impulse toward mystical experience, and a psychological approach to meditative practice. Nonetheless, the links from Ledi to Thetgyi to U Ba Khin to Goenka, along with Ledi's formative influence on the context in which Mingun and Mahasi operated, led to the training of Goldstein, Kornfield, and Salzberg and, subsequently, the teaching of Kabat-Zinn. This was not a predetermined course by any means. Full of uncertainty and the agency of teachers along the way, I have not followed all the paths that have led to one predominant "life" of insight practice in the United States.[94] But Ledi's career was a critical starting point that set a path of development that made this situation possible.

During a 1997 presentation on the "mainstreaming" of meditation in American society, Kabat-Zinn showed a slide of a Buddha statue and made the following comment about it:

> This comes out of the Buddhist tradition, but people might be interested to know that in some fundamental way, this statue or other artistic representations of a similar kind, don't actually represent the deity, although in some traditions they're spoken of that way. But the fundamental representation here is of a state of mind, and that state of mind is best characterized by this word: *awake*. All of a sudden everybody goes, "Oh, I didn't know that. Well that makes sense," and there's no more barrier.[95]

The barrier Kabat-Zinn refers to here is to an understanding of the true significance of a Buddha image by those unfamiliar with Buddhism and meditation. In order to make the image meaningful, he denies its material reality in favor of what he sees lying behind it. He makes the statue, so to speak, disappear, replaced by a psychological state of awareness to which it purportedly refers. There is no doubt that a Buddha image conveys the sense of someone who has woken up to reality. But the tangible facticity of the statue at the Botataung, which began this chapter, does not represent just a state of mind. Knowing what we know now, after an examination of Ledi's role in the development of mass meditation, the Botataung Buddha cannot be so easily dismissed. He has, after all, words emblazoned on his very palms, forcing one to acknowledge a message far more complex and culturally rooted than Kabat-Zinn's use of the word "awake" can express.

Kabat-Zinn's Buddha and the *Athi-Thati* at the Botataung are both, however, the result of complex path dependencies that owe much to Ledi. Ending this book about his transformative effects on Buddhism with a consideration of his influence beyond Burma shows that the ongoing development of modern forms of Buddhism and meditative practice depend on the past, even as people's improvisations create radically new forms. This calls our attention to the irremediable tension between past and present in which all modern people find themselves. Such a fruitful tension would shape Ledi's efforts and those after him. It led to a Buddha who holds up his hands to give equal weight to knowledge and insight practice for all, and yet also to a conception of practice in which the Buddha seems to disappear altogether.

Glossary

(P) indicates Pali terms, and (B) indicates Burmese terms. The transliterations of Burmese terms appear in brackets.

Abhidhamma (P)—Higher *dhamma*, meaning the seven books in the third basket (*piṭaka*) of canonical literature, the Abhidhamma Piṭaka, and, by extension, the system of thought that develops from the canonical texts and later Abhidhamma literature, which seeks to describe reality in ultimate terms.

Abhidhammapariyāya (P)—Literally, "with an Abhidhamma perspective," meaning to approach matters from the ultimate perspective of the basic and real, though ephemeral, constituents of existence.

Abhisamācārika (P)—That of praiseworthy conduct, meaning moral actions that go beyond basic morality defined as "the fundamentals of good conduct" (see definition of *ādibrahmacariya* below).

Acinteyyāni (P)—The unthinkables, meaning those issues which are fruitless to ponder. They are the extent of the powers of a Buddha (*buddhavisaya*), the extent of the powers of one in the meditative absorptions (*jhānavisaya*), the possible results of karma (*kammavipāka*), and the nature of the world (*lokacintā*), especially its beginning.

Adhicitta (P)—Higher consciousness, meaning states of absorption in *jhāna* that depend on the basis of higher virtue (*adhisīla*).

Adhipaññā (P)—Higher wisdom, meaning liberative insight that depends on higher virtue and consciousness.

Adhisīla (P)—Higher virtue, meaning virtuous action that forms the basis of higher consciousness and wisdom.

Ādibrahmacariya (P)—The fundamentals of good conduct, defined in the *Visuddhimagga* as eight actions: those of the body (not killing, stealing, or engaging in sexual misconduct), those of speech (refraining from lying, malicious speech, harsh speech, and gossip), and a proper livelihood that does not require immoral actions of body or speech.

Aggamahāpaṇḍita (P)—Award conferred by the British on a learned monk. The title means "the foremost great learned one."

Anāgāmī (P)—A non-returner, the third of four levels of attainment of awakening. A "non-returner" is so-called because he or she will be reborn only in a heavenly realm before achieving awakening.

Ānāpāna (P)—Inhalation and exhalation of the breath.

Ānāpānasati (P)—Insight meditation using mindfulness of the inhalation and exhalation of the breath.

Anattā (P)—No-self, one of the three marks of existence.

Anicca (P)—Impermanence, one of the three marks of existence.

Anna (B)—Unit of currency in colonial Burma. Sixteen *annas* equal one rupee.

Apāyabhūmi (P)—The woeful plane, one of four possible planes of existence. This plane includes hell, the animal realm, the realm of hungry ghosts (*peta*), and the realm of the "titans" (*asuras*).

Āpo (P)—The element of water, one of the four principle elements (see *mahābhūtāni* below) that make up all physical matter.

Araññavāsī (P)—A forest-dwelling monk.

Athi [*a si*] (B)—Knowledge, perception, or knowing.

Attadiṭṭhi (P)—The view that one possesses an essential self.

Atthuppatti (B)—Biography.

Ayakauk [*a ra kok'*] (B)—Burmese-language primers on Abhidhamma doctrine.

Batha (B) [*bhā sā*]—Religion, but the word can also mean language, a topic of study, or custom.

Bhāvanā (P)—Cultivation or development, mental or spiritual. It is the general term for meditation.

Bhikkhu (P)—A Buddhist monk.

Bhūmi (P)—A plane of existence in Buddhist cosmology.

Bhūmicatukka (P)—The four planes of existence in which rebirth is possible. One can be reborn in the woeful plane (*apāyabhūmi*), the sensuous blissful plane (*kāmasugatibhūmi*), the fine-material-sphere plane (*rūpāvacarabhūmi*), or the immaterial-sphere plane (*arūpāvacarabhūmi*).

Bodhipakkhiyadhammas (P)—The thirty-seven factors of awakening.

Brahmacariya (P)—Moral conduct.

Buddhavacana (P)—The word of the Buddha.

Cakkhu (P)—Eye.

Cetasikas (P)—Mental factors; there are fifty-two that combine with consciousness and physical matter in the Abhidhamma system to make up all experience.

Citta (P)—Consciousness, either as a bare state of cognizance or as a more complex mental state of knowing combined with mental factors.

Cittakkhaṇa (P)—A moment of consciousness.

Cittavīthi (P)—The process of consciousness.

Dāna (P)—Generosity, particularly in giving to the *saṅgha*.

Dhamma (P)—The nature of reality or the Buddhist teachings; also, a mental or physical phenomenon.

Dhammadesanā (P)—A teaching on the *dhamma*.

Dhammarāja (P)—A righteous king who rules by and in support of the *dhamma*.

Dhātu (P)—An element; the four primary physical elements are earth (*paṭhavī*), water (*āpo*), fire (*tejo*), and wind (*vāyo*). The term can also refer to a realm of existence in Buddhist cosmology.

Dhutaṅga (P)—Optional ascetic practices that a monk can undertake for set periods of time.

Dīpanī (P)—A manual or handbook that explains some matter of Buddhist doctrine or practice.

Dosa (P)—Hatred or anger.

Dukkha (P)—The suffering or unsatifactoriness that marks all existence.

Dussana (P)—Hostility.

Gaing-dauks [*guiṇ‘" thauk‘*] (B)—Monk-officials who administered sub-districts as part of the royal ecclesiastical hierarchy.

Gaing-oks [*guiṇ‘" up‘*] (B)—Monk-officials who administered districts as part of the royal ecclesiastical hierarchy.

Gāmavāsī (P)—A town-dwelling monk.

Ganthadhura (P)—The burden of books. A term used to describe a monk's focus on the study of the dhamma as his main avocation.

Hetu (P)—Root, meaning in the Abhidhamma system either a wholesome or unwholesome condition that leads to conditioned states.

Hti [*thi*] (B)—The finial placed on a *stūpa*.

Jambūdīpa (P)—The island of the rose-apple tree; this is the land in Buddhist cosmology where human beings live.

Jhāna (P)—Deep absorptive states achieved through calming (*samatha*) meditation.

Kalāpa (P)—A corporeal unit of matter in the Abhidhamma system, often equated to a subatomic particle in contemporary literature, that is primarily comprised of the four primary elements (*dhātus*).

Kāmadhātu (P)—The sense-sphere realm in Buddhist cosmology that contains both the woeful planes of existence (*apāyabhūmi*) and the blissful planes of existence (*kāmasugatibhūmi*).

Kāmasugatibhūmi (P)—The blissful planes of existence, comprising seven realms, the human realm and six realms of gods.

Kamma (P)—Meritorious and demoritorious actions of body, speech, and mind that lead to good and bad effects in one's current life or in future lives.

Kamma vā (B)—The Burmese word for the Pali *kammavācā*; texts used for recitation in official acts of the *saṅgha*.

Kammaṭṭhāna (P)—An object upon which one focuses in meditation.

Kammavācā (P)—Texts used for recitation in official acts of the *saṅgha*.

Kasiṇa (P)—An object used for meditation, particularly circular disks of colored earth used to develop the meditator's concentration.

Kāyagatāsati (P)—Mindfulness of the body, a common focus in the practice of insight meditation (*vipassanā*).

Khaṇa (P)—A moment in time in the Abhidhamma system.

Khaṇikasamādhi (P)—Momentary concentration, a relatively low level of concentration prior to access concentration (*upacārasamādhi*) or full absorption (*jhāna*), in which the object of meditation is kept in mind moment by moment, but one is not absorbed in it.

Konbaung (B)—The dynasty of kings that ruled all or parts of Burma from 1752–1885.

Kriyā (or *Kiriya*) (P)—Functional, referring to forms of consciousness that are neither the result of wholesome or unwholesome consciousnesses.

Kui raṅ‘ (B)—A novice monk, called in Pali a *sāmaṇera.*

Kusala (P)—Wholesome, meritious action.

Kyaṅ‘ vat‘ (B)—Rules of conduct in the monastic code of the Vinaya.

Lak‘ san‘" (B)—"Finger manuals," meaning synoptic handbooks on the Abhidhamma; there are nine in the Burmese classification.

Lobha (P)—Greed.

Maggañāṇa (P)—Knowledge of the path, a transcendent moment of insight in meditation when all the thirty-seven factors of the path are fully realized in a moment of awakening.

Mahābhūtāni (P)—The four great essentials, meaning the elements (*dhātus*) of earth (*paṭhavī*), water (*āpo*), fire (*tejo*), and wind (*vāyo*).

Mahadansaye [*mahā dān‘ cā re"*] (B)—The clerk of religious affairs, who, under the *mahadanwun,* the officer of religious affairs, supervised monastic behavior in the royal capital of Mandalay.

Mahadanwun [*mahā dān‘ wan‘*] (B)—The officer of religious affairs, who, assisted by the clerk of religious affairs (*mahadansaye*), supervised monastic behavior in the royal capital of Mandalay.

Mahāthera (P)—A great elder, a respected older monk.

Majjhimadesa (P)—The middle land, meaning the country of central India.

Māra (P)—The personification of all desire; the one who tempts the Buddha as he pursues awakening under the Bodhi tree.

Māyākāra (P)—A magician.

Micchādiṭṭhi (P)—A wrong view, meaning one not in accord with the *dhamma.*

Moha (P)—Delusion.

Muddā (P)—A stylized hand gesture by a Buddha that conveys a message.

Nāma (P)—Literally, name, meaning mind or mentality.

Nats (B)—Spirits, both malevolent and beneficent, in Burmese Buddhist cosmology.

Nibbāna (P)—Awakening or enlightenment.

Nikāya (P)—A group of collection, either of suttas in the canon or of monks in lineal affiliation.

Nimitta (P)—An image or sign developed in the cultivation of concentration (*samādhi*) in meditation.

Nippariyāyadhammadesanā (P)—"A literal or unembellished discourse on the dhamma," meaning speaking in ultimate terms, as in the Abhidhamma.

Nirutti (P)—Etymological analysis.

Nissaya (P)—Burmese texts that translate and explain Pali works, often on a systematic word-by-word basis.

Nuiṅ' ṅaṃ (B)—Land, territory, or country.

Paccaya (P)—Condition; in the Abhidhamma system it refers to the twenty-four conditional relations that give rise to all mental and physical phenomena.

Paññā (P)—Wisdom or understanding of the dhamma.

Pārājika (P)—Refers to a person who has broken one of the first four rules of the *pātimokkha* of the Vinaya: no sex, no stealing, no killing, and no false claiming of spiritual attainments. The transgression of these four rules entails automatic expulsion from the *saṅgha*.

Paramattha (P)—The ultimate, meaning that which is truly real.

Pāramī (P)—A perfection; there are ten, which must be fulfilled for awakening.

Pariññā (P)—Profound or full knowledge. There are three levels of such knowledge: *ñāta-pariññā* or "realized profound knowledge," *tīraṇa-pariññā* or "the profound knowledge of analysis," and *pahāna-pariññā* or "the profound knowledge of dispelling."

Paritta (P)—A sutta for chanting for the purpose of protection.

Pariyatti (P)—The study of Buddhist texts and teachings.

Pasādarūpa (P)—Sensitive matter that forms the bases for sense consciousnesses.

Pathama cā khya (B)—"First teacher," a title conferred upon a monk in recognition of his skill in instruction.

Paṭiccasamuppāda (P)—The doctrine of the dependent origination of all things through a twelve-fold series of events.

Pātimokkha (P)—The 227 monastic rules contained within the Vinaya.

Paṭipatti (P)—The practice of the Buddhist teachings, including meditation.

Paṭisandhicatukka (P)—The set of four types of consciousness (*citta*) that lead to rebirth in the four planes of existence.

Paṭivedha (P)—Realization of the Buddhist teachings.

Paṭṭhāna (P)—The twenty-four conditional relations which lead to the arising of all mental and physical phenomena.

Phalañāṇa (P)—Knowledge of the fruit, a moment of dwelling in a transcendent *jhānic* state, following the full realization of the thirty-seven factors of the path in meditation.

Piṭaka (P)—Literally, basket, meaning one of the three collections within the canon.

Pongyi [*bhun'" krī"*] (B)—A monk.

Puñña (P)—Merit, meaning good *kamma* gained from wholesome deeds.

Puññakhetta (P)—Field of merit, referring to a person, most often a monk, who is a source of good *kamma* as the recipient of generosity or other good deeds.

Pya (B)—A Burmese unit of currency.

Rajjana (P)—Attachment.

Rūpa (P)—Form, meaning physicality or materiality.

Rūpakāya (P)—A relic of the Buddha.

Rupee (B)—A unit of currency; one rupee equals sixteen *annas*.

Sa zo [*cā chui*] (B)—The title of the head monastic student in a monastery who instructs his fellow students.

Sabhāva (P)—Possessing one's own nature, meaning an object that does not depend on something else for its origination.

Saṃ khip' (B)—A term cognate to the Pali *saṅkhepa,* meaning gist, condensed version, or summary.

Saṃ pok' (B)—Texts that render complex terms and concepts in single syllables to serve as mnemonic devices.

Samādhi (P)—Concentration of the mind.

Sāmaṇera (P)—A novice monk, who follows ten rules of behavior instead of the full 227; called in Burmese a *koyin* [*kui raṅ'*].

Samatha (P)—Calming meditation that aims at concentration (*samādhi*); usually yoked as a pair with insight meditation (*vipassanā*).

Samathayāna (P)—The vehicle of calming meditation, meaning the use of calming meditation to carry the meditator far on the path to awakening.

Sammuti (P)—That which is conventional, referring to conventional truth, the everyday perception of reality, versus perception of the truly real, ultimate (*paramattha*) reality.

Saṃsāra (P)—The round of rebirth, driven on by *kamma*.

Saṅgāyanā (P)—A general convocation of the *saṅgha* of monks in which the Buddhist canon is recited.

Saṅgha (P)—The community of ordained monks and nuns.

Saṅgīti (P)—A general convocation of the *saṅgha* of monks in which the Buddhist canon is recited.

Sāsana (P)—The complex of Buddhist teachings and institutions started by the Buddha.

Sati (P)—Mindfulness, a key component of insight practice (*vipassanā*).

Satipaṭṭhāna (P)—The four establishings or bases of mindfulness used in insight meditation. These are body (*kāya*), feeling (*vedanā*), consciousness (*citta*), and aspects of the path (*dhammā*).

Sayadaw (B)—A term of respect for accomplished monks, meaning literally "royal teacher." As this literal translation indicates, originally it was a title reserved for monastic teachers of the king, but the term came to be given to any monk held in high esteem.

Sikkhā (P)—Training, meaning the three trainings in "higher virtue" (*adhisīla*), "higher consciousness" (*adhicitta*), and "higher wisdom" (*adhipaññā*).

Sīla (P)—Virtuous behavior, ethics, morality, or good conduct.

Sotāpanna (P)—A stream-enterer, one who has attained the first of the four levels of attainment of awakening.

Stūpa (Sanskrit)—A conical or mound-like shrine that houses relics of the Buddha.

Suddhavipassanā (P)—Mere insight meditation, meaning meditative practice aiming at insight that is not based on prior calming (*samatha*) practice.

Sukkhavipassaka (P)—One of dry insight, meaning a meditator who practices insight meditation without first developing concentration through calming meditation (*samatha*).

Sutta (P)—A discourse of the Buddha given in everyday language.

Tejo (P)—Fire, one of the four elements (*dhātus*).

Thathanabaing (B)—The leader of the saṅgha in Burma, appointed by the king, except for the final incumbent, who was picked by an assembly of monks in 1903.

Theravāda (P)—The way of the elders, used to refer to the Pali-text-based Buddhism of South and Southeast Asia, though the term came into common usage only in the twentieth century.

Thudhamma (B)—A *nikāya* or group of monks who gained control of the Burmese *saṅgha* under King Bodawpaya (1782–1819) and were the only significant lineal grouping of monks in Burma until King Mindon's reign (1853–78).

Ṭīkā (P)—A subcommentary.

Ṭīkā maw [*ṭīkā mau*] (B)—"The subcommentary that surpasses," referring to Ledi Sayadaw's *Paramatthadīpanī* as surpassing the subcommentary entitled the *Abhidhammatthavibhāvinī*.

Ṭīkā jaw [*ṭīkā kyau*] (B)—"The famous subcommentary," referring to the *Abhidhammatthavibhāvinī*.

Tilakkhaṇa (P)—The three marks, referring to the three fundamental qualities of all existence as impermanent (*anicca*), suffering-filled (*dukkha*), and essenceless (*anattā*).

Tipiṭaka (P)—The three baskets, meaning the three-fold division of the Buddhist canon into the collection of sermons (Sutta Piṭaka), the monastic discipline (Vinaya Piṭaka), and the philosophical works of the Abhidhamma Piṭaka.

Uddhacca (P)—Restlessness.

Upacārasamādhi (P)—Access concentration, the state of a calm and collected mind just on the threshold of absorption (*jhāna*).

Upādāyarūpa (P)—Derived materiality, meaning all material substance that originates in dependence on the four great essentials (*mahābhūtāni*).

Upāsaka/upāsikā (P)—A male/female lay follower of Buddhism.

Upasampadā (P)—Ordination as a full Buddhist monk.

Upekkha (P)—Equinimity.

Uposatha (P)—The days of the new and full moon when monks gather to recite the communal rules (*pātimokkha*) of the saṅgha, and lay people often visit temples and monasteries for merit making, socializing, and other religious activities.

Vā (B)—The period of the rains retreat, when monks settle in a residence and devote themselves more rigorously to study and meditation; equivalent to Pali *vassa*.

Vassa (P)—The period of the rains retreat, when monks settle in a residence and devote themselves more rigorously to study and meditation.

Vāyo (P)—Wind, one of the four elements (*dhātus*).

Vedanā (P)—Feeling or sensation.

Vicikicchā (P)—Doubt.

Vinaya (P)—The monastic discipline, one of the three baskets (*piṭaka*) of the Pali canon.

Vipāka (P)—Result or resultant, used in the Abhidhamma system to refer to a category of consciousness (*citta*) that is the result of other wholesome or unwholesome consciousnesses.

Vipallāsa (P)—Distorted or corrupted view, in the sense of being distorted or corrupted by greed, hatred, and delusion.

Vipassanā (P)—Insight meditation, the meditative process of observing a chosen object to understand its and, by extension, all objects' impermanent, suffering-filled, and essenceless natures.

Vipassanādhura (P)—The burden of insight practice. A term used to describe a monk's focus on the practice of insight meditation as his main avocation.

Vipassanāyāna (P)—The vehicle of insight, meaning the meditative process in which one practices insight meditation without first developing concentration through calming meditation (*samatha*).

Visuddhi (P)—Purification, used to refer to the seven purifications in the process of awakening.

Yakkha/yakkhinī (P)—A demon/demoness.

Yap' hlai (B)—"Fan down," referring to a style of preaching in which the monk does not cover his face with a fan while preaching, in order to engage the audience directly.

Yap' toṅ' (B)—"Fan up," referring to a style of preaching in which a monk covers his face with a fan while he preaches, in order to minimize any personal rapport with the audience.

Yogi (P)—A meditator.

Yojana (P)—A measurement of distance, reckoned to be about seven miles.

Notes

INTRODUCTION

1. Horner 1962, 5–6; Jayawickrama 2000, 108; see also Malalasekera 1997, 2:991.
2. Stadtner 2011, esp. 74–76; Pe Maung Tin 1934; and Moore, Mayer, and Win Pe 1999, esp. 101–54; Edwards 2006. The Shwedagon is also often called a *stūpa* in English, using the common Sanskrit term, or in Burmese a *paya* (*bhu rā"*). It is a conical or mound-like monument that houses relics or objects of remembrance of the Buddha.
3. Scholars have noted the recent provenance of "Theravāda" as a general term for the Buddhism of Southeast Asia, probably gaining predominance around the middle of the twentieth century (Skilling 2009a). I use the label, on occasion, to refer to a distinguishable form of Buddhism. To do otherwise would create confusion, as it is now a common and indigenous term. What is at stake is not so much a historical issue, that is, using a term that is historically more accurate, but, rather, the proper conceptual use of terms that avoids a reification that implies the Buddhisms of Southeast Asia are unchanging. My use of Theravāda is always circumscribed within discussions that highlight the historical contingency of the form it denotes.
4. See, for example, Bechert 1988, 1:50; Winston L. King 1980, 120–23; Carrithers 1983, 223; Bond 1988, 149–51; Gombrich and Obeyesekere 1988, 238; Holt 1991a; Houtman 1990a, esp. part 1; 1999, 8, 203; Sharf 1995, 253; 1998, 105; Cousins 1996, esp. 41; Lopez 2002, xxviii–xxix; and Jordt 2007, 20–23. For the Tibetan case, see Dreyfus 2003, 168–69.
5. There was no line to South America. This is odd, since the map depicts centers in the Goenka tradition, and, in fact, the Goenka organization lists on its website three permanent meditation centers in South America (in Peru, Venezuela, and Brazil), as well as a schedule for many courses at temporary

sites throughout the continent. See http://www.dhamma.org/en/worldmap.html (accessed June 28, 2010).

6. Stewart 1949, 15.
7. The Buddhist canon is called the "three baskets" (*tipiṭaka*), because it is divided into three collections. The first is the Vinaya Piṭaka, the rules and regulations of monks and nuns; the second is the Sutta Piṭaka, the sermons of the Buddha given in discourses; and the third is the Abhidhamma Piṭaka, the exposition and analysis of reality, given in technical language that refers only to what is considered ultimately real. More on the nature and composition of the Abhidhamma is given in chapter 2.
8. Long before colonial incursions, the Burmese had divided the land mass roughly comprising the area of modern Myanmar into two halves, Upper and Lower Burma. This division reflected political configurations, because separate kingdoms had arisen in the two areas and people in the different parts had often fought with one another. These political configurations also mapped roughly onto ethnic divisions (between Mons in the south and ethnic Burmese in the north) and geographic differences (with much less rainfall, for instance, in Upper Burma versus Lower). This split of the country in the Burmese consciousness was supported by the colonial takeover, which gained control over the country in a piecemeal fashion that followed the same division (first Lower Burma was taken, in two steps, then Upper Burma in one fell swoop). Additionally, the subsequent colonial partition of the country into districts and parts also reflected the bipartite split. See Schober 2011, 160 n.7; Lieberman 2003, 23–25, 85.
9. For a snapshot of the effects of colonial rule, see Charney 2009, 5–13.
10. Cousins 1996, 41; see also Gethin 1998, 179.
11. For a clear expression of the orthodox view of the relation of samatha to vipassanā, in which vipassanā follows the attainment of a certain level of calm, see Winston L. King 1980 and Nyanaponika 1996. Some scholars have questioned the commonly held view. Bronkhorst (1986) has argued that samatha practices may indeed have been the distinctive contribution of the Buddha, and Cousins (1984) has pointed out the possibility presented in the texts for samatha to lead one very close to awakening, rather than being simply a preparatory exercise. For more information on the details of meditation as depicted in the canonical and paracanonical sources, see Cousins 1973, 1996; Griffiths 1981; Schmithausen 1981; Anālayo 2003.
12. The *Visuddhimagga* is a formative work in Theravāda Buddhism, one that provides a coordinative vision of the doctrinal tradition as a whole, but with a perspective rooted in the philosophical works of the third part of the Buddhist canon, the Abhidhamma. As Buddhaghosa states in the prologue to his commentaries on the four *nikāya*s or collections of Buddhist scripture: "The *Visuddhimagga* stands between and in the midst of all four collections (Nikāyas) and will clarify the meaning of such things stated therein" (quoted in Ñāṇamoli 1999, xxxiv). Structured according to the three-fold division

of morality (*sīla*), concentration (samādhi) and wisdom (*paññā*), as well as the seven purifications that culminate in awakening, the work also serves as a detailed exegetical manual of meditation theory. Its enduring influence and the detail in its analysis of meditation means we will return often to its teachings in the pages that follow.

13. For instance, Francois Bizot has shown that an esoteric (sometimes called "tantric") tradition of meditation existed in Southeast Asia well before recent times, though never as a large-scale movement. See *Le Figuier à Cinq Branches* (1976). See Crosby 2000 for an assessment of Bizot's works, as well as Cousins 1997. I note other indications of the practice of meditation prior to the modern era in Burma, Thailand, and Sri Lanka in subsequent chapters.
14. In the *Visuddhimagga* Buddhaghosa allows for the possibility of divergences in how meditators pursue the path to liberation (see, for instance, Vism. XVIII 3–5; Ñāṇamoli 1999, 605–6), but he assumes as normative the cultivation of deep calm first, and only afterwards insight. See also Winston L. King 1980, 116. Chapter 5 has a detailed discussion of this issue.
15. Ledi 1915, 64.
16. These lineages see themselves as going back to the Buddha but explain that the vagaries of history have washed away the names of the teachers prior to Ledi. Goenka, whose family is of Indian extraction and Hindu, was born in Burma and learned meditation in Yangon. In the early 1960s, he moved to India and set up his headquarters near Mumbai. Goenka and earlier teachers in his lineage are discussed further in the conclusion.
17. Goenka 1998, 101. I have not been able to locate a source where Ledi says this.
18. The sutta is located at DN 22. I take the translation of *satipaṭṭhāna* as "establishing of mindfulness" from Anālayo 2003, 29–30; see also Gethin 2001, 30.
19. Nyanaponika 1996, 85–86; see also Maung Maung 1980, 113–14.
20. There are, however, important exceptions to this historiographical situation. Htin Aung (1966) offers valuable information on the turn to meditation in the latter half of the nineteenth century, though his examination is very brief. E. Michael Mendelson's *Sangha and State* (1975) offers much useful information, but his work focuses on meditation only as it touches upon matters of sectarian division, politics, and nationalism. Winston L. King (1980, 116–44), in his study largely dedicated to an ahistorical structural analysis of meditation, does briefly discuss developments in meditation as a social phenomenon in Burma with reference to Ledi. Maung Maung (1980, esp. chapter 8), though focused on politics and nationalism, offers valuable details on meditation teachers in the 1930s. Gustaaf Houtman's groundbreaking thesis and his subsequent book (1990a, 1997) on meditation and modern politics in Burma, among other works by him, offer the most detailed views of meditation's development in Burma from the nineteenth century. He does discuss at some length the contributions of Ledi, and, as will become evident, his work is an important resource for my project. But he orients his work toward laying the

groundwork for his anthropological research and thus its goal carries it away from a focus on what Ledi's written output reveals about insight meditation's origins or its relationship with the Burmese Buddhist doctrinal tradition.

21. Marx put the idea of tradition's effects in gripping if gloomy language: "Men make their own history, but they do not make it as they please; they do not make it under self-selected circumstances, but under circumstances existing already, given and transmitted from the past. The tradition of all dead generations weighs like a nightmare on the brains of the living" (Marx 2008 [1852], 15).
22. Chakrabarty 2002, esp. xx.
23. Some people look particularly to acultural factors, such the growth of capitalism, technological developments (e.g., steamships and printing presses), and rationalized bureaucratic structures. Others focus on cultural factors, including a sense of self-conscious reflexivity, of a disjuncture between the present and the past, and of disenchantment and demystification. These sets of factors are not necessarily mutually exclusive, of course, and are often combined in complex ways. See Ivy 2005; Tanabe and Keyes 2002, introduction; Kaviraj 2005; Blackburn 2010, esp. 211. For studies of colonialism's effects in Burma, see Schober 2006 and 2011; Turner 2009; and Ikeya 2011.
24. The term *premodern* can mask the significance of the past by lumping together and homogenizing forms of Buddhism with different characters, histories, and trajectories all under one label. Kaviraj notes the term can denote the initial conditions out of which modernity arises, or it can describe the situation which modernity replaces (Kaviraj 2005, 515–16).
25. Hla Pain 1967, 456; see also Aung Mon 2007, 702–4. Aung Mon bases much of his presentation of Wunnita's life on Hla Pain.
26. Wunnita, whose lay name was Hla Tin, sold traditional Burmese medicine in the town of Thaton for his livelihood. No details for his death are given in the *Ledi Lineage* because at the time it was written in 1967 he was still alive (Hla Pain 1967, 467).
27. Hla Pain 1967, 458.
28. See Hla Pain 1967, *ṇa*. I should note that here "*ṇa*" indicates a page number. While Western books often use roman numerals for introductory material, Burmese use the letters of the Burmese alphabet.
29. In the preface, the author has "Ledi" prefaced to his name, "Ledi U Hla Pain," indicating his allegiance to the lineage of Ledi. The *Ledi Lineage* mentions that he was active in Buddhist matters in Sagaing (Hla Pain 1967, *ṭha*).
30. U Aung Mon was kind enough to invite into me his home to discuss Ledi's life when I was in Yangon in 2005.
31. I use the title "Ledi Sayadaw" to avoid confusion, but, in fact, it is anachronistic, because it is a title Ledi achieved later in his life, in the 1880s. Like many august monks, the first part of his title derives from the place with which he is associated—in Ledi's case, the "Ledi forest" near Monywa. The second word in his title is a term of respect for accomplished monks, mean-

ing literally "royal teacher." As this literal translation indicates, originally, "sayadaw" (*cha rā to*) was a title reserved for monastic teachers of the king, but the term came to be given to any monk held in high esteem.

32. Wunnita 1956, 6.
33. Burmese writers have produced numerous biographies of the Buddha. For a list of major biographies, see Houtman 1990a, 294. There are also numerous translations and rewritings of the Jātakas, the stories of the Buddha's previous lives. Depictions of the Jātakas can be seen in the wall murals of the temples in Pagan, dating from the early eleventh century (Houtman 1990a, 293–94).
34. See Reynolds 1976 for an overview of biography in the Theravāda tradition. Also see Tambiah 1984, 81–153.
35. Houtman 1997, 311.
36. Houtman has noted this in his study of the Burmese biography of a meditation teacher in the lineage of Ledi, U Ba Khin. The blurring between history and biography leads in U Ba Khin's 614-page biography to only 27 pages being actually devoted to U Ba Khin's life. The rest concerns his lineage. Houtman (1997, 312) argues that this proportion of pages reflects an understanding of the "insubstantiability" of any one individual in light of the concept of no-self and a desire to show that U Ba Khin cannot be restricted to one particular life.
37. This controversy is explored in chapter 2.
38. Reynolds 1976, 5, quoted in Houtman 1997, 320.
39. Houtman 1990a, 204.
40. His name could be translated "one who ascends to the top."
41. Wunnita 1956, 7–8.
42. Ibid., 4.
43. Ibid., 9.
44. For descriptions of the education of young boys in village Burma, see J. G. Scott 1963, 14–20; Mendelson 1975, 150–57; and Mi Mi Khaing 1962, 75–78.
45. Wunnita 1956, 9–10.
46. A more detailed explication of the texts studied in Burmese monastic education will be given in chapter 2.
47. Wunnita 1956, 10.
48. Ibid., 10; see also Hla Pain 1967, 32–35.
49. Charney 2006.
50. Wunnita 1956, 17–18.
51. Cady 1958, 88–89.

CHAPTER ONE

1. Ledi had actually arrived in Mandalay in July 1867. He stayed in the Thit-sein (Sac' chim'') Monastery while preparing to win a place in Thanjaun (Aung Mon 2007, 120).

2. Wunnita 1956, 18.
3. *Ratanā puṃ man ta le"* (Chit San Win 2003, 31–33). Perhaps it was especially dazzling because Mandalay was a fairly new city, founded only twelve years earlier in 1857 (Cady 1958, 24).
4. Aung Mon 2007, 118–19; Wunnita 1956, 20.
5. Chit San Win 2003, 32.
6. Pranke 2004, 4.
7. For the initial arguments for textual superiority on the part of Thudhamma monks, see Charney 2006, 39–47. See also Ferguson 1975, 196–200. The name Thudhamma comes from the "Thudhamma pavilion" used to re-ordain monks into this lineage. The pavilion took the name "Thudhamma" as a reference in the Burmese Buddhist tradition to such a structure believed to exist in the Tāvatiṃsa heaven (Pranke 2004, 1).
8. Pranke 2004, 2.
9. The importance of literati control over texts is a central argument of Charney 2006. This emphasis on texts—their memorization, recitation, translation, and exegesis—fits within a larger trend in the Theravāda world. Anne Blackburn notes the importance of textual command in her studies of the rise of the Siyam Nikāya in Lanka (2001; 2003).
10. Bodawpaya's ruling on this matter was not the first to be made by a Burmese king. Alaungpaya (ruled 1752–60) took the side of the one-shoulder faction, while the king Singu (ruled 1776–82) favored the two-shoulder monks (Pranke 2004, 3).
11. Ibid., 9–10; Charney 2006, 100–101. A well-developed system of village monasteries was long in place by Ledi's time (Lieberman 2003, 188).
12. Charney 2006, 50–58.
13. Ibid., 15. Alexey Kirichenko has called into question Charney's argument for the Lower Chindwin as a region with a distinctive community of monks seeking to win favor at the court. Kirichenko (2011, 14) argues that the Chindwin area contained competing groups within it and that the formation of monastic factions in networks took place thanks not only to a process of integration and centralization, but also due to a tension in which the court sought to keep the countryside subordinate and at some distance.
14. Charney 2006, 28–34.
15. Ibid., 28; Blackburn 2003, 136; and Tambiah 1984, 53–77.
16. Hla Pain 1967, 55.
17. Aung Mun 2007, 118.
18. Ibid., 131–33; Ferguson 1975, 230–31; Houtman 1990a, 273.
19. Aung Mon 2007, 122. It is not clear how many monks resided at Thanjaun, but Myo Myint (1987, 162) estimates that there were ten thousand monks in Mandalay at this time. See also Kirichenko 2011, 14.
20. Wunnita 1956, 23.
21. Ibid., 20.
22. Hla Pain 1967, 55. See also Aung Mon 2007, 138–39.

23. Dhammasami 2004, 51.
24. He had come to power in 1853 at the age of thirty-nine as the result of a coup against his brother, King Pagan, a deeply unpopular ruler in the latter part of his reign, thanks to the Second Anglo-Burmese War then being waged against the British. Unlike Pagan, Mindon had a more realistic view of the superior military capabilities of the British compared to the Burmese, and he was eager to end the war with the loss of the lower half of the country (Myint-U 2001, 104–5; see also Myo Myint 1987, 22–72).
25. Myint-U 2001, 106; Myo Myint 1987, 160–61; and Charney 2006, 201–2.
26. Ferguson 1975, 235.
27. Myint-U (2001, 149) notes that royal records indicate Mindon presided over at least one religious ceremony a month, besides sponsoring and attending many more.
28. Cady 1958, 8. To underline the fundamental nature of this aspect of the king's rule, Smith (1965, 21) notes that in the coronation ceremony for the king the litmus test for his qualification to rule was the question asking him whether he would protect Buddhism. Even recent regimes have partaken of this sense of obligation to protect Buddhism. The 1961 constitution of Burma obligates the government to protect the marble slabs on which the Buddhist canon is inscribed at the Kuthodaw Stūpa in Mandalay (Stadtner 2011, 297). The incising of the canon, which was done under Mindon's direction, is discussed below.
29. Myo Myint 1987, 88.
30. Charney 2006, 217; Ferguson 1975, 236.
31. Myo Myint 1987, 184.
32. Lieberman 2003, 191.
33. Myo Myint 1987, 169–70; Charney 2006, 208–9. Mindon's thathanabaing followed up the king's edict with further orders in March of the same year, 1856, forbidding monks to eat elephant and horse meat, among other things, and directing monastic officials in the capital to report monks committing any prohibited activity (Charney 2006, 208–9). Mindon would issue further orders to shore up monastic discipline in 1867, probably as a means to assert his authority after the coup attempt of 1866 (Charney 2006, 216).
34. The thathanabaing and the Thudhamma Council met every *uposatha* (the days of the waxing and waning of the moon) to adjudicate disagreements in the saṅgha over such matters as property disputes and doctrinal issues (Myo Myint 1987, 174).
35. Dhammasami 2004, 113.
36. Myo Myint 1987, 169.
37. For example, the Bhamo Sayadaw, a monk famous for his learning and irascibility, objected so strenuously that Mindon exiled him back to his hometown of Bhamo. See Htin Aung 1966, 19; Mendelson 1975, 99; Ferguson 1975, 221–26. Dhammasami (2004, 115–17) suggests that even the thathanabaing himself was uneasy over the king's attempt at purification.

38. Charney 2006, 212–14; Ferguson 1975, 226–28.
39. Charney 2006, 213; Mendelson 1975, 102.
40. Ferguson 1975, 230–35.
41. Htin Aung 1966, 17–18.
42. See Charney 2006, 160–61; Cady 1958, 33, 101–2; Hpo Hlaing 2004, 39; Myo Myint 1987, 199.
43. Charney 2006, 11.
44. One of Mindon's queens, for example, had a great interest in science and mathematics, and learned some astronomy from an Englishman (Charney 2006, 156–57).
45. Today, in Burma, however, Hpo Hlaing is probably best known for the traditional Burmese medical textbook that he wrote, the *Udobhojana Saṅgaha,* which is admired for its clear and simple style (Hpo Hlaing 2004, 80).
46. Unfortunately, this monastery was destroyed in a fire (Hpo Hlaing 2004, 34).
47. Hpo Hlaing 2004, 28–29, 32.
48. Ibid., 27–29. The students first went to St. Cyr and to the École Polytechnique in 1859 (Myint-U 2001, 114).
49. Hla Pain 1967, 63–64; Aung Mon 2007, 163.
50. Hla Pain 1967, 65.
51. Ibid., 64; Aung Mon 2007, 163–64.
52. King Mindon and the next king, Thibaw, both placed Hpo Hlaing under house arrest for causing offense. Once, in 1873, Hpo Hlaing suggested to Mindon that he was hastening the downfall of the kingdom by indulging in too much sex. It was said that the king was so incensed that he grabbed a spear hanging on the wall—the very same one that had been used to kill Hpo Hlaing's father—and threatened him with it. Hpo Hlaing apparently stuck out his chest and said "Please execute me, your majesty" (Myo Myint 1987, 145–46; Hpo Hlaing 2004, 56). Another time during Mindon's rule, Hpo Hlaing was suspended from service because he suggested that the king should receive a salary like any other government official (Myo Myint 1987, 145–46). During the reign of the next king, Thibaw, Hpo Hlaing wrote a text entitled *Rājadhammasaṅgaha,* in which he argued for a form of constitutional monarchy. This text won for him his final banishment from the court in 1878; he died in 1883, two years before the arrival of the British and the same year Ledi left Mandalay (see Myo Myint 1987, 128–30).
53. The biographer Hla Pain says that Ledi's writing offended some traditionalists and that, in his willingness to disagree, he was perceived by some as something of a "leftist" (*lak' vai*) (Hla Pain 1967, 66). See also Houtman 1999, 203.
54. Aung Mon 2007, 169–70. If one adds up all the purported councils in Theravāda cultures, there are far more than five. Different texts offer different tabulations. The idea of four councils prior to Mindon's is found in the *Sāsanavaṃsa.* For an account of differing lists of councils, see Hallisey 1991, esp. 146–47.

55. They met in Rājagaha to do so (Prebish 1974, 240–41).
56. These points are technical matters of behavior related to Vinaya rules, such as whether one can preserve salt in a horn, hold several *uposathas* within a defined area meant only for one group of monks, eat a meal in one village and then go to another for another meal, drink unfermented wine, and handle gold and silver (Prebish 1974, 246–47).
57. Ibid., 253–54. The Theravāda tradition understands that Asoka convened the third council, and he has served as the preeminent model for later kings' convenings of councils. It should be noted that Mindon's royal order announcing the Fifth Council, as well as the later historical chronicle documenting it, connect every council to a king's sponsorship (Than Tun 1984–90, 9:178; Maung Maung Tin 1968, 383).
58. Ibid., 382–83.
59. No council had taken place in Burma before Mindon, but kings in the medieval period had used the third council as a model in their attempts to defrock monks and regain economic resources (Hallisey 1991, 144). It should be noted that the Fifth Council, however, was not accepted as legitimate by other Theravāda cultures. As Mendelson puts it, "To non-Burmese it was purely a Burmese affair" (Mendelson 1975, 277). See also Dhammasami 2004, 124. The Thai chronicle *Saṅgītiyavaṃsa* calculates nine councils without including Mindon's (Hallisey 1991, 146–47).
60. This coup delayed Ledi's journey to Mandalay, the king barely survived, many ministers were killed too, and Hpo Hlaing only escaped death because he happened to be away from the palace (Hpo Hlaing 2004, 33–34).
61. Myo Myint 1987, 188.
62. Mindon had to allow British steamers to navigate the full course of the Irrawaddy up to the town of Bhamo, far above Mandalay, and had to accept a British envoy at the court (Cady 1958, 107). Mindon also had to let the British envoy, Albert Fytche, use two golden umbrellas during his visit, a practice usually reserved only for royalty (Myo Myint 1987, 188).
63. Tilakaratne (2000, 175) argues that councils are akin in this regard to recitations of the monastic rules (pātimokkha) by monks at the local level every two weeks to insure unity.
64. Mendelson 1975, 113.
65. "While the Fifth Sangayana is often honored in Burmese literature as the crowning achievement of a really great Buddhist king, it did not bring even momentary unity to the Sangha. In my opinion, it was too late to accomplish such ends" (Ferguson 1975, 239). Also see Myo Myint, who says, "In terms of unifying the divided Sangha, the Fifth Buddhist Council was only a qualified success" (Myo Myint 1987, 189); Mendelson 1975, 113.
66. Charney suggests that what was forged here for the first time was a distinctively modern relationship between saṅgha and state, as there have been multiple groupings of monks since that time up to the present day (Charney 2006, 219).

67. Ibid., 99.
68. Kirichenko 2011, 5.
69. Myo Myint 1987, 184–86.
70. Ibid. Dhammasami (2004, 125) reports that there was the belief that the exceptional act of carving on stone was done to protect the scriptures in the event that Upper Burma fell to the British.
71. I would like to thank Charles Hallisey and Donald Swearer, who both pointed out to me this point about the appeal of chanting, and to an anonymous reader who noted the importance of chanting as a sort of consecration that insures that a merit-making act is effective.
72. See Cady 1958, 103; Ray 2002, 249; Dhammasami 2004, 124.
73. Anisakhan Sayadaw n.d., 25; my italics. See also the speech included in the volume by U Win, the minister for religious affairs, paraphrased by U Hla Maung: "In our country of the Union of Burma, the Fifth Great Council was held at Mandalay in 2415 B.E. by 2,400 learned Mahātheras under the leadership of the Venerable Mahāthera Jāgarābhivaṃsa and with the generous support of King Mindon. At the Great Council the bhikkhus recited the revised Tipiṭaka and the Texts were recorded on marble slabs, so that the Teachings of the Buddha may remain for a great length of time" (Hla Maung n.d., 30).
74. Wunnita 1956, 22.
75. Dhammasami 2004, 51.
76. Ibid., 48.
77. Hla Pain 1967, 64; Aung Mun 2007, 165.
78. Ibid., 201; Wunnita 1956, 22; see also Dhammasami 2004, 51.
79. Aung Mon 2007, 223–24; Wunnita 1956, 24–25. Aung Mon notes (2007, 223) that the Thanjaun Sayadaw had teachers in the monastery use it in their instruction.
80. Aung Mon 2007, 185.
81. Wunnita 1956, 25–26. This text is a subcommentary to a commentary (entitled the *Abhidhammatthavibhāvinīṭīkā*) on the Abhidhamma compendium entitled the *Abhidhammatthasaṅgaha.*
82. Houtman 1990a, 38.
83. Lieberman 1984, 194–95; Pranke 2010 (2011), 455–56. Pranke suggests that Waya-zaw-ta's followers may have been defrocked and punished because claims to spiritual attainments were a form of lèse-majesté, as they put advanced students above the king in spiritual terms, something unacceptable to a king who claimed bodhisatta status (Pranke 2010 [2011], 456–57).
84. Medhawi's books were, in fact, presented in terms of the Theravāda philosophy of the Abhidhamma (Pranke 2010 [2011], 457). As we see in the following chapters, Ledi also relied on this resource for his articulation of meditation.
85. Pranke 2010 (2011), 458–60.
86. Pranke 2004, 28–29; 2010 (2011), 458–59.
87. Ibid., 456.

88. Charney 2006, 211; Htin Aung 1966, 19–20.
89. Houtman 1990a, 269–70. Mindon also admired and supported a female student of Htut-kaung, Saya Kin, known for her meditative abilities, who died in 1878 (Houtman 1990a, 40–41).
90. Ibid., 286.
91. We can also see an interest in meditation emerging in Lower Burma in Mindon's time through the list of publications maintained by the British. At least a small number of pamphlets and books were published. For example, a book entitled *Bawah-na-wadeh Deepanee* by a "Moung Shwe Tso" in 1877; it was thirty-seven pages long. In 1878 the "Bishop of Shwe-gyeen" (the Shwegyin Sayadaw?) had published a book called *Kamathon or Analytical Meditations*. See Government of Burma 1868–1941.
92. Mendelson 1975, 102.
93. Houtman 1990a, 268.
94. Htin Aung 1966, 21–22; Pranke 2010 (2011), 460.
95. Mendelson 1975, 107.
96. The Hngettwin Sayadaw was unable to make any headway for his views in royal Burma, in fact, and he eventually moved to Lower Burma. There the Hngettwin sect of monks was established officially in 1885 and survives up to the present day. For discussion of the formation of the Hngettwin sect and its later history, see Mendelson 1975, 105–11. For a consideration of the significance of the Hngettwin Sayadaw's actions in the context of the late royal era, see Htin Aung 1966, 20–22.
97. The Maungdaung Sayadaw implies in his book that the topic of meditation is a novel one, as he remarks that previous writers did not consider Buddhism in all of its profundity because they did not include the topic of meditation. For the descriptions of these works, I am relying upon Houtman 1990a, 40.
98. Hpo Hlaing also wrote another book on meditation around the same time. It is called the *Ten Kinds of Vipassanā Insight* (*Vipassanā ñāṇ' chay' pā"*). Unfortunately, I have not been able to locate a copy.
99. Kirichenko 2009, 38.
100. Hpo Hlaing 1953, *kha*. Aung Mon notes that he had the time to write the book because Mindon had dismissed him (temporarily, as it turned out) from duties because of his stated opinion that it was acceptable to drink alcoholic beverages for medicinal purposes (Aung Mon 2007, 175–76).
101. Hpo Hlaing 1956, *kha*.
102. Ibid.; Houtman 1999, 201.
103. *Koṅ'" mvan' lvay' kū hmat' yū krañ'' hrū* (Hpo Hlaing 1956, *kha*).
104. Charney has called such an intellectual move part of the Burmese "literati spirit" (2006, 233).
105. Hpo Hlaing 1956, 2.
106. Ibid., 10–15.
107. Ibid., 10.
108. Ibid., 172.

109. Ibid.
110. Houtman 1990a, 40.
111. Mindon did invite to live in Mandalay two monks, mentioned earlier, who were well-known as meditators, the Thilon and the Shwegyin Sayadaws. But his interest in them stemmed from his admiration for their reputations for purity in adherence to the Vinaya and for their administrative abilities (Dhammasami 2004, 115).
112. Houtman 1990a, 38–41. See also Pranke 2004, 30–32 and Lieberman 1976. Recall that the *Sāsanavaṃsa* was written in 1861.
113. Law 1986, 152. See Bode 1897, 151, for the Pali passage.
114. Thibaw had been a monk since the age of seven and only disrobed to get married (Cady 1958, 111).
115. The influential minister the Kinwun Mingyi, who would later host Ledi for talks on breath meditation at his house, colluded with Sinpyumashin to put Thibaw on the throne, as he and others hoped to control him and introduce reforms. But Thibaw's queen, Supayalat, who in Burmese historiography has the reputation, along with her mother, as the dominant force in her husband's life and in his court, is said to have convinced Thibaw to wipe out any other claimants to the throne. The stories of numerous princes beaten to death inside rugs—so as not to spill a drop of royal blood—and other atrocities were frequently cited by the British business interests in Rangoon, eager to take the upper half of Burma for commercial reasons. Thibaw's decimation of the court allowed for the appointment of ministers and court officials who would follow Thibaw's and Supayalat's wishes, subverting the Kinwun's hopes of behind-the-scenes control. See Hall 1956, 125–26; Cady 1958, 111ff.; Myint-U 2001, 173–77.
116. Nisbet 1901, 173.
117. Scott and Hardiman 1900, 96.
118. Aung Mon 2007, 228; Chit San Win 2003, 41.
119. Aung Mon 2007, 230.
120. Hla Pain 1967, 75–76.
121. Aung Mon 2007, 233–36. Shwesigoun has a stūpa which has remained popular up to the present day.
122. Cady 1958, 116–17.
123. Ibid., 120. The demand to allow a British resident included the requirement that when the resident visited the king he be allowed to keep on his shoes. This was a deeply disrespectful act for the Burmese. Wearing shoes would become a flashpoint decades later when Europeans insisted on wearing their shoes at the Shwedagon Pagoda, and the matter sparked a nationalist outcry.
124. Scott and Hardiman 1900, 96.
125. Aung Mon 2007, 261.
126. Khin Maung Nyunt 1999, 65.
127. Ledi 2004c, 31. A passage from the *Great Monk Ledi* further supports the idea that Ledi connected beef eating to political events in Burma. Prior to writing

"The Letter on Cows," in his own earlier forswearing of beef, Ledi is supposed to have said: "Young monks, soon foreigners will take over Myanmar. When they rule, many animals that serve us will likely be hurt and die. Among the animals that serve us, cows are the masters of life for us. They are like our mothers and our fathers. For us they are of much benefit, and so, starting from this day, I will not eat beef. You also should not eat beef" (Wunnita 1956, 28). Guy Lubeigt (2005, 394) argues that this quote was a nationalistic interpolation from the socialist era, but the version which I have of the *Great Monk Ledi* was published—with the quote—in 1956, prior to socialist times.

128. Chit San Win 2003, 70. King Alaungpaya (ruled 1752–60) had forbidden the killing of animals for sacrifice to spirits (Ferguson 1975, 184).
129. See van der Veer 1994, chapter 3, esp. 91–92.
130. Also spelled Viḍūḍabha. For more on the king, see Malalasekera 1997, 3:876–77.
131. *Nats* are spirits; *Sakka* (also called Indra in Sanskrit texts and *si krā"* in Burmese) is the king of the *nats* in the Burmese Buddhist pantheon; the *Brahmas* are celestial beings who live in heavenly realms (Spiro 1967, 133).
132. Spelled "Savatthi" in the Pali texts.
133. Ledi uses the word *gaṅ' gā,* which can refer to the Ganges River, but it seems likely he uses the word here simply as a poetic way to refer to a river, because in the well-known story of King Viṭaṭū the king and his army camp in the dry riverbed of the Aciravatī and drown in the night when water comes unexpectedly (Malalasekera 1997, 3:877).
134. In other words, each received their just karmic desserts in turn.
135. These are parents, spouses, teachers, friends, religious teachers, and workers.
136. Ledi 2004c, 31–32.
137. This story appears in the *Dhammapada Aṭṭhakathā* i 346–349, 357–367. See Malalasekera 1997, 3:876–77. Other Theravāda thinkers have used the story to explain group calamities. See Walters 2003, 12–13, for examples.
138. Ledi 2004c, 32.
139. Ibid., 37.
140. Walters 2003, 11. Walters notes that, given the social nature of most acts of merit, "it makes perfect sense the community should have a karmic dimension" (2003, 10), and he presents evidence going back to the canonical texts for such a belief.
141. Ledi 2004c, 36.
142. He continued his campaign throughout his life against beef eating—indeed, against eating any meat in ideal circumstances.
143. See also Aung Mon 2007, 279ff.
144. The *uposatha* days are the days of the new and full moon when monks gather to recite the communal rules (pātimokkha) of the saṅgha, and lay people often visit temples and monasteries for merit making, socializing, and other religious activities.
145. Wunnita 1956, 29–30.

146. Hla Pain 1967, 81; Aung Mon 2007, 288.
147. Ibid., 280.
148. Wunnita 1956, 30; Aung Mon 2007, 284–85. It should be said, however, that the buildings which exist now are quite different from the structures in which Ledi and his students lived. It is said that Ledi forbade any building worth more than 200 kyats, a relatively modest amount of money at the time, and so he and his pupils lived in bamboo structures (Htay Htay Lwin 1998, 2). At present, the monastery covers a large area with many cement buildings. Because of the growth of Monywa, it is no longer in the forest, but fully in the town amid houses, shops, and dusty streets.
149. Charney 2006, 28–29.
150. Ajaan Mun began his wanderings around 1896. Based upon an analysis of Mun's biography, Tambiah describes him as follows: "Mun preferred *living alone and moving constantly* as a homeless seeker" (Tambiah 1984, 85). Even with his frequent traveling, however, Mun did manage to teach and to set up "a network of cells of disciples" (305).
151. For information on the lives of these and other Thai forest monks, see Taylor 1993 and Tiyavanich 1997.
152. Carrithers 1983, 72, but see the whole of chapter 4 for an analysis of Paññānanda's life and monastic career.
153. Carrithers contrasts Paññānanda with the German-born Nyanatiloka, who lived as a forest monk in Sri Lanka and produced a great deal of erudite scholarship.
154. Carrithers 1983, 14.
155. He wrote the *Pāramīdīpanī* (*Manual on the Perfections*), while still at Thanjaun. At the Ledi monastery, he also wrote the *Uposathasīla Vinicchaya* (*Decision on Observance Day Morality*), the *Lakkhaṇadīpanī* (*Manual on the Marks of Existence*), and the *Puṇṇovādakammaṭṭhān'"* (*Meditation Object of Puṇṇovāda*), which is discussed below and in more detail in chapter 5.
156. Ledi 2003a, 634.
157. Aung Mon 2007, 404–9.
158. Hla Pain 1967, 103; Wunnita 1956, 39; Aung Mon 2007, 404–5.
159. Wunnita 1956, 40; Aung Mon 2007, 414–16.
160. Wunnita 1956, 41.
161. In traditional Buddhist cosmology, Jambūdīpa is the realm of humans. *Jambūdīpa* is a variant spelling of *Jambudīpa.*
162. These are the eight absorptive states of concentration (samādhi), each more rarified than the last, pursued within the realm of calming (samatha) meditation.
163. *Va sī bhau* (Pali: *vasībhāva*) refers to the five "masteries" over the jhānas of "adverting" (*āvajjanavasitā*), "attainment" (*samāpajjanavasitā*), "resolution" (*adhiṭṭhānavasitā*), "emergence" (*vuṭṭhānavasitā*), and "reviewing" (*paccavekkhaṇāvasitā*). See Bodhi et al. 2000, 342; also Ñāṇamoli 1999, 150.
164. In Buddhist cosmology, the Brahma gods occupy particularly high realms of

heavenly existence and live exceptionally long and pleasant lives. They do not dwell, however, in the highest realms, as Ledi indicates when he refers to realms above Brahma.

165. Wunnita 1956, 41. My thanks to U Saw Tun and John Okell for their assistance in translating this poem.
166. The other three are no sex, no killing, and no stealing.
167. J. G. Scott 1963, 119: "If a pyin-sin [monk] committed any one of the four cardinal sins, he would most assuredly be unfrocked and turned out of the monastery doors to the mercy of the people, and they would certainly stone him, and, in Upper Burma, probably put him to death."
168. Aung Mon 2007, 428.
169. Ledi 1999b, vi; Aung Mon 2007, 441. Ledi's meditation was apparently going well. Here his biographies have a rare report of a supernatural event. One day, the monastery's lay attendant (*kappiya*), Maung Tha Mun, happened to see Ledi in his hut, meditating while floating about three feet above the ground. When he told U Tiloka and the other monks in residence about this, they rushed over and observed the event as well (Aung Mon 2007, 441; Hla Pain 1967, 125).
170. Htay Htay Lwin 1998, 10. As Ledi's successor as abbot at his original monastery, Nyanabatha would later become the second Ledi Sayadaw after the first's death (Aung Mon 2007, 436 n.3).
171. Aung Mon 2007, 469; Ledi 1999b, vi.
172. Ibid.; Aung Mon 2007, 481–83; 502–3. The first cave was on Shwe Taung U (Hrve toṅ' ū") Mountain and the other was on Lat-pan-taung (Lak' pan'" toṅ'") Mountain.

CHAPTER TWO

1. His real name was U Tun Pe. He was an ex-monk (his monastic name was U Naginda) and a disciple of the head of the Dwara sect of monks, U Ukkaṃvaṃsamālā (Myin Swe n.d., *kai*).
2. *Kecivāda e* ran' sū* (Nat Tha 1910, 3).
3. Myin Swe n.d., *khai-kho'*. The student was U Maung Gyi, also known as Ledi Pandita. He will appear again at the start of chapter 4.
4. Aung Mon 2007, 474; Ledi 2003b, *ḍha*. As noted in the previous chapter, Ledi had actually finished writing the book some years before, in 1897 (Aung Mon 2007, 428; Ledi 2003b, *ḍha*).
5. Hla Pain 1967, 115; Aung Mon 2007, 647–49; Myin Swe n.d., *khī*.
6. Prominent newspapers were the *Hanthawaddy,* the *Myanmar Taya,* and the *Mahabodhi* (Myin Swe n.d., *gai-go'*). Unfortunately, I have been unable to locate these articles in my search through the archives of Yangon University. The microfiche and microfilm archives are in a poor state and much has been lost. The British Library does not have these newspapers at such an early date, for the debates seem to have taken place prior to 1915.

7. Wunnita 1956, 52.
8. Ibid., 52–54. Cooler heads prevailed and a burning was not held. See also Aung Mon 2007, 555–56.
9. *Ṭīkā cac' pvai krī"* (Hla Pain 1967, 115). Another Burmese scholar, writing in the 1960s, described the reaction to the *Paramatthadīpanī* as more intense than the explosion of an atomic bomb: *Aṇu mrū buṃ thak' praṅ'" than' cvā pok' kvai saññ'* (Myin Swe n.d., *khā*).
10. Gethin 1998, 203. The seven books of this part of the canon are the *Dhammasaṅgaṇī* (*Enumeration of Phenomena*), the *Vibhaṅga* (*Book of Analysis*), the *Dhātukathā* (*Discourse on the Elements*), the *Puggalapaññati* (*Concepts of Individuals*), the *Kathāvatthu* (*Points of Controversy*), the *Yamaka* (*Book of Pairs*), and the *Paṭṭhāna* (*Book of Conditional Relations*).
11. The *Dhammasaṅgaṇī* lays the basis for the articulation of the Abhidhamma system as a whole by cataloging the eighty-two dhammas in exhaustive fashion. The *Vibhaṅga* contains eighteen essays on the organizational categories of Buddhist thought, such as the five aggregates (*khandha*) and dependent origination (*paṭiccasamuppāda*). The *Dhātukathā* relates all phenomena to the doctrinal categories of aggregates, sense bases, and the physical elements. The *Puggalapaññati*, a bit of an outlier in the canon, is the least "Abhidhammic," as it touches upon conventional matters, in order to classify people into different types of individuals and groups. The *Kathāvatthu* is a refutation of views held by non-Theravādins. The *Yamaka* seeks analytical precision by examining doctrinal concepts within the range of their application in the Abhidhamma system and in relation to other terms. The last, seventh book, the *Paṭṭhāna*, completes the system by explaining how the previously enumerated entities produce all phenomena through precisely twenty-four "conditional relations," that is to say twenty-four ways of combining (Bodhi et al. 2000, 11–12; for a detailed description of all these works, see Buswell and Jaini 1996, 90–97).
12. Bodhi et al. 2000, 76.
13. See ibid., 79, table 2.1, for a list of all the factors.
14. Among the eighty-nine consciousnesses, there are eight supramundane consciousnesses, four of path and four of fruition (Bodhi et al. 2000, 69–70). However, these path and fruition consciousnesses can be divided further on the basis of their jhānic attributes, yielding twenty in each category, leading to an alternate tabulation of types of consciousness as 121 (Bodhi et al. 2000, 71).
15. Ibid., 31–32. Resultant and functional consciousnesses have no moral valence and so are called "undetermined" (*abyākata*).
16. Ibid., 237–38.
17. As Rupert Gethin puts it, "The Abhidhamma method, in contrast [to the method of the suttas], presents the Buddha's teachings without making concessions to time or place or audience, and in technical terms that are precisely defined to ensure analytical exactitude" (1998, 207).

18. See, e.g., Vism. XXI 126.
19. Bodhi et al. 2000, 6.
20. Gimello 1983, 74.
21. Bodhi et al. 2000, 15.
22. Von Hinüber 2000, 162.
23. Malalasekera (1928, 173) suggests as the most likely time-frame the tenth to early twelfth centuries, as do Bechert 1979 and Norman 1983. Rupert Gethin (Gethin and Wijeratne 2002, xiv) notes, however, that a well-known commentary on the *Saṅgaha* understands Anuruddha to be a contemporary of another commentator named Jotipāla. If one accepts this Jotipāla as the same one mentioned in the *Cūlavaṃsa* from the sixth century, it is possible that the *Saṅgaha* could be dated as early as the sixth or early seventh century CE.
24. Bodhi et al. 2000, 15. Snodgrass (2007, 195) says that the Sri Lankan saṅgha urged the publication of the *Saṅgaha* by the Pali Text Society in 1881, the year the society was founded, because it was considered the best introduction to Buddhist philosophical thinking. It was published in 1910 in a translation by the Burmese scholar Shwe Zan Aung and Caroline Rhys-Davids.
25. These categories of concern follow Bhikkhu Bodhi's characterization. See Bodhi et al. 2000, 3.
26. Ibid., 19.
27. This is done through six categories: root (*hetu*), feeling (*vedanā*), function (*kicca*), door (*dvāra*), object (*ārammaṇa*), and base (*vatthu*).
28. See Bodhi et al. 2000, 19.
29. Ibid., 285.
30. These are the two ways to describe the process of conditioned arising. Dependent origination is the relatively simpler system that explains the twelve conditioning states that give rise to conditions in a causal structure. The system of twenty-four conditional relations explains not only the conditioning states and their resultant states, but the forces within the conditioning states that cause the results. See Bodhi et al. 2000, 293–94.
31. Ibid., 20.
32. Ibid., 17; Gethin and Wijeratne 2002, xvi.
33. Gethin and Wijeratne 2002, xvi. No critical editions of either the *Saṅgaha* or the *Vibhāvinī* have been produced (Gethin and Wijeratne 2002, xvii). I use the Pali version of the *Saṅgaha* and the English translation included in Bodhi et al. 2000, which I have checked against the version of the *Saṅgaha* contained in the Burmese Chaṭṭhasaṅgāyanā (Sixth Council) version. I refer as well to the translations by Gethin and Wijeratne (2002) and Shwe Zan Aung (1910). For the translation of the *Vibhāvinī* I have used the English translation of Gethin and Wijeratne.
34. Only nineteen of the 245 corrections in the *Paramatthadīpanī* concern another text. Two corrections concern the twelfth-century *Abhidhammatthsaṅgahaṭīkā* (also called the *Porāṇaṭīkā*); thirteen con-

cern the *Vibhāvinī* and the *Poraṇaṭīkā;* and four the *Vibhāvinī* and the *Visuddhimaggamahāṭīkā.*

35. *Saṅgruih' mahāṭīkā sac' pāṭh'.* The earliest edition I have found is a 1907 version, published by the Kavi myak' hman' Press. I also have a 2003 version of the text published in Burma, and have referred as well to the Chaṭṭhasaṅgāyanā version. Additionally, I have referred to the unpublished manuscript of the English translation of the *Paramatthadīpanī* by Dhammācariya U Nandamālābhivaṃsa, the abbot of Mahathukayoun Monastery in Sagaing, Burma. All translations from the *Paramatthadīpanī,* however, are mine.
36. In identifying these works as commentarial literature, I take three features as determinative, as defined by Paul Griffiths: first, that the text stands in a subordinate position to a dominant root text, indicated by the use of direct quotation, paraphrase, and summary; second, that the subordinate quality of the commentarial text should dominate; and third, that the order of the earlier work should determine the order of the commentary (Griffiths 1999, 81).
37. For example, in the dispute over whether novice monks must cover both shoulders or only one during certain appearances before the laity, described in the previous chapter, the non-canonical text *Cūḷaganṭhipada,* which supported the view that monks needed only to cover one shoulder, had aroused great controversy during the reign of King Bodawpaya (ruled 1782–1819) (Pranke 2004, 2–3). Later, during Mindon's reign, the Okpo and Hngettwin Sayadaws both caused intense controversies with their arguments over proper practice and worship (see Htin Aung 1966, 20–24).
38. Ledi 2003b, 1.
39. Wunnita 1956, 34–35; Aung Mon 2007, 428. His notes filled over forty palm-leaf manuscripts and accordion-folded paper notebooks (*parabaik*).
40. Gethin and Wijeratne 2002, 2.
41. Myin Swe n.d., *au.*
42. Although the text itself among all versions of the *Paramatthadīpanī* is the same, the tally of critiques can vary somewhat, depending on whether one classifies certain points as parts of a single larger correction or as separate corrections. Chit San Win (2003, 118–19) tabulates 245, as does the version of the *Paramatthadīpanī* included in the Sixth Council version of the *tipiṭaka* at http://www.tipitaka.org. The 2003 version of the *Paramatthadīpanī* identifies 270 critiques.
43. I thank Alexey Kirichenko for bringing this group of texts to my attention. He suggests, further, that Ledi may have been building on the tradition of the *khalita vicāraṇā* in the *Paramatthadīpanī* (personal communication, November 4, 2012).
44. Gethin and Wijeratne (2002, 124) translate *asāraṃ* as "lacking in substance." Nandamālābhivaṃsa (n.d., 213) translates the term as "nonsense."
45. The debate was over the existence of a "present moment" in cognition be-

tween its state of arising and its state of dissolution; see Gethin and Wijeratne 2002, 121. The commentaries on the Abhidhamma texts are believed to have been composed by the fifth-century monk, Buddhaghosa, the same man who wrote the *Visuddhimagga*.

46. Gethin and Wijeratne 2002, 209.
47. Ibid., xiv.
48. Ledi 2003b, *kha*.
49. Chit San Win 2003, 115.
50. Wunnita 1956, 53.
51. Ledi's scope was certainly broad enough to have allowed larger arguments about the *Vibhāvinī*. He has critiques of it from its explication of birth to its analysis of death. For example, Ledi says it mistakenly omits the first state of consciousness of a reborn being in its recounting of the states of consciousness at birth (Ledi 2003b, 37–38), and, at the other end of a being's lifespan, he says it unnecessarily limits the range of possible sense experiences at death (Ledi 2003b, 340).
52. Gimello describes this literature as having "oddly flat, abstract, detached, and circumlocutory prose. As literature it is quite unpalatable, some would say downright repellent" (1983, 74).
53. Bodhi et al. 2000, 235.
54. See *Aṭṭhasālinī* 2.584, and also Vism. XI 98–100; Ñāṇamoli 1999, 361–62.
55. Gethin and Wijeratne 2002, 216.
56. Ledi 2003b, 350.
57. Bodhi et al. 2000, 32–39.
58. Gethin and Wijeratne 2002, 17.
59. Ibid.
60. Ledi 2003b, 48–49.
61. Nat Tha 1910, 31–32.
62. Talaingoun Sayadaw 1909, 30.
63. I follow Bodhi et al. (2000, 34, 37) in translating *somanassa* as "pleasant mental feeling" and *domanassa* as "unpleasant mental feeling."
64. Talaingoun 1909, 30. My thanks to Rupert Gethin who assisted me in the translation of this passage.
65. Shwe Zan Aung 1910, 160 n. 2; Gethin and Wijeratne 2002, 234–35.
66. The mind is a sense as well, usually listed as the sixth. But since the object of its apprehension is a thought, it does not fall under analysis in the materiality section (*rūpasaṅgaha*) of the *Paramatthadīpanī*. See Ledi 2003b, 381–82.
67. Ibid., 340.
68. Cox 1995, 71.
69. See Cox 1995; Jaini 1959, 532–47. For another example of how a profound change started with a small manipulation, see Cox 1992, in which she discusses the changing understanding of mindfulness (*smṛti/sati*) through the reinterpretation of key terms in Abhidharma literature.
70. The argument for an intervening moment of existence (*ṭhiti*) between arising

and degeneration of all matter was a controversial innovation, in fact, condemned by the *Mūlaṭīka* (Shwe Zan Aung, "Buddhism and Science," http://www.thisismyanmar.com/nibbana/szaung04.htm [accessed November 4, 2011]).

71. Bodhi et al. 2000, 14–15.
72. Ronkin 2005, 2.
73. Nandamālābhivaṃsa n.d., ix.
74. Ledi argues, contrary to the *Vibhāvinī*, that a delusional consciousness (citta) always comes into being automatically (*asasankhārika*). The Talaingoun Sayadaw agrees with Ledi, saying that deluded consciousnesses have "sharp natures" which inherently promote action, even if they are so unstable they cannot generate the clarity of purpose on the part of the actor to actually do anything (Talaingoun 1909, 30–31).
75. Myin Swe n.d., *kā"*.
76. Hla Pain 1967, 116.
77. Myin Swe n.d., *khi*.
78. I have not been able to locate a textual source for this tale. Peter Skilling related the story to me in an email, and subsequently I heard it in 2005 in Burma from several monks. I might add that this is a story meant to stress only the Burmese love for the Abhidhamma: The Thais are not known in Burma for a particular love of the Vinaya, nor Sri Lankans for the suttas.
79. Than Tun 1978, 82; Ray 2002, 192–95; Pruitt 1994, 19; Bode 1909, 102.
80. Bode 1909, 58. In his history of Buddhism in Burma, Bischoff calls the seventeenth century "the dawn of the Abhidhamma age" (1995, 21).
81. Bischoff 1995, 20; Ray 2002, 210–12; J. A. Stewart 1949, 9.
82. Ray 2002, 213; Bischoff 1995, 21. The system was created by the monk U Devacakkhobhasa.
83. Charney 2006, 40–41; Ū" Jotika 1978, *ci*. The Masoyein Sayadaw captures well the sense the Burmese have of the importance of these texts for Burma's Abhidhamma tradition: "Because there were the well-known *ayakauk* in the union of Myanmar, the great tradition of the Abhidhamma has endured and increased, so as to reach [us] today without disappearing. In the Theravāda countries of Thailand and Sri Lanka which did not have the *Mātikā ayakauk, Dhātukathā ayakauk, Yamuik' ayakauk*, and *Paṭṭhān'" ayakauk,* the great tradition of the Abhidhamma could not endure as much as it should endure, could not shine and blaze forth as much as it should" (Ū" Jotika 1978, *cu-cū*).
84. Saddhātissa 1989, xv. See also Gethin and Wijeratne 2002, xv; Bodhi et al. 2000, 16.
85. Dhammasami 2004, 45–56. An emphasis on the Abhidhamma did not mean monks would neglect other aspects of the tradition, of course. For an overview of the monastic educational system in precolonial times, see Dhammasami 2004.
86. The term "finger manual" has gained currency outside of Burma in the modern period (Malalasekera 1928, 108).

87. Besides the *Saṅgaha* by Anuruddha, the compendiums are the *Nāmarūpapariccheda,* also by Anuruddha; the *Paramatthavinicchaya*, authorship uncertain, though perhaps also by Anuruddha; the *Abhidhammāvatāra*, by Buddhadatta; the *Rūpārupavibhāga*, also by Buddhadatta; the *Saccasaṅkhepa*, by Dhammapāla; the *Mohavicchedanī*, by Kassapa; the *Khemapakaraṇa*, by Khema; and the *Nāmacāradīpaka*, by Sadhamma (Bodhi et al. 2000, 15).
88. Ananda Metteyya 1911, 133. Recall that *uposatha* days are the days of the new and full moon when monks gather to recite the communal rules (pātimokkha) of the saṅgha, and laypeople often visit temples and monasteries.
89. Ledi 2001, 540.
90. Ibid., 548.
91. These four are the extent of the powers of a Buddha (*buddhavisaya*), the extent of the powers of one in the meditative absorptions (*jhānavisaya*), the possible results of karma (*kammavipāka*), and the nature of the world (*lokacintā*), especially its beginning.
92. The Buddha also says that he has taught everything that one needs to know in order to achieve awakening. He explains that a Buddha is not a teacher who teaches with "a closed fist," i.e., with some information hidden (*ācariyamuṭṭhi*). This is said in the *Mahāparinibbānasutta* (DN 16).
93. This is a fish said to be one thousand leagues long (Malalasekera 1997, 2:1014).
94. Bodhi et al. 2000, 9; *Aṭṭhasālinī* 13.
95. Ledi 2003b, 1–2.
96. This heaven is on the summit of the central mountain of Meru in the Buddhist cosmological system. For a detailed description, see Sadakata 2004, 56–57.
97. Ledi 2001, 160–61. My italics.
98. The Buddha went to the heaven specifically to preach to his mother, Mahāmāyā, who had been reborn there when she died just a week after the Buddha was born. But the audience was not limited to that realm; gods (*devas*) gathered from ten thousand world systems to hear the preaching of the ultimate truth (Bodhi et al. 2000, 10).
99. He doled it out to his disciple most renowned for his intellectual understanding of the dhamma, Sāriputta (Bodhi et al. 2000, 10).
100. Bodhi et al. 2000, 5, quoting *Aṭṭhasālinī* 2, *Expositor* 3. For more details see Watanabe 1983 and Ronkin 2005, 32 n. 37.
101. Ferguson 1975, 240. These were the Taungdaw and Shwegyin Sayadaws, but the Shwegyin refused the title.
102. Smith 1965, 49.
103. Mendelson 1975, 180.
104. Quoted in Smith 1965, 42.
105. Htin Aung 1966, 16.

106. White 1913, 185.
107. Htin Aung 1966, 16.
108. Two monks, the Pakan Sayadaw and the Mogaung Sayadaw, were each supported by factions as the legitimate thathanabaing, and each attempted to act in the role. The confusion that ensued forced the colonial government to issue a circular stating that no one had been officially recognized as the thathanabaing (Smith 1965, 49).
109. Smith 1965, 49–50. Kirichenko (2010) specifies that new monastic alliances, patrons, and organizations catalyzed by the colonial situation, rather than colonial government policy itself, accounts for the weakening of the role of the thathanabaing.
110. Smith 1965, 52. It does seem that the number of monks went into a long decline after the arrival of the British (Smith 1965, 52; Mendelson 1975, 121–22). But note that monks were unevenly distributed in the country. In Upper Burma every village had a monastery, but in Lower Burma, which had had colonial rule since 1855 and gained much of its population due to immigration in the same period, the infrastructure was not well developed and so there were far fewer monks. In 1891, three-fourths of the villages there had no monastery (Furnivall 1956, 103). The movement of people to Lower Burma and the marked absence of village monasteries in the region likely contributed to the sense that throughout Burma monks and their monasteries were on the wane.
111. Furnivall 1956, 200–201.
112. Ibid., 57; Bode 1909, 94.
113. In 1891, there were 4,324 government-recognized monastic schools and 890 lay; in 1918, 2,977 monastic and 4,650 lay; by 1938, 976 and 5,255 respectively (Cady 1958, 179; Mendelson 1975, 159). By 1936, 80 percent of students who attended monastic schools did so for two years or less (Cady 1958, 179).
114. Mendelson 1975, 160; Charney 2006, 182; see also Dirks 2001, 147.
115. The British felt they encouraged the vice of gambling (Furnivall 1956, 109).
116. See Furnivall 1956, 106–19.
117. Bode 1909, 95.
118. Burmese kings had been aware of the potential power of printing before this time; Charney (2006, 182–84) notes that King Bodawpaya tried to acquire a press around 1815 and King Bagyidaw tried again in the 1830s. For an overview of early publishing in Burma, see Charney 2006, 182–86; Allott, Herbert, and Okell 1989, 9–10. For an examination of Mindon's efforts to secure printing capabilities and start a Burmese newspaper in Mandalay, see Charney 2006, 195–200.
119. Stewart 1949, 13.
120. Malalgoda 1976, 184; Charney 2006, 182–83. In fact, the first Buddhist press in Sri Lanka (in Colombo) was purchased from missionaries (Malalgoda 1976, 219). The Serampore Mission in India sent presses to Burma in the early

nineteenth century. The first, sent to the royal court, sank in the Irrawaddy River in 1813. The second was established in Rangoon in 1816 (Allott, Herbert, and Okell 1989, 9).

121. It seems that often Christian publications were sought by Burmese simply as admired physical objects—as "collector's items"—and so the bigger the book the better, regardless of its content (Charney 2006, 192–93).
122. Allott, Herbert, and Okell 1989, 9; Stewart 1949, 13.
123. Htin Aung 1966, 28.
124. Colston 1910, 76. The vigorous turn to the use of the technology of printing is similar to that which developed in Sri Lanka after the purchase of the first Buddhist press there in 1855 by the Society for the Propagation of Buddhism in Colombo, which devoted itself "mainly to the publication and distribution of polemical tracts, pamphlets and periodicals" (Malalgoda 1976, 221).
125. Stewart 1949, 13. Of course, Ledi spread his teachings textually before the advent of a vigorous print culture. For instance, the "Letter on Cows" was first hand-copied. Ledi (2004c, 38) makes reference in the letter to duplications of it being circulated. The system of distribution for hand-copied documents was well established and efficient in Burma, ensuring that a document could reach a significant audience. Still, the extent of duplication did not approach that possible with the modern printing press.
126. For a discussion of the move from a hierarchical and segmented Buddhism to one "flattened" and based upon doctrine for the masses, see Kirichenko 2009.
127. In regard to monks' knowledge of Pali, J. G. Scott remarks, perhaps somewhat hyperbolically: "Very few of the religious could string a sentence together in Pali, far less speak the language" (1963, 37).
128. Not all looked at matters this way—some believed that the sāsana's degeneration was inevitable and would be sudden. Ledi argued strongly against such a view. In the *Sāsanavisodhanī* he said: "Some say, 'When a thousand years have passed, just on that next day the great sāsana disappears all at once. Starting from that day, there is no *Buddhasāsana*.' One should not believe this" (Ledi 1954, 1:52).
129. Nattier 1991, 56.
130. For an overview of stories of decline in Buddhism, see Nattier 1991.
131. See Malalasekera 1997, 2:304; Nattier 1991, 56–57.
132. Sri Lankan texts, such as the *Sāratthasaṅgaha* (thirteenth century) and the *Saddhammaratnākara* (fifteenth century), also contain narratives of decline. For more information on these texts, see von Hinüber 2000.
133. The *Anāgatavaṃsa* is of uncertain date and provenance. The Burmese version concerning the decline of Buddhism was found in a library in Rangoon, edited by the Russian scholar Ivan Minayeff, and printed in the *Journal of the Pali Text Society* in 1886 (Turner 2009, 62 n. 20). Skilling (2009b, 121 n. 1) has pointed out the *Anāgatavaṃsa* is a literary genre, not one text specifically; Collins refers to "the *Anāgatavaṃsa* family of texts" (Collins 1998, 359). Most

of the texts in this family, in fact, focus not on the disappearance of Buddhism but on the hopeful arrival of the next Buddha, Metteyya. Hence the meaning of the title *Anāgatavaṃsa*, "History of the Future."

134. Turner 2009, 64. For a discussion of the price of books and the purchasing power of Burmese in the colonial period, see chapter 3.
135. Ledi 2001, 402.
136. Ibid.
137. Htin Aung 1966, 15–16, see also 24, noted in Turner 2009, 57; Cady 1958, 171; and Smith 1965, 38. For more recent views on decline in Burmese Buddhism, see Mendelson 1975, 270, and Jordt 2007, 26.
138. Hansen 2007, 5.
139. Carbine 2011, 153.
140. Ū" Jotika 1978, *cu.*
141. Ibid., *cai.* My italics.
142. Bastian 2004, 122.
143. Than Tun 1984–90, 9:729–30.
144. Carbine (2011, 148) notes that these CDs are purely decorative and not meant to be played. See also Bischoff 1995, 21.
145. As noted above, the Buddha gave the Abhidhamma as an uninterrupted discourse in the Tāvatiṃsa heaven over the three months of the rains retreat. It was in the seventh year after his awakening. The last day of the rains retreat, then, is understood as the day the Buddha returned to the human realm with the teaching of the Abhidhamma completed (Bodhi et al. 2000, 10).
146. Aung Mon 2007, 767.
147. Hla Pain 1967, 232.
148. Myin Swe n.d., *ghū.*
149. At the Mahasatipatthana Temple in Malden, Mass., in the fall of 2006, the monk U Zawtika [Ū" Jo ti ka] (not the same monk as the author of the history of the Abhidhamma referenced above) told me that advanced Burmese students study the *Paramatthadīpanī.*
150. Hla Pain 1967, 232.

CHAPTER THREE

1. White 1913, 197.
2. The record of places Ledi stayed during the yearly three-month rains retreats (*vā* or *vassa*) during this period shows this clearly. In 1903, just as he began his career on the national stage, he resided three miles to the west of Monywa on Lat-pan-taung Mountain, but a year later he was hundreds of miles south in the city of Pyinmana (Ledi 1999b, vi). The year after that, he was back up north in the town of Myingyan, some seventy miles south of Mandalay. But, in 1906, he was once again hundreds of miles south in the city of Pyi. The next year he resided in Minhla, some two hundred miles from

Monywa, and he also traveled hundreds of miles west to the coast of Arakan to preach in Sittwe. The year after that, Ledi went far south, to Mawlamyain, over five hundred miles from Monywa, and in 1909 he stayed in Thapaun, near Pathein, some 119 miles west of the colonial capital of Rangoon. It was not until 1910 that he finally made it back to his old monastery in Monywa. In 1911, however, he went close to five hundred miles south again to Rangoon, then the next year back up some four hundred miles to Sagaing. After these nine years, in which Ledi moved thousands of miles and never stayed in the same place two years in a row, he resided for three years in Mandalay. Then, in 1916, he spent the retreat period again in the middle part of the country in Pyinmana. In 1917, he finally returned to the Ledi Monastery in Monywa, for what would be the last time. In 1918 the rains retreat was in Myittha, about fifty miles south of Mandalay, and then the next year he went back down to Rangoon. He spent the 1920 retreat in Katun in the delta region and the next up north, again in Sagaing. His final rains retreat, in 1922, was again in Pyinmana. See Ledi 1995, *da-na.*

3. *The Burman Buddhist* 1908b, 27.
4. Wunnita 1956, 107.
5. White 1913, 198.
6. *The Burman Buddhist* 1908b, 28.
7. Nyanissara 1999, 30–31. Ledi sent some disciples to accept the award, perhaps in a canny move to avoid too close an association with the colonial power.
8. Hpo Hlaing 2004, 40–41. Public drinking had once been common, in fact, but fell out of favor and was replaced by the consumption of pickled tea. See Harvey 1967, 314–15. Lieberman argues that the prohibition of alcohol formed part of a program of growing centralized political and cultural control that emphasized Theravādin orthodoxy (Lieberman 2003, 196).
9. Schober 2007, 61.
10. Charney 2006, 193. Missionaries did have significant success among non-Burman ethnic groups.
11. *The Burman Buddhist* 1908a, 17–18.
12. Ananda Metteyya 1903b, 142.
13. Ledi 2012, 182; Ledi 2003a, 370.
14. Ledi 1954, 2:84.
15. Dirks 2001, 146.
16. Ledi 2012, 182.
17. Ledi 2003a, 370.
18. Ledi 1954, 2:82.
19. Ibid., 82–83.
20. Turner 2009, 212.
21. Ledi 2001, 192.
22. Ibid., 193.

23. The missionary said: "There may be a succession of conservative movements like that of the Ledi Saya Daw. But they will only retard and not arrest the disintegrating tendency [of Buddhism]" (Purser and Saunders 1914, 91).
24. Hla Pain 1967, 189–90.
25. A local Bassein (now called Pathein) newspaper reported in 1907 that Ledi chanted Abhidhamma texts to rid a village of disease (in "Bassein," *Burma Echo*, June 22, 1907, quoted in Turner 2009, 211). Ledi also gave advice to villagers to invite other monks to recite (Aung Mon 2007, 636).
26. Stewart 1949, 15. Stewart was later professor of Burmese at the University of London.
27. Hla Pain 1967, 233. Charles Hallisey has pointed out to me that it is unusual to use the *kammavācā* to dispel danger. *Kammavācā* are typically used only for ritualized acts, such as ordaining monks or establishing a monastery. In a personal communication (April 4, 2012), William Pruitt pointed out that the recitation of *kammavācā* is understood to call down beneficent gods (*devas*) and purify an area, and so could be understood to offer protection from disease.
28. Tambiah 1976, 212; see also Winichukul 1994.
29. Ledi 2012, 182.
30. Payne 2002, 159.
31. Ledi 2003a, 507.
32. This is an expression coined by Stephen Jay Gould, that indicates there is no real conflict at all between religion and science: "The lack of conflict between science and religion arises from a lack of overlap between their respective domains of professional expertise—science in the empirical constitution of the universe, and religion in the search for proper ethical values and the spiritual meaning of our lives." http://www.stephenjaygould.org/library/gould_noma.html (accessed May 4, 2010). This expression is discussed in Lopez 2008, 34.
33. In 1918, Ledi's lay pupil Shwe Zan Aung, whom we encountered in the last chapter, wrote an article for the *Journal of the Burma Research Society* in which he argued for the supremacy of Buddhism over science. We can see in his analysis a similar approach to that of Ledi, and he sums up his article by saying: "In conclusion, Buddhism as a philosophy underlies all sciences" (Shwe Zan Aung 1918, 106).
34. See Taylor 1999, esp. 25. I will return to this point at the end of chapter 5, in light of the discussion there of the specifics of Ledi's vision of meditation in lay life.
35. Indeed, at times figures such as Dharmapala and even Ledi, too, sensing this perceived weakness on Christianity's part, have capitalized on it by asserting Buddhism's consonance with the scientific worldview. See Lopez 2008, 32.
36. See the first chapter of Lopez 2008 for a discussion of arguments among Buddhists and others (particularly Christian missionaries) over the reality of Mt. Meru in light of scientific knowledge.

37. Chakrabarty 2000, 14.
38. Ledi 1954, 1:120.
39. Ibid., 118. On the development of the idea of Buddhism as comprising beliefs in the Sri Lankan context, see Lopez 1998.
40. Houtman 1990b and Kirichenko 2009.
41. This was similar to the situation in Sri Lanka. See Carter 1993, 19–23.
42. This is not to say that Ledi invented the word. Kirichenko has found its use as early as 1852 in a Christian document (Kirichenko 2009, 33). It should be noted also that *batha* is not the only term that Ledi and other Burmese used for Buddhism. *Sāsana* and *Buddhasāsana* were also used frequently. But, whatever other terms were also used, the growing predominance of *batha* reflects a broader shift in the understanding of what it meant to be Buddhist.
43. Bishop Bigandet, writing in the mid-nineteenth century, claimed the average period for a boy to be ordained was one to two years (quoted in Stewart 1949, 10).
44. Ibid.
45. See Schober 2007.
46. Htin Aung 1966, 11. This seems to have been a situation similar to that of traditional Buddhism in Sri Lanka (Rāhula 1966, 254).
47. Kirichenko 2009, 26.
48. Ananda Metteyya 1903b, 142.
49. Speaking of the case of Sri Lanka, David Scott has noted that "'Buddhism,' the 'religion,' was constituted *as such* in an *adversarial* relation in as much as *all* 'religion' necessarily is" (1996, 14). Italics in original.
50. Ledi 2001, 127.
51. Kirichenko 2009, esp. 37–38.
52. Wunnita 1956, 107.
53. Ibid., 129.
54. Aung Mon 2007, 498.
55. *The Burman Buddhist* 1909, 172.
56. Ledi 2012, 182.
57. Vism. XXI 126.
58. Jordt 2007, 22.
59. Khaṅ' E" 2002, 268; Ledi 2004d, 711–13; Ledi 1986, *ta-dha*.
60. Ledi 1986, *ta-kha*.
61. Wunnita 1956, 170–71.
62. Bennison 1928, 96–97. One rupee equaled sixteen annas.
63. Purser and Saunders 1914, 88.
64. Stewart 1949, 13–14.
65. Ledi 2003a, 371.
66. P. J. FitzPatrick, quoted in Duffy 2011, 12.
67. This is not to say that printed texts would mean the layperson would want to cut out the monk from his or her religious life in favor of a text. Ledi re-

mained, for instance, a figure of great veneration, and we will see below that his sermons attracted huge audiences. Monastic preachers, *dhammakathikas*, were generally very popular.

68. Ledi 1986, 263.
69. Chit San Win 2003, 66.
70. Htin Aung 1966, 33–34; Chit San Win 2003, 24. This situation was similar to traditional preaching events (*dharmadesanā*) in Sri Lanka, where understandable doctrinal content was negligible and the generation of merit was of the greatest importance (Seneviratne 1999, 46–47).
71. Hla Pain 1967, 195; Maung Maung (1980, 111) says the fans were often a yard in diameter.
72. *The Burman Buddhist* 1908c, 50–51.
73. The *General Catalogue* lists a book by U Wunnita called *Ledi Yathle,* which translates literally as "Ledi Fan Down" and is glossed in English as "Ledi's Practical Sermons." Unfortunately, I have not been able to locate this work.
74. Purser and Saunders 1914, 88. The missionary ends by claiming that Ledi's style is the result of borrowing the "Christian manner of preaching" (Purser and Saunders 1914, 88). I know of no source that would suggest any overt influence on his style from missionaries. On the other hand, the Sri Lankan movement for modern, short sermons, led by Dharmapala, seems to have been explicitly modeled on Christian practice (Seneviratne 1999, 49). See the discussion below.
75. Stewart 1949, 15.
76. For a detailed description of the Thingazar Sayadaw's life, as well as a collection of his stories, see Htin Aung 1966.
77. Hla Pain 1967, 196. Maung Maung (1980, 111) notes that some monks used the titles of popular songs or movies for their sermons.
78. Mendelson 1975, 215; a detailed plot synopsis is on 214–21.
79. Malalgoda 1976, 226.
80. Ibid.
81. Seneviratne 1999, 49.
82. Stewart 1949, 15.
83. Lubeigt 2005, 393.
84. For instance, as one writer observed: "It is worthy of note to mention here that the well-known Ledi Sayadaw has, by his preaching, helped to a certain extent to check the vice of the opium habit" (Aung Tun 1909, 136).
85. See Htin Aung 1966.
86. Seneviratne 1999, 53–54.
87. Chit San Win 2003, 25.
88. Hla Pain 1967, 188.
89. Aung Mon (2007, 575) notes that sayadaws often attracted groups of lay followers, but the extent of the attraction to groups associated with Ledi was much more extensive than was usual.
90. Ledi 1999b, vii; Aung Mon 2007, 580–81.

91. Htay Htay Lwin 1998, 75. This was the case for Ledi's *Dhat' kammaṭṭhān'* text, for instance, which concerned the doctrinal exposition of the meditation on the basic elements and the dependent origination groups (Htay Htay Lwin 1998, 66, 74–75).
92. Ibid. For detailed descriptions of traditional pedagogy in Burma, particularly the emphasis on memorization and recitation, see Mendelson 1975, 150–61; see also Schober 2007.
93. See Aung Mon 2007, 452, 532, 547, 564, 566, 586, 693, and 743.
94. Colston 1910, 80.
95. Turner 2009, 21–22.
96. Founded on April 16, 1900, by two men, one of whom was Maung Thaw, the person who submitted the questions to Ledi that would result in his writing of the *Uttamapurisa* (Ananda Metteyya 1903a, 168).
97. Mendelson 1975, 197.
98. The YMBA existed in Sri Lanka as well, founded there in 1898 by C. S. Dissanayake. It seems that the Sri Lankan YMBA viewed the Burmese YMBA as a branch of itself, but this was not the understanding in Burma, where YMBA members saw themselves as entirely independent (Schober 2005b, 22 n. 5).
99. Schober 2007, 63. For example, the Sāsanādhāra Society had a school, named "Buddhaghosa's School," which taught government-approved topics along with Buddhism (Ananda Metteyya 1903a, 172). Education was an important issue for the YMBA in Sri Lanka, too (Bond 1988, 65).
100. Schober 2005b, 5. The leading figures in the organization in the late nineteenth and early twentieth centuries were highly educated elites of Burmese society, who were based in major cities, such as U May Oung, a barrister educated at Cambridge, and U Kin, later knighted (Cady 1958, 179).
101. Schober 2011, 58.
102. Malalgoda 1976, 240.
103. Ibid., 232–37.
104. Frost 2002, 959.
105. *The Burman Buddhist* 1908a, 1.
106. Schober 2007, 64; Schober 2011, esp. chapter 4; Mendelson 1975, 196.
107. Commenting on transformations in Burmese Buddhism in the early years of the twentieth century, Ananda Metteyya brings all the aspects of Ledi's efforts together in a general description of what he calls "the new Buddhist Revival": "There are many evidences of the progress of this new Buddhist Revival: the appearance of great Monks, like the well-known Ledi Sayadaw, who, remaining no longer hidden in their Monasteries, go forth among the people and intensely stir them to better their ways; all over the land, again, there are new societies, forming for various religious purposes in the new spirit of the age. Even the subject of religious education, too long neglected, save by the merest handful of far-seeing women and men, is now beginning to secure attention" (Bennett 1929, 110–11).
108. In their book *Buddhism Transformed,* Gombrich and Obeyesekere describe

laicization as "the hallmark of modern Buddhism" and see it as the gradual takeover of spheres of action, particularly meditation, once largely limited to monks (Gombrich and Obeyesekere 1988, 324). Schober has argued that lay meditation has led to a laicization of Theravāda because meditative accomplishments on the part of laypeople obviate the need for the saṅgha (Schober 1995, 314–15).

109. "In the absence of kingship, the saṅgha and ambitious lay reformers, such as the early-twentieth-century figure Anagarika Dharmapala, have clearly stepped in to orient the religious lives of the laity in a much more emphasized *lōkōttara* direction. There has occurred, in the process, a 'monasticization' of lay Buddhism" (Holt 1991b, 219). Speaking of Buddhism in the 1980s, Houtman has said: "It has been remarked in much of the literature on 'modern Buddhism' across Theravāda Southeast Asia that a process of 'laicization' has taken place, whereby the layman has come to play a central role in Buddhism. Considering the way some unordained meditators have a tendency to mark in language their status as 'core' Buddhists by using monastic language and by classifying themselves as monks as described above, one would be better off suggesting the reverse, namely that there has been a 'monasticization' of the unordained" (Houtman 1990b, 125).

110. In fairly recent times (the 1980s), Gustaaf Houtman even observed some lay meditators referring to themselves as "true monastics" and speaking of themselves with Burmese vocabulary usually reserved for the ordained (Houtman 1990b, 124). To use such vocabulary was not common, however, and controversial, as Houtman notes.

111. Collins and McDaniel 2010, 1375.

112. Wunnita 1956, 109; Ledi 1986, *u*. To form this organization, Ledi drew members from earlier missionary organizations, the Yangon-based organization *Buddha thāthana samāgama a phvai'* (founded in 1903) and the Mandalay-based *Man ta le" mrui' buddha thāthana a thaṅ'"* (founded in 1899) (Aung Mon 2007, 705–8).

113. See Tambiah 1976; Hansen 2007, esp. 18–44; Seneviratne 1999; and Malalgoda 1976, esp. 239.

114. Wunnita 1956, 107.

115. Collins 1998, 460. In another speech at the founding of the Foreign Missionary Society, the head lay member of the organization, U Kyaw Yan, correlated lay efforts to the missionary efforts of the most esteemed and powerful lay figure in the Theravāda tradition, Asoka, the exemplary Buddhist king (Wunnita 1956, 119). Jonathan Walters (1992) has argued that, contrary to modern perceptions, Buddhism only became a missionary religion in the modern period under the influence of colonialism. By the time of Ledi's missionary organization, however, the Burmese understood missionary action as a traditional practice with a pedigree stretching back to the Buddha.

116. Jordt (2007, 27) has observed that the lay organization which runs the large

and influential Mahasi meditation center has continued in the role of the king.

117. Houtman has noted that this "ideal" of a clear differentiation between monk and layperson has remained up to recent times, even among ardent lay meditators (Houtman 1990b, 125).
118. Ledi 1995, 365–66.

CHAPTER FOUR

1. Hla Pain 1967, 155. My thanks to Charles Carstens and U Saw Tun for helpful comments on this translation. For more on Maung Gyi, also known as Ledi Pandita, who became well known and highly influential in his own right in Burma, see Ikeya 2011, 60ff.
2. Hla Pain 1967, 155.
3. My analysis of the *Summary* depends upon two copies of the text, one from 2004 and another from 1986 that includes Ledi's autocommentary. There appear to be no differences in the text of the *Summary* verses in either version.
4. Ledi 1986, 19. Besides the *Summary,* Ledi also wrote a *saṃ khip'* on the Vinaya, and between 1904 and 1910 the British catalogue of published books records eight other *saṃ khip'* by different authors (Government of Burma 1846–1941).
5. The *Summary* with autocommentary is listed among Ledi's works inscribed in stone at his monastery, though I have not been able to find any information on when the autocommentary was written or first published. The 1986 edition of the *Summary* includes the autocommentary without any information on its history, save to say on the title page that the book includes "the explication of the great sayadaw."
6. The *Summary* went through nine printings in the years 1904–7:

Pub. Date	Price (in annas)	No. of copies
1904	12	3,000
1905	3	3,000
1906	3	6,000
1906	12	3,000
1906	3	6,000
1906	2	10,000
1906	12	3,000
1907	3	6,000
1907	4	10,000

Other texts about the *Saṅgaha* had appeared by the time Ledi wrote the *Summary,* and more would follow. For the years 1900 to 1910, 47 of the 133 works published on some topic of Abhidhamma concern the *Saṅgaha.* But none of these works enjoyed anything close to the success of the *Summary.* See Government of Burma 1846–1941.

7. Hla Pain 1967, 155.
8. Ledi 1986, 19–20.
9. See Ledi 2001, 304–5, and his extensive discussion in Ledi 1996, 525–50. Both examples are discussed in the next chapter.
10. Ledi 2012, 182.
11. I thank Bhikkhu Anālayo for pointing out to me this interpretation of Ledi's statement.
12. *The Burman Buddhist* 1908b, 28.
13. I would like to thank Hiroko Kawanami, who drew my attention to this aspect of the poem's appeal.
14. These texts are also called *niyaṃ.*
15. "Mnemotechnical devices" in Griffith's phrase, speaking of other religious literature (1999, 46).
16. The *hetu* (root) conditions are the conditioning factors of greed (*lobha*), hatred (*dosa*), or delusion (*moha*), which were discussed in chapter 2, or their opposites of non-greed, non-hatred, or non-delusion. *Adhipati* (predominance) means four possible states (desire, energy, consciousness, and investigation) which dominate co-arising conditioned states. Kamma means volitions (*cetanā*) within the eighty-nine classes of consciousness. *Āhāra* means nutriments that support the coexistence of mind and matter. *Indriya* are fifteen immaterial faculties, such as pleasure, pain, and mindfulness. Jhāna means the seven factors of initial application, sustained application, zest, one-pointedness, joy, displeasure, and equanimity. Finally, *magga* means the twelve path factors of right view, intention, speech, action, livelihood, effort, mindfulness, and concentration, and also wrong view, intention, effort, and concentration. For details on these conditions, see Bodhi et al. 2000, chapter 8.
17. I thank D. Christian Lammerts, who spoke with several learned monks in Burma about *saṃ pok'* on my behalf and provided me with this example and others (personal communication, July 6, 2011).
18. Ledi 1986, 156, after v. 390.
19. To mention another example, in verse fifty-four Ledi says *"phas', ve, sañ', ce | e, jī, mana"* for *"phassa, vedanā, saññā, cetanā | ekaggatā, jīvitindre, manasikāra"* (Ledi 1986, 39). These are contact, feeling, perception, volition, one-pointedness, life faculty, and attention. They are the so-called "universal mental factors" (*sabbacittasādhāraṇa*) because they are common to all of the eighty-nine consciousness.
20. Hiroko Kawanami reported to me that Burmese nuns, in fact, had to struggle for decades to gain access to some closely guarded Abhidhamma memorization texts used at large monasteries in Mandalay, such as Mahagandayoun Monastery (personal communication, June 24, 2011). Presumably, these

texts went beyond the basics available in a work like the *Summary*. There are, of course, examples of the use of abbreviation in Buddhist texts for purposes other than study that had a reach into lay lives, such as the esoteric use of syllables, drawn from the Abhidhamma, for protection. See Swearer 1995; see also McDaniel 2008, 228–46.

21. The straight lines that separate words in this and other verses are present in the Burmese and indicate the feet within a verse. They are called *pud' ka le"*. I include them here and in longer translated quotations below to give a sense of the organization of verses.
22. Ledi 1986, 242. The eight recollections are of Buddha, dhamma, saṅgha, morality, generosity, the qualities of the gods, death, and awakening. Perception is perception of the disgustingness of food, and analysis is analysis of the four great essentials in all physical matter.
23. Ledi 1986, 239.
24. These are the qualities of mind the Buddha possesses in limitless measure (hence called "immeasurables" or "illimitables") and which all Buddhists are encouraged to develop without limit. See Bodhi et al. 2000, 89–90.
25. See the discussion in Collins 1998, 46–53.
26. This idea akin to the conception of Sanskrit in the Hindu sphere.
27. Collins 1998, 49–50.
28. Sheldon Pollock has defined this distinction between cosmopolitan and vernacular languages in a way that applies well to the Burmese situation: "*Cosmopolitan* and *vernacular* can be taken as modes of literary (and intellectual, and political) communication directed toward two different audiences, whom lay actors knew full well to be different. The one is unbounded and potentially infinite in extension; the other is practically finite and bounded by finite audiences" (Pollock 2000, 593–94).
29. Many Pali texts were written after Ledi's commentary, up to the present day, but none have commanded widespread attention. Burma had made a decisive shift to the Burmese vernacular in its literature by at least the seventeenth century (Bode 1909, 48). Even at that time many Burmese translations were made of the *Saṅgaha* (Bode 1909, 61).
30. Collins 1998, 53.
31. Schober 2005b, 10; Sarkisyanz 1965, 108.
32. One can be reborn in the woeful plane *(apāyabhūmi),* the sensuous blissful plane (*kāmasugatibhūmi*), the fine-material-sphere plane (*rūpāvacarabhūmi*), or the immaterial-sphere plane (*arūpāvacarabhūmi*).
33. Bodhi et al. 2000, 194. These are consciousnesses that determine the nature of one's birth by linking the new life to the old one that has just passed, determine the character of the subsequent flow of the life-continuum (*bhavaṅga*), and that comprise the final consciousness before another rebirth takes place. The precise make-ups of these consciousnesses depend on one's kamma and place in the Buddhist cosmology. See Bodhi et al. 2000, 124–28.
34. These are productive, supportive, obstructive, and destructive kamma. Pro-

ductive kamma produces results directly; supportive kamma enables, catalytically, another karmic act to come to fruition; obstructive kamma is that deed that prevents another kamma from producing a result; and destructive kamma produces its own result directly and also prevents another kamma from coming to fruition (Bodhi et al. 2000, 200–202).

35. There are three "timely" (*kālamaraṇa*) deaths, due to the natural end of one's lifespan, the extinguishing of the karmic force that drives life on, or both. An "untimely" (*akālamaraṇa*) death is one in which life is cut off by a karmic fruition even before the natural end of one's lifespan (Bodhi et al. 2000, 220).
36. *Peta*s are often referred to as "hungry ghosts." The term means "the departed," i.e., the dead. They wander the earth, invisible to most people, searching for food, yet never able to satiate themselves. They are often depicted with needle-size mouths and tremendous pot bellies (Sadakata 2004, 54).
37. Sometimes called "titans," *asura*s are beings similar to the *peta*s (Bodhi et al. 2000, 190).
38. These four great kings rule over realms associated with the four directions of east, south, north, and west (Bodhi et al. 2000, 191).
39. This is Tāvatiṃsa, where the Buddha preached the Abhidhamma to his mother. The ruler of this realm is Sakka, also known as Indra (Bodhi et al. 2000, 191).
40. So named because Yāma is king of this realm.
41. This is called in Pali *Tusita*. It is the realm in which the *Bodhisatta*, the Buddha-to-be, lives during his penultimate life before his human life in which he achieves awakening.
42. These gods are so called because they produce objects of enjoyment with their minds (Bodhi et al. 2000, 191).
43. These gods do not produce objects of enjoyment with their own minds, but control the objects created for them by those serving them (Bodhi et al. 2000, 191–92).
44. Bodhi et al. 2000, 189–90.
45. Lopez 2004, 3.
46. In a later section of this chapter, the lifespans of beings in the sense-realms are discussed, but not the spatial details Ledi gives in the *Summary*. See Bodhi et al. 2000, 196–97; Ledi also discusses the lifespans of beings in these realms; see Ledi 1986, 122ff.
47. These measurements are in *yojanas*. The *Concise Pali-English Dictionary* and *The Pali Text Society Dictionary* measure a *yojana* at about seven miles, so the "air basis" of the cosmos would be approximately 6,720,000 miles.
48. As the next verse indicates, these are the names of hell realms. This verse and the next list the eight great hells. The Sañjīva or "reviving" hell is one where residents are cut apart with blades and then revived to be chopped up over and over again. Kāla is an abbreviation for the Kālasutta or "black string" hell. In this hell a string black with ink is used to measure a being's body.

The body is then cut up according to the lines. In the Saṃghāta or "dashing together" hell all sorts of tortures are inflicted on the denizens. There are two Roruva hells or hells of "weeping." Various sufferings cause the crying of the inhabitants, giving rise to the name (Sadakata 2004, 47–50).

49. The two Tāpana or "heating" hells involve torture by fire, as implied by the name. Finally, Avīci is the lowest and worst hell, for there torture is unceasing, without even the break in the others necessitated by reconstituting the body of the denizen after the mode of torture has destroyed it (Sadakata 2004, 47–50). Note that the Burmese believed that it was inevitable that hunters and fishermen would end up in this realm because of the evil of their livelihoods (Scott 1963, 100 n. 1). This is pertinent to this project because Ledi will discuss the spiritual potential of people with these lowly jobs in the context of meditation (see chapter 5).
50. *Baṅ', prā, lak', than'* stand for, respectively, *Baṅ' pup'* (excrement), *Prā pū* (hot ash), *Lak' paṃ* (red silk cotton tree), and *Than' lyak'* (dagger). These hells are filled with the things indicated by their name. So in the excrement hell one must wade through lakes of feces teeming with maggots that eat one to the bone. The hot ash hell burns one to a crisp. The red silk cotton tree hell is one where the beings in it must climb up and down red silk cotton trees, which have leaves that are blades (the leaves always turn to face in the direction the person is climbing, whether up or down). Denizens of the dagger hell are also sliced up, as they attempt to make their way through a forest of four-sided blades (Sadakata 2004, 51–52).
51. The seven abbreviations in this verse stand for the seven realms of the Human Realm, the Realm of the Four Great Kings, the Realm of the Thirty-three Gods, the Realm of the Yāma gods, the Delightful Realm, the Realm of the Gods Who Rejoice in (Their Own) Creations, and the Realm of the Gods Who Lord over the Creations of Others (Bodhi et al. 2000, 189–90). Ledi calls these places ones of power because these are places where Māras, personifications of sense-desire, hold sway (Ledi 1986, 116).
52. Ledi 1986, 112–16.
53. See J. G. Scott 1963, 133ff.
54. Ledi 2004c, 32.
55. Ledi 1908, 96.
56. The seven purifications are purification of virtue (*sīlavisuddhi*), purification of mind (*cittavisuddhi*), purification of view (*diṭṭhivisuddhi*), purification by overcoming doubt (*kaṅkhāvitaraṇavisuddhi*), purification by knowledge and vision of the right and wrong paths (*maggāmaggañāṅadassanavisuddhi*), purification by knowledge and vision of the way (*paṭipadāñāṅadassanavisuddhi*), and purification by knowledge and vision (*ñāṅadassanavisuddhi*). See Gunaratana 1980, 283–301, for an overview of the purifications.
57. Bodhi et al. 2000, 347.
58. Ibid., 348. The requisites can also be described as consisting of eight items: three robes, an alms bowl, a water strainer, a needle, a belt, and a razor.

59. Ledi 1986, 235–37.
60. In Vism. I 10 (see also VIII 173), Buddhaghosa explains that higher virtue is shown by moral behavior, higher consciousness by the development of concentration (samādhi), and higher wisdom by the development of liberative understanding of the dhamma. See Ñāṇamoli 1999, 8.
61. Ibid., 750 n. 9.
62. Vism. I 27; Ñāṇamoli 1999, 15.
63. Ledi 1986, 237. The *dhutaṅga* rules are optional ascetic practices such as wearing robes made of cast-off clothing, dwelling at the foot of a tree in the forest, and never lying down to sleep. For discussion of all thirteen, see Vism. II 1–10. An *upajjhāya* (preceptor) and *ācariya* (teacher) instruct novices and junior monks. The layperson usually follows five precepts: no killing, stealing, no sexual misconduct, no lying or false speech, and no intoxicants. The eight precepts or sīlas change the rule about sexual behavior to one of celibacy and add three more: no eating after midday, no attending entertainments or using perfumes, and no high or luxurious beds. The ten sīlas are typically for novices; they are often called "rules of training" (*sikkhāpada*): no killing, no stealing, no sex, no lying or false speech, no intoxicants, no eating after midday, no attending entertainments, no wearing jewelry or perfumes, no sleeping on high or luxurious beds, and no handling of gold and silver (Gethin 1998, 87, 110).
64. Griffiths 1999, 40–46.
65. Gadamer (2006, 282) makes the point that tradition, to survive, must be embraced and cultivated creatively. We will return to this issue in the conclusion.
66. Ledi 1986, 263–64. I would like to thank John Okell for his assistance in the translation of this poem.
67. Aung-Thwin 2008, 209.
68. Ledi 1986, 263. It is interesting that Ledi includes chapter 5, the planes of existence chapter, in the Sutta Piṭaka. The chapter's main focus on the processes of consciousness driven by enumerated configurations of mental factors makes it highly Abhidhammic, given its focus on "ultimate" (*paramattha*) entities.
69. See Turner 2009, 105–6.
70. The "nat realm" (*nat' praññ'*) (Ledi 1986, 263).
71. Ibid.
72. A meditation manual by the well-known Burmese monk and meditation master U Pandita (born 1921) is entitled *In This Very Life* (1993).
73. Solitary Buddhas (*paccekabuddhas*) are those that reach full enlightenment but do not teach and so do not establish a sāsana.
74. Aung Mon 2007, 740–43.
75. Ledi started the first *Summary* study group in 1903 in Pyinmana (Aung Mon 2007, 538) and then continued to found groups on trips around Burma (Aung Mon 2007, 575).

76. Jordt 2007, 22.
77. Wunnita 1956, 51; Hla Pain 1967, 155.
78. Turner 2009, 103.
79. Htay Htay Lwin states that the eighth Ledi Sayadaw, U Indaka, became well known for reinstituting *Summary* study groups in 1980, after they had disappeared during World War II (Htay Htay Lwin 1998, 63). Recall that Ledi's successor as abbot at his original monastery, U Nyanabatha, became the second Ledi Sayadaw after the first's death (Aung Mon 2007, 436 n. 3). The current abbot of the Ledi Monastery, U Kelatha (Kelāsa), who is therefore also called Ledi Sayadaw, is the ninth.
80. Htay Htay Lwin 1998, 60–61.
81. Government of Burma 1908, 35.
82. Ledi 1986, 263.
83. Htay Htay Lwin 1998, 24.
84. From "Moulmein," *Burma Echo*, December 7, 1907, quoted in Tuner 2009, 105.
85. Wunnita 1956, 67.
86. Turner 2009, 104–5.

CHAPTER FIVE

1. Ledi 2001, 328–29. This is from the *Manual on the Factors of Awakening (Bodhipakkhiyadīpanī)*, a work discussed below.
2. *Pakati lū pugguil' paṅ' phrac' sau laññ'" ra han'" chui ra e** (Ledi 2001, 400).
3. Cousins 1996, 35.
4. Gombrich and Obeyesekere 1988, 237; Bond 1988, 59. Dharmapala started his own self-devised meditation practice around 1890, using mantra recitation and other techniques quite different from the approach to meditation in Burma (Frost 2002, 956).
5. Carrithers 1983, 11.
6. This was done in anticipation of the upcoming Buddha *jayanti,* or 2,500th anniversary of the Buddha's death. The *jayanti* was also understood traditionally to be the halfway point in the lifespan of the sāsana (Gombrich and Obeyesekere 1988, 238). The first Burmese delegation of meditation monks, including U Sujāta, an assistant to Mahasi, arrived in 1955 (Bond 1988, 132). There was apparently the teaching of the Mahasi method of meditation in 1939 to a limited extent, but at that time it seems to have attracted little attention (Gombrich and Obeyesekere 1988, 237). The revival of meditation among forest monks by the Sri Lankan monk Ñāṇārāma depended, as well, on his learning to meditate from a Burmese monk, U Javana, in 1958 (Carrithers 1983, 237–38).
7. See Tiyavanich 1997; Tambiah 1976, 1984.
8. Jim Taylor 1993, 42. Tambiah states: "Mongkut neither as monk nor later as king was a meditation enthusiast" (Tambiah 1987, 214). See also Tambiah 1976, 209.

9. See Jackson 1988.
10. Tambiah (1987, 211) says that Burmese methods of meditation, especially the Mahasi method (discussed in detail in the conclusion), spread mainly to Bangkok-area monasteries that were unconnected to the Thai forest movement. From Wat Mahāthāt in Bangkok, one of the largest monasteries in Thailand, the abbot Phra Phimolatham established branch monasteries to teach Burmese-style meditation in the 1950s and 60s (Tambiah 1984, 170–71). See also Sharf 1995, 254; Kornfield 1996. For the Dhammakāya, see Rachelle Scott 2009.
11. Pranke 2010 (2011), 460.
12. See Government of Burma 1868–1941, the record of August 24, 1877. There were 1,700 copies printed on April 20, 1877, by "Moung Shwe Tso," who in the record is described as "Moung Tsoh, *Friend of Moulmein* Press, Lower Main Road, Moulmein." Each copy of the book cost 8 annas.
13. Wunnita 1956, 108.
14. The exception is the *Manual on No-Self* (*Anattadīpanī*). Ledi states in the introductory paragraph to that work that he wrote it in December of 1901 at the request of the monk Nyanavamsa [Ñāṇavaṃsa], a resident of the city of Aloun [A luṃ], who wanted a clear and easy presentation of the method for meditating on the feelings (*vedanās*) in accordance with the sacred texts (Ledi 1995, 457; see Aung Mon 2007, 491–92).
15. For the *Meditation Object of Puṇṇovāda,* see Ledi 2003a, 634. Aung Mon notes that it was first published in an anthology of Ledi's *dīpanīs* in 1924 (Aung Mon 2007, 420 n. 2). For the *Manual on the Path to Knowledge,* see Ledi 1995, 364. Such hermits, called in Burmese ya-thay [*ra the'*], though not ordained, often wear dark brown robes and observe some precepts and austerities (Mendelson 1961, 569).
16. Saya Myo was practicing meditation during the rains retreat at Ledi's monastery in Monywa when he requested the *Manual on Meditation Objects.* See Ledi 1996, 525; Aung Mon 2007, 514–15. For the *Manual on Breath Meditation,* see Ledi 1995, 297; Aung Mon 2007, 539.
17. Ledi 1995, 367; Aung Mon 2007, 522–23.
18. For the *Manual on the Factors of Awakening,* see Ledi 2001, 417; Aung Mon 2007, 532. In the epilogue, Ledi says he wrote the *Big Book on Meditation Objects* at the request of a lay Abhidhamma teacher, named Saya Thay, as an elaboration of the chapter on meditation in the *Summary of the Ultimates.* Aung Mon's biography quotes from a letter addressed to Ledi by Saya Thay, in which he explains that he has had no trouble teaching the other chapters of Ledi's poem, but that his students (over twenty men and more than thirty women) cannot grasp the full meaning of the chapter on meditation (Aung Mon 2007, 543).
19. Aung Mon 2007, 580. It is called the *"New" Book on the Meditation Object of the Elements* because his book the *Meditation Object of Puṇṇovāda* is considered

his first on the elements as the object of meditation (Aung Mon 2007, 580 n. 5).

20. Ledi 2001, 75.
21. Ibid., 296–300.
22. J. G. Scott 1963, 100 n. 1.
23. Ledi 2001, 309. Calming is samatha, insight is vipassanā, and reflection is *manasikāra*. Here, reflection means the attention directed toward the object of meditation that enables the cultivation of concentration and insight. See Ledi's comments in the *Manual of Insight Meditation* (1915, 39).
24. Ledi 2001, 304.
25. Ibid., 308.
26. Ibid., 307.
27. Ledi 1995, 23.
28. In discussing lay morality in the *Factors*, in fact, Ledi (2001, 312–13) refers to the categories of spiritual cultivation called the three trainings (*sikkhās*), discussed also in the *Summary:* higher virtue (*adhisīla*), higher consciousness (*adhicitta*), and higher wisdom (*adhipaññā*).
29. Quotations of the *Manual on Insight Meditation* are from U Nyana's (Ñāṇa's) English translation, since this translation was published during Ledi's life and presumably in consultation with him. Based on my review of the Burmese text, it seems that Nyana sticks closely to the meaning Ledi intended, though for key phrases I have used my own translations. U Nyana, a monk from the Masoyein Monastery in Mandalay, was Ledi's student and also worked with him on a Pali dictionary (Hla Pain 1967, 223). Besides *Insight Meditation,* he translated some of Ledi's other works into English, including the *Manual of Relations* (*Paṭṭhānuddesadīpanī*) and parts of the *Manual of the Way* (*Niyāmadīpanī*). Of the most importance, he seems to have acted as Ledi's conduit to English-speakers. He translated the correspondence to Ledi from C.A.F. Rhys-Davids, and also translated Ledi's responses to Rhys-Davids into English.
30. There is no certain record of it in Burmese until 1932, but it is likely that it was published long before this date, given that a Burmese version was at hand and Ledi's works typically went into print very quickly (Ledi 1915, i). The *General Catalogue* records a work by Ledi published in Prome in 1927 entitled *The Insight Meditation Handbook* (*Vipassanā lak' cvai kyam'"*). I have never encountered a book of this title in any source concerning Ledi. Perhaps it is a variant title given to the *Manual on Insight Meditation?* I have not yet found a copy to answer this, but if it is then it pushes its recorded appearance back by five years. In the record for the first quarter of the year ending March 31, 1927, the book is described rather vaguely as "A Catechism on the Fundamental Principles of Buddhist Philosophy." It was published on January 1 of that year, and 1,350 copies were printed. It is 50 pages long and cost 1 anna and 8 pies.

31. Aung Mon 2007, 682; Ledi 2012.
32. Aung Mon 2007, 680; see also 842ff. Ledi's answers to C.A.F. Rhys-Davids are found in Ledi 2004b, 67–208. English-language translations are in Ledi 2012 and Ledi 1999b, 126–31.
33. Mills wrote the introduction to Dudley Wright's 1912 *A Manual of Buddhism.* In one letter to Mills, for instance, Ledi explained the nature of the physical makeup of reality (rūpa and *ākāsa*), as well as the formation of the order of monks and nuns (Ledi 2004b, 40–66).
34. Ledi 2012, 182.
35. Ledi 1915, 10.
36. Rhys-David's introduction to the Pali Text Society edition of the *Abhidhammatthasaṅgaha* privileges the Burmese hierarchy and estimation of Abhidhamma commentaries, for instance. It should be noted that much of Ledi's influence on Rhys-Davids was mediated through his pupil Shwe Zan Aung, who worked closely with Rhys-Davids on the English translation of the *Abhidhammatthasaṅgaha.* For more on her dealings with Shwe Zan Aung, see Snodgrass 2007. One could call this a moment of "intercultural mimesis" (Hallisey 1995, 33) or "mutuality" (O'Hanlon 1988, 217).
37. Ledi 2001, 411.
38. Ñāṇamoli 1999, 442. Buddhaghosa calls the information in the *Visuddhimagga*'s *paññābhūmi* or "realm of wisdom" chapters the "soil" in which purification of the meditator grows like a trunk. It is a telling divergence from Ledi's approach described below, however, that Buddhaghosa discusses the development of morality and concentration before investigation of the soil. In chapter 1, we noted, too, the monk Medhawi wrote a number of vernacular works on meditation in Abhidhamma terms in the mid-eighteenth century (Pranke 2010 [2011], 457).
39. Gethin points out: "Indian culture as a whole is in origin 'oral'; indeed, a penchant for analyzing something in terms of a neat categorized list is characteristic of much traditional Indian learning, and the oral origins of Indian learning continued to inform its structure long after its exponents had begun to commit it to writing" (1992, 149).
40. Ledi 1999a, 107–8.
41. Ledi 2003a, 608–13. As the title suggests, Ledi takes the approach given in the *Puṇṇovāda Sutta* (MN 145).
42. Ledi 1995, 313. These are the bases formed of sensitive matter (*pasādarūpa*) on which the five physical senses and the mind depend. The mind has as its base the *hadayavatthu* or "heart base." See Bodhi et al. 2000, 144–45.
43. These are the properties of heat and cold born from karma, consciousness, physical processes, and nutriments within the body, as well as the properties of heat and cold external to the body (Ledi 1995, 336–37).
44. Ledi notes these are organized in a complementary fashion to the element of fire, so there are the two basic types of physical substance, solid and liquid, born from the nutriments (*āhāra*) of edible food, sense impressions,

volitional thought, and consciousness within the body, as well as solids and liquids external to the body (Ledi 1995, 339).

45. Ibid., 313.
46. Ibid., 458–63. Although Ledi says at the start of the work that he wrote it to explain the role of the feelings in meditation, he adds in the conclusion that he called the text an explanation of no-self because he wanted to explain to people the liberating knowledge of anattā (543).
47. The Pali Text Society Dictionary defines *pariññā* as "accurate or exact knowledge, comprehension, full understanding" (PTSD 1999, 425). Ñāṇamoli in his translation of the *Visuddhimagga* translates the word as "full-understanding" (Ñāṇamoli 1999, 891). The translation "profound knowledge" is the one used by Ledi's translator, U Nyana, in his translation of the *Manual on Insight Meditation.* I have chosen to use Nyana's translation because it seems likely Nyana discussed his translation with Ledi, since he was Ledi's student and corresponded with him. Furthermore, the expression "profound knowledge" conveys the sense of a comprehensive understanding that goes beyond the merely factual to impact the reader on a salvific level.
48. Ledi 1996, 525.
49. See, respectively, Ledi 1996, 525–50, 550–604, 604–21, 622–25, and 625–57.
50. The sutta is at MN 118.
51. Ledi 1995, 409.
52. Ibid., 412–13.
53. Ledi 2001, 312–13. This set of thirty-seven factors comprises, first, the four establishings of mindfulness (*satipaṭṭhānas*) used in insight meditation. These are body (*kāya*), feeling (*vedanā*), consciousness (citta), and aspects of the path (dhammas), such as the hindrances (*nīvaraṇas*). Next are the four right efforts (*padhānas*), which are to overcome unwholesome states that have arisen, avoid those that have not arisen, support wholesome states that have arisen, and try to arouse wholesome states that have not arisen. Then come the four means to power (*iddhipādas*); these are the strong desire (*chandiddhipāda*) to attain the goal, the resolution to use full effort (*vīriyaddhipāda*), an ardent focus (*cittiddhipāda*) on the task, and a keen knowledge (*vīmaṃsiddhipāda*) of the nature and value of wisdom. Next are the five spiritual abilities (*indriyas*): faith (*saddha*), energy (*vīriya*), mindfulness (sati), concentration (samādhi), and wisdom (*paññā*). After that are the five spiritual powers (*balas*), which are the same as the abilities but as applied to root out the false view of an essential self. The seven factors of enlightenment (*bojjhaṅgas*) come next; they are mindfulness (sati), investigation (*dhammavicaya*), energy (*vīriya*), joy (*pīti*), calm (*passaddhi*), concentration (samādhi), and equanimity (*upekkhā*). Finally, there is the eightfold path (*magga*).
54. Ledi 2001, 304–5; my italics.
55. Ibid., 328.
56. See Ledi 2012, 181–82.

57. See, for example, MN 140, the *Dhātuvibhaṅga Sutta*, and DN 22, the *Satipaṭṭhāna Sutta*.
58. Ibid., 309.
59. Ledi 1995, 2–4.
60. Ibid., 23. As noted earlier, to realize fully these three marks of impermanence (anicca), suffering (dukkha), and not-self (anattā) as the fundamental qualities of existence is to achieve awakening.
61. As noted in the previous chapter, Ledi classifies the meditation chapter of the *Abhidhammatthasaṅgaha* as part of the Sutta Piṭaka (Ledi 1986, 263), but, framed as it is within an exegesis of the Abhidhamma system, it still partakes of a general Abhidhamma perspective.
62. Ledi divides the *Meditation Object of the Elements* into two parts. The first is in Pali and the second in Burmese. In the Pali section, the first three pages are lists of the features of each of the four elements. There is first an *uddesa,* or basic list of the four elements, then a *niddesa* or more detailed description of each element. Finally, there is a *paṭiniddesa,* which further elaborates on their qualities. After the Pali-language section, Ledi provides a *nissaya,* a word-by-word commentary in Burmese for the Pali. After the word-by-word commentary, Ledi goes into even greater detail in Burmese on the elements and how they work together to form physical matter (rūpa).
63. Ledi 1995, 438.
64. Ledi 1915, 16. "Hallucination" as the translation of *vipallāsa* is the translator U Nyana's choice. It might be rendered "distorted view" or "corrupted view," in the sense of being distorted or corrupted by greed, hatred, and delusion. Ledi had made much the same point about the value of the Abhidhamma five years earlier in his book the *Manual of Light* (*A liṅ‘" kyam‘"*): "As for these two ways, the way of the world is useful in the world, but it cannot go beyond the world. But the way of the Abhidhamma can go beyond the world. It can reach to the highest world" (Ledi 2001, 437).
65. Ledi 1995, 535. In the *Visuddhimagga,* the hallucinations (*vipallāsas*) only receive significant discussion in chapter 14, the first chapter of the *paññābhūmi* section. And the profound knowledges (pariññās) are not discussed until chapter 20 on the purification by knowledge and vision of the right and wrong paths (*maggāmaggañāṅadassanavisuddhi*).
66. Ledi 1915, 42. In the *Manual on No-Self,* Ledi provides the reader with an analysis of the arising and passing away of feelings through the process of dependent origination (*paṭiccasamuppāda*) as a means to acquire this knowledge (Ledi 1995, 467–89).
67. See Ledi 1995, 489–534.
68. Ledi 1915, 50.
69. Ibid.
70. Ibid., 45.
71. Collins 1998, 51.
72. Collins 1992, 127.

73. Ledi 2001, 312; my italics.
74. Griffiths 1981, 618.
75. Thitagu Sayadaw U Nyanissara, "Abhidhamma and Vipassana," http://www.thisismyanmar.com/nibbana/dhamaj2.htm#ABHIDHAMMA (accessed September 22, 2011).
76. Ledi 1995, 387–89.
77. For the breath, it is often said to resemble, among other things, a star, smoke, or the disc of the moon (Gunaratana 2002, 57). See Vism. IV 31; Bodhi et al. 2000, 331–32.
78. Ledi 1995, 387–89.
79. Ibid., 407. The notion of "momentary concentration" would be critical to the meditation method of another monk, the Mahasi Sayadaw, discussed below. See Cousins 1996, 43–47.
80. Ledi 1995, 405–6.
81. Ledi made the same point that same year in the *Manual on the Factors of Awakening* (Ledi 2001, 324). He also discusses the details of the possibility of such practice with minimal concentration earlier in the *Manual on No-Self* and the *Manual on Nutriment* (*Āhāradīpanī*). I focus on the *Manual on Breath Meditation* to demonstrate this aspect of Ledi's innovations because it is his most practice-oriented work and in it he presents the possibility clearly and concisely.
82. Ledi (2001, 308–9) also assures people in the *Manual on the Factors of Awakening* that one can cultivate wisdom even without cultivating calm and concentration, though ideally one would follow the order of the seven purifications. See also Winston L. King 1980, 120; Houtman 1990a, 187–89; Chit Tin 1999a, 13.
83. Throughout the work Ledi also says that the details of method are in the hands of the practitioner. For example, he says a person can count the breaths if it helps to focus the attention, but it is not required; one can count out loud or remain silent; and he says one can keep track of the breath by using a string of beads, but their use is optional (Ledi 1995, 385). The meditator can also decide for him- or herself how long to meditate each day and when to switch from calming to insight practices (Ledi 1995, 406–8).
84. For canonical warrant, see AN 4.170; see also Vism. I 6, and discussion in Cousins 1984, 59–61.
85. See, for instance, Vism. XXI 112. Justification for this alternative is apparently based upon an interpretation of the *Patisambhidāmagga* II 92–103. For a detailed explanation of the argument, see Cousins 1996, esp. 48–50, and also Cousins 1984, 60–64.
86. Vism. XVIII 1–2; Ñāṇamoli 1999, 605. Winston L. King (1980, 116) suggests that the structure of the *Visuddhimagga* implies that not cultivating concentration prior to insight work is a "second-grade possibility."
87. In fact, the "dry" meditator will experience at least the "supramundane *jhāna*" (*lokuttarajhāna*), which arises as the state of mind that sees with the

penetrative focus necessary to achieve awakening at the end of the process leading to insight (Gunaratana 1980, 275).

88. Ledi 1995, 408–10.
89. Ibid., 408–9.
90. "In terms of ultimate reality [*paramattha*], in the in-breath and the out-breath there are only these four qualities of hardness, coherence, heat, and movement. It is the wisdom of ultimate reality which perceives fully each of these four qualities. . . . One gains the pure wisdom to see that there are just these four elements" (Ledi 1995, 409–10).
91. Vism. XVIII 5–8; Ñāṇamoli 1999, 606–7.
92. Ledi 2001, 160. Speaking only of the first of the profound knowledges (i.e., *ñāta-pariññā*), Ledi says in the *Manual on Insight Meditation:* "If only the Four Great Essentials out of twenty-eight material phenomena are discerned accurately in the aforesaid manner, it may be said that the function of *Ñāta-pariññā* as regards *Rūpa* (form), is accomplished" (Ledi 1915, 42).
93. Ledi 2001, 161.
94. Ledi 2012, 182.
95. See also Ledi's stress of the four elements in his overview of meditation in *Visodhanī* (Ledi 1954, 1:32–35).
96. Ledi 1915, 64.
97. In the *Manual on the Factors of Awakening* Ledi had said that one could start insight practice right away and include in the process of such practice the mindfulness of the body that engenders the necessary concentrative control over the mind, "if he is a person *of true effort and knowledge*" (Ledi 2001, 324; my italics). Again, it is hard work in the realm of learning that makes the difference.
98. Ledi 1915, 64.
99. To state that one could achieve awakening in the midst of picayune activities is not unprecedented. For instance, Buddhaghosa gives the example of a monk who looks up when he hears a woman laugh loudly. When he sees her teeth he perceives their foulness and attains arhatship:

    He saw the bones that were her teeth,
    And kept in mind his first perception;
    And standing on that very spot
    The elder became an Arahant. (Vism. I 55; Ñāṇamoli 1999, 23)

    The *Paramattha-mañjūsā*, the commentary on the Vism., says that this realization is possible because the monk "had developed the preliminary work well" (Pm. 41–42; given in Ñāṇamoli 1999, 752 n. 15).
100. Ledi 1915, 65.
101. Ledi 1995, 68.
102. Ledi 1915, 68–69. *Vipariṇāma* is the radical change that takes place when something comes into existence or goes out of existence. Thus *vipariṇāma* is about the beginning and the ending of something. But in between the overt and

obvious arising and passing away of objects which is *vipariṇāma*, change still takes place. This is *aññathābhāva*, the small-scale, often undetectable changes all things constantly undergo. To differentiate between these two forms of change, Ledi gives the example of the flame of a lamp. The arising of the flame and its dying out are *vipariṇāma*. The quivering of the flame while it is burning, as its properties change and shift, is *aññathābhāva* (Ledi 1915, 50–51).

103. Ledi 2001, 161.
104. Ledi 1995, 408.
105. Ledi 2001, 316–17, 416.
106. For the canonical understanding of mindfulness, see MN 53; also Anālayo 2003, 46–49.
107. Many writers follow the German-born monk Nyanaponika's (1901–94) original use of the term, though his full discussion of sati, which encompasses much more than "bare attention," is more sophisticated than others' use of the term would suggest. See Nyanaponika 1996, 24–27 and 30–31. See also Bodhi 2011, 28–30.
108. Ledi 1915, 70.
109. Houtman 1985, 91.
110. As Gadamer observed: "Even where life changes violently, as in ages of revolution, far more of the old is preserved in the supposed transformation of everything than anyone knows, and it combines with the new to create a new value" (Gadamer 2006, 282–83).
111. Ledi 2001, 400. Ledi is referring to verse 142 of the *Dhammapada* where the Buddha says that a person, even if lay, can be called a monk or Brahmin if he is controlled, chaste, and dedicated to harmlessness. But, of course, it was not until the modern era that the Buddha was understood in Burma—or, for that matter, across the Theravāda world—to be calling for a lay life in many respects akin to that of monks.
112. Ledi 2001, 304–5.
113. Arnold 1994, 86. It is this view that leads to J. Alfred Prufrock's life measured out in coffee spoons, hearing the sound of the eternal footman snickering.
114. Taylor 2001, esp. 186–87.
115. Wunnita 1956, 41.
116. Chakrabarty 2002, 23.
117. Sharma 2002, 282.
118. Ledi 1915, 64.
119. Wunnita 1956, 41.
120. See the discussion in Mendelson 1975, 262–64.
121. See Jordt 2007, esp. chapter 5.

CONCLUSION

1. Stadtner 2011, 113–16.
2. The statue was donated by the well-known Burmese actor U Kyaw Hein.

Kyaw Hein announced he was quitting acting to become a monk in 2008 (Nilar 2008). *Athi* can also mean the sort of liberative realization (*paññā*) that stems from meditative practice, but its positioning on the Buddha's hands suggests knowledge as a means to realization. What is more, knowing as the product of practice implies a grounding in the dhamma that brings the word back to learning.

3. Hla Pain 1967, 237.
4. Aung Mon 2007, 878–79. The Thai monk fled in terror when he realized what his ministrations had done.
5. Chit Tin 1999a, 11. Ledi did collect one more accolade shortly before his death. The British government awarded him a Doctor of Literature degree at the opening ceremony of Yangon University in 1922. He did not accept the award in person, though some of his disciples attended the ceremony and received it on his behalf (Nyanissara 1999, 30–31).
6. Taylor 2001, 183.
7. As William Sewell puts it, path dependence means that "what has happened at an earlier point in time will affect the possible outcomes of a sequence of events occurring at a later point in time" (Sewell 1996, 263).
8. Taylor 1989, 514–15; Mahoney 2000, 510. This view is in some sympathy with Tambiah's notion of the relations of continuities and transformations in his works on Thai Buddhism. He argues that "even the great revolutions in modern history have after initial cataclysmic phases, returned to routinisation in which older forms are seen to persist or are reinstituted." He goes on to assert that "certain kinds of persistence *coexist* with certain kinds of changes of state, and such amalgams and syntheses of varying kinds and varying degrees of cohesion and tension characterise much of the so-called flow of history" (Tambiah 1987, 194). This view of the relations between past and present suggests that enduring structural patterns surface to constrain change, while I am stressing continuities as the very agents of change; I do not see any persisting deep structure, but forces of causation that sometimes have long-lasting effects.
9. Asad 2000, 31.
10. Blackburn calls this assumption the "sea-change model" (Blackburn 2010, 200; see also xii–xiii).
11. Marx, "The British Rule in India" at http://www.marxists.org/archive/marx/works/1853/06/25.htm (accessed December 2, 2011). Here is a more recent expression of this idea: "[The] colonial rupture is the social, psychological, cultural, and economic equivalent of a paradigm shift, inaugurating a new regime of knowledge. Words and relations on either side of the colonial rupture are incommensurate" (Baker et al. 1995, 1047).
12. Marx 1978 [1888], 476.
13. For Homi Bhabha (1994, esp. 153–59), resistance to subjugation in the face of colonial power responds in terms that, while ambivalent, are presented by the colonial masters. To give another example, Gayatri Spivak has argued

that it is questionable whether the subaltern figure, particularly women, can "speak," in the sense that he or she can gain an objective position from which to critique colonial perspectives (Spivak 1995, 34–35). For a critique of such a strong sense of subjugation, particularly as presented by Bhabha, see Parry 1987, esp. 43. For an overview of these sorts of post-colonial thinkers and the development of their positions, see Richard King 1999, 200–207. See Whitaker 1999, especially the introduction, for an excellent summation and critique of this approach from a philosophical angle. See also Dirks 1992, 7.

14. Whitaker 1999, xvii–xviii.
15. For ways of understanding the past's relation to the present in colonial studies and in the study of Asian religion, see Jordt 2007, xiii; Blackburn 2001, 7–8; McDaniel 2008, 97–99; Pollock 1993, 97; Hallisey 1995, 49–50; Pieterse and Parekh 1995, 2.
16. Gadamer (2006, 300) remarks that people "are always already affected by history" and that one's historical consciousness is "situated in the web of historical effects."
17. I equate Ledi's application of Buddhist ideals with Sudipta Kaviraj's argument that modernizing political systems in Asia apply what he calls "relevant principles" in an improvisational fashion (Kaviraj 2005, 522).
18. Improvisation thus makes sense within a background understanding that is akin to a *habitus,* defined as "the durably installed generative principle of regulated *improvisations*" (Bourdieu 2006, 78). My italics.
19. Doniger 2009, 21.
20. The sociologist William Sewell has observed: "The term *modern* often serves as a label for those processes or agents that are deemed by the analyst to be doing the work of the future in some present, while *traditional* labels those equally current forces in the present that the analyst regards as doing the work of the past" (Sewell 1996, 247).
21. Kaviraj 2005, 501.
22. Guha 1988, 40, quoted in Chakrabarty 2000, 15.
23. Gadamer 2006, 282: "The fact is that in tradition there is always an element of freedom and of history itself. Even the most genuine and pure tradition does not persist because of the inertia of what once existed. It needs to be affirmed, embraced, cultivated."
24. There was a slump in rice prices between 1927 and 1930; Indian-Burmese riots took place in 1930; and the Saya San rebellion convulsed the nation from 1930 to 1931 (Houtman 1990a, 44).
25. Maung Maung 1980, 115. Mohnyin started his studies and meditative training under Ledi in 1901. He entered the Mohnyin forest, from which his title comes, in 1911 (Hla Pain 1967, 341–42). He stayed in the forest for ten years before venturing out again at around the age of forty-nine. From 1934 until the start of World War Two, he preached every year in Rangoon (Maung Maung 1980, 262 n. 8).
26. Kornfield 1996, 194. Maung Maung (1980, 115) notes that he even followed

Ledi's lead and made up simple verses on topics which, when he was preaching, he made people repeat after him until he was sure that they had memorized them.

27. Kornfield 1996, 201.
28. Another monk-disciple of Ledi, the Theikchadaung Sayadaw, first taught Saya Thetgyi, but Thetgyi went on to receive training from Ledi himself (Houtman 1990a, 284).
29. From the Vipassanā Research Institute website, http://www.vri.dhamma.org/general/thetgyi.html (accessed July 18, 2008).
30. Chit Tin 1999a, 25–26. My italics.
31. Thetgyi first taught U Ba Khin in January of 1937 (Chit Tin 1999a, 18).
32. He had studied for thirteen years with Ledi, and it is said he only visited his family during the first two years of this time (Chit Tin 1999a, 19).
33. Chit Tin 2003, 11, 40.
34. The government had issued a notice on October 10, 1950, that any government department could establish a Buddhist shrine room for religious activities (Chit Tin 1999a, 49).
35. Confalonieri 1999, 25.
36. U Ba Khin also took instruction from another monk, Webu Sayadaw (1896–1977), who was reputed to be an arhat. They met in July 1941 (Chit Tin 1999a, 32). Webu, as a lateral insertion in the lineage, has added further monastic filiation and authority to U Ba Khin, especially as he is considered to have been awakened. I have found no information about who taught Webu meditation. His discourses focus on mindfulness of the breath (*ānāpāna*) (Bischoff 2003, 4–5). Ledi remains, however, at the base of the chain of teachers and, as will be discussed below, seems to have been the formative influence on U Ba Khin's method.
37. Ledi discusses the kalāpas, too (see Ledi 1995, 450–51), but he favors discussion of the basic elements (*dhātu*s) that comprise the kalāpas, as we have seen.
38. Confalonieri 1999, 114.
39. For a description of the organization of the ten days, see ibid., 93–100.
40. Ibid., 111.
41. Ibid., 25.
42. No doubt his position as an important government official helped him to spread his message, too (Houtman 1997, 317).
43. U Ba Khin did require all practitioners to follow the eight precepts (Chit Tin 1999b, 53).
44. Ibid., 1.
45. I focus on Goenka next because his organization clearly shows important transformations of insight meditation and because it has been highly influential. Goenka, however, was by no means the only disciple of U Ba Khin empowered to teach, or the only teacher to spread the Ba Khin lineage beyond Burma's borders. U Ba Khin approved a number of people to teach, including

the Westerners John Coleman, Ruth Denison, and Robert Hover. What is more, the Burmese woman Daw Mya Thwin, known as Sayamagyi ("revered teacher"), is understood by many to be the direct lineage holder of U Ba Khin (Chit Tin 1999a, 125–26). She lives and teaches now in the United Kingdom at the International Meditation Center–UK, which is closely affiliated with the original International Meditation Center in Yangon. In the early 1980s, Daw Mya Thwin, the American teacher John Coleman, and other Burmese teachers at the IMC split with Goenka and his followers. Two issues seem to have been at the heart of the split: Goenka's refusal to allow any charge for courses and his approval of a newsletter produced by his followers with the statement that meditation was an "art of living." In opposition to Goenka, teachers at the IMC felt it was acceptable to suggest a donation, and they believed the description of meditation as a way to live an ideal life diminished meditation as a practice meant to lead beyond living within the round of rebirth. See Mya Thwin, Coleman, Tint Yee, and Ba Pho 1982.

46. Recall the point in chapter 3 that Ledi helped "doctrinize" Buddhism through his use of the term *Buddha batha.* If Ledi were to hear Goenka's claim, I think he would be highly sympathetic to the point that the Buddha's teaching is universally applicable, but his attitude to Christian missionaries and other religions suggests this would not negate his belief in the distinctive superiority of Buddhist views for all.
47. Hart 1987, 18.
48. From http://www.vri.dhamma.org/general/vipintro.html (accessed July 18, 2008).
49. As I noted above, the predominating focus on the kalāpas is an innovation of U Ba Khin, though one based on Ledi's stress on the four great elements, which comprise a kalāpa.
50. Cadge 2005, 35. For descriptions of Goenka retreats among those on the "hippie trail," see Rahula 1985 and Lerner 1977.
51. Cadge 2005, 36.
52. See http://www.dhamma.org/en/alphalist.shtml (accessed September 19, 2012).
53. Ṭhe" Hluiṅ' 1993, 510; see also Kornfield 1996, 83–116.
54. The disciple was named U Paduma (Ṭhe" Hluiṅ' 1993, 636).
55. See Kornfield 1996, 209–34, and Ṭhe" Hluiṅ' 1993, 629–48.
56. The Mingun Sayadaw was based in Thaton, in lower Burma. His location makes him the neat geographical counterpart to Ledi: Ledi always had his base in Upper Burma, in Monywa first and later in Pyinmana. In 1985, Houtman estimated that Sunlun, Mogok, and the Mingun Sayadaw's student, the Mahasi Sayadaw (discussed below), had, collectively, between six and seven hundred meditation centers. For information on Mingun's lineage, see Maung Maung 1980, 113–14.
57. Houtman 1985, 91.
58. Ibid., 311.

59. Jordt 2007, 23.
60. Ibid., 64.
61. For Mahasi's description of his method, see Mahasi 1979. For two compelling descriptions of personal experiences of the Mahasi method, see Shattock 1958 and Rahula 1985.
62. Some decades after Ledi's death in 1923, U Ba Khin teachers and Mahasi teachers stopped teaching in the same center in England in part because they disagreed on the amount of calming practice that students needed to learn (Houtman 1990a, 188). That said, the amount of calming required before turning to insight practice in the U Ba Khin/Goenka method is still quite low, usually defined as the ability to keep one's mind on respiration at the nostrils for about five minutes.
63. Cadge 2006, 11.
64. Kornfield 2007, 33.
65. "Insight Meditation at 25," *Shambala Sun,* http://www.shambhalasun.com/index.php?option=content&task=view&id=1755 (accessed August 14, 2012). Salzberg was there as part of an independent-study program in India through the State University of New York, Buffalo (Salzberg 2011, 4–5).
66. Kornfield went to teach there after meeting Trungpa at a cocktail party in Cambridge, Massachusetts, in 1973 (Cadge 2005, 28). Goldstein arrived at the invitation of Ram Dass, whom he met in a café in Berkeley, California (Rawlinson 1997, 590).
67. From a 1976 flyer of IMS quoted in Cadge 2005, 29.
68. Cadge 2005, 29. In later years, IMS added a center on adjacent grounds, called the Forest Refuge, to house practitioners on extended retreats of several weeks or even months. An affiliated center was also founded on nearby property, dedicated to combining meditation with explicit study, the Barre Center for Buddhist Studies.
69. Cadge 2005, 29.
70. Rawlinson 1997, 590. Kornfield echoed this point, speaking about ritual and other traditional observances: "We left much of the Eastern culture, ritual, and ceremony behind also in Asia . . . we felt that for Americans it was an unnecessary barrier. It seemed to us that for our culture the simplicity and straightforwardness of mindful practice itself would speak best to the heart of those seeking practice" (Cadge 2005, 29).
71. Fronsdal 1998, 171. Kornfield puts a fine point on the idea that a true understanding of Buddhism includes the practice of meditation, when he dismisses most Buddhists (and Christians) as not really grasping the heart of their religion: "But just as only a small minority of the Christians in this country really understand and practice their religion, so too do only a small minority of Asian Buddhists understand and practice theirs" (Kornfield 1996, 6).
72. Five hundred thousand people from Theravāda countries came to America between 1977 and 2000 (Cadge 2005, 19–20).

73. Native-born Americans, usually white, middle or upper class, and focused on meditative practice, are sometimes called "convert Buddhists," since they typically come to Buddhism by choice in adulthood, as opposed to "immigrant" or "cradle" Buddhists born to Buddhism. This is not to say that all convert Buddhists are white or well off, or that cradle Buddhists are not interested in meditation. The use of these categories here serves the heuristic purpose of describing a broad demographic distinction at present, but these terms have received much critical reflection and critique as enduring divisions. See Tweed 2002, 22; Seager 2002, 116ff.; Fronsdal 1998, 178; and Numrich 2003.
74. Thus, the Mahasi Sayadaw would visit the U.S. in 1979 in response to an invitation from Western-born insight teachers, but would also help establish an ethnic Burmese Buddhist organization in the San Francisco Bay Area by leaving behind two Burmese monks (Cadge 2005, 31). Bhante Henepola Gunaratana arrived in America in the late 1960s and took up residence at the Washington Buddhist Vihara, ministering mainly to Sri Lankan and other Asian Buddhists. Eventually, however, he would found the Bhavana Society in West Virginia, a monastery and retreat center which draws many Westerners interested only in practice, as well as more traditional Theravāda Buddhists interested in supporting monastics (see Gunaratana 2003, 248).
75. Fronsdal 1998.
76. Kornfield 2007, 35.
77. Ibid., 39. Mahasi Sayadaw, his prominent successor U Pandita, and Munindra subsequently taught at the center, and their visits are critical to IMS's understanding of its lineage of teaching. The leaders of IMS, however, have always been explicit that they have no formal affiliation with Mahasi (Cadge 2005, 224 n. 51).
78. Cadge 2005, 35.
79. This therapeutic orientation has received support from a larger orientation in American culture toward the therapeutic (Metcalf 2002, 353).
80. Salzberg 2011, 3.
81. This justification of meditation as a means to recovery and health fits with what Catherine Albanese has called the metaphysical strand in American religious life. This is a form of religiosity that emphasizes the mind and its power and represents a "yearning for salvation understood as solace, comfort, therapy, and healing" (Albanese 2001, 13–15).
82. Fronsdal 1998, 172.
83. Gombrich and Obeyesekere 1988, 237.
84. Confalonieri 1999, 46.
85. Kornfield 1993, 244, quoted in Fronsdal 1998, 170. See also Metcalf 2002, 354ff.
86. Another notable voice is Mark Epstein, whose book *Thoughts without a Thinker* (1995) is a classic of this perspective.
87. One influential psychology paper defines it as "a kind of nonelaborative,

nonjudgmental, present-centered awareness in which each thought, feeling, or sensation that arises in the attentional field is acknowledged and accepted as it is" (Bishop et al. 2004, 4, quoted in Gilpin 2008, 232). Chapter 6 of Epstein's (1995) book, which concerns mindfulness, is entitled "Bare Attention."

88. I do not mean to suggest that I am questioning the value of this understanding of mindfulness for therapy. Many rigorous studies show clearly the benefits of such mindfulness practice (see Arias et al. 2006). This will be true, too, for the method of Jon Kabat-Zinn discussed below. My point is that, whatever its value, this use of mindfulness and, more broadly, the sort of insight practice that depends upon it are real divergences from Buddhist conceptions that came earlier, including that of Ledi. Mace (2008) has noted that in psychological studies and therapeutic settings the concept of mindfulness often contains unacknowledged factors beyond bare attention.
89. Kate Linthincum, "Teacher Who Helped Shape Buddhism Is Still on a Quest," *Los Angeles Times* May 29, 2010, http://articles.latimes.com/2010/may/29/local/la-me-beliefs-buddhist-20100529 (accessed August 15, 2012).
90. Gilpin 2008, 238. Although Kabat-Zinn's first book for a popular audience, *Full Catastrophe Living: Using the Wisdom of Your Body and Mind to Face Stress, Pain, and Illness* (1990), does not present his technique in Buddhist terms, his next book, *Wherever You Go, There You Are: Mindfulness Meditation in Everyday Life* (2005), does acknowledge Buddhist teachings as an important source for his understanding of mindfulness.
91. Gilpin 2008, 234.
92. For eating, see Jan Chozen Bays, *Mindful Eating: A Guide to Rediscovering a Healthy and Joyful Relationship with Food* (2009); for childraising, see Susan Greenland, *The Mindful Child: How to Help Your Kid Manage Stress and Become Happier, Kinder, and More Compassionate* (2010); for mindfulness and sex, there is Claudia Blake, *The Joy of Mindful Sex: Be in the Moment and Enrich Your Lovemaking* (2010).
93. Ledi 2001, 411.
94. As Charles Taylor puts it in describing his study of the rise of secularism: "I am treating secularity as something which is path dependent. But this path is immensely complex, more an interlocking skein of highways and byways than a single giant autobahn" (Taylor 2010, 721).
95. Kabat-Zinn 1998, 483.

Bibliography

Ledi Sayadaw's Works in Burmese and Pali

Ledi Sayadaw (Lay‘ tī chā ra to). 1907. *Paramatthadīpanī* [Manual of the Ultimates]. Ran‘ kun‘: Ka pi myak‘ hman‘ cā puṃ hnip‘ tuik‘.

———. 1908. "Yac‘ myui" ta rā" tau" [A Sermon about Intoxicants]. *Dhammadesanā ta rā" sa taṅ‘" cā* [Dhamma Teachings Magazine] 1 (4): 93–97.

———. [1923]. *Lay‘ tī pucchā a phre poṅ‘" khyup‘ kyam‘" krī"* [Big Anthology of Ledi's Answers to Questions]. Ran‘ kun‘: Amyui" thā" cā puṃ hnip‘ tuik‘.

———. 1951. *Vipassanādīpanī* [Manual on Insight Meditation]. Ran‘ kun‘: Haṃ sā va tī puṃ hnip‘ tuik‘.

———. 1951. *Dhammadīpanī* [Manual on the Dhamma]. Ran‘ kun‘: Mran‘ mā' a laṅ‘" sa taṅ‘" cā puṃ hnip‘ tuik‘.

———. 1954. *Sāsana visodhanī, pathama-tatiya tvai* [Purification of the Sāsana, vols. 1–3]. Ran‘ kun: Haṃ sā va tī puṃ hnip‘ tuik‘.

———. 1986. *Paramattha saṃ khip‘* [Summary of the Ultimates]. Ran‘ kun‘: Mahā lay‘ tī cā pe thin‘" sim‘" re" a phvai'.

———. 1995. *Lay‘ tī dīpanī poṅ‘" khyup‘, dutiya tvai* [Anthology of Ledi Manuals, vol. 2]. Ran‘ kun‘: Lay‘ tī dīpanī thvan‘" kā" pran‘' pvā" re" a phvai'.

———. 1996. *Lay‘ tī dīpanī poṅ‘" khyup‘, tatiya tvai* [Anthology of Ledi Manuals, vol. 3]. Ran‘ kun‘: Lay‘ tī dīpanī thvan‘" kā" pran‘' pvā" re" a phvai'.

———. 1999a. *Lay‘ tī Nibbān‘* [Ledi Nibbāna]. Ran‘ kun‘: Mi khin‘ e rā va tī cā up‘ tuik‘.

———. 2001. *Lay‘ tī dīpanī poṅ‘" khyup‘, pathama tvai* [Anthology of Ledi Manuals, vol. 1]. Ran‘ kun‘: Lay‘ tī dīpanī thvan‘" kā" pran‘' pvā" re" a phvai'.

———. 2003a. *Lay‘ tī dīpanī poṅ‘" khyup‘, catuttha tvai* [Anthology of Ledi Manuals, vol. 4]. Ran‘ kun‘: Lay‘ tī dīpanī thvan‘" kā" pran‘' pvā" re" a phvai'.

———. 2003b. *Paramatthadīpanī* [Manual of the Ultimates]. Ran' kun': Lay' tī dīpanī thvan'" kā" pran'' pvā" re" a phvai'.

———. 2004a. *Paramattha saṃ khip'* [Summary of the Ultimates]. Ran' kun': Lay' tī dīpanī thvan'" kā" pran'' pvā" re" a phvai'.

———. 2004b. *Nuiṅ' ṅaṃ khrā" pucchā a phre poṅ'" khyup'* [Anthology of Answers to the Questions of Foreigners]. Ran' kun': Lay' tī dīpanī thvan'" kā" pran'' pvā" re" a phvai'.

———. 2004c. *Gambhīra kabyā kyam'"* [Book of Profound Poetry]. Ran' kun': Lay' tī dīpanī thvan'" kā" pran'' pvā" re" a phvai'.

———. n.d. *Vipassanādīpanī* [Manual on Insight Meditation]. Ran' kun': Ratanā mui" puṃ hnip' tuik'.

Ledi Sayadaw's Works in Translation

Ledi Sayadaw. 1915. *The Vipassanā Dīpanī or The Manual of Insight.* Translated by U Ñāṇa. Mandalay: The Society for Promoting Buddhism in Foreign Countries.

———. 1961. *L'enseignement de Lêdi Sayadaw: Bouddhisme du Théravâda.* Translated by Charles Andrieu. Paris: Michel.

———. 1999b. *The Manuals of Dhamma.* Bombay: Vipassana Research Institute.

———. 1999c. *Alin-Kyan: The Manual of Light.* Translated by U Tin U. Portsmouth, UK: Private printing by S. S. Davidson.

———. 2004d. *The Manuals of Buddhism.* Yangon: Mother Ayeyarwaddy Publishing House.

———. 2012. "Two Letters from Ledi Sayadaw to Mrs Rhys-Davids." Translated by U Nyana and Maung Myo and edited by William Pruitt and Erik Braun. *The Journal of the Pali Text Society* 31:155–82.

———. n.d. *Dhamma Dipani.* Translated by Han Htay and edited by Bhikkhu Pesala. Accessed at http://www.aimwell.org/Books/Ledi/Dhamma/dhamma.html.

———. n.d. *A Manual of the Excellent Man: Uttamapurisa Dipani.* Translated by U Tin Oo and edited by Bhikkhu Pesala. Accessed at http://www.aimwell.org/Books/Ledi/Uttama/uttama.html.

Other Pali and Burmese Sources

Aung Mon [Oṅ' Mvan']. 2007. *Kye" zū" hraṅ' lay' tī cha rā to bhu ra krī" bhava phrac' tau cañ'* [Life Story of the Great Monk and Benefactor Ledi Sayadaw]. Ran' kun': Mrat' Chu Mvan'.

Bode, Mabel. 1897. *Sāsanavaṃsa* [History of the Sāsana]. London: H. Frowde.

Chaṭṭha Saṅgāyana Pāli Tipiṭaka (including the *Visuddhimagga,* the

Abhidhammatthasaṅgaha, the *Abhidhammatthavibhāvinīṭīkā*, and the *Paramatthadīpanī*). http://www.tipitaka.org.

Chit San Win [Khyac' caṃ waṅ'"]. 2003. *Lay' tī aṅ'" naṃ bhe" hma khraṅ' se' maṅ'" hin'" saṃ* [The Roar of the Majestic Lion from the Shore of the Ledi Lake]. Ran' kun': Mra va tī.

Hla Pain [Hla Puiṅ']. 1967. *Lay' tī gantha waṅ' kyau mya" sa muiṅ"* [History of the Famous People in the Ledi Lineage]. Man ta le": Sukhavatī puṃ hnip' tuik'.

Hpo Hlaing [Bhui" Hluiṅ']. 1953. *Vimuttirasa kyam'"* [Taste of Liberation]. Ran' kun': Haṃ sā va tī puṃ hnip' tuik'.

———. 1956. *Kāyanupassanā kyam'"* [Meditation on the Body]. Ran' kun': Haṃ sā va tī puṃ hnip' tuik'.

Jotika, Ū". 1978. *Abhidhamma sa muiṅ'" khyup'* [An Abbreviated History of the Abhidhamma]. Ran' kun': Sāsanā re" ū" cī" ṭhāna puṃ hnip' tuik'.

Khaṅ' E", Ū". 2002. *Cā chui tau myā" atthuppatti* [Biographies of Famous Writers]. Ran' kun': Rā praññ' cā up' tuik'.

Maung Maung Tin [Moṅ' Moṅ' Taṅ']. 1968. *Kun'" boṅ' chak' mahā raja vaṅ' tau krī", tatiya tvai* [The Great Royal Chronicle of the Konbaung Period, vol. 3]. Ran' kun': Lay' tī maṇḍuiṅ' puṃ hnip' tuik'.

Myin Swe [Mraṅ' Chve]. n.d. *Saṅ' gruih' hnaṅ" saṅ' gruih' mahā ṭīkā sac' cac' tam'"* [An Accounting of the Saṅgaha and the New Great Commentary on the Saṅgaha]. No publication information.

Nat Tha [Nat' Sā"]. 1910. *Atisundara kyam'"* [The Very Good Book]. Ran' kun': Sā sa nā lak' ā ra piṭakat' puṃ hnip' tuik'.

Paññasāmi. 1897. *Sāsanavaṃsa* [The History of the Sāsana]. Edited by Mabel Bode. London: H. Frowde.

Phe Moṅ' Taṅ' and Pāmokkha Ū". 2003. *Mran' mā cā pe sa muiṅ'"* [The History of Myanmar Literature]. Ran' kun': Ca pay' ū" cā pe phran" khyī re".

Saddhātissa, H., ed. 1989. *Abhidhammatthasaṅgaha and Abhidhammatthavibhāvinīṭīkā* [Compendium of the Topics of the Abhidhamma and the Exposition of the Topics of the Abhidhamma]. Oxford: Pali Text Society.

Talaingoun Sayadaw [Ta luiṅ'" kun'" cha rā to]. 1909. *Aṅ' ku ra ṭīkā* [The Sprout Commentary]. Ran' kun': Praññ' krī" maṇ ḍuiṅ' piṭakat' puṃ hnip' tuik'.

Ṭhe" Hluiṅ', Ū". 1993. *Ra han tā hnaṅ" pugguil' thū" myā"* [Extraordinary Monks and Lay People]. Ran' kun': Buddha athaṃ cā pe.

Wunnita, U [Vaṇṇita, Ū"]. 1956. *Lay' tī cha rā to ther' mrat' krī" e* mahātheruppatti kathā* [The Biography of the Great Monk Ledi Sayadaw]. Ran' kun': Haṃ sā va tī puṃ hnip' tuik'.

Western Language Translations and Sources

Albanese, Catherine. 2001. *A Republic of Mind and Spirit: A Cultural History of American Metaphysical Religion*. New Haven: Yale University Press.

Allott, Anne, Patricia Herbert, and John Okell. 1989. "Burma." In *South-East Asia Languages and Literatures: A Select Guide,* edited by Patricia Herbert and Anthony Milner. Honolulu: University of Hawai'i Press.

Anālayo. 2003. *Satipaṭṭhāna: The Direct Path to Realization.* Birmingham, England: Windhorse.

Ananda Maitreya Thero. 1956. "The Dawn and Spread of Buddhism." *The Light of Dhamma* 3 (3): 11–16.

Ananda Metteyya. 1903a. "Buddhist Activities." *Buddhism: An Illustrated Quarterly Review* 1 (1): 168–74.

———. 1903b. "The Awakening." *Buddhism: An Illustrated Quarterly Review* 1 (1): 140–44.

———. 1911. "The Compendium of Philosophy." *The Buddhist Review* 3 (3): 131–36.

Andersen, Benedict. 1991. *Imagined Communities: Reflections on the Origin and Spread of Nationalism.* New York: Verso.

———. 1992. "The Changing Ecology of Southeast Asian Studies in the United States, 1950–1990." In *Southeast Asian Studies in the Balance,* edited by C. Hirschman, Charles Keyes, and K. Hutterer. Ann Arbor: The Association for Asian Studies.

Anisakhan Sayadaw. n.d. "Verses of Adoration Read by the Venerable Anisakhan Sayadaw." In *The Chaṭṭha Sangāyanā Souvenir Album.* Rangoon: Union Buddha Sāsana Council Press.

Arias, Albert J., Karen Steinberg, Alok Banga, and Robert L. Trestman. 2006. "Systematic Review of the Efficacy of Meditation Techniques as Treatments for Medical Illness." *Journal of Alternative and Complementary Medicine* 12 (8): 817–32.

Arnold, Matthew. 1994. *Dover Beach and Other Poems.* Mineola, N.Y.: Dover Publications.

Asad, Talal. 2000. "Agency and Pain: An Exploration." *Culture and Religion* 1 (1): 29–60.

Aung Tun. 1909. "The Use and Abuse of Opium." *The Burman Buddhist* 2 (6 & 7): 133–36.

Aung-Thwin, Michael. 2008. "Mranma Pran: When Context Encounters Notion." *Journal of Southeast Asian Studies* 39 (2): 193–217.

Baker, Houston A., Jr, Teresa Dovey, Rosemary Jolly, and Herbert Deinert. 1995. "Colonialism and the Postcolonial Condition." *PMLA* 110 (5): 1047–52.

Barry, Randall K. 1997. *ALA-LC Romanization Tables: Transliteration Schemes for Non-Roman Scripts.* Washington, D.C.: Library of Congress.

Bastian, Adolf. 2004. *A Journey in Burma, 1861–1862.* Translated by Walter E. J. Tips and edited by Christian Goodden. Bangkok: White Lotus Press.

Bays, Jan Chozen. 2009. *Mindful Eating: A Guide to Rediscovering a Healthy and Joyful Relationship with Food.* Boston: Shambhala Publications.

Bechert, Heinz. 1970. "Theravada Buddhist Sangha: Some General Observations on Historical and Political Factors in Its Development." *Journal of Asian Studies* 29 (4): 761–78.

———. 1973. "Sangha, State, Society, Nation: Persistence of Traditions in 'Post-traditional' Buddhist Societies." *Daedalus* 102 (1): 85–95.

———. 1979. "Remarks on Four Buddhist Sanskrit Works Composed in Sri Lanka." In *A Memorial Volume in Honor of Bhikkhu Jagdish Kashyap.* Delhi: B.R. Publishing Corporation.

———. 1984. "Buddhist Revival in East and West." In *The World of Buddhism: Buddhist Monks and Nuns in Society and Culture,* edited by Heinz Bechert and Richard Gombrich. London: Thames and Hudson.

———. 1988 [1966]. *Buddhismus, Staat und Gesellshaft in den Ländern Theravada-Buddhismus.* 3 vols. Berlin and Göttingen: Seminars für Indologie und Buddhismuskunde der Universität Göttingen.

Bennett, Alan [Ananda Metteyya]. 1929. *The Religion of Burma and Other Essays.* Adyar, Madras, India: Theosophical Publishing House.

Bennison, J. J. 1928. *Report of An Enquiry into the Standard and Cost of Living of the Working Classes in Rangoon.* Rangoon: Govt. Printing and Stationery, Burma.

Bigandet, Paul A. 1858. *The Life or Legend of Gaudama, the Buddha of the Burmese, with Annotations.* Rangoon: Thos. Stowe Ranney.

Bhabha, Homi 1994. *The Location of Culture.* New York: Routledge.

Bischoff, Roger. 1995. *Buddhism in Myanmar.* Kandy: Buddhist Publication Society.

———. 2003. *Selected Discourses of the Webu Sayadaw.* N.p.: The Sayagyi U Ba Khin Memorial Trust.

Bishop, S. R., M. Lau, S. Shapiro, L. Carlson, N. D. Anderson, J. Carmody, Z. V. Segal, S. Abbey, M. Speca, D. Velting, and G. Devins. 2004. "Mindfulness: A Proposed Operational Definition." *Clinical Psychology: Science and Practice* 11 (3): 230–41.

Bizot, Francois. 1976. *Le Figuier à cinq branches, recherche sur le Boudhisme Khmer.* Paris: École Française d'Extrême-Orient.

Blackburn, Anne M. 2001. *Buddhist Learning and Textual Practice in Eighteenth-Century Lankan Monastic Culture.* Princeton: Princeton University Press.

———. 2003. "Localizing Lineage: Importing Higher Ordination in Theravadin South and Southeast Asia." In *Constituting Communities: Theravada Buddhism and the Religious Cultures of South and Southeast Asia,* edited by John Holt, J. N. Kinnard, and J. S. Walters. Albany: State University of New York Press.

———. 2010. *Locations of Buddhism: Colonialism and Modernity in Sri Lanka.* Chicago: University of Chicago Press.

Blake, Claudia. 2010. *The Joy of Mindful Sex: Be in the Moment and Enrich Your Lovemaking.* New York: De Capo Press.

Bode, Mabel. 1909. *The Pali Literature of Burma.* London: Royal Asiatic Society.

Bodhi, Bhikkhu, trans. 1995. *The Middle Length Discourses of the Buddha: A Translation of the Majjhima Nikāya.* Boston: Wisdom Publications.

———. 2011. "What Does Mindfulness Really Mean? A Canonical Perspective." *Contemporary Buddhism* 12 (1): 19-38.

Bodhi, Bhikkhu, Mahathera Narada, U Rewata Dhamma, eds. and trans. 2000. *A Comprehensive Manual of Abhidhamma: The* Abhidhammatthasangaha *of Acariya Anuruddha*. Seattle: BPS Pariyatti Edition.

Bond, George D. 1988. *The Buddhist Revival in Sri Lanka: Religious Tradition, Reinterpretation, and Response*. Columbia: University of South Carolina Press.

Bourdieu, Pierre. 2006. *Outline of a Theory of Practice*. Cambridge: Cambridge University Press.

Brockman, Norbert. 2011. *The Encyclopedia of Sacred Places*. Santa Barbara: ABC-CLIO.

Bronkhorst, Johannes. 1986. *The Two Traditions of Meditation in Ancient India*. Stuttgart: Franz Steiner Verlag.

Buddhadatta, A. P. 1994. *Concise Pali-English Dictionary*. Delhi: Motilal Banarsidass.

The Burman Buddhist. 1908a. "Buddhist Schools." 1 (1): 16–22.

———. 1908b. "Literature in Burma." 1 (2): 27–28.

———. 1908c. "Modern Preaching." 1 (3): 50–51.

———. 1908d. "Buddha Gaya Resthouse." 1 (5): 99–100.

———. 1909. "Literature in Burma." 1 (8): 171–72.

Buswell, Robert E., and Padma S. Jaini. 1996. *Abhidharma Buddhism to 150 A.D.* Delhi: Motilal Banarsidass.

Cadge, Wendy. 2005. *Heartwood: The First Generation of Theravada Buddhism in America*. Chicago: University of Chicago Press.

Cady, John F. 1958. *A History of Modern Burma*. Ithaca, N.Y.: Cornell University Press.

Carbine, Jason A. 2004. "An Ethic of Continuity: Shwegyin Monks and the Sasana in Contemporary Burma/Myanmar." Ph.D. diss., University of Chicago.

———. 2011. *Sons of the Buddha: Continuities and Ruptures in a Burmese Monastic Tradition*. New York: Walter de Gruyter.

Carrithers, Michael. 1983. *The Forest Monks of Sri Lanka: An Anthropological and Historical Study*. Delhi: Oxford University Press.

Carter, John Ross. 1993. *On Understanding Buddhists: Essays on the Theravāda Tradition in Sri Lanka*. Albany: State University of New York Press.

Chakrabarty, Dipesh. 2000. *Provincializing Europe: Postcolonial Thought and Historical Difference*. Princeton: Princeton University Press.

———. 2002. *Habitations of Modernity*. Chicago: University of Chicago Press.

Charney, Michael W. 2006. *Powerful Learning: Buddhist Literati and the Throne in Burma's Last Dynasty, 1752–1885*. Ann Arbor: Centers for South and Southeast Asian Studies, University of Michigan.

———. 2009. *A History of Modern Burma*. New York: Cambridge University Press.

Chit Tin, ed. 1999a. *Truth Must Triumph: A History of the Worldwide Dhamma Mission of Sayagyi U Ba Khin*. N.p.: The Sayagyi U Ba Khin Memorial Trust.

———, ed. 1999b. *Dhamma Texts By Sayagyi U Ba Khin*. N.p.: The Sayagyi U Ba Khin Memorial Trust.

———, assisted by William Pruitt. 2003. *Buddhism as a Way of Life and Other Essays.* N.p.: The Sayagyi U Ba Khin Memorial Trust.

Collins, Steven. 1992. "Notes on Some Oral Aspects of Pali Literature." *Indo-Iranian Journal* 35 (2–3): 121–35.

———. 1998. *Nirvana and Other Buddhist Felicities: Utopias of the Pali Imaginaire.* Cambridge: Cambridge University Press.

Collins, Steven, and Justin McDaniel. 2010. "Buddhist 'Nuns' (*mae chi*) and the Teaching of Pali in Contemporary Thailand." *Modern Asian Studies* 44 (6): 1373–1408.

Colston, E. J. 1910. "Some Recent Social Movements in Burma." *The Imperial and Asiatic Quarterly Review and Oriental and Colonial Record* 29 (57–58): 68–87.

Confalonieri, P., ed. 1999. *The Clock of Vipassana Has Struck: The Teachings and Writings of Sayagyi U Ba Khin with Commentary by S. N. Goenka.* Seattle: Vipassana Research Publications.

Cousins, Lance S. 1973. "Buddhist *Jhāna*: Its Nature and Attainment According to the Pali Sources." *Religion* 3:115–31.

———. 1984. "Samatha-yana and Vipassana-yana." In *Buddhist Studies in Honour of Hammalava Saddhātissa,* edited by Gatare Dharmapala, Richard Gombrich, and K. R. Norman. Nugegoda, Sri Lanka: Hammalava Saddhatissa Felicitation Volume Committee.

———. 1996. "The Origin of Insight Meditation." *The Buddhist Forum* 4:35–58.

———. 1997. "Aspects of Esoteric Southern Buddhism." In *Indian Insights: Buddhism, Brahmanism, and Bhakti,* edited by Peter Connolly and Sue Hamilton. London: Luzac Oriental.

Cox, Collette. 1992. "Mindfulness and Memory: The Scope of *Smrti* from Early Buddhism to the Sarvastivadin Abhidharma." In *The Mirror of Memory: Reflections on Mindfulness and Remembrance in Indian and Tibetan Buddhism,* edited by Janet Gyatso. Albany: State University of New York Press.

———, trans. 1995. *Disputed Dharmas: Early Buddhist Theories on Existence: An Annotated Translation of the Section of Factors Dissociated from Thought from Sanghabhadra's Nyayanusara.* Tokyo: International Institute for Buddhist Studies.

Crosby, Kate. 2000. "Tantric Theravada: A Bibliographic Essay on the Writings of François Bizot and Other Literature on the Yogavacara Tradition." *Contemporary Buddhism* 1 (2): 141–98.

Dhammasami. 2004. "Between Idealism and Pragmatism: A Study of Monastic Education in Burma and Thailand From the Seventeenth Century to the Present." Ph.D. diss., Oxford University.

Dirks, Nicholas B. 1992. "Introduction." In *Colonialism and Culture,* edited by Nicholas B. Dirks. Ann Arbor: University of Michigan Press.

———. 2001. *Castes of Mind: Colonialism and the Making of Modern India.* Princeton, N.J.: Princeton University Press.

Doniger, Wendy. 2009. *The Hindus: An Alternative History.* New York: Penguin Books.

Dreyfus, Georges B. J. 2003. *The Sound of Two Hands Clapping: The Education of a Tibetan Buddhist Monk.* Berkeley and Los Angeles: University of California Press.

Duffy, Eamon. 2011. *Ten Popes Who Shook the World.* New Haven: Yale University Press.

Edwards, Penny. 2006. "Grounds for Protest: Placing Shwedagon Pagoda in Colonial and Postcolonial History." *Postcolonial Studies* 9 (2): 197–211.

Eisenstadt, S. N. 2002. "Multiple Modernities." In *Multiple Modernities,* edited by S. N. Eisenstadt. New Brunswick, N.J.: Transaction Publishers.

Epstein, Mark. 1995. *Thoughts without a Thinker: Psychotherapy from a Buddhist Perspective.* New York: Basic Books.

Ferguson, John P. 1975. "The Symbolic Dimensions of the Burmese Sangha." Ph.D. diss., Cornell University.

Fronsdal, Gil. 1998. "Insight Meditation in the United States: Life, Liberty, and the Pursuit of Happiness." In *The Faces of Buddhism in America,* edited by Charles S. Prebish and Kenneth K. Tanaka. Berkeley and Los Angeles: University of California Press.

Frost, Mark. 2002. "'Wider Opportunities': Religious Revival, Nationalist Awakening and the Global Dimension in Colombo, 1870–1920." *Modern Asian Studies* 36 (4): 937–67.

Furnivall, John S. 1939. "The Fashioning of the Leviathan." *The Journal of the Burma Research Society* 24 (3): 1–138.

———. 1956. *Colonial Policy and Practice: A Comparative Study of Burma and Netherlands India.* New York: New York University Press.

Gadamer, Hans-Georg. 2006. *Truth and Method.* New York: Continuum.

Gethin, Rupert. 1992. "The Matikas: Memorization, Mindfulness and the List." In *In the Mirror of Mindfulness,* edited by Janet Gyatso. Albany: State University of New York Press.

———. 1998. *The Foundations of Buddhism.* Oxford: Oxford University Press.

———. 2001. *The Buddhist Path to Awakening.* Oxford: Oneworld Publications.

Gethin, Rupert, and R. P. Wijeratne, trans. 2002. *Summary of the Topics of Abhidhamma (Abhidhammatthasangaha).* Oxford: Pali Text Society.

Gilpin, Richard. 2008. "The Use of Theravāda Buddhist Practices and Perspectives in Mindfulness-Based Cognitive Therapy." *Contemporary Buddhism* 9 (2): 227–51.

Gimello, Robert. 1983. "Mysticism in Its Contexts." In *Mysticism and Religious Traditions,* edited by Steven T. Katz. New York: Oxford University Press.

Goenka, S. N. 1998. *The Satipatthana Discourses.* Seattle: Pariyatti Publishing.

Gombrich, R. F. 1988. *Theravada Buddhism: A Social History from Ancient Benares to Modern Colombo.* London: Routledge & Kegan Paul.

———. 1991 [1971]. *Buddhist Precept and Practice: Traditional Buddhism in the Rural Highlands of Ceylon.* Delhi: Motilal Banarsidass.

Gombrich, R. F., and Gannath Obeyesekere. 1988. *Buddhism Transformed: Religious Change in Sri Lanka.* Princeton: Princeton University Press.

Government of Burma. 1868–1941. *Catalogue of Books and Pamphlets Published in Burma.* Rangoon: Government of Burma.

———. 1908. *The Third Quinquennial Report of Public Instruction in Burma for the Years 1902–1903—1906–1907.* Rangoon: Office of the Superintendent, Government Printing.

Greenland, Susan K. 2010. *The Mindful Child: How to Help Your Kid Manage Stress and Become Happier, Kinder, and More Compassionate.* New York: Free Press.

Griffiths, Paul J. 1981. "Concentration or Insight: The Problematic of Theravada Buddhist Meditation Theory." *Journal of the American Academy of Religion* 49:605–24.

———. 1999. *Religious Reading: The Place of Reading in the Practice of Religion.* New York: Oxford University Press.

Guha, Ranajit. 1988. "On Some Aspects of the Historiography of Colonial India." In *Selected Subaltern Studies,* edited by Ranajit Guha and Gayatri Spivak. New York: Oxford University Press.

Gunaratana, Henepola. 1980. "A Critical Analysis of the Jhanas in Theravada Buddhist Meditation." Ph.D. diss., American University. Reformatted at http://www.buddhanet.net/pdf_file/printguna.pdf (accessed September 18, 2012).

———. 2002. *Mindfulness in Plain English.* Boston: Wisdom Publications.

———, with Jeanne Malmgren. 2003. *Journey to Mindfulness: The Autobiography of Bhante G.* Somerville, Mass.: Wisdom Publications.

Gunawardana, R.A.L. 1979. *Robe and Plow.* Tucson: University of Arizona Press.

Hall, D.G.E. 1956. *Burma.* London: Hutchinson's University Library.

Hallisey, Charles. 1991. "Councils as Ideas and Events in the Theravada." *The Buddhist Forum* 2:133–48.

———. 1995. "Roads Taken and Not Taken in the Study of Theravāda Buddhism." In *Curators of the Buddha: The Study of Buddhism Under Colonialism,* edited by Donald S. Lopez. Chicago: University of Chicago Press.

———. 2005. "Buddhist Ethics: Trajectories." In *The Blackwell Companion to Religious Ethics,* edited by William Schweiker. Malden, Mass.: Blackwell Publishing.

Hansen, Anne R. 2007. *How to Behave: Buddhism and Modernity in Colonial Cambodia, 1860–1930.* Honolulu: University of Hawai'i Press.

Harris, Elizabeth J. 2006. *Theravāda Buddhism and the British Encounter: Religious, Missionary and Colonial Experience in Nineteenth Century Sri Lanka.* New York: Routledge.

Hart, William. 1987. *The Art of Living: Vipassana Meditation as Taught by S. N. Goenka.* New York: HarperSanFrancisco.

Harvey, G. E. 1967. *History of Burma: From the Earliest Times to 10 March 1824, the Beginning of the English Conquest.* London: Longmans Green and Co.

Hinüber, Oskar von. 1983. *Notes on the Pali Tradition in Burma.* Göttingen: Vandenhoeck & Ruprecht.

———. 2000. *A Handbook of Pali Literature.* Berlin: Walter de Gruyter.

Hla Maung, trans. [no date.] "An Address of Praise Read by the Honorable U Win,

Minister for Religious Affairs and National Planning at the Opening Ceremony of the Chaṭṭha Sangāyanā Held on the Visakha Day of 2498 B.E." In *The Chaṭṭha Sangāyanā Souvenir Album*. Rangoon: Union Buddha Sāsana Council Press.

Hla Pe. 1985. *Burma: Literature, Historiography, Scholarship, Language, Life, and Buddhism*. Singapore: Institute of Southeast Asian Studies.

Holt, John. 1991a. "Protestant Buddhism? A Review of *Buddhism Transformed*." *Religious Studies Review* 17 (4): 307–12.

———. 1991b. *Buddha in the Crown: Avalokiteśvara in the Buddhist Traditions of Sri Lanka*. New York: Oxford University Press.

Horner, I. B., trans. 1962. *The Book of Discipline (Vinaya-Pitaka)*, vol. 4: *Mahāvagga*. London: Luzac & Company.

Houtman, Gustaaf. 1985. "The Burmese *Wipathana* Meditation Tradition Self-conscious: A History of Sleeping Texts and Silent Buddhas." *Groniek* 92 (July): 87–97.

———. 1990a. "Traditions of Buddhist Practice in Burma." Ph.D. diss., University of London.

———. 1990b. "How a Foreigner Invented Buddhendom in Burmese: From *tha-tha-na* to *bok-da ba-tha*." *Journal of the Anthropological Society at Oxford* 21 (2): 113–28.

———. 1997. "Beyond the Cradle and Past the Grave: The Biography of Burmese Meditation Master U Ba Khin." In *Sacred Biography in the Buddhist Traditions of South and Southeast Asia*, edited by Juliane Schober. Honolulu: University of Hawai'i Press.

———. 1999. *Mental Culture in Burmese Crisis Politics: Aung San Suu Kyi and the National League for Democracy*. Tokyo: Tokyo University of Foreign Studies Institute for the Study of Languages and Cultures of Asia and Africa.

Hpo Hlaing. 2004. *Rajadhammasangaha*. Translated by L. E. Bagshawe. Accessed at http://www.burmalibrary.org/docs/THE_RAJADHAMMASANGAHA.pdf.

Htay Htay Lwin. 1998. "The History of the Maha Ledi Nikaya." Masters thesis, University of Mandalay.

Htin Aung. 1966. *Burmese Monk's Tales*. New York: Columbia University Press.

Ikeya, Chie. 2011. *Refiguring Women, Colonialism, and Modernity in Burma*. Honolulu: University of Hawai'i Press.

Ivy, Marilyn. 2005. "Modernity." In *Critical Terms for the Study of Buddhism*, edited by Donald Lopez. Chicago: University of Chicago Press.

Jackson, Peter A. 1988. *Buddhadasa, a Buddhist Thinker for the Modern World*. Bangkok: Siam Society.

Jaini, Padma. 1959. "The Origin and Development of the Viprayukta-samskaras." *Bulletin of the School of Oriental and African Studies* 22 (3): 532–47.

Jayawickrama, N. A. 2000. *The Story of Gotama Buddha: The Nidāna-kathā of the Jātakaṭṭhakathā*. Oxford: The Pali Text Society.

Jordt, Ingrid. 2001. "Mass Lay Meditation and State-Society Relations in Post-Independence Burma." Ph.D. diss., Harvard University.

———. 2007. *Burma's Mass Lay Meditation Movement: Buddhism and the Cultural Construction of Power.* Athens: Ohio University Press.

Kabat-Zinn, Jon. 1990. *Full Catastrophe Living: Using the Wisdom of Your Body and Mind to Face Stress, Pain, and Illness.* New York: Delta.

———. 1998. "Toward the Mainstreaming of American Dharma Practice." In *Buddhism in America,* compiled by Al Rapaport and edited by Brian D. Hotchkiss. Boston: Charles E. Tuttle Co., Inc.

———. 2005. *Wherever You Go, There You Are: Mindfulness Meditation in Everyday Life.* New York: Hyperion.

Kaviraj, Sudipta. 2005. "An Outline of a Revisionist Theory of Modernity." *Archive of European Sociology* 46 (3): 497–526.

Keyes, Charles. 1983. "Merit-Transference in the Kammic Theory of Popular Theravada Buddhism." In *Karma,* edited by Charles Keyes and E. V. Daniel. Berkeley and Los Angeles: University of California Press.

Khin Maung Nyunt. 1999. *An Outline History of Myanmar Literature.* Yangon: Cā pe bi mān' a phvai'.

King, Richard. 1999. *Orientalism and Religion: Postcolonial Theory, India, and 'The Mystic East.'* New York: Routledge.

King, Winston L. 1964a. *In the Hope of Nibbana: Theravada Buddhist Ethics.* LaSalle, Il.: Open Court.

———. 1964b. *A Thousand Lives Away: Buddhism in Contemporary Burma.* Cambridge: Harvard University Press.

———. 1980. *Theravada Meditation: The Buddhist Transformation of Yoga.* University Park: Pennsylvania State University Press.

Kirichenko, Alexy. 2009. "From *Thathanadaw* to Theravada Buddhism: Construction of Religion and Religious Identity in Nineteenth- and Early Twentieth-Century Myanmar." In *Casting Faiths: Imperialism and the Transformation of Religion in East and Southeast Asia,* edited by Thomas DuBois. New York: Palgrave-Macmillan.

———. 2010. "Taunggwin Hsayadaw and the Transformation of Monastic Hierarchies in Colonial Burma." Paper presented at the Theravada Buddhism under Colonialism: Adaption and Response Conference, Nalanda-Srivijaya Center, ISEAS, Singapore.

———. 2011. "Dynamics of Monastic Mobility and Networking in Upper Myanmar of the Seventeenth and Eighteenth Centuries." Paper presented at the Buddhist Dynamics in Premodern Southeast Asia Conference, Nalanda-Srivijaya Center, ISEAS, Singapore.

Kornfield, Jack. 1993. *A Path with Heart.* Boston: Bantam Books.

———. 1996. *Living Dharma: Teachings of Twelve Buddhist Masters.* Boston: Shambhala Publications.

———. 2007. "This Fantastic, Unfolding Experiment." *Buddhadharma: The Practitioner's Quarterly* (Summer): 32–39.

Law, Bimala Churn, trans. 1986. *The History of the Buddha's Religion (Sasanavamsa).* Delhi: Sri Satguru Publications.

Lerner, Eric. 1977. *Journey of Insight Meditation: A Personal Experience of the Buddha's Way*. New York: Schocken Books.

Lieberman, Victor B. 1976. "A New Look at the *Sāsanavaṃsa*." *Bulletin of the School of Oriental and African Studies* 39 (1): 137–49.

———. 1984. *Burmese Administrative Cycles: Anarchy and Conquest, c. 1580–1760*. Princeton: Princeton University Press.

———. 1987. "Reinterpreting Burmese History." *Comparative Studies in Society and History* 29 (1): 162–94.

———. 1997. "Introduction to Special Issue: The Eurasian Context of the Early Modern History of Mainland South East Asia, 1400–1800." *Modern Asian Studies* 31 (3): 449–61.

———. 2003. *Strange Parallels: Southeast Asia in Global Context, c. 800–1830*. Cambridge: Cambridge University Press.

Linthicum, Kate. 2010. "Teacher Who Helped Shape Buddhism Is Still on a Quest." *Los Angeles Times*, May 29. http://articles.latimes.com/2010/may/29/local/la-me-beliefs-buddhist-20100529 (accessed August 15, 2012).

Lopez, Donald S. 1998. "Belief." In *Critical Terms for Religious Studies*, edited by Mark C. Taylor. Chicago: University of Chicago Press.

———, ed. 2002. *Modern Buddhism: Readings for the Unenlightened*. London: Penguin.

———, ed. 2004. *Buddhist Scriptures*. New York: Penguin Books.

———. 2008. *Buddhism and Science: A Guide for the Perplexed*. Chicago: University of Chicago Press.

Lubeigt, Guy. 2005. "Introduction of Western Culture in Myanmar in the 19th Century: From Civilian Acceptance to Religious Resistance." In *Essays in Commemoration of the Golden Jubilee of the Myanmar Historical Commission*, edited by Than Tun. Yangon: Ministry of Culture.

Mace, Chris. 2008. *Mindfulness and Mental Health: Therapy, Theory, and Science*. New York: Routledge.

Mahasi, Sayadaw [Ū" Sobhaṇa]. 1979. *The Satipatthana Vipassana Meditation: A Basic Buddhist Mindfulness Exercise*. Rangoon: Department of Religious Affairs.

Mahoney, James. 2000. "Path Dependence in Historical Sociology." *Theory and Society* 29 (4): 507–48.

Mahoney, James, and Daniel Schensul. 2006. "Historical Context and Path Dependence." In *Oxford Handbook of Contextual Political Analysis*, edited by Robert E. Goodin and Charles Tilly. Oxford: Oxford University Press.

Malalasekera, G. P. 1928. *The Pali Literature of Ceylon*. London: Royal Asiatic Society.

———. 1997. *Dictionary of Pali Proper Names*, vols. 1–3. Oxford: Pali Text Society.

Malalgoda, K. 1976. *Buddhism in Sinhalese Society, 1750–1900: A Study of Religious Revival and Change*. Berkeley and Los Angeles: University of California Press.

Marx, Karl. 1936. *Capital*. New York: The Modern Library.

———. 1978 [1888]. "Manifesto of the Communist Party." In *The Marx-Engels Reader*. New York: W.W. Norton & Company.

———. 2008 [1852]. *The Eighteenth Brumaire of Louis Bonaparte.* Rockville, Md.: Wildside Press.

Maung Maung. 1980. *From Sangha to Laity: Nationalist Movements of Burma, 1920–1940.* New Delhi: Manohar.

McDaniel, Justin. 2008. *Gathering Leaves and Lifting Words: Histories of Buddhist Monastic Education in Laos and Thailand.* Seattle: University of Washington Press.

McHale, Sean F. 2004. *Print and Power: Confucianism, Communism, and Buddhism in the Making of Modern Vietnam.* Honolulu: University of Hawai'i Press.

Mehm Tin Mon. 1995. *The Essence of Buddha Abhidhamma.* Yangon: Mya Mon Yadanar.

Mendelson, E. Michael. 1961. "A Messianic Buddhist Association in Upper Burma." *Bulletin of the School of Oriental and African Studies* 24 (3): 560–80.

———. 1975. *Sangha and State in Burma: A Study of Monastic Sectarianism and Leadership.* Edited by John Ferguson. Ithaca, N.Y.: Cornell University Press.

Metcalf, Franz Aubrey. 2002. "The Encounter of Buddhism and Psychology." In *Westward Dharma: Buddhism beyond Asia,* edited by Charles S. Prebish and Martin Baumann. Berkeley and Los Angeles: University of California Press.

Mi Mi Khaing. 1962. *Burmese Family.* Bloomington: Indiana University Press.

Moore, Elizabeth, Hansjorg Mayer, and Win Pe. 1999. *Shwedagon: Golden Pagoda of Myanmar.* London: Thames & Hudson.

Mya Thwin, John E. Coleman, Tint Yee, and Ba Pho. 1982. "A Notice of Clarification." *Vipassana Newsletter, IMC-UK* (Spring): 1–3.

Myanmar Language Commission. 1996. *Myanmar-English Dictionary.* Yangon: Department of the Myanmar Language Commission.

Myint-U, Thant. 2001. *The Making of Modern Burma.* Cambridge: Cambridge University Press.

Myo Myint. 1987. "The Politics of Survival in Burma: Diplomacy and Statecraft in the Reign of King Mindon." Ph.D. diss., Cornell University.

Ñāṇamoli, Bhikkhu, trans. 1999. *The Visuddhimagga: The Path of Purification.* Seattle: BPS Pariyatti.

Nandamālābhivaṃsa, Dhammācariya U. n.d. "*Paramatthadipani* (The Exposition of the Higher Truth): A Translation from Original Pali Text with Annotation and Introduction." Manuscript.

Nattier, Jan. 1991. *Once Upon a Future Time: Studies in a Buddhist Prophecy of Decline.* Berkeley: Asian Humanities Press.

Nilar. 2008. "Life as Monk for Actor Kyaw Hein." *The Myanmar Times,* July 28–August 3, vol. 22, no. 429, http://mmtimes.com/n0429/t001.htm (accessed September 10, 2010).

Nisbet, John. 1901. *Burma under British Rule—and Before,* vol. 1. Westminster, U.K.: A. Constable.

Norman, K. R. 1983. *Pali Literature: Including the Canonical Literature in Prakrit and Sanskrit of All the Hinayana Schools of Buddhism.* Wiesbaden: Harrassowitz Verlag.

Numrich, Paul. 2003. "Two Buddhisms Further Considered." *Contemporary Buddhism* 4 (1): 55–78.

Nyanaponika Thera. 1996. *The Heart of Buddhist Meditation.* York Beach, Me.: Samuel Weiser, Inc.

Nyanissara, Ashin (Sitagu Sayadaw). 1999. *A Short Biography of the Venerable Ledi Sayadaw.* Mandalay: [No publisher information].

Obeyesekere, G. 1963. "The Great Tradition and the Little in the Perspective of Sinhalese Buddhism." *The Journal of Asian Studies* 22 (2): 139–53.

———. 1970. "Religious Symbolism and Political Change in Ceylon." *Modern Ceylon Studies* 1 (1): 43–63.

O'Hanlon, R. 1988. "Recovering the Subject: Subaltern Studies and Histories of Resistance in Colonial South Asia." *Modern Asian Studies* 22 (1): 189–224.

Pandita, U. 1993. *In this Very Life: The Liberation Teachings of the Buddha.* Translated by Venerable U Aggacitta and edited by Kate Wheeler. Boston: Wisdom Publications.

Paññāsāmi. 1986. *Sāsanavaṃsa.* Translated by Bimala Churn Law. Delhi: Sri Satguru Publications.

Parry, Benita. 1987. "Problems of Current Theories in Colonial Discourse." *Oxford Literary Review* 9:27–58.

Payne, Richard. 2002. "Buddhism and the Sciences: Historical Background, Contemporary Developments." In *Bridging Science and Religion,* edited by Gaymon Bennett and Ted Peters. London: SCM.

Pe Maung Tin. 1934. "The Shwe Dagon Pagoda." *The Journal of the Burma Research Society* 24 (1): 1–91.

Pieterse, Jan Nederveen, and Bhikhu Parekh. 1995. "Introduction." In *The Decolonization of Imagination: Culture, Knowledge, and Power,* edited by Jan Nederveen Pieterse and Bhikhu Parekh. Atlantic Highlands, N.J.: Zed Books.

Pollock, Sheldon I. 1993. "Deep Orientalism? Notes on Sanskrit and Power Beyond the Raj." In *Orientalism and the Postcolonial Predicament,* edited by Carol Breckenridge and Peter van der Veer. Philadelphia: University of Philadelphia Press.

———. 2000. "Cosmopolitan and Vernacular in History." *Public Culture* 12 (3): 591–625.

———. 2006. *The Language of the Gods in the World of Men: Sanskrit, Culture, and Power in Premodern India.* Berkeley and Los Angeles: University of California Press.

Pranke, Patrick A. 2004. "The 'Treatise on the Lineage of Elders': Monastic Reform and the Writing of Buddhist History in Eighteenth-Century Burma." Ph.D. diss., University of Michigan.

———. 2010 (2011). "On Saints and Wizards: Ideals of Human Perfection and Power in Contemporary Burmese Buddhism." *Journal of the International Association of Buddhist Studies* 33 (1–2): 453–88.

Prebish, Charles S. 1974. "A Review of Scholarship on the Buddhist Councils." *The Journal of Asian Studies* 33 (2): 239–54.

Pruitt, William. 1994. *Étude linguistique de nissaya birmans: traduction commentée de textes bouddhiques.* Paris: Presses de l'Ecole Française d'Extrême-Orient.

Purser, W.C.B. and K. J. Saunders. 1914. *Modern Buddhism in Burma: Being an Epitome of Information Received from Missionaries, Officials and Others.* N.p.: Christian Literature Society, Burma Branch.

Rāhula, Walpola. 1966. *History of Buddhism in Ceylon: The Anuradhapura Period, 3d Century BC–10th Century AD.* Colombo: Gunasena.

Rahula, Yogavacara. 1985. *One Night's Shelter: From Home to Homelessness, The Autobiography of an American Buddhist monk.* Colombo: Printed by the Public Trustee of Sri Lanka.

Rawlinson, Andrew. 1997. *The Book of Enlightened Masters: Western Teachers in Eastern Traditions.* Chicago: Open Court.

Ray, Niharranjan. 2002 [1946]. *An Introduction to the Study of Theravada Buddhism in Burma: A Study in Indo-Burmese Historical and Cultural Relations from the Earliest Times to the British Conquest.* Bangkok: Orchid Press.

Reid, Anthony. 1993. *Southeast Asia in the Age of Commerce, 1450–1680.* New Haven: Yale University Press.

Reynolds, Frank. 1976. "The Many Lives of the Buddha." In *The Biographical Process: Studies in the History and Psychology of Religion,* edited by D. Capps and F. Reynolds. The Hague: Mouton.

Ronkin, Noa. 2005. *Early Buddhist Metaphysics: The Making of a Philosophical Tradition.* New York: RoutledgeCurzon.

Sadakata, Akira. 2004. *Buddhist Cosmology: Philosophy and Origins.* Tokyo: Kosei Publishing Company.

Salzberg, Sharon. 2011. *Real Happiness: The Power of Meditation, a 28-Day Program.* New York: Workman Publishing.

Sarkisyanz, Manuel. 1965. *Buddhist Backgrounds of the Burmese Revolution.* The Hague: M. Nijhoff.

Schmithausen, Lambert. 1981. "On Some Aspects of Descriptions of 'Liberating Insight' and 'Enlightenment' in Early Buddhism." In *Studien zum Jainismus und Buddhismus: Gedenkschrift für Ludwig Alsdorf,* edited by L. Alsdorf, K. Bruhn and A. Wezler. Wiesbaden: Franz Steiner.

Schober, Juliane. 1995. "The Theravada Buddhist Engagement with Modernity in Southeast Asia: Whither the Social Paradigm of the Galactic Polity?" *Journal of Southeast Asian Studies* 26: 307–25.

———. 2005a. "Buddhist Visions of Moral Authority and Civil Society: The Search for the Post-Colonial State in Burma." In *Burma at the Turn of the Twenty-First Century,* edited by Monique Skidmore. Honolulu: University of Hawai'i Press.

———. 2005b. "The Theravada Buddhist Engagement with Modernity: Colonialism and the Young Men's Buddhist Association (1906–1920) in Burma." Paper presented at the annual international meeting for the American Academy of Religion, November, 2005.

———. 2006. "Buddhism and Modernity in Myanmar." In *Buddhism in World*

Cultures: Contemporary Perspectives, edited by S. Berkwitz. Santa Barbara: ABC-Clio.

———. 2007. "Colonial Knowledge and Buddhist Education in Burma." In *Buddhism, Power and Political Order,* edited by Ian Harris. New York: Routledge.

———. 2011. *Modern Buddhist Conjunctures in Myanmar: Cultural Narratives, Colonial Legacies, and Civil Society.* Honolulu: University of Hawai'i Press.

Scott, David. 1996. "Religion in Colonial Civil Society: Buddhism and Modernity in 19th-century Sri Lanka." *Cultural Dynamics* 8 (1): 7–23.

Scott, J. G. [Shwe Yoe]. 1963. *The Burman: His Life and Notions.* New York: Norton.

Scott, J. G., and J. P. Hardiman. 1900. *Gazetteer of Upper Burma and the Shan States in Five Volumes.* part 1, vol. 1. Rangoon: Superintendent, Government Printing, Burma.

Scott, Rachelle. 2009. *Nirvana for Sale? Buddhism, Wealth, and the Dhammakaya Temple in Contemporary Thailand.* Albany: State University of New York Press.

Seager, Richard Hughes. 2002. "American Buddhism in the Making." In *Westward Dharma: Buddhism Beyond Asia,* edited by Charles S. Prebish and Martin Baumann. Berkeley and Los Angeles: University of California Press.

Seneviratne, H. L. 1999. *The Work of Kings: The New Buddhism in Sri Lanka.* Chicago: University of Chicago Press.

Sewell, William H. 1996. "Three Temporalities: Towards an Eventful Sociology." In *The Historic Turn in the Human Sciences,* edited by Terrence McDonald. Ann Arbor: University of Michigan Press.

Sharf, Robert. 1995. "Buddhist Modernism and the Rhetoric of Meditative Experience." *Numen* 42:228–83.

———. 1998. "Experience." In *Critical Terms in Religious Studies,* edited by Mark C. Taylor. Chicago: University of Chicago Press.

Sharma, Arvind, ed. 2002. *Modern Hindu Thought: The Essential Texts.* New York: Oxford University Press.

Shattock, E. H. 1958. *An Experiment in Mindfulness.* London: Rider.

Shwe Zan Aung. 1910. *Compendium of Philosophy.* Revised and edited by C.A.F. Rhys-Davids. London: Pali Text Society.

———. 1918. "Buddhism and Science." *Journal of the Burma Research Society* 8 (2): 99–106.

Skilling, Peter. 2009a. "Theravāda in History." *Pacific World* 3 (11): 61–94.

———. 2009b. *Buddhism and Buddhist Literature of South-East Asia: Selected Papers,* edited by Claudio Cicuzza. Bangkok and Lumbini: Fragile Palm Leaves Foundation.

Smith, Donald E. 1965. *Religion and Politics in Burma.* Princeton: Princeton University Press.

Snodgrass, Judith. 2007. "Defining Modern Buddhism: Mr. and Mrs. Rhys-Davids and the Pāli Text Society." *Comparative Studies of South Asia, Africa and the Middle East* 27 (1): 186–202.

Spiro, Melford. 1967. *Burmese Supernaturalism.* Englewood Cliffs, N.J.: Prentice-Hall.

———. 1982. *Buddhism and Society: A Great Tradition and Its Burmese Vicissitudes.* Berkeley and Los Angeles: University of California Press.

Spivak, Gayatri. 1995. "Can the Subaltern Speak?" In *The Post-Colonial Studies Reader,* edited by Bill Ashcroft, Gareth Griffiths, and Helen Tiffin. New York: Routledge.

Stadtner, Donald. 2011. *Sacred Sites of Burma: Myth and Folklore in an Evolving Spiritual Realm.* Bangkok: River Books.

Steedly, Mary. 1999. "The State of Culture Theory in the Anthropology of Southeast Asia." *Annual Review of Anthropology* 28:431–54.

Stewart, A.T.Q. 1972. *The Pagoda War: Lord Dufferin and the Fall of the Kingdom of Ava, 1885–86.* London: Faber.

Stewart, J. A. 1949. *Buddhism in Burma.* London: School of Oriental and African Studies.

Swearer, Donald. 1995. "A Summary of the Seven Books of the Abhidhamma." In *Buddhism in Practice,* edited by Donald Lopez. Princeton: Princeton University Press.

Tambiah, Stanley J. 1970. *Buddhism and the Spirit Cults of North-East Thailand.* Cambridge: University of Cambridge Press.

———. 1976. *World Conqueror and World Renouncer: A Study of Buddhism and Polity in Thailand against a Historical Backdrop.* Cambridge: Cambridge University Press.

———. 1984. *The Buddhist Saints of the Forest and the Cult of Amulets.* Cambridge: Cambridge University Press.

———. 1987. "At the Confluence of Anthropology, History, and Indology." *Contributions to Indian Sociology* 21 (1): 187–216.

Tanabe, Shigeharu, and Charles Keyes. 2002. "Introduction." In *Cultural Crisis and Social Memory,* edited by Shigeharu Tanabe and Charles Keyes. Honolulu: University of Hawai'i Press.

Taylor, Charles. 1989. *Sources of the Self: The Making of the Modern Identity.* Cambridge, Mass.: Harvard University Press.

———. 1999. *A Catholic Modernity? Charles Taylor's Marianist Award Lecture, with Responses by William M. Shea, Rosemary Luling Haughton, George Marsden, and Jean Bethke Elshtain.* Edited by James L. Heft. New York: Oxford University Press.

———. 2001. "Two Theories of Modernity." In *Alternative Modernities,* edited by Dilip Goankar. Durham, N.C.: Duke University Press.

———. 2010. "Charles Taylor Replies." *New Blackfriars* 91 (1036): 721–24.

Taylor, Jim. 1993. *Forest Monks and the Nation-state: An Anthropological and Historical Study in Northeastern Thailand.* Singapore: Institute of Southeast Asian Studies.

Taylor, Robert. 1987. *The State in Burma.* Honolulu: University of Hawai'i Press.

Than Tun. 1978. "History of Buddhism in Burma A.D. 1000–1300." *Journal of the Burma Research Society* 61, parts 1 and 2.

———. 1984–90. *The Royal Orders of Burma, A.D. 1598–1885*. 10 vols. Kyoto: Center for Southeast Asian Studies.

Tilakaratne, Asanga. 2000. "*Saṅgīti* and *Sāmaggī*: Communal Recitation and the Unity of the Saṅgha." *Buddhist Studies Review* 17 (2): 175–97.

Tiyavanich, Kamala. 1997. *Forest Recollections: Wandering Monks in Twentieth-Century Thailand*. Honolulu: University of Hawai'i Press.

Turner, Alicia. 2009. "Buddhism, Colonialism, and the Boundaries of Religion: Theravada Buddhism in Burma, 1885–1920." Ph.D. diss., University of Chicago.

Tweed, Thomas A. 2002. "Who Is a Buddhist? Night-Stand Buddhists and Other Creatures." In *Westward Dharma: Buddhism Beyond Asia,* edited by Charles S. Prebish and Martin Baumann. Berkeley and Los Angeles: University of California Press.

Van der Veer, Peter. 1994. *Religious Nationalism: Hindus and Muslims in India*. Berkeley and Los Angeles: University of California Press, 1994.

Vetter, T. 1988. *The Ideas and Meditative Practices of Early Buddhism*. Leiden: E.J. Brill.

Walters, Jonathan S. 1992. "Rethinking Buddhist Missions." Ph.D. diss., University of Chicago.

———. 2003. "Communal Karma and Karmic Community in Theravāda Buddhist History." In *Constituting Communities: Theravada Buddhism and the Religious Cultures of South and Southeast Asia,* edited by John Clifford Holt, Jacob N. Kinnard and Jonathan S. Walters. Albany: State University of New York Press.

Watanabe, F. 1983. *Philosophy and Its Development in the Nikayas and Abhidhamma*. Delhi: Motilal Banarsidass.

Whitaker, Mark. 1999. *Amiable Incoherence: Manipulating Histories and Modernities in a Batticaloa Tamil Hindu Temple*. Amsterdam: VU University Press.

White, Herbert T. 1913. *A Civil Servant in Burma*. London: E. Arnold.

Winichukul, Thongchai. 1994. *Siam Mapped: A History of the Geo-Body of a Nation*. Honolulu: University of Hawai'i Press.

Wolters, O. W. 1999 [1982]. *History, Culture, and Region in Southeast Asian Perspectives*. Ithaca, N.Y.: Southeast Asia Program Publications, Cornell University.

Wyatt, David. 1969. *The Politics of Reform in Thailand: Education in the Reign of King Chulalongkorn*. New Haven: Yale University Press.

Index

abbreviation text (*saṃ pok'*), 106–7, 109, 131, 210n20
abhidhamma: books of, 194nn10–11; changes in, 60; conceptual reach of, 64–66; decline of Buddhism and, 5, 66, 70–73, 75, 81, 103–4, 118, 201n128; defined, 4, 46–49, 66, 180n7; Gethin, Rupert, on, 194n17; Gimello, Robert, on, 48, 197n52; importance for meditation of, 55, 130–31, 133–37, 140, 142, 144–45, 154, 218n38; lay study of, 64, 89, 96, 116, 119–21, 130, 152; Ledi's teaching of, 13; origin of, 64–65, 199n98, 202n145; prestige of, in Burma, 4, 62–64, 72–73, 101, 103, 118, 198n78, 198n80, 198n83; recitation of, 27, 204n25; Ronkin, Noa, on, 60; science and, 80–81; social and religious problems and, 7; style of, 55, 197n52; teaching of, 62; Western knowledge and, 31–32, 80, 87, 129. See also *Abhidhammatthasaṅgaha* (*Compendium of the Ultimates*); decline of Buddhism; great essentials (*mahābhūtas*); insight meditation; meditation; *Paramatthadīpanī* (*Manual on the Ultimates*); *Paramattha saṃ khip'* (*Summary of the Ultimates*); *Vibhāvinī* (*Abhidhammatthavibhāvinīṭīkā*)
Abhidhammatthasaṅgaha (*Compendium of the Ultimates*), 12, 188n81; content of, 48–49; date of, 195n23; education and, 46, 63–64; fisherman's recitation of, 134; Pali Text Society edition of, 218n36; relationship to *Paramatthadīpanī* and *Vibhāvinī*, 48, 50–52, 54–55, 57, 62, 68, 75; relationship to *Paramattha saṃ khip'*, 89, 103, 105–16
abhisamācārika (that of praiseworthy conduct), 115
abstention from beef eating, 36–38. See also *kamma* (karma)
access concentration (*upacārasamādhi*), 137–38
adhicitta (consciousness, higher), 114–15, 214n60, 217n28
adhipaññā (wisdom, higher), 114–15, 214n60, 217n28
adhisīla (virtue, higher), 114–15, 214n60, 217n28
ādibrahmacariya (fundamentals of good conduct), 114–15
Alaungpaya, King, 184n10, 191n128
Albanese, Catherine, 229n81
anāgāmī (non-returner), 29
Anagarika Munindra, 163, 229n77
Anālayo, Bhikkhu, 210n11
Ananda Metteyya, 86, 97–98, 207n107
aññathābhāva (change, small-scale), 142, 223
anubandhanā (connection), 137
Anudīpanī, 73